Nigerian Pidgin in Lagos

Language contact, variation and change in an African urban setting

Dagmar Deuber

2005

Battlebridge Publications
137 Queen Alexandra Mansions
Bidborough St, London WC1H 9DL, UK
(0044) / (0) 20 7278 1246

110 Egodamulla
Ahungalla
Sri Lanka
(0094) / (0) 9122 64820

All rights reserved

ISBN 1 903292 10 7

Cover design
Jeehoon Kim

Cover photograph
Bariga Market, Lagos

Printing
Latimer Trend & Company Ltd, Estover Rd, Plymouth PL6 7PY, UK

Contents

The CD	iv
Acknowledgements	v
Transcription conventions	vii
Map 1a Nigeria. Major geographical features and state divisions 1976-87	viii
Map 1b Nigeria – Present state divisions	ix
Map 2 Nigeria – Languages	x
Map 3 Metropolitan Lagos	xi
Four locations in Lagos where NigP is typically spoken	xiii

1	Introduction	1
2	Language contact, variation and change: theoretical and methodological background	13
3	Nigerian Pidgin in its sociolinguistic context	45
4	Aspects of language variation and change in Nigeria	59
5	Educated NigP in face-to-face speech and radio broadcasts: the corpus study	71
6	Nigerian Pidgin as spoken by less educated speakers: analysis of additional recordings	161
7	Language planning for Nigerian Pidgin: problems and prospects	183
8	Conclusions and future outlook	201

Appendix **A**:	The questionnaires	211
Appendix **B**:	Results of the questionnaire study of corpus extracts	219
Appendix **C**:	Interviews (summary only; full version on CD)	247
Appendix **D**:	Samples of written Nigerian Pidgin	249

References	255
Index	269

The CD

The accompanying CD-ROM (see inside of back cover) is a mixed mode CD, which can be used both in a computer CD-ROM drive and a CD player. Track 1 is for the computer. The remaining tracks are for the CD player. A detailed list of the tracks and files on the CD is given below.

Computer-readable files (Track 1)

Folder "Texts"
The complete corpus (40 text files)

Folder "Background information"
Background information on each text in the corpus (40 *Word* files)

Folder "Samples"
Samples from the corpus with English translations and clickable audio (6 *Word* files):
Text V01-3
Text D01-2
Text C04-1
Text N04-1
Text A02-1
Text R03-1 71-173

"Appendix C" (PDF)

"List of speakers" (PDF)

Tracks for CD player

Track 2: Text V01-3
Track 3: Text D01-2
Track 4: Text C04-1
Track 5: Text N04-1
Track 6: Text A02-1
Track 7: Text R03-1 71-173

Acknowledgements

The data for this study were collected during field trips to Nigeria in 1997 (3 months) and 2000 (6 months). The field trip in 2000 was funded by a doctoral research grant (HSP III) from the German Academic Exchange Service (Deutscher Akademischer Austauschdienst). The field trip in 1997 was financed in part by a special grant from the German National Academic Foundation (Studienstiftung des deutschen Volkes), which supported my studies from 1993 to 1999 and which, furthermore, provided me with a doctoral scholarship from 2001 to 2003. I would like to express my gratitude to both of these organizations.

I also wish to thank Prof. Abiodun Adetugbo, then Head of the English Department at the University of Lagos, for receiving me as a visiting research student in the department in 2000 and providing all necessary support. Special thanks are due to all the lecturers and postgraduate students in the department who contributed to the research; I would like to single out Patrick Oloko, who was ever ready to bring his native speaker competence in Nigerian Pidgin to bear on my transcription and translation problems, Harry Olufunwa, who gave particularly eloquent and detailed answers to my many questions on the status, functions and prospects of Nigerian Pidgin, and Raphael Uzoezie, who kindly shared his insights into code-switching in the Nigerian environment with me, but others made valuable contributions as well.

Furthermore, I am grateful to Mr. Edime, Deputy Director of Radio Nigeria 3, Lagos, for giving me the opportunity to gain a detailed insight into work in the station's Pidgin Section in the course of an internship in 2000 as well as for giving me permission to reproduce the materials I obtained from the station; the kind collaboration of the staff of the Pidgin Section, especially Smart Esi, the Head of the Section, and God'swill Adheke Joseph is also appreciated. Khadijah Tuggar at the African Radio Drama Association, Lagos, generously arranged for copies of recordings and scripts of the radio drama serial *Rainbow City* to be made available to me and granted me permission to reproduce them, which is gratefully acknowledged. Kola Ogunjobi kindly let me have copies of recordings and scripts of the radio drama serial *One Thing at a Time*; for permission to reproduce these materials I am grateful to the Society for Family Health, Lagos.

Among my Nigerian friends who were present during one or both of the two field trips and provided various kinds of help in matters of daily living, I would like to mention especially Patrick Oloko (once again), Nkechi Okoroanyanwu, Sylvester Ejeh and the Adekunle family.

My very sincere appreciation is extended to all those who contributed to the research as informants and/or assistants. While they are too numerous to be listed here, the names of all contributors of speech samples and research assistants except of course those who wished to remain anonymous will be mentioned in appropriate places in this work.

At Freiburg University I am especially grateful to my supervisor, Prof. Christian Mair, for his encouragement, support and advice throughout the project. Among my colleagues I would like to mention in particular Andrea Sand and Andreas Sedlatschek, who discussed issues related to my work with me on various occasions, and Lars Hinrichs, who helped a lot in reproducing the maps and photographs.

Parts of this work have benefited from Edgar Schneider's detailed comments on a paper in which some of the research results were first presented. Charles Mann commented on the same paper and discussed other questions about Nigerian Pidgin with me as well.

I would also like to thank Julia Washbourne and Graham Nash for proofreading the thesis on which this book is based.

My whole family has been a constant source of encouragement and support. Although I know that they would not wish me to emphasize the role they have played, I would nevertheless like to specially mention at least my husband, who, with his expertise in things African, has contributed to my work in subtle but important ways.

Finally, I thank Philip Baker for his helpful comments and all the work he did in preparing the text for publication.

Transcription conventions

[<<text code], [text code>>]	Beginning, end of text
[<text code-subtext no.], text code-subtext no.>]	Beginning, end of subtext
$Name/code:	Turn start and speaker identification
$?:	Turn start where speaker cannot be identified
/	Intonation unit boundary suggesting nonfinality
//	Intonation unit boundary suggesting finality (as at end of declarative sentence)
?	Intonation unit boundary suggesting question
-text-	Embedded intonation unit
--	Truncated sentence/intonation unit
text& &text	Sentence/intonation unit continued (when interrupted)
#	Truncated word
(text)	False start
{text} {text}	Overlapping speech
[DESCRIPTION: text]	Speech with special quality
[?text?]	Uncertain transcription
[?numberWORDS?]	Unintelligible speech (approximate number of words)
[+text+]	Non-NigP speech
[I.L.numberWORDS]	Untranscribed speech in indigenous language (approximate number of words)
[==]/[=DESCRIPTION=]	Part of recording omitted
[~]	Long pause (ordinary pauses are not marked)
"text"	Quotation or word cited as word
[DESCRIPTION]	Noise/action
[[COMMENT]]	Transcriber's comment

The symbol "$" marking turn start/speaker identification is used only in the text files on the CD. In the printed texts and examples and the *Word* files on the CD the speaker name/code is set off by boldface.

Intonation unit boundaries are marked only in transcriptions of spontaneous speech. In scripted texts conventional punctuation is used.

The symbols for sentence/intonation unit continued and overlapping speech are indexed with numbers if they occur several times in succession (e.g. &2 &2, {2text} {2text}).

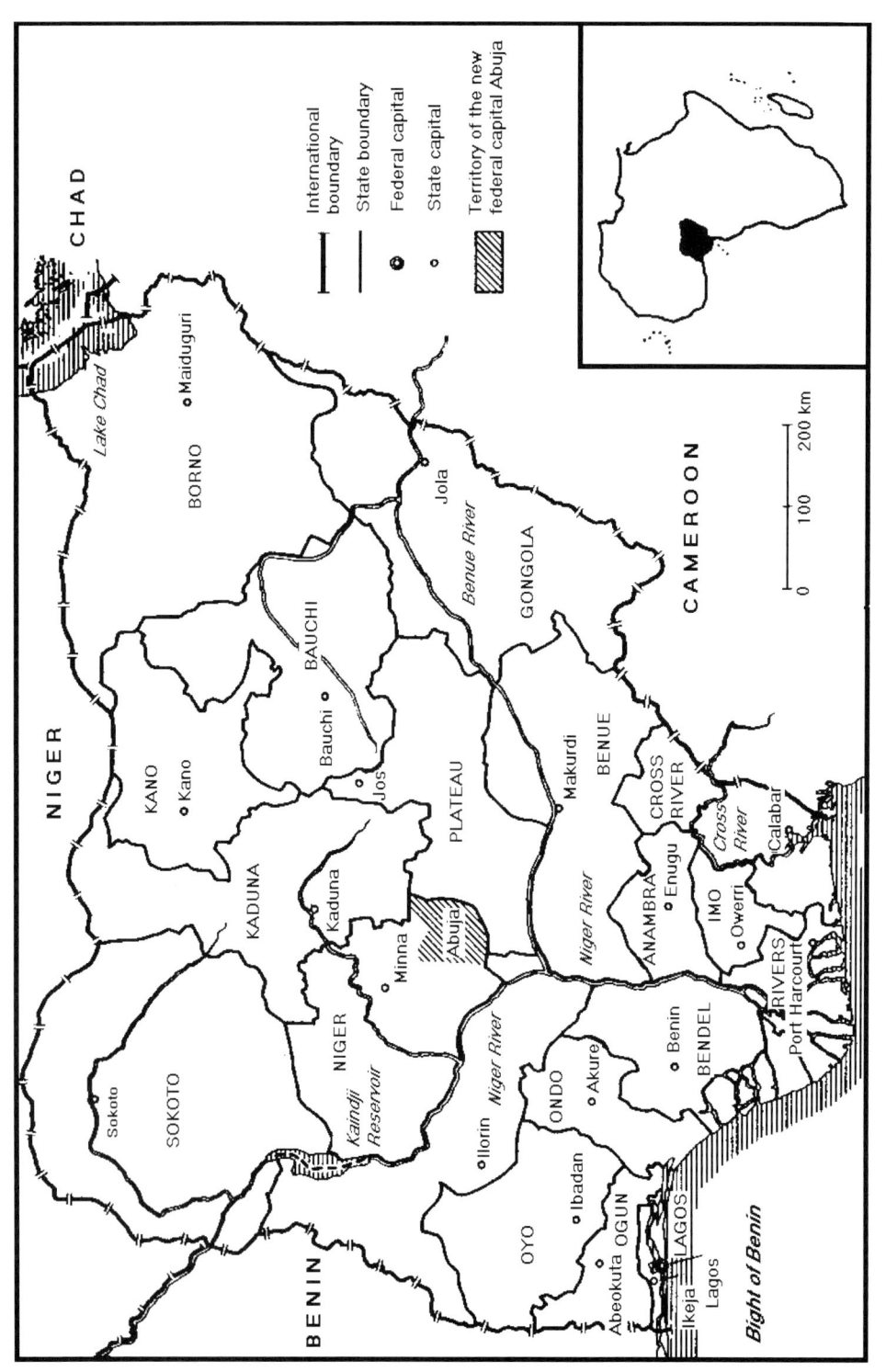

Map 1a. *Nigeria: Major geographical features and state divisions 1976-1987*
Source: Adapted from Statistisches Bundesamt (1983: 6)

Map 1b. *Nigeria: Present state divisions*
Source: Falola (1999: 2)

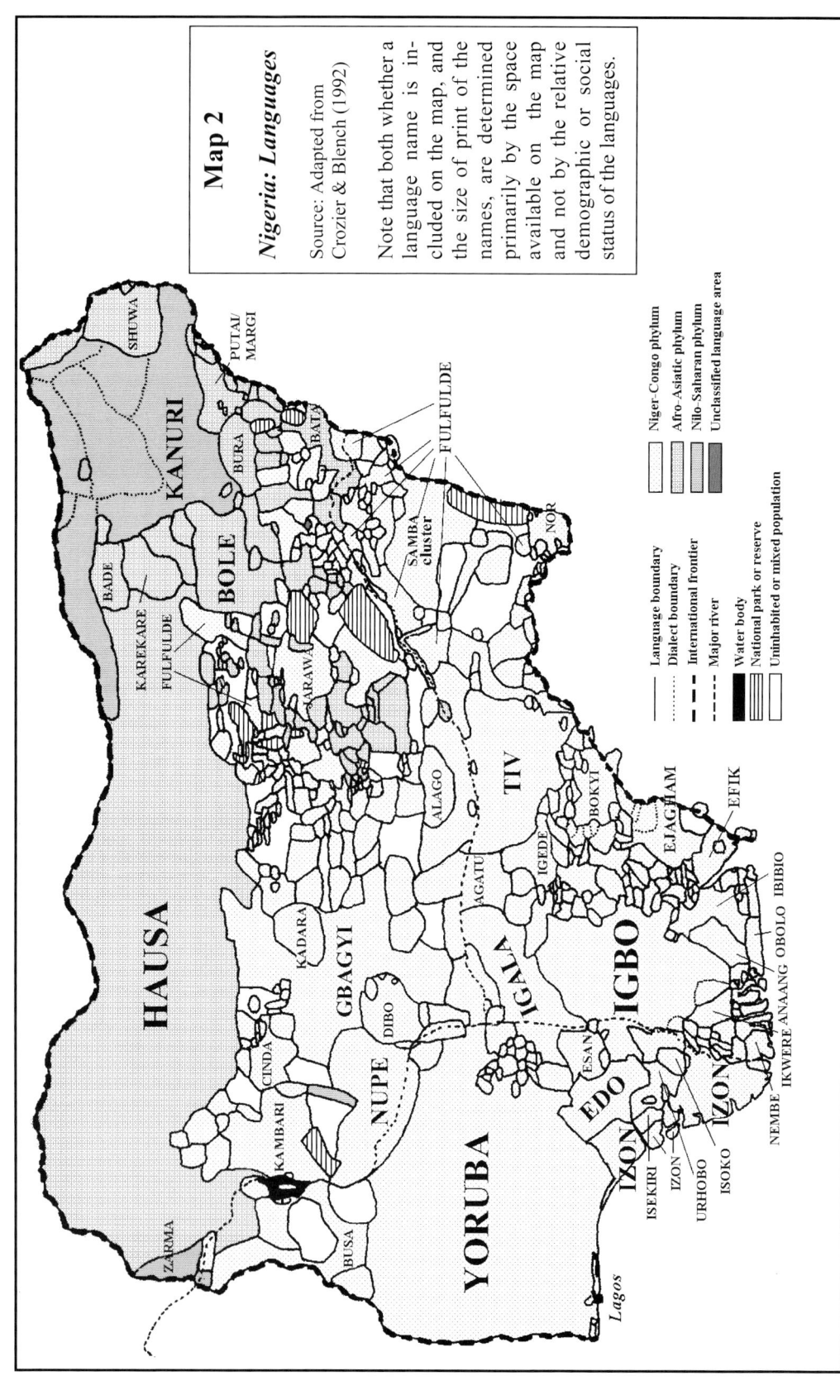

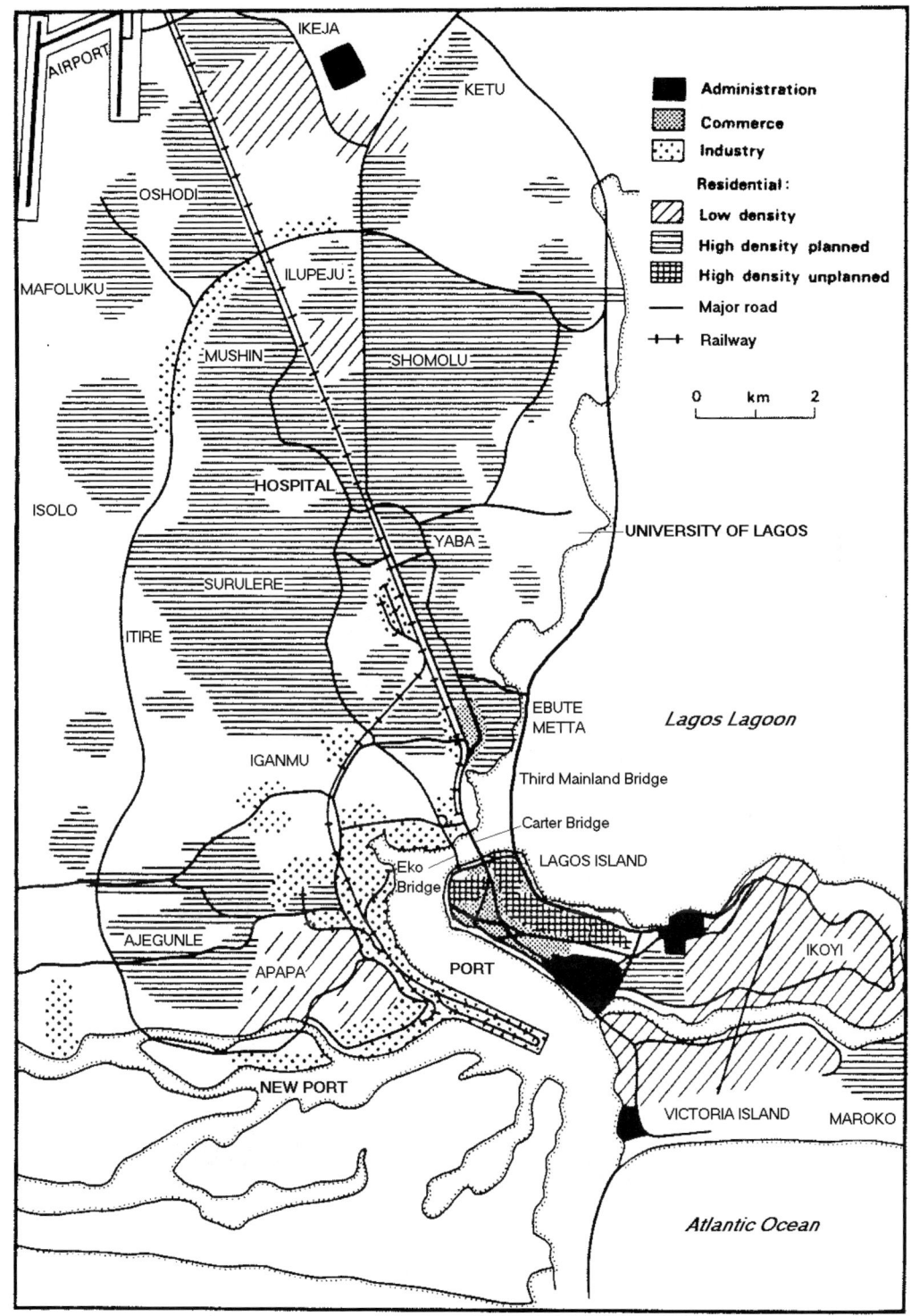

Map 3 *Metropolitan Lagos*

Source: Adapted from O'Connor (1983: 194); Barbour et al. (1982: 97); Peil (1991: 23)

The author wishes to thank John Benjamins Publishing Co. for permission to reproduce Table 5.7 and Figures 5.5, 5.10, 5.11(a/b), 5.12(a/b), 5.14(a/b), which first appeared (as Table 2 and Figures 1-5) in her article "'First year of nation's return to government of make you talk your own make I talk my own': Anglicisms versus pidginization in news translations into Nigerian Pidgin" published in *English World-Wide* 23 (2002), pp 195-222.

Four locations in Lagos where NigP is typically spoken

Iyana Ipaja Expressway

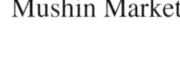

Mushin Market

Bariga Market

Ojuelegba Motor Park

1

Introduction

1.1 Nigerian Pidgin: terminological issues

Nigerian Pidgin is a structurally and functionally expanded pidgin, insofar as the term *pidgin* is appropriate at all. It is widely spoken in the country as a second language but has a growing number of first language speakers as well. Thus, like most of the English-lexified contact languages in West Africa (cf Holm 1989: 409), as well as Tok Pisin and related contact languages in the South Pacific (cf Mühlhäusler 1997: 9), it cannot easily be assigned to any of the traditional categories of "Pidgin" (spoken as a second language) or "Creole" (spoken as a first language). The common designations for the language, "(Nigerian) Pidgin" or "(Nigerian) Pidgin English",[1] therefore reflect the actual sociolinguistic situation only to some extent. Even more misleading is the popular term *Broken*. Prejudices that Nigerian Pidgin is some form of broken English persist to some extent in popular perceptions, but, as Agheyisi (1988: 233) observes,

> All serious and informed views about NPE [Nigerian Pidgin English] agree on its status as a distinct language in its own right, while recognizing its special relationship (historical and social) with English, on the one hand, and the indigenous languages in Nigeria, on the other.

In view of such observations on its relatively independent status, the language will be referred to as "Nigerian Pidgin" (NigP) rather than "Nigerian Pidgin English" in this book.

1.2 The origin and development of Nigerian Pidgin

While it is uncontroversial that the use of English-lexified contact varieties has a long tradition in what is today Nigeria, the exact circumstances of the formation and spread of modern NigP are a matter of debate. The points of controversy are the respective roles played by an early trade jargon and Sierra Leonean Krio.

Restructured English became established throughout coastal West Africa as the dominant medium of communication in trade relations between Africans and Europeans in the 18th century, supplanting an earlier Pidgin Portuguese (Holm 1989: 411). In the area of

---

[1] In the linguistic literature one also finds the terms *Anglo-Nigerian Pidgin* (Mann 1993a ff) and *Ẹnpi* (Omamor 1997).

present-day Nigeria, the trade contacts were concentrated in the Niger Delta and the Cross River estuary, i.e. in the eastern part of the coastal region (cf Map 1a). An English-lexified jargon is attested for this part of the coast from the middle of the 18th century (Huber 1999: 121; cf also Forde 1956). For the southwest, there are no 18th-century attestations of restructured English, but an English-based jargon apparently arose in Lagos after it had become a British colony in 1861 (Huber 1999: 121). The local jargon was, according to historical sources quoted in Huber (1999: 95, 120), not the only variety of restructured English in use in late 19th-century Lagos; there was also a Sierra Leonean variety. This can be explained by the presence of "recaptives" from Sierra Leone, i.e. Africans released at the port of Freetown from slave ships intercepted by the British after they had declared the slave trade illegal in 1808 (cf Holm 1989: 412). From the 1840s, important numbers of recaptives had settled in Lagos and other towns in the southwestern part of present-day Nigeria, bringing a knowledge of Sierra Leonean Krio with them (Huber 1999: 119ff). Another factor to be considered in connection with the role of Krio in 19th century Nigeria are Sierra Leoneans working for the British government:

> In 1821 the British government took over all British trading settlements in West Africa and began to expand and consolidate its control of certain areas. Until outright annexation of its protectorates towards the end of the century, however, the majority of Britain's administrators, missionaries, traders and teachers in its sphere of influence were Sierra Leonean Creoles rather than British-born subjects. This greatly increased the influence of Krio on West African Pidgin English in what became Nigeria and the German colonies of Togo and Kamerun. (Holm 1989: 412)

Folk wisdom has it that the early southeastern trade jargon is the direct ancestor of modern NigP. The following quotation from one of my interviews with NigP speakers (cf Appendix C, interview 5, ll 181-96) is typical of popular views of the origin of NigP:

> Di thing wey bring Pidgin be say, for Port Harcourt, when oyibo come dere, and dis Nigeria from dere, dem sit togeder, Nigeria no hear oyibo well well, e speak am for Pidgin. Den oyibo dey try, try small small come catch am. For Port Harcourt, na dere e start well well, before e come enter go Nigeria. Because if you reach Port Harcourt, na di language wey dey for Port Harcourt be dat. [...] So for Port Harcourt, Warri, all dis Ijo side, dem dey talk am well well.

> 'The way Pidgin originated was, in Port Harcourt, when the white people came there, and these Nigerians from there, they made contact, and the Nigerians didn't understand the white people's language very well, so they spoke it as Pidgin. Then the white people gradually learned it, too. In Port Harcourt, that's where it really started, and then it spread across Nigeria. Because if you go to Port Harcourt, that is the language there. So, in Port Harcourt, Warri, all these Ijo areas, they speak it a lot.'

Elugbe & Omamor (1991: 12f, 19f) also maintain that NigP developed out of the early trade jargon, with some Krio influence. They believe that in the multilingual southeastern part of the coastal region the Europeans' African trading partners must have found the jargon useful as a medium of communication among themselves (1991: 12). This would mean that "tertiary hybridization" (cf Whinnom 1971) or the use of the contact variety among different groups of substrate speakers – the crucial factor for the development of a stable Pidgin out of a jargon – took place at an early stage. The account given by Faraclas (1996:

3f) of the origin and development of NigP is in most respects similar to Elugbe & Omamor's scenario. Faraclas cites both the trade with the Europeans and the activities of missionaries from Sierra Leone as factors in the development of NigP. He emphasizes, however, that "at every stage of its history, Nigerian Pidgin has been used primarily as a means of communication among Nigerians rather than between Nigerians and traders, missionaries and other foreigners" (p 3). In addition, he puts forward the hypothesis that pre-existing pidgins based on Nigerian languages probably played a part in the development of NigP. Elugbe & Omamor (1991: 19) consider this unlikely.

A revision of the received wisdom is offered by Huber (1999). On the basis of historical evidence relating mainly to the Gold Coast (roughly the part of the West African coast which today belongs to Ghana) he argues that the early trade jargons were highly limited in terms of both their number of speakers and their uses. He shows that communication between Europeans in the trading posts and Africans in the surrounding communities took place mainly through a small number of African middlemen, so that direct linguistic contacts between the two groups were minimized. Furthermore, he points out that white men's African wives or concubines, as well as their offspring, retained strong ties with the local African population; they continued to speak African languages, and the jargon remained an additional language for communication with Europeans. On the basis of historical linguistic data, Huber then documents the diffusion of an important number of Krio features in several varieties of West African Pidgin, including the Nigerian, Ghanaian and Cameroonian varieties. In contrast to Holm (1989; see the quotation above), Huber points out that the number Sierra Leoneans serving the British government was quite small and considers their role of in the diffusion of these features "at least doubtful" (p 123). His conclusion regarding the origin of modern NigP is therefore that it must have originated in the southwest, where the more numerous receptives settled, with the English-based Pidgin that had developed there and Krio as the major elements in its formation.[2] It was in the southwest, he argues, that tertiary hybridization first occurred, as the Krio-influenced variety of NigP was used for communication between Sierra Leoneans and Nigerians, and later also between Nigerians themselves, whereas the early southeastern jargon had been restricted to Afro-European communication.

Today, the Niger Delta – the zone that used to comprise Bendel and Rivers State, and particularly the Warri-Sapele area in what is now Delta State (cf Maps 1a/b) – is considered the heartland of NigP, although the southwestern metropolis of Lagos as well as Cross River State in the far southeast or its capital, Calabar, are often cited as part of the major NigP-speaking zone as well (Agheyisi 1984a: 212f; Elugbe & Omamor 1991: 12; Mann 1996: 94, 97). Huber (1999: 124f) is aware of this but believes that the present-day situation is only seemingly at odds with his account of the origin of NigP. He hypothesizes that the Krio-influenced variety of NigP which had developed in the southwest in the late 19th century spread along the coast with the extension of British interests and ultimately became more important in the multilingual southeast than in the Yoruba-dominated southwest (cf Map 2).

---

[2] The Krio features in Ghanaian and Cameroonian Pidgin are explained by Huber as the result of the spread of the Krio-influenced Nigerian variety in the course of early 20th century labour migrations.

The question of origins has been dealt with at some length here because it will become relevant in the discussion of present-day variation in NigP. However, it is not my aim to contribute to the debate regarding NigP's origin, and I will take both of the main possibilities that have been outlined into consideration, i.e. an origin in the southeastern trade contacts and an origin in the Lagos colony (with an important Krio element).

NigP has remained in contact with both with its lexifier and its substrate languages throughout its history. English became the official language of the country under the British colonial rule and has retained this function to the present day, while most Nigerians continue to speak an indigenous language as their first language.

Since about 1960, the time of Nigeria's independence, NigP has moved beyond its original role as an auxiliary medium of communication in restricted informal contexts where neither English nor an indigenous language could bridge a communicative gap. It is now common for educated Nigerians to use it in their informal conversations, and the language has also acquired some functions in formal domains (cf Agheyisi 1984a, 1988; Mann 1993b).

1.3   Previous studies of Nigerian Pidgin

The two earliest published studies of NigP, an overview article by Bernard Mafeni and Rebecca Agheyisi's doctoral dissertation, both date from 1971. Since then, NigP has received considerable attention from linguists.

Scholarly articles have been published in increasing numbers since the early 1980s. Many of them focus on structural aspects (e.g. Egbe 1980; Ofuani 1981a; Faraclas et al. 1984; Faraclas 1984, 1986, 1987, 1991; Mann 1993a; Poplack & Tagliamonte 1996; Tagliamonte, Poplack & Eze 1997), but the functions and status of the language have also been investigated (e.g. Shnukal & Marchese 1983, Donwa-Ifode 1984, Mann 1993b). Another field of interest has been language planning. Status planning has attracted the greater amount of attention (e.g. Ndolo 1989, Gani-Ikilama 1990, Adegbija 1994), but issues in corpus planning have been discussed as well (see especially Agheyisi 1988).

A number of book-length studies, mostly PhD theses, have also appeared. These include Elugbe & Omamor's *Nigerian Pidgin: Background and Prospects* (1991), a broad study dealing with historical, structural and sociolinguistic aspects, Faraclas's comprehensive grammar of the language (1996), and the more specialized studies by Eze (1980) and Oloruntoba (1992).

In spite of the amount of scholarship available, one may point out a number of ways in which research on NigP has so far been limited or biased. These are described below.

(a) *The geographical scope of empirical studies:* Scholars have so far concentrated on NigP as spoken in the Niger Delta. All of Faraclas's important structural work is on NigP in Rivers State; the corpus on which most of his studies are based, including the 1996 grammar, was recorded in Port Harcourt. Sociolinguistic studies conducted in various locations in the Delta are Shnukal & Marchese (1983), Donwa-Ifode (1984) and Oloruntoba (1992). Data from Lagos and Calabar, the two main NigP-speaking centres outside the Delta, have so far been cited only in Agheyisi's (1984a) study of variation in NigP and

Mann's (1996, 1998, 2001) reports of results of a sociolinguistic survey he conducted; in both cases, these data are combined with data from the Delta region.[3]

(b) *The data and its analysis in studies of NigP grammar:* There are a number of studies which are based mainly or solely on introspection. For example, Agheyisi (1971: 3f) mentions introspection as one of her data sources, besides the judgments of three informants and examples from novels and a radio drama serial (*Safe Journey*). In the absence of any remark on the source of the data, one would assume that introspection is also the primary basis of Elugbe & Omamor's (1991: chapter 4) structural description of the language. In itself, introspection is of course a valid approach, but it harbours the danger of bias, and Elugbe & Omamor have in fact been criticized for adopting a "possessive, defensive, emotional and puristic attitude" to NigP (Jibril 1995: 234). In those studies which are based on corpora of authentic speech, the tendency has been to interpret the data mainly in qualitative terms by isolating typical patterns (see especially Faraclas 1996). Quantitative analyses have so far not played a major role in studies of NigP grammar, with the exception of the work done by Poplack & Tagliamonte. These authors have been able to show that at least in the variety of NigP they investigate (see (c) below), certain grammatical markers are not nearly as important as previous studies suggest.

(c) *Social variation:* Agheyisi (1984a) is an insightful study of social varieties in NigP, and there is an article by Faraclas (1986; expanded as Faraclas 1991) which focusses on social variation in a specific aspect of NigP grammar (the pronoun system). The predominant tendency – explicit or implicit – has, however, been to concentrate on a core variety often identified as the speech of fluent, not highly educated speakers and to occasionally refer to other varieties (Agheyisi 1971, Eze 1980, Faraclas 1996) or even to virtually ignore social variation (Elugbe & Omamor 1991, chapter 4). The work of Poplack & Tagliamonte is exceptional in that it is based on a corpus of educated NigP (as spoken by Nigerian immigrants in Canada).

(d) *Domains of NigP use:* The interest of researchers has so far been directed primarily towards informal, mostly conversational speech. The work of Faraclas, as well as that of Poplack & Tagliamonte, is based on corpora in which this is the only type of language use represented. Radio broadcasts, arguably the most important more formal domain where NigP is now used, have received much less attention. Previous authors such as Agheyisi (1984a, 1988), Elugbe & Omamor (1991; also Elugbe 1995) and Jibril (1995) make only some isolated remarks on NigP use in this domain and give a few text samples. Some authors have studied written NigP on the basis of selected text samples from newspaper columns or literary texts (Ofuani 1981b, Huber & Görlach 1996, Omamor 1997; also Elugbe & Omamor 1991, Jibril 1995). The aim of these studies is mostly to uncover deviations from "proper" NigP. Omamor (1997) in particular is very critical of the way NigP is used in such texts. She concludes that literary NigP is mostly a gross distortion of the language ("pseudopidgin"). In the same vein, Elugbe & Omamor (1991) reject the idiosyncratic type of language used in the newspaper column *Wakabout*, supposed to be

---

[3] Agheyisi (1984a: 231n4) explains that the speech samples on which her article is based were collected mainly in Lagos and Benin City. Mann's (1996, 1998, 2001) survey was conducted in several urban centres in southern Nigeria; these include Lagos and Calabar as well as Warri, Benin City, and Port Harcourt in the Delta.

written in a form of NigP, as "most definitely not NP [Nigerian Pidgin]" (p 72) because of a number of "violations of the rules of NP grammar" (p 70). Jibril (1995: 234f) considers this analysis exaggerated.

1.4   Aims and scope of the present study

The present study looks at NigP in its relationship with English within the language contact situation brought about by Nigeria's multilingual sociolinguistic set-up. A central aim is to determine the nature and extent of English influences in present-day NigP, especially as spoken by educated speakers, on the lexical, grammatical and discourse levels. In particular, I would like to investigate whether a linguistic continuum of the type found in the anglophone Caribbean has also developed, or is developing, between NigP and English.

A second major issue that will be addressed is the linguistic consequences of the expanding use of NigP in more formal domains, exemplified by radio broadcasts. This second area of investigation overlaps to a great extent with the first, as radio broadcasts are produced by educated speakers. However, there are important additional questions. Is a tendency towards "pseudopidgin" – whatever its exact role in written texts – manifest in the broadcasts? Do they show ways in which NigP can be adapted structurally to its new functions? To what extent does a comparison of radio broadcasts with face-to-face speech reveal register differences?

Furthermore, it is clear that the two aspects outlined above impinge on the status of NigP as well. For example, if NigP or at least certain varieties of the language can be shown to undergo major restructuring in the direction of English, this will weaken claims as to its status as a major language in its own right. If radio broadcasts supposedly in NigP turn out to propagate "pseudopidgin", this will seriously undermine the functional expansion of the language, while a more or less successful use in this domain will enhance its functional potential. The study seeks to address such interrelations between micro- and macro-sociolinguistic aspects, and the functions and status of NigP, its potential for further development and the prospects for language planning are therefore issues to be discussed as well.

1.5   The research setting: metropolitan Lagos

Lagos State is the smallest state of the Nigerian federation in terms of area, but it has the highest number of inhabitants (results of the most recent census, held in 1991, as reported in Statistisches Bundesamt 1992: 34). The great majority of the state's population (93%, according to 1991 census results cited in Abiodun 1997: 195) lives in the urban agglomeration of metropolitan Lagos.

The city of Lagos became the capital when Nigeria was created by the amalgamation of the Northern and Southern British Protectorates in 1914. Although it now no longer serves as the seat of the federal government, it remains the country's primary city in all other respects:

> Despite the movement of the federal capital to Abuja in 1990, metropolitan Lagos is still the main economic, social, and financial centre and the hub of international communications. Consequently it is the most important point for the dissemination of information and innovation throughout the country. It is also the nerve-centre of manufacturing industries and commercial activities [...] and is unrivalled by any other urban centre in Nigeria. (Abiodun 1997: 198)

While the opportunities offered by the city have always attracted migrants from other parts of the country, it is since the 1950s that population growth, due mainly to migration although natural increase is also high, has really become intense (Peil 1991: 16, 20), and by 2003 the population of metropolitan Lagos was estimated to be about 10 million (United Nations 2004). Many migrants have come from the surrounding Yoruba states and the Yoruba are still the predominant ethnic group in Lagos (Peil 1991: 30), but the presence of other ethnic groups has also shaped it, and it is now essentially a heterogeneous metropolis, although with visible Yoruba roots (ibid. p 193).

Metropolitan Lagos comprises an island area (Lagos Island, Ikoyi, Victoria Island) and a large and growing area on the adjoining mainland, which are connected by three bridges (cf Map 3). For various reasons, where one lives in Lagos is not always a reliable indicator of one's social status (Peil 1991: 26, 154), but the following generalizations can be made (cf Peil 1991: 26ff, 151ff): Ikoyi and Victoria Island, as well as parts of Apapa and Ikeja in the southern and northern part of the mainland, respectively, are expensive residential districts. Surulere and parts of Yaba in the central part of the mainland are among the areas that have mostly middle income residents. Low income areas include Lagos Island, Ajegunle in the southern part of the mainland, many districts in the central part of the mainland (e.g. Mushin, Shomolu) and some northern suburbs (e.g. Agege, situated to the north of Ikeja).

Metropolitan Lagos is the main research setting and all the speech samples were obtained there. The macro-sociolinguistic part of the study also includes some data from Calabar. The choice of metropolitan Lagos as the main research setting was motivated by three principal factors:

(a) As observed in 1.3, scholars have so far focussed on NigP's heartland in the Niger Delta. However, if the development and prospects of NigP in Nigeria at large are at issue, other areas, particularly those where NigP has been gaining ground in recent times, must be taken into consideration as well. Outside its heartland, NigP is primarily an urban phenomenon (cf Agheyisi 1984a: 212; Mann 1993: 169). Mafeni (1971: 98) has made the following observation in this connection:

> Nigerian Pidgin is essentially a product of the process of urbanization. [...] The rapidly growing towns of Nigeria have increasingly become the melting pots of the many tribes and races which constitute Nigeria, and Pidgin seems to be a very widely spoken lingua franca [...].

Lagos is perhaps the best example of the spread of NigP due to urbanization. In view of the historical evidence adduced by Huber (1999), it is difficult to maintain Elugbe & Omamor's (1991: 12) position that NigP is "decidedly a recent phenomenon in metropolitan Lagos". However, it is probably safe to say that the widespread use of NigP in Lagos is due to the large-scale migration to the city in recent times.

(b) With its mixed population, Lagos offers the researcher the unique opportunity to obtain a sample of NigP as spoken by people with diverse backgrounds while studying language use in a particular setting.

(c) The cities in general and Lagos in particular also offer the best opportunity to study English influences in NigP. English is usually acquired through formal education, and in urban areas, the proportion of the population that does not have any formal education (13.9% and 25.4% for males and females, respectively, according to National Population Commission 2000: 16) is much lower than in rural areas (31.2% and 43.4% for males and females, respectively; ibid.).[4] In addition, the southwest region where Lagos is situated has the highest proportion of persons with a secondary or tertiary education (ibid.). Lagos itself is described by Peil (1991: 194) as having "one of the best-educated populations in Africa". The urban population also has greater access to mass media, in which English is widely used.

1.6 Data and methodology

Since the study encompasses several different aspects of NigP use, it also has to combine different data sources and methodological approaches. The main division is between macro- and micro-sociolinguistic data and methods. The macro-sociolinguistic data were collected during a first field trip to Nigeria from July to October 1997. The main research methods I employed were questionnaires and interviews. In the course of the field trip, I also compiled a collection of illustrative samples of written and spoken NigP. Most of the speech samples for the micro-sociolinguistic analyses were, however, recorded during a second field trip from April to October 2000, although I did include a few suitable samples from the earlier collection.

The fieldwork for the micro-sociolinguistic part of the study was subdivided into two principal stages. The first was the compilation of a computerized corpus of spoken educated NigP comprising face-to-face speech and radio broadcasts. The second was the elicitation of reactions of NigP speakers to extracts from the corpus by means of a questionnaire. The questionnaire was designed to elicit, among other things, lexical and grammatical items considered English elements. These data form the basis of my own subsequent quantitative and qualitative analyses of the corpus. A third but relatively minor aspect were additional recordings of less educated speakers. Further data from the second field trip include a few more interviews on sociolinguistic questions to complement those conducted in 1997 and the insights I gained into the production of NigP radio broadcasts in the course of an internship in the Pidgin Section of Radio Nigeria 3, Lagos, between May and August 2000.

Details of field methods and data analysis are explained in the respective chapters in which the data are discussed.

---

[4] The figures apply to persons age six and over.

1.7 Outline of the study

Chapter 2 is devoted to theoretical and methodological issues. Chapter 3 describes the functions and status of NigP in the context of the multilingual sociolinguistic set-up in Nigeria in general and Lagos in particular. In Chapter 4, I begin to look at the linguistic side of the language contact situation in Nigeria; the chapter provides an overview of relevant aspects of language variation and change which takes into account NigP and English as well as the indigenous languages. Chapter 5 is the core of the study: the analysis of the corpus of educated NigP. Selected additional recordings of less educated speakers are analysed in Chapter 6. Chapter 7 deals with questions of language planning. The concluding Chapter 8 draws together the main findings from the empirical parts of the study and relates them to the theoretical issues raised in Chapter 2; the prospects for the future development of the language contact situation in Nigeria are briefly discussed as well.

The study includes four appendices, which present the questionnaires (Appendix A), the full range of data from the elicitation test (Appendix B), transcripts of interviews (Appendix C) and samples of written NigP (Appendix D). Appendices A, B and D as well as an overview of the content of Appendix C are printed in the book. The full Appendix C appears on the accompanying CD. The CD also contains the complete corpus, detailed background information on all the texts and speakers, and selected sample texts from the corpus with sound.

1.8 Orthography

How best to represent the recorded speech samples in writing is by no means a straightforward issue in any research on spoken language (cf e.g. Edwards & Lampert 1993). In the present case, the problem was compounded by the fact that NigP does not have a standardized orthography. Which type of spelling to use was in fact one of the most difficult questions I faced in devising a transcription system for the study. A phonetic transcription according to IPA conventions was out of the question. Since phonetics and phonology are not among my research interests, it would have complicated the transcription process and reduced readability unnecessarily. A basically phonemic orthography of the type proposed and used by some linguists (e.g. Elugbe & Omamor 1991, Faraclas 1996) might have been a satisfactory solution in some respects, but practical factors militated against it: since such a system has so far been employed only by specialists, I could not expect my research assistants and informants to be able to use it in helping to transcribe and analyse the large amount of data. In the end, I had to settle for an English-based spelling system of the type used in non-scholarly writing in NigP, such as radio scripts, public enlightenment texts, newspaper columns and literary texts (one example each of these types of texts is given in Appendix D). This had several practical advantages for my work: it is easy to use, compatible with any standard software and readable to the educated layperson. But of course, the decision to use a transcription system of this type was not entirely unproblematic. As there are no fixed conventions, writers are not always consistent in their spelling, but I needed a consistent transcription and therefore had to devise a system of my own that would be maximally close to the spelling my informants were familiar with from popular usage and at the same time maximally systematic.

To arrive at such a system, I have employed the following strategies: I have generalized the very common tendency in writing in NigP to replace <th> by <d> where it represents /ð/ in English[5] (where English has /θ/, writers of NigP texts sometimes use <t>, but this is much less common, and I have retained <th>).[6] No other general adaptations have been made. Where there is no obvious motivation, adaptations of individual words have also been avoided. For example, *bodi* in the news script in Appendix D (Text D 1, l 17) is spelled *body* in the version of the same text that is part of the corpus, and I do not use spellings like *bicos/becos* (Text D 2, l 14/Text D 3, l 10) and *bifor* (Text D 2, ll 7, 15, 37, 52) but *because* and *before*. However, there are also cases where an English spelling is not available, where an adaptation commonly made in NigP writing is useful to avoid homography, or where a deviation from the etymological principle in the spelling of an English-derived word is justifiable on phonological grounds. In such cases, I have usually adopted what appeared to be the most common variant in my collection of NigP writing. For example, the Portuguese-derived NigP words for 'child' and 'know' are spelled *pikin*[7] and *sabi*, respectively. The imperfective aspect auxiliary and locative copula is spelled *dey*[8] and the relative clause introducer *wey*.[9] I have also taken over from my collection of NigP writing the spelling *don* for the perfective aspect auxiliary,[10] while *done* is reserved for the lexical verb 'be cooked'. The definite article is spelled *di*; *di* is a common spelling for the article (which in NigP is generally pronounced /di/, regardless of whether the following word starts with a vowel or a consonant),[11] and it is thus distinguished from *de* as a variant of the third person plural pronoun *dem*. *Siddon, comot* and *throway* are the spellings I have adopted for the NigP simple verbs derived from English *sit down, come out* and *throw away*, respectively.

---

[5] The NigP sound system as described, for example, by Elugbe & Omamor (1991: 75ff) and Faraclas (1996: 255ff) lacks the interdental fricatives, and the alveolar stops are used in their place. In educated speech the interdental fricatives sometimes occur (cf also Agheyisi 1984a: 218), but this is not a subject for the present study.

[6] Cf also the texts in Appendix D. In Texts D 1 and D 4, <th> representing /ð/ in English is consistently replaced by <d>. In Text D 2, this replacement can also be observed in almost all instances; the only exceptions are *their* (l 28) and *that* (l 69). In Text D 3, <d> is used in all instances of the third person plural personal and possessive pronoun (*dem*), all instances of the (singular) demonstratives (*dis, dat*), most instances of the definite article, and in *broda* (l 38), while <th> occurs in two instances of the definite article (ll 50, 55) and in *other* (ll 31, 34, 52), *there* (l 27) and *than* (l 43). Where English has /θ/, <th> is generally retained in all of these texts. The only exception one may cite is *trowey* (from *throw away*; Text D 1, l 6).

[7] Cf especially Text D 2. A variant which is also quite common (although it does not occur in the texts in Appendix D) is *pickin*.

[8] This is also the predominant spelling in the texts in appendix D: In Texts D 1, D 2 and D 4, *dey* is used throughout. In Text D 3, a distinction is made between the auxiliary, spelled *de* (ll 14, 16, 18, 19, 23, 31, 47, 60, 62, 63), and the copula, spelled *dey* (ll 40, 42, 68).

[9] This spelling is also used consistently in all texts in Appendix D.

[10] This is also the spelling used in the texts in Appendix D wherever the item occurs.

[11] In Text D 1 and D 2 in Appendix D, the spelling *di* is used in all instances of the definite article, while the writer of Text D 3 uses mostly *de* (ll. 42 43, 48, 54, 55) and in two instances *the* (ll 50, 55). (In Text D 4 the definite article does not occur.)

The use or non-use of English inflectional endings (e.g. plural *-s*) is reflected in the transcripts, as is the presence or absence of initial and final consonants in function words when this distinguishes the English and NigP variants (e.g. *he* versus *e*). I also decided to indicate striking cases of vowel epenthesis (e.g. *helep* versus *help*).

Longer stretches of speech in English (as identified according to a set of criteria that will be specified in the course of the analyses) are transcribed in English orthography without adjustments. Indigenous language elements (the larger ones of these especially are mostly Yoruba) are handled similarly as English ones.[12] Single items (except personal names) in otherwise NigP/English discourse are always adapted orthographically. For example, I use <sh> for the postalveolar fricative and <kp> for the voiceless labio-velar plosive instead of the respective Yoruba graphemes, <ṣ> and <p>, and I do not use diacritics, so that, for instance, Yoruba *ṣẹlè* 'happen' and *ọlọ́pàá* 'police' are spelled *shele* and *olokpa*, respectively.[13] In the longer stretches of indigenous language speech that were identified such adaptations are not made.[14]

The main gate to the University of Lagos campus,
the author's base while conducting field research in 1997 and 2000

---

[12] I would like to thank my research assistant Atinuke Obakoya for her help with Yoruba transcriptions. Thanks are further due in this connection to Prof. Gboyega Alaba and Mr K O Oladeji of the Department of African and Asian Studies, University of Lagos, who gave advice on orthographic details.

[13] In the case of the Yoruba question-introducing particle *ṣé*, I have also added a *y*, adapting it to *shey* (cf *dey*, *wey*) in order to distinguish it from the English pronoun *she*.

[14] However, in the electronic version of the corpus, the diacritics are omitted, as they are not compatible with the plain text format chosen to facilitate automatic analyses. In the extracts from the corpus and additional texts printed in subsequent chapters of the study the diacritics are included.

2

Language contact, variation and change: theoretical and methodological background

2.1   Introduction

As stated in Chapter 1, the present study is a sociolinguistic investigation of a currently creolizing expanded pidgin which coexists with its lexifier. It has also already been mentioned that a central concern of the study is to test the applicability to the Nigerian case of an important concept in Pidgin/Creole (P/C) studies, the (post-)Creole or (post-)Pidgin continuum. In addition to the continuum as a model of linguistic variation in P/C-lexifier contact situations, the related notion of decreolization or depidginization as a special type of language change which may take place in a P/C coexisting with its lexifier will be examined as well.

Regarding the relationship between sociolinguistics and P/C studies, Rickford (1988: 54f) has observed that

> linguists studying pidgins and creoles often appear to make insufficient use of sociolinguistic principles and methods and to make little reference to data from non-creole communities. When we discuss language attitudes, or language maintenance and shift, or code switching, or change in progress, or virtually any sociolinguistic topic in particular creole-speaking communities, we rarely refer to parallel cases which have been studied in Paraguay or Tanzania or Austria or Montreal or New York City or to theories and models which have been developed in relation to these [...]. It is as if we were convinced that the pidgin/creole cases were unique unto themselves.

The view that P/Cs are unique has also been challenged with regard to their structure. Mufwene (e.g. 1986a, 1994, 1997, 2000) argues that Creoles (as well as pidgins, cf Mufwene 1997) can be defined on the basis of the specific sociohistorical circumstances of their genesis, but that there are no structural features which set them apart from other languages.[1] He also rejects the notion of decreolization as a type of change unique to Creoles:

> Insofar as creoles are natural language varieties – and the structural changes they allegedly have been subjected to under the influence of their lexifiers are not different from those changes noncreole varieties have experienced under similar conditions – it does not seem

---

[1]   For a contrary view, see McWhorter (1998, 2000).

necessary to devise a special category of decreolization phenomena to discuss them. (Mufwene 1994: 72)

The present study is informed by the view that a P/C need not behave differently from any other language in a given situation. This has two important implications. First, although the study discusses concepts that have been developed in the framework of P/C studies, it is not confined to these but draws on concepts from the broader field of language contact studies and the general discipline of sociolinguistics as well. The present chapter provides a selective discussion of theories, concepts and methods that have been developed within each of these (of course partially overlapping) frameworks. I will concentrate on those aspects that are relevant to the concerns of this study, beginning with the (post-)P/C continuum and then moving on to other theoretical and methodological issues. The second implication is that concrete cases that will be considered for comparison are not only other P/Cs coexisting with their lexifiers but also non-P/C languages involved in a similar contact situation with English as NigP. One does not even have to look to other communities for comparable non-P/C cases, as Nigeria's indigenous languages offer themselves for comparison. (While selected other P/C cases will be discussed in the present chapter, the way Nigeria's indigenous languages are affected by the contact with English is a topic that is reserved for Chapter 4.)

2.2 The concepts of the (post-)P/C continuum and decreolization versus alternative views on linguistic variation and change in P/C-lexifier contact situations

2.2.1 Linguistic variation in the anglophone Caribbean

Since the concept of the (post-)Creole continuum was developed primarily in relation to the situation in the anglophone Caribbean, I will begin with a consideration of linguistic variation in that area.

The Caribbean countries in which an English-based Creole is spoken and English is the official language are generally characterized by a high degree of linguistic variation. The span of variation is, however, greater in countries such as Jamaica and Guyana, where there exists a "conservative" Creole, and smaller in Trinidad, Barbados and other countries whose Creole is an "intermediate" variety closer to English.[2] (In a few cases, the situation is further complicated by additional, unrelated varieties; this applies in particular to Belize, where Spanish and Amerindian languages are spoken, and the islands of Dominica and St. Lucia, where a French-based Creole is widely used.[3]) Sebba (1997: 210f) illustrates the type of linguistic variation that can be observed in the anglophone Caribbean by the following Jamaican sample sentences, which represent versions of the same sentence ranging from the one in the broadest Creole (at the top in my arrangement) to the standard English one (at the bottom):

---

[2] The classification is taken from Winford (1993: 4).
[3] For an overview of the language situation in the anglophone Caribbean see e.g. Winford (1991).

>   me a nyam
>   me a eat
>   me eatin'
>   I eatin'
>   I is eatin'
>   I am eating

The example shows lexical (*nyam* vs *eat*) and morphosyntactic variation (*me* vs *I*; *a* + V vs V*in'* vs invariant *is* + V*in'* vs inflected *be* + V*ing*). The fact that there is a whole range of different versions intermediate between the broadest Creole and the standard English one is due to two factors: the transition from Creole to English forms occurs at different points in the spectrum for the different features considered (*nyam* occurs only in one version while *me* occurs in three), and there are intermediate forms which are not compatible with either broad Creole or standard English (V*in'* and invariant *is* + V*in'*). The wide range of variation illustrated here does not, however, mean that the different forms can be combined randomly. For example, a sentence such as *I am nyaming* does not normally occur (Sebba 1997: 214).

2.2.2   *Development and applications of the Creole continuum concept*

The formulation of the concept of a (post-)Creole continuum (later extended to "(post-)pidgin-continuum") as a model for the kind of variation described above is often associated with David DeCamp's seminal article "Toward a generative analysis of a post-creole speech continuum" (1971). However, neither the idea of a spectrum of variation between a restructured variety and its lexifier nor the term *continuum* to describe it were new when this article was published and DeCamp himself had already contributed to research in the area (see the discussion in Holm 1988: 54ff).

The 1971 article and DeCamp's earlier work in the area are based on the example of Jamaica. A major contribution to the development of the continuum model and its associated methodology has also been made by Derek Bickerton (especially in Bickerton 1973a) on the basis of Guyanese data. The Jamaican and Guyanese continua are often regarded as the prototypical cases, but the concept has been applied to other P/C-lexifier contact situations both within and outside the anglophone Caribbean as well.

In line with the usage of many subsequent studies, which reflects criticism of the diachronic assumptions in DeCamp's original formulation of the concept (see 2.2.5), the term *Creole continuum* will be used in the following discussion instead of DeCamp's *post-Creole continuum*.

2.2.3   *The Creole continuum as a model of synchronic variation*

The most fundamental and enduring claim of the Creole continuum concept as originally developed by DeCamp and Bickerton is the non-discrete character of the synchronic variation that can be observed between the Creole and the lexically related standard language. In an often-quoted passage, DeCamp (1971: 350) writes that "in Jamaica there is no sharp cleavage between creole and standard" but rather a "linguistic continuum" or "continuous spectrum of speech varieties". He adds (p 354) that the situation does not literally represent a continuum because the number of speakers is finite and the number of variable linguistic features limited, and explains (ibid.):

> By calling it a continuum I mean that given two samples of Jamaican speech which differ substantially from one another, it is usually possible to find a third intermediate level in an additional sample. Thus it is not practicable to describe the system in terms of two or three or six or any other manageable number of discrete social dialects.

In the terminology that has come to be associated with the model mainly through Bickerton (1973a, 1975b), the broad Creole is referred to as the basilect, the standard variety as the acrolect and the intermediate varieties as the mesolect(s).[4]

The linguistic continuum has clear social correlates. DeCamp (1971: 358) observes that in his illustrative "mini-continuum" (ibid. p 355), the informant who uses only standard features is a well-educated urban shopowner, the one who uses only Creole ones is an illiterate peasant, and the positions of the other informants, who use standard and Creole features to varying degrees, also correlate roughly with their social status. However, he argues (ibid. p 355) that the linguistic varieties and features that form the continuum can (and should) be ordered on the basis of linguistic data alone and that such correlations – widely confirmed by sociolinguistic studies in the anglophone Caribbean, cf Winford (1991: 572) – are only a second step. Bickerton in his work on the Guyanese continuum strongly emphasizes the primacy of the linguistic over the social (cf e.g. Bickerton 1973a: 666, 1975b: 6). This approach has been much criticized (cf e.g. Sankoff 1977: 299ff). Rickford (1987: 31) points out that such criticism does not invalidate the model itself, since more socially oriented work is possible in a continuum framework as well.

Both DeCamp (1971: 354) and Bickerton (1973b: 20) were of the opinion that most of the variation in the respective communities they studied corresponded to a single dimension Creole vs standard but did envisage the possibility of a multidimensional continuum. In Rickford's (1987) description of the continuum model, unidimensionality becomes an essential feature, like non-discreteness (p 32). The view of the unidimensionality of variation in a Creole continuum was, however, controversial even at that time. It had been challenged in particular by Le Page & Tabouret-Keller (1985) on the basis of data mainly from the more multilingual countries of Belize and St. Lucia. Rickford (1987: 24ff) argues that a multidimensional continuum is incompatible with the technique of implicational scaling[5] (see 2.2.4) and suggests that complex variation of the type studied by these authors could be handled by a combination of unidimensional continua.

The claim of non-discreteness on which the continuum model hinges has not remained unchallenged either. Scholars who argue for two discrete systems, Creole and English, do not deny that the kind of variation described in 2.2.1 exists in the anglophone Caribbean but explain it in terms of "borrowing and interference" (Bailey 1971: 342) or "code-shifting" (Lawton 1980). Rickford (1987: 16ff) discusses these and similar views and comes to the conclusion that the continuum model is more adequate. More recently, there seems to have

---

[4] The terms *basilect* and *acrolect* had been used earlier by Stewart (1965). DeCamp (1971) did not use any of these terms.
[5] Le Page & Tabouret-Keller (1985) do not use this technique. They are concerned with the socio-psychological motivations for speakers' linguistic choices – their "acts of identity" – and not the systematic patterns of linguistic variation that implicational scales reveal.

been a certain convergence between continuum critics and advocates. Winford (1997) offers a weaker version of the discrete systems approach by arguing that linguistic variation in the anglophone Caribbean is produced by "the interaction of relatively self-contained though not completely discrete grammars" (p 260).[6] Patrick (1999: 292) defends what he describes as "a moderate version of the pro-continuum position", having found extensive, though not complete, continuity, or non-discreteness, in his Jamaican data. This does not mean that code-switching is ruled out, as Patrick (ibid. p 10) makes clear: "My approach is consistent with the existence of (occasional, or even frequent) genuine code-switching [...]. I do not deny that it takes place, but merely argue that not every mesolectal utterance can be attributed to this process." For the purposes of the present study, I will accept that some form of a continuum model is a valid characterization of the linguistic situation in places such as Jamaica and Guyana.

2.2.4 The Creole continuum: methodological approaches

DeCamp (1971) introduced the technique of implicational scaling for the systematic analysis of variation in Creole continua. His "mini-continuum" based on the output of seven speakers has been widely reproduced in a rearranged form on the basis of his description of the technique. The version in Table 2.1 is from Rickford (1980).

Table 2.1 Implicational scale for the Jamaican Creole continuum

Features Idiolects	D	C	A	F	E	B
4	-	-	-	-	-	-
3	-	-	-	-	-	+
7	-	-	-	-	+	+
2	-	-	-	+	+	+
6	-	-	+	+	+	+
1	-	+	+	+	+	+
5	+	+	+	+	+	+
KEY to Features	D	C	A	F	E	B
- (or "Creole") =	/d/	/t/	pikni	no ben	nana	nyam
+ (or "English") =	/d~ð/	/t~θ/	child	didn't	granny	eat

Source: Rickford (1980: 186), based on DeCamp (1971: 356f)

The rearrangement of DeCamp's features and speakers (or idiolects) in this form clearly reflects the assumption on which the technique is based, namely that the continuum can be conceptualized as a series of lects which differ from each other in only one feature and in such a way that the occurrence of one form implies the use of certain others. For example, in Table 2.1, the use of one English form implies the use of all other English forms to the right. This explains why, as pointed out in 2.2.1, the different forms cannot be combined randomly.

---

[6] Note that for the case of Guyana, though not for other cases, he posits three, not two, underlying systems (see Winford 1997: 235f).

Bickerton (1973a, 1975b) elaborated the technique in several ways. His scales allow more than two variants of a feature as well as intra-lectal variation and do not randomly combine features from different subsystems such as lexis and morphosyntax. A number of other Creolists have made use of implicational scales as well (see Rickford 1980: 167 for a list of studies from the 1970s using the technique), but it has become increasingly clear that there are valid alternative methods of analysing variation in Creole continua. Rickford (1980) points out the difficulty of correlating scales constructed for different subsystems and sees in the quantitative variationist approach (cf 2.5) a promising alternative to implicational scales. He himself had already used quantitative methodology – in addition to implicational scales – in his study (1979) of variation in the Guyanese continuum. A number of other scholars studying Creole continua in the anglophone Caribbean have worked in the quantitative framework as well (see Winford 1991 for an overview). While researchers applying quantitative variationist methodology to Creole continua have had to grapple with certain problems (see 2.5.1), this direction of research has continued to yield noteworthy results (cf especially Patrick's (1999) book-length study of the Jamaican mesolect in a quantitative variationist framework).

2.2.5 *The diachrony of the Creole continuum and the concept of decreolization*

DeCamp (1971) explains the Creole continuum by extending Hall's (1962) P/C life-cycle beyond the Creole stage. In his view, the continuum represents a "post-creole stage" in which the Creole gradually merges with its lexifier. Two conditions must, according to DeCamp, be fulfilled for this stage to occur: the lexifier must be the official language of the community in which the Creole is spoken, and a formerly rigid social stratification must have started to break down. Bickerton (1973a), who shares this assumption, describes the resultant emergence of the Creole continuum in the following words:

> The creole continuum owes its existence to the fact that, after emancipation, the social, political, and economic barriers between whites and non-whites were gradually but progressively weakened – while white norms remained, at least until very recently, dominant in the community as a whole. In consequence, a slowly increasing segment of the creole-speaking population was provided with both opportunity and motivation to modify its linguistic behavior in the direction of the approved variety. (p 644)

In the view of DeCamp and (the early) Bickerton, then, the pre-emancipation state was a dichotomous Creole versus standard situation. The mesolects are more recent and result from a process of "decreolization" whereby the Creole gradually loses its basilectal features (cf especially Bickerton 1973a, 1980).

Alleyne (1971, 1980) gives a different explanation of the origin of the Creole continuum. In his view, the mesolect is not a post-emancipation development. Rather, both more standard-like and more divergent varieties had emerged in the plantation society due to its occupational stratification. The plantations were organized in such a way that some groups among the African population (domestic slaves and, to a somewhat lesser extent, artisans) had more contact with Europeans than others (field slaves). Therefore, Alleyne argues, the different groups manifested different degrees of "acculturation" or adaptation to the Europeans' culture and language. However, he believes that although intermediate speech forms developed, they played only a subordinate role at that time because of the numerical predominance of the field slaves, who had least contact with Europeans. The mesolect, according to Alleyne, became important only after emancipation, when more and more speakers of the basilect had the motivation and opportunity for greater acculturation.

Bickerton has since been converted to the position that the mesolect is not a recent development. Crucial to the change in his thinking were, as he says in Bickerton (1983), the insights he gained from Baker & Corne (1982; see the discussion in 2.2.6) into the role of demographic factors in Creole development. A central point which he admits he earlier overlooked is that plantation societies with a slave majority did not come into existence overnight but that Europeans were in the majority in the initial period of the colonies' history so that the conditions for second language learning by non-Europeans were more favourable than at later stages. His new theory is that

> the creole continuum came into existence 'backwards', so to speak – those varieties closest to English originating from the earliest contact, and those furthest from English, from the phase in which the original model was most drastically diluted by a massive and rapid increase in the non-European population. (Bickerton 1988: 272)

Mufwene (1996, 2001)[7] also regards the Creole continuum as the result of a process of progressive restructuring of the lexifier rather than of decreolization of the basilect. Following Chaudenson (1992), he divides the history of the colonies in question before the abolition of slavery into two periods. In the initial "homestead" phase (Chaudenson's *société d'habitation*) Europeans constituted the majority of the population in the colonies. Most of the slaves lived on small farms where they had enough direct contact with Europeans to be able to develop relatively close approximations of their speech. The second phase came with the shift to the plantation system (Chaudenson's *société de plantation*). Due to the massive importation of new labour, the African population soon outgrew the European. Most Africans had little direct contact with native speakers of the lexifier. Therefore, already restructured varieties often became the model for newly arrived Africans. In this way, according to Mufwene, the basilect crystallized, without necessarily replacing less restructured varieties. This process, which Mufwene refers to as "basilectalization", was, he argues, most drastic during the critical transition to the plantation phase and then continued gradually up to the abolition of slavery or the total collapse of the plantation system.

Like Bickerton (1983, 1984, 1988) in his later theory inspired by Baker & Corne (1982), Mufwene (2001) considers the different speed with which, and extent to which, the ratio of Europeans to non-Europeans shifted towards the latter group in each colony to be important factors for the differences between today's Creoles in the degree of divergence from the lexifier. In one of the examples he provides to illustrate this, Mufwene (2001: 39) draws a comparison between Jamaica and Barbados, colonized by the English in 1655 and 1627, respectively. The former switched to the plantation system faster than the latter. By the mid-18th century the proportion of Africans to Europeans was over ten to one in Jamaica, but only two to one in Barbados. Therefore, according to Mufwene, a basilect comparable to those of other Caribbean territories seems to have developed in Barbados

---

[7] Mufwene (1996) is integrated into Mufwene (2001) as chapter 2. Subsequent references will be to the 2001 version.

only on a smaller scale than in Jamaica, and this is why, in contrast to Jamaica's basilect, it has disappeared.

In sum, the view that the mesolects of present-day Creole continua go back to the period of slavery and did not develop out of an earlier dichotomous Creole vs standard situation via decreolization of the former has found increasing support. It has also become increasingly clear that the different degrees of divergence from the lexifier of today's Creoles (or their basilects) do not necessarily reflect different degrees of decreolization. This is not to say that the demographic developments mentioned above are the only factor accounting for these differences (a claim made neither by Bickerton nor by Mufwene),[8] nor, of course, that a Creole coexisting with its lexifier will not continue to be influenced by it in some way. However, the early life-cycle theory is clearly no longer the cornerstone of views on variation and change in contact languages – at least as far as the Creole continua of the anglophone Caribbean are concerned.

2.2.6 *The concepts of the Creole continuum and decreolization and the French-based Creoles: English and French Creolist perspectives*

DeCamp (1971: 349f) contrasts the Jamaican Creole continuum with the discontinuity between Creole and French in the diglossia situation in Haiti, citing Ferguson (1959), and argues that unlike Jamaican Creole as a variety in the process of merging with the standard language, Haitian Creole seems to continue without any substantial change. The characterization of the Haitian case as diglossia has since been rejected by a Haitian linguist, Yves Dejean (1983, 1993) – not because he does not consider Haitian Creole and French discrete linguistic systems,[9] but because he finds that Ferguson's sociolinguistic criteria are not fulfilled. I will therefore separate the two issues. The linguistic relationship between French-based Creoles and French will be discussed in this section. Diglossia will be dealt with as a separate topic in 2.3.

According to Valdman (1968, 1973, 1991), the alleged clear line of demarcation between Haitian Creole as well as other French-based Creoles and French and the immunity of these Creoles to decreolization are to some extent an idealization on the part of "English Creolists". His view on the relationship between Haitian Creole and French is that

> although there is little evidence at the morphosyntactic level of the appearance of mesolectal features between the creole and the lexifier standard, putative mesolectal phonological features and massive lexical borrowing are indeed drawing the two languages closer together. (Valdman 1991: 76)

However, in the relative absence of morphosyntactic features that could be described as mesolectal, it remains true that Creole and French in Haiti can be characterized as two discrete systems (Valdman 1991: 85), with educated Haitians bilingual in Creole and French frequently switching between the two systems in their conversations or discussions (Valdman 1968: 314, 1991: 80; Dejean 1993: 74). Lefebvre (1974) shows that essentially

---

[8] Cf also Parkvall's (2000) critical examination of the relation between demographics and language restructuring.

[9] In fact, Dejean argues that Creole and French in Haiti are not only discrete varieties but distinct languages (which of course also disqualifies Haiti as a case of diglossia according to Ferguson's model).

the same state of affairs obtains in the French overseas territory of Martinique, and Chaudenson (1979: 129) suggests that among the French-based Creoles, it may be only Réunion Creole (which overall shows a relatively high degree of proximity to French and is classified by Holm 1989: 392 as a semi-Creole) that is linked to French by a continuum of the type described for Guyana by Bickerton (1973a, 1975b).[10]

Bickerton, for his part, did not restrict his early view of the process of decreolization and the Creole continuum as its outcome to English-based Creoles. He maintained (1980: 109) that "decreolization is a phenomenon which is found wherever a creole language is in direct contact with its associated superstrate language". To counter objections to this view on the basis of the apparent counterexample of the French-based Creoles, he went on to argue that "much evidence, from Valdman 1968 on suggests that decreolization is active in Haiti and elsewhere" and dismissed Lefebvre's (1974) observations on the discrete character of Creole and French in Martinique on account of the methodology of the study. In support of his theory he further cited the fact that Réunion Creole is closer to French than the other French-based Indian Ocean Creoles, arguing that this correlated with the fact that Réunion had remained politically associated with France while the other territories in the Indian Ocean where a French-based Creole is spoken (i.e. Mauritius, Rodrigues and the Seychelles) had not. This view more or less accords with that of Chaudenson (1974). Chaudenson (1974 and later publications) argues that Mauritian Creole (of which the Rodrigues and Seychelles varieties are uncontroversially offshoots) is derived from early Réunion Creole. The different nature of present-day Mauritian Creole and Réunion Creole is, according to Chaudenson (1974: 448f), mainly the result of later developments in Réunion Creole. These are ascribed by Chaudenson (1974: 449) to two principal factors. The first is the larger white population element in Réunion. The second is the fact also alluded to by Bickerton (1980: 109) that French influence continued in this island after 1814 (all four territories were captured by the British during the Napoleonic wars, and only Réunion was returned to France). Chaudenson (1974: 449) adds that the French influence in Réunion had become particularly pronounced during the last 20 years (Réunion became a French overseas territory in 1946) and that the development of Réunion Creole in the direction of French is due primarily to this fact. However, in Chaudenson (1979: 121f) he points out that the growing influence of French since the time when Réunion became a French overseas territory cannot have been decisive, since one should then be able to observe a parallel development in the French overseas territories of Martinique and Guadeloupe in the Caribbean. Therefore, he goes on to argue, the primary factor must have been that in Réunion there also exists traditionally a variety of French with only some Creole features ("français créolisé"), the speech form of the white proletariat which developed in the eighteenth century (see Carayol & Chaudenson 1978). This unique configuration, as Chaudenson (1979: 33) also points out, makes the case of Réunion quite different from that of Jamaica or Guyana, although there are superficially similar continua. Furthermore, it is not even generally accepted that Réunion Creole is a more decreolized variety which has a common origin with Mauritian Creole. Baker & Corne (1982) argue that the two varieties are largely independent developments and that the different degrees of

---

[10] Cf also Carayol & Chaudenson's (1977) implicational analysis of phonological variation in the continuum of Réunion.

restructuring of French in Réunion and Mauritius can be explained by differences in the early settlement history of the two islands. As Baker points out in his contribution to the study (Baker & Corne 1982: 251), in Réunion more than half of the population was made up of free citizens during the first 50 years, whereas in Mauritius slaves outnumbered the free population before the end of the first decade of settlement. It is this view of the development of the Indian Ocean Creoles which Bickerton has now adopted (cf Bickerton 1984: 177f). Thus, instead of "French Creolists" finding further evidence to support his earlier theory, as envisaged by Bickerton (1980: 109), research on French-based Creoles has contributed to the growing awareness among "English Creolists" that the developments which have led to the different degrees of divergence from the lexifier among present-day Creoles (or varieties of a Creole) cannot be reduced to a single universal decreolization process.

2.2.7 The issue of P/C continua in anglophone West Africa

The theory of the Creole continuum and decreolization developed by DeCamp (1971) and in particular by Bickerton in his early work with its claim of universal applicability was extended from the anglophone Caribbean not only to French-based Creoles in the Caribbean as well as the Indian Ocean, but also to English-based P/Cs in West Africa and the Pacific. In her book *Pidgins and Creoles* (1974), in which a whole chapter (chapter 4) is devoted to the pidginization-creolization-decreolization life-cycle, Loreto Todd claimed that a continuum was to be found in all areas of the world where an English-based Creole or expanded pidgin coexists with its lexifier (p 51f). The only qualification she made was that the process of decreolization was more advanced in the West Indies than in West Africa or Papua New Guinea because of the early establishment of compulsory education in English in the former area (p 63). Bickerton himself also addressed the question of expanded pidgins coexisting with their lexifier. In a paper on Tok Pisin presented at a conference in 1973 – two years before Papua New Guinea's independence – (published as Bickerton 1975a),[11] he argued on the basis of his theory and two other examples of P/C-lexifier contact situations that once Papua New Guinea became independent and there was an increase in social mobility, a continuum would probably develop in Papua New Guinea as well. The two other examples he referred to in that paper are Guyana and Nigeria. His early view of the development of the Guyanese continuum has already been discussed in 2.2.5. For Nigeria he claimed that until independence, there were no varieties intermediate between English and NigP, but that since then, a continuum had emerged. Its existence, although not documented in the linguistic literature, was, he said, "patently obvious to anyone who has read the novels of Achebe or the plays of Solinka [sic; read Soyinka], or who has listened to Nigerian radio serials such as *Save* [sic] *Journey*" (p 26).[12]

While Bickerton has now turned away from the view of the continuum as part of a life-cycle of contact languages which underlies his description of the Nigerian situation in Bickerton (1975a), similar descriptions of the Nigerian situation are still found in the more

---

[11] I am grateful to Peter Mühlhäusler for drawing my attention to this paper and for making it available to me.
[12] On the language of *Safe Journey* see 3.3.

recent literature. Todd (1994: 3181) illustrates the continuum phenomenon by the following Nigerian example:

> *A bin kam, kariam go.*
> *A kɔm, kariam go.*
> *A kɔm, kariam awe.*
> *A kem an kari it awe.*
> I came and carried it away.

Hudson (1996: 65) quotes this example to illustrate variation in what he refers to as the "post-creole continuum of Nigeria", while Sebba (1997: 128) discusses the Nigerian case under the heading "The Post-Pidgin Continuum".

There has been no reference so far to the specialized literature on NigP. This is no coincidence. First of all, the influence of English on the language has so far not been a major issue in research on NigP (cf 1.3). Besides, the existence of a NigP-English continuum is not a matter of general agreement among NigP specialists, although a few observations have been made which seem to point in that direction. One of the scholars who have worked on the language, Rebecca Agheyisi, has explicitly denied the existence of such a continuum. In Agheyisi (1971: 30) she mentions a "'middle variety' of English" between the extremes of standard English and NigP used on certain occasions by uneducated speakers in urban Nigeria, but she makes it clear that this is essentially a learner variety of English with some NigP interference, which, she argues, is best described as "non-standard Nigerian English". In Agheyisi (1984a) she shows that there are also educated speakers' learner varieties of NigP with English interference but emphasizes that

> the relationship that exists between these varieties and NSE [Nigerian Standard English] cannot be described as that of a continuum, in the same sense that creole-speaking communities in the Caribbean region [...] have been shown to manifest this phenomenon. In other words, the NPE [Nigerian Pidgin English] variety which has been designated here as interlanguage PE [Pidgin English] does not constitute a 'mesolect' in a possible continuum that might be said to have the Pidgin-proper variety as the 'basilect' and NSE as the 'acrolect'. (p 230)

Faraclas, in contrast, seems to tend more towards a continuum view, although he does not claim explicitly that there exists in Nigeria a mesolect comparable to those found in the anglophone Caribbean. In Faraclas (1984: 68) he relates the situation in Nigeria to the life-cycle view of P/C development by saying that "the RPE [Rivers Pidgin English] speech community as well as those of the languages resembling it (Cameroon Pidgin English, other varieties of Nigerian Pidgin English, etc.) encompass the entire pidginization-creolization-decreolization continuum". In Faraclas (1986: 3; also later publications) he divides NigP "for convenience of description", as he says, into "three sets of social varieties (acrolectal or decreolized, mesolectal or creolized, and basilectal or pidginized)". As he explains in various publications (e.g. 1986: 6, 1991: 510, 1996: 2), he describes as "acrolectal" those varieties of NigP which are used by speakers who also have a good command of standard English and which therefore display standard English influence; as "mesolectal" he describes the varieties spoken by those who use NigP in most of their daily interactions or have acquired it as their first language; and as "basilectal" he describes the varieties typical of uneducated second language speakers who use NigP only in a limited number of contexts (especially in markets) and whose speech is influenced by the Nigerian languages that they speak as their first languages. Thus, while the terms *acrolectal, mesolectal* and *basilectal* might be taken to suggest the existence of a continuum, the way these terms are used by Faraclas in his attempt to accommodate two dimensions of variation – between NigP and the superstrate and between NigP and the various substrates – in the terminology designed for a unidimensional model obviously represents a departure from the terminological conventions of the pioneering continuum studies.

Since several other English-based contact languages in West Africa – specifically, Sierra Leonean Krio, Cameroonian Pidgin and Ghanaian Pidgin – can (depending on one's view on the extent to which their histories and that of NigP are interconnected, cf 1.2) be considered as more or less directly related to NigP, it is also of interest in the present context what has been said about the issue of continua in relation to these varieties. As has already been mentioned, Todd (1974) has postulated the existence of continua in West Africa generally, and while in Todd (1994) she gives the Nigerian example quoted above, O'Donnell & Todd (1991: 52f) refer to a Cameroonian continuum. There is also an overview article on Cameroonian Pidgin or Kamtok by Todd & Jumbam (1992) in which considerable attention is given to social variation. Todd & Jumbam start out from a distinction between basilectal, mesolectal and acrolectal varieties of Kamtok. Among the features of acrolectal speech they mention are the use of English and French lexical items and, in the grammar, the occasional observance of English gender and case distinctions in pronouns not made in the basilect, variable use of the *-s* suffix to mark the plural of nouns, a tendency to mark possessive relations in the noun phrase by *-'s* or *of* ("especially in fixed phrases") and the use of a larger set of prepositions. However, they also mention that English influence does not affect all areas of the grammar equally. For example, they report that in two hours of acrolectal speech, they found only one occurrence of a non-Kamtok auxiliary (*will*) and no single instance of an *-ed* or *-ing* form. This seems to be a remarkable example of stability and an aspect which makes the case of Cameroonian Pidgin quite different from that of English-based Creoles in the Caribbean. Todd & Jumbam (1992: 10) predict, though, that Cameroonian Pidgin will gradually lose many of its basilectal features. Like these authors for Cameroonian Pidgin, Huber (1999) also refers to basilectal, mesolectal and acrolectal varieties in his description of Ghanaian Pidgin, but he points out that "although a number of differences exists between 'basilectal' and more 'acrolectal' GhaPE [Ghanaian Pidgin English] [...], the structural differences are not so vast as to warrant speaking of a continuum in the sense that this term is usually used by Creolists with reference e.g. to the situation in the Caribbean" (p 140). For Krio the issue of English influence and the possibility of a continuum has been discussed e.g. by Williams (1975). Williams documents two aspects of standard English influence in Krio, namely the loss of negative concord and a more extensive use of prepositions. However, he also mentions that there is little or no variation in the auxiliary and pronominal systems and argues that Krio is not undergoing the kind of drastic restructuring that would warrant the term *decreolization* and that, although there are anglicized varieties of the language, the case of Krio does not represent a true continuum situation. Johnson (1992) also refers to an English-influenced variety of Krio used by the educated. He believes that this variety represents "an early stage of decreolization" (p 26), adding in a note that decreolization is to be understood as the process whereby a Creole gradually merges with the corresponding standard language and that this process could lead to a "post-creole continuum" as in Jamaica. Thus, although their existence is sometimes taken for granted, at present there is in actual fact little hard evidence of P/C continua in Nigeria and the other parts of anglophone West Africa that I have discussed,[13] and such statements as have been made about continua or decreolization in these areas seem to owe a great deal to the early work of DeCamp and Bickerton.

The situation outlined above raises the question of how the theories of the development of Creole continua of Alleyne, Mufwene and, in his later work, Bickerton relate to the situation in West Africa. As these authors are primarily concerned with plantation Creoles, this is a question which has so far not been given much consideration, but a few pertinent remarks have nevertheless been made. Alleyne (1980: 183f) argues that the situation in the West African trading stations essentially paralleled those on the New World plantations, with different groups of Africans having different kinds of relations with Europeans and, in consequence, differential access to their language, but he does not discuss the West African situation in any detail. Bickerton (1988: 269ff) draws a somewhat more elaborate comparison between "fort situations" such as those in West Africa and "plantation situations" such as those in the Caribbean. In both situations, he identifies a stage of relatively intimate contacts between Europeans and non-Europeans, in which the conditions for second language learning by the latter were not too unfavourable. As has already become clear in 2.2.5, in those colonies where Europeans settled in important numbers and established plantation economic systems this stage corresponds to the initial European-majority phase. In the fort situation such intimacy would, according to Bickerton, have been found in the households established by European traders with African women. He also finds in the fort situation a parallel to the "dilution" stage, which came about in the plantation situation when large numbers of new slaves were imported (see 2.2.5), namely the spread of second language versions of the European language from racially mixed households to servants, local merchants and others whose contacts with Europeans were more limited. Bickerton therefore argues that in spite of the differences between the two types of contact situation, the linguistic processes which occurred in them must have been essentially the same. Although he does not say so explicitly, one may then expect continua of varieties reflecting different degrees of restructuring of the lexifier to have developed in the fort situation in the same way as, according to Bickerton's newer theory, they did in the plantation situation. Mufwene (1997, 2001), in contrast, emphasizes the differences rather than the similarities between the two types of contact situations. He draws a fundamental distinction between the "settlement colonies" in the New World and the Indian Ocean and the "trade colonies" (later turned into "exploitation colonies") in Africa and the Pacific.

---

[13] A different case is Liberian. This has a history distinct from the varieties discussed above (cf Holm 1989: 421ff), with far more African-American settlers than in the Sierra Leone colony (see below in the text), and while, according to Holm (1989: 409), Krio and Nigerian, Cameroonian and Ghanaian Pidgin are mutually intelligible to a considerable extent, the same is not true of these varieties and Liberian. Liberian actually comprises several restructured varieties of English; Singler (1997) distinguishes the following: Settler English (the variety spoken by the descendants of the African-Americans), Kru Pidgin English (spoken by Kru sailors and migrant workers, a variety which differs markedly from the other Liberian varieties) and Vernacular Liberian English (spoken by the rest of Liberia's English-speaking population, a variety in whose development Settler English has played an important role). The latter can, according to Singler (1997: 225), be seen as comprising a full-fledged continuum, with special mesolectal features that are found neither in the basilect nor in the acrolect. This seems to be a unique case in West Africa.

According to Mufwene, these two different colonial situations involved very different kinds of interactions between Europeans and non-Europeans:

> Settlement colonies started with intimate interactions between the two parties. Segregation was subsequent to the increase in the sizes of the European population and the larger proportions of non-Europeans. Multilingualism led the Africans to adopt the languages of the groups in power as their vernaculars. These were restructured during the appropriation process. Trade colonies were characterized by random contacts between the European traders and their African counterparts. The adoption of European languages under these conditions of limited, occasional exposure to them allowed the development of what have also been identified as "broken languages", a reflection of the minimal uses to which elements of their lexifiers were put. (Mufwene 2001: 171)

Mufwene (1997: 41f) therefore argues that the Creoles of the New World and Indian Ocean had a very different development from expanded Pidgins like Tok Pisin and NigP which today function like Creoles. While, according to Mufwene, the former are the result of a gradual process of restructuring which gave rise to varieties diverging more and more from the lexifier (i.e., there was no antecedent pidgin), the latter developed out of jargons (or incipient/unstable pidgins, Mufwene's preferred terms) resulting from sporadic trade contacts. This accords with the traditional view of the origin of NigP (cf 1.2) viz, that it is the result of the appropriation and subsequent expansion by substrate speakers of a contact variety which initially served the purpose of Afro-European communication in the context of trade. Although Mufwene does not explore this aspect, one may then not necessarily expect the development of a spectrum of restructured varieties but, as the lexifier would have played only a minor role compared to its influence in the settlement colonies, probably a solid crystallization of a variety that one would describe as basilectal if such a spectrum existed.

Mufwene's view of the relations between Europeans and non-Europeans in the trade colonies is certainly more in consonance than Bickerton's with the picture of early Afro-European contacts in West Africa painted by Huber (1999) with reference to the Gold Coast (see 1.2). However, it has to be remembered that according to Huber, present-day West African Pidgins are not direct descendants of the early trade jargons at all but have been shaped to a great extent by Krio. It is therefore necessary to take a look at the origin of Krio itself. This is also a matter of some controversy. Huber (1999: 75f) mentions as the main theories the "domestic hypothesis" and the "Jamaican hypothesis". The argument of the "domestic hypothesis", which has been proposed by Hancock (e.g. 1986), is that the origin of present-day Krio has to be sought in Creole communities which emerged along the Upper Guinea Coast (i.e., the Gambia and Sierra Leone river estuaries and adjacent areas) in the 17th century as a result of domestic unions between British men and African women. Huber (1999) examines this view in detail and comes to the conclusion that it is supported neither by linguistic nor by sociohistorical evidence (p 118). According to the more widely accepted "Jamaican hypothesis", Krio is derived from the language of the about 500 Jamaican Maroons who arrived in Freetown in 1800.[14] Huber (1999), who supports a New

---

[14] See e.g. Hancock (1986: 73f) for a list of references to studies supporting a New World and particularly a Jamaican origin of Krio, and McWhorter (1995) for a more recent articulation of the "Jamaican hypothesis". (Note that this hypothesis does not preclude a West African origin of the English-based New World Creoles – McWhorter 1995 in fact agrees with Hancock on this controversial point.)

World origin, also notes (p 70) that not much consideration has so far been given to the other group of New World settlers in the Sierra Leone colony, the Nova Scotians (former American slaves whom the British had temporarily resettled in Nova Scotia). These, he points out (ibid. p 61), arrived a few years before the Maroons and in about twice their number, so that their speech may well have been an important factor in the development of Krio. By far the most important population group in the early Sierra Leone colony in numerical terms were, however, the liberated Africans or "recaptives" (cf 1.2), of whom tens of thousands arrived during the 19th century. Huber (1999: 70ff) argues that, considering their number alone, one may well assume them to have dominated the linguistic scene, but that the social organization of the Sierra Leone colony makes it more likely that they were eventually assimilated into the New World settlers' society.[15] This would mean that Sierra Leonean Krio and the present-day West African Pidgins on which, according to Huber, Krio exerted a decisive influence are ultimately New World Creoles. What does this scenario imply for the degree of restructuring at the early stages, which is of primary interest to the present study? According to Huber (1999: 62), indications are that the majority of the Nova Scotians must have been familiar either with some form of Virginian Black English or with Gullah, but Huber also points out (ibid. p 72) that the exact degree of restructuring of their language is uncertain. As regards the Jamaican Maroons, it is well known that their language was even further removed from the lexifier than that of the field slaves on the plantations. It is therefore not surprising that there is evidence that their speech differed to some extent from that of the Nova Scotians, a distinction which was apparently maintained for some time before it was eventually blurred (Huber 1999: 72f; Holm 1989: 414). Thus, while the Nova Scotians constitute a factor of uncertainty, it is clear that if the Maroons, as traditionally assumed, played a major role in the development of Krio, Krio would be a transplanted New World Creole but certainly not a transplanted Creole continuum. Furthermore, it was, according to Huber (1999: 71ff), the already restructured varieties of the New World settlers which became the immediate target for the recaptives from the time when they began to have opportunities for social advancement (circa 1830). Unlike in the New World colonies, European native speakers of English did not make up more than a very minor proportion of the Sierra Leone colony's population at any stage (cf Huber 1999: 65). Nor did Europeans settle in important numbers in the Lagos colony (cf Peil 1991: 7f), which Huber sees as the primary locus of the development of the Krio-influenced pidgin that, according to him, is the ancestor of present-day NigP and also spread to Ghana and Cameroon (see 1.2). Thus, not only in the trade period, but also after outright colonization did these colonies have a very different linguistic ecology from that of the Caribbean colonies at the initial period of colonization. Therefore, if the Caribbean Creole continua go back to the early days of the colonies that were established in that area, the historical perspective presented above suggests that in most parts of anglophone West Africa, the existence of similar continua can at least not be taken for granted.

---

[15] This is, however, another aspect of the development of Sierra Leonean Krio that not all scholars are agreed on (cf Huber 1999: 73n15).

2.2.8 *Continuum or discrete varieties? Tok Pisin and English in Papua New Guinea*

In the discussion of the question of P/C continua in West Africa in the preceding section I also referred to Tok Pisin in Papua New Guinea. Like NigP, Tok Pisin is an expanded pidgin to which the notion of the P/C continuum has been transferred on the basis of the life-cycle view of P/C development. Also like NigP, it represents a case where one may not necessarily expect such a spectrum of variation if the prototypical continua in the anglophone Caribbean reflect different degrees of restructuring of the lexifier in the early history of Caribbean Creoles rather than a more recent process of decreolization. It is thus of great interest to the present study whether Bickerton's (1975a) prediction that a continuum would soon emerge in Papua New Guinea has been borne out. In the following I will therefore take a look at more recent studies which deal with the Papua New Guinean case of contact between a P/C and its lexifier.

Mühlhäusler (1982: 453ff) discusses the "postpidgin/(postcreole) stage" in Tok Pisin's development, i.e. the period in which the language has increasingly been exposed to the influence of English. This stage is not to be equated with a post-P/C continuum: he argues that such a continuum has not emerged in Papua New Guinea, although borrowing from English into Tok Pisin is taking place. Mühlhäusler therefore calls into question the idea that the consequence of renewed contact between a P/C and its lexifier is of necessity a development whereby the P/C becomes more and more like the lexifier and is eventually absorbed by it. His data, he says, rather suggest that a new third system is emerging as a result of the contact situation: the sociolect of "Urban Tok Pisin" or "postpidgin Tok Pisin". To illustrate this variety, Mühlhäusler provides an extract from a conversation recorded on the campus of the University of Papua New Guinea. Among the features of the text that he draws attention to are code-switching between Tok Pisin and English, a high proportion of lexical items recently borrowed from English, and the use of borrowed conjunctions (e.g. *bikos, when*) and of English plural *-s*.

Romaine (1992: 323) believes that a "post-creole continuum" has recently emerged in Papua New Guinea, but the existence of this continuum is again disputed in more recent studies by Siegel (1997) and Smith (2000, 2002). Smith (2000) describes the kind of English elements he has found in a corpus of the Tok Pisin speech of young first language Tok Pisin speakers attending English-medium educational institutions. Like Mühlhäusler (1982), Smith finds that code-switching and borrowing are taking place. He observes that the speakers sometimes insert whole phrases in English into their Tok Pisin or calque English idiomatic expressions, that they draw freely on the English lexicon to express modern concepts, that some conjunctions have been borrowed from English, and that there seems to be an increasing tendency to mark the plural of nouns by *-s*. However, he also reports that he does not find the range of intermediate syntactic forms typical of Creole continua (p 283). While not excluding the possibility that the situation may change with prolonged bilingualism in the two languages, he concludes that at present Tok Pisin and English do not form a continuum but remain distinct languages (p 287). In the discussion of the findings from the comprehensive analysis of his corpus in Smith (2002), he also emphasizes that in spite of the undeniable influence of English on Tok Pisin, there is clear discontinuity between the two systems (p 210). According to Siegel (1997), this is exactly the situation which obtains not only in Papua New Guinea but also in the other Melanesian countries where English-based contact languages are spoken. Siegel (1997: 201) also considers the historical implications of this situation:

> The absence of extensive depidginization or decreolization in Melanesia may also support the view that a post-creole continuum is not the result of decreolization, but reflects a spectrum of variation that has existed since much earlier stages of development [...]. [...] Thus, according to this view, we would not expect to find a pidgin-to-English continuum in Melanesia because there never has been one.[16]

Several studies of Tok Pisin thus confirm my thesis that the continuum model as it has been established for the anglophone Caribbean is not necessarily transferable to other P/C-lexifier contact situations.

2.3   Di- and triglossia

In the discussion of the Creole continuum above I have also mentioned diglossia (2.2.6). Diglossia is sometimes taken as the opposite of a continuum situation, but, as has already been pointed out in 2.2.6, it is in fact not directly comparable to the continuum model because it is a broader concept. In contrast to the Creole continuum as a model of linguistic variation between a Creole and its lexifier, diglossia (at least in its original sense) is based on both linguistic and sociolinguistic criteria, and it was not developed specifically for Creole-lexifier contact situations. However, as has already become clear in 2.2.6, it is one of the models that have been applied to contact situations of this kind, and since, furthermore, the present study considers both linguistic and social aspects of the contact situation, it is of interest here. In this section I will therefore take a closer look at this concept. In addition, I will discuss triglossia, an extension of diglossia to certain situations in which three languages (or languages types) or three varieties of a language coexist in a society. Since the situation under investigation in the present study involves not only the P/C and its lexifier but also a third factor, the indigenous languages, this concept is obviously of interest as well.

2.3.1   *Development and applications of the concepts of di- and triglossia*

The term *diglossia* was coined by Ferguson (1959) on the model of the French *diglossie*, which had been used earlier in French scholarship on Greek and Arabic. It was Ferguson's (1959) article that established diglossia as a sociolinguistic concept. His description of the concept is based on four paradigmatic cases: classical and colloquial Arabic, the *katharévusa* and *dhimotikí* varieties of Greek, standard and Swiss German, and Creole and French in Haiti. In each of these cases there are what Ferguson considers two highly divergent varieties of the same language. These coexist in the respective communities, with their functions strictly compartmentalized. While the applicability of this description to one of Ferguson's defining cases, that of Haiti, has been denied (see 2.2.6), scholars have also used *diglossia* to describe a wide range of other cases which often do not fit Ferguson's

---

[16] Siegel (ibid.) also points out that the codification of the different dialects of Melanesian Pidgin has helped to keep them distinct from English.

description. In the process, the concept has undergone numerous reinterpretations and extensions. These cannot all be discussed here,[17] but it is important to note that diglossia has been extended from two highly divergent varieties of the same language to two (or more) functionally differentiated elements of a community's linguistic repertoire with any degree of linguistic relatedness, i.e. there may be distinct languages or merely a standard language with dialects (cf e.g. Fishman 1967; Fasold 1984: chapter 2). Fasold (1984) refers to this extended version as "broad diglossia" and to the case described by Ferguson as "classic diglossia".

The term *triglossia* (or its French equivalent *triglossie*) is first attested in the early 1970s in the work of Abdulaziz Mkilifi (1972), Lafont (1971: 93n1), and Whiteley (1973: 174). Among these authors, only the first describes a triglossic situation, namely the one in Tanzania, in detail. His description of the Tanzanian case established triglossia as an important model for speech communities in sub-Saharan Africa in which local vernaculars coexist with an indigenous lingua franca as well as the language of a former colonial power (cf Johnson 1978; Pasch 1997; Haust & Dittmar: 1998: 81[18]). This is, however, not the only type of situation to which the concept of triglossia has been applied. Like diglossia, it has been used to describe quite different cases, and there are competing versions. While Abdulaziz Mkilifi's model involves distinct languages and is based on sociolinguistic criteria alone, Youssi's (1995) description of Arabic in Morocco in terms of triglossia, with three varieties of the language, includes linguistic as well as functional aspects, like Ferguson's (1959) diglossia.

Linguistic aspects of di- and triglossia are not relevant to the present study, since they apply only to what are considered varieties of the same language. Unless NigP and English can be shown to form a continuum, there is no need to question the scholarly view that they are distinct languages (cf 1.1). In the following, I will therefore describe only the sociolinguistic aspects of Ferguson's diglossia, and the triglossia model for sub-Saharan Africa established by Abdulaziz Mkilifi's study of the sociolinguistic situation in Tanzania.

2.3.2 *Sociolinguistic features of diglossia*

Ferguson (1959) describes the following five sociolinguistic features of diglossia:

(a) *Function:* The functions of the two varieties, termed H (High) and L (Low) by Ferguson, are in complementary distribution. To illustrate this, Ferguson gives a table with examples of communicative situations, indicating which variety, H or L, would be used in each. This is reproduced below as Table 2.2. As is clear from the table, H is used for more formal and serious types of communication while L serves more informal and less serious functions. Ferguson (1959: 328) emphasizes that the functions of H and L overlap only very slightly; he considers this functional specialization one of the most important features of diglossia.

(b) *Prestige:* H is regarded as superior to L.

---

[17] See e.g. Mackey (1986) for a concise overview.
[18] Haust & Dittmar's (1998: 81) "double overlapping diglossia" is another term for the kind of situation that Abdulaziz Mkilifi (1972) refers to as triglossia (cf Fasold 1984: 45).

(c) *Literary Heritage:* There is a sizable and highly esteemed body of literature in H, written either in a distant period in the community's history or in another community in which H is the standard language.

(d) *Acquisition:* H is learned through formal education. L is acquired as the mother tongue.

(e) *Standardization:* H has a high degree of standardization. L is not standardized.

Table 2.2 Choice of varieties in diglossia

	H	L
Sermon in church or mosque	x	
Instructions to servants, waiters, workmen, clerks		x
Personal letter	x	
Speech in parliament, political speech	x	
University lecture	x	
Conversation with family, friends, colleagues		x
News broadcast	x	
Radio "soap opera"		x
Newspaper editorial, news story, caption on picture	x	
Caption on political cartoon		x
Poetry	x	
Folk literature		x

Source: Ferguson (1959: 329)

2.3.2 Sociolinguistic features of triglossia

In the following, Abdulaziz Mkilifi's (1972) description of the Tanzanian triglossia situation as he found it at the time of his study[19] will be discussed under the five headings used in 2.3.2, which were taken over from Ferguson (1959).

(a) *Function:* Abdulaziz Mkilifi defines triglossia as a language situation in which three languages are involved whose functions are complementary in some areas but also overlap to some extent. In his Tanzanian example, the three languages are the vernacular of each ethnic group, Swahili and English. The vernaculars are associated primarily with informal intra-group interaction in a rural environment. Swahili is the language of communication at the national level and representative of a more urban type of African culture. It is used not only in informal interaction among members of different ethnic groups but also in the lower levels of the education system and to some extent in official business. English is the language of higher education and the dominant medium of official business and commercial and legal transactions. The mass media and religious services are contexts where the functions of Swahili and English overlap.

(b) *Prestige:* The language associated with socioeconomic prestige is English. The vernaculars are languages of "ethnocultural identification and solidarity" (Abdulaziz Mkilifi 1972: 203). Outside the ethnic group Swahili becomes the language of "affective

---

[19] The study is based on interviews with fifteen informants whose reports Abdulaziz Mkilifi considers fairly representative of the patterns of language acquisition and use of urban Tanzanians at that time, particularly those aged thirty or over.

socialization" (ibid. p 201), so that "among the younger and more detribalized speakers there is a merging of role and value distinctions based on Swahili and the vernacular, with Swahili systems often predominating" (ibid. p 204). One may thus say that the vernaculars and Swahili have covert prestige in different contexts: the former within the ethnic group and the latter in wider social life.

(c) *Literary heritage:* Ferguson's description of literary heritage in diglossia applies to English in Tanzania. Literature in Swahili exists but is limited, and Swahili-English bilinguals prefer to read in English.

(d) *Acquisition:* The vernacular is acquired in the home environment. Some also acquire a knowledge of Swahili at pre-school age, but the most important context of exposure to Swahili in childhood is the primary school. The learning of English takes place mainly in secondary school.

(e) *Standardization:* Swahili is standardized but not developed to such an extent that it can cover the domains of a modern technological culture.

2.4   Code-switching, borrowing and interference

In the discussion of the P/C continuum concept in 2.2, reference was repeatedly made to other concepts from the general field of language contact studies such as code-switching, borrowing and interference which have also been used in the description of P/C-lexifier contact situations. These will now be examined in more detail.

2.4.1   *Code-switching*

Code-switching involves the use of more than one language within a single discourse. If the switches from one language to another occur at sentence boundaries, it is generally agreed that the phenomenon is to be referred to as code-switching. Some authors, e.g. Poplack (1980 and other publications) and Myers-Scotton (1993b, 1993c and other publications) also refer to language alternation within the same sentence as code-switching. Others, e.g. Bokamba (1988), use the term *code-mixing* for the latter phenomenon.[20] In the present study a broad definition of code-switching such as the one found in the work of Poplack and Myers-Scotton is adopted.

Code-switching became an important topic in language contact research in connection with the development of the discipline of sociolinguistics in the 1960s. Since then, studies of the phenomenon have been conducted in a wide range of settings all over the world. Multilingual sub-Saharan Africa is well represented, with the work of Carol Myers-Scotton, one of the leading figures in code-switching research, based mainly on African data. The topic has been approached from two basic angles: the structural and the functional. What follows is not a comprehensive discussion of developments in these two lines of research but merely an overview of the basic terms and concepts from both which are relevant to the present study.

---

[20]   Myers-Scotton (1993b, 1993c) also explicitly includes alternation between varieties of the same language in her definition of code-switching. Some authors use the term *code-shifting* in this case (cf e.g. Görlach 1991: 79f).

From the structural point of view, Poplack (1980) distinguishes three types of code-switching: inter-sentential switching, tag-switching and intra-sentential switching. The distinction between inter-sentential switching and intra-sentential switching (i.e. what some authors refer to as code-mixing) has already been mentioned above. Poplack's additional category of tag-switching is the insertion of discourse markers such as *you know* in one language into discourse in another.

In a pioneering study in the functional direction, Blom & Gumperz (1972) introduce a distinction between situational code-switching, which reflects changes in the speech situation, and metaphorical code-switching, where the aim is to allude to the values associated with a particular code. In a later study by Gumperz (1982: chapter 4) what appears to be the equivalent of metaphorical code-switching is referred to as conversational code-switching. Gumperz (1982: 60f) contrasts conversational code-switching with situational code-switching. Whereas in situational code-switching the use of different codes corresponds to different speech events or clearly identifiable parts of a speech event, conversational code-switching is characterized by code alternation within the same unit of verbal interaction. The connection between social context and language use is therefore less direct than in situational code-switching, as in conversational code-switching speakers "build on their own and their audience's abstract understanding of situational norms, to communicate metaphoric information about how they intend their words to be understood" (p 61). Several specific functions of conversational code-switching can be distinguished (Gumperz 1982: 75ff):

(a) *Quotations:* Switching between different codes marks a passage that is identifiable as a direct quotation or reported speech.

(b) *Addressee specification:* By switching to another code a speaker directs an utterance to one of several possible addressees.

(c) *Interjections:* Code-switching marks an interjection or sentence filler (cf Poplack's tag-switching).

(d) *Reiteration:* What has been said in one code is repeated (literally or in modified form) in another. In this way the message is emphasized or elaborated.

(e) *Message qualification:* The main message is expressed in one code; in qualifying constructions added to the statement another code is used.

(f) *Personalization versus objectivization:* Code-switching serves to mark contrasts like personal opinion versus objective fact or specific instances versus general truth.

Gumperz (1982: 93) emphasizes that code-switching is more than a device to mark off a certain stretch of discourse; the direction of the shift may have a meaning as well. For example, the opposition between personal opinion and generally known fact can be said to reflect the "'we'/'they' code opposition" (ibid. p 94), i.e. the distinction between in-group and out-group language.

Like the studies by Blom & Gumperz (1972) and Gumperz (1982), Myers-Scotton's "markedness model" of code-switching (see Scotton 1983, 1986, 1988a, 1988b; Myers-Scotton 1993a, 1993c) builds on societal norms which designate certain code choices as expected or unmarked for specific situations and on the symbolic values associated with different codes. If, in a given situation, a speaker switches to a marked code ("code-switching as a marked choice", according to Myers-Scotton), he/she intends to redefine the situation in terms of the values implied by this code. The symbolic import of such switching recalls Blom & Gumperz's (1972) metaphorical code-switching or Gumperz's (1982) conversational code-switching. However, while, as the discussion above has shown, Gumperz (1982) stresses the message- or discourse-related aspects of such switching, Myers-Scotton foregrounds the use of marked code-switching as a social-interactional device; its purpose, according to her model, is to change the social distance between participants in a speech event: it can encode anger or put somebody in their place by emphasizing a status gap, or, conversely, it can establish solidarity. Blom & Gumperz's (1972) and Gumperz's (1982) situational switching has a closer parallel in Myers-Scotton's model, namely "sequential unmarked code-switching", i.e. speakers make a series of unmarked code choices in accordance with changes in one or more aspects of the speech situation (in particular the participants or the topic). Myers-Scotton's model also includes another type of unmarked code-switching: "code-switching itself as the unmarked choice". This phenomenon has also been observed by Poplack (1980), who speaks of code-switching as an "overall discourse mode" (p 614). In this mode is not each specific switch which has a social meaning, but the pattern of continuous switching itself. According to Myers-Scotton, such switching occurs mainly in informal in-group interactions among bilingual peers in some, but not all, bi- or multilingual communities. One type of community where she observes it is prevalent is multilingual Third World societies with an exogenous official language, as is typically the case in sub-Saharan Africa. Myers-Scotton argues that code-switching itself as the unmarked choice enables a speaker to encode dual identities. For example, in the African setting, by continuously switching between the official language and an African language a speaker can identify himself/herself as educated while at the same time affirming his/her identity as an African, or as a member of a particular ethnic group.

In the present study, the following terms will be used for the four functional types of code-switching that emerge from the literature as discussed above:
- situational code-switching (for what is referred to by this term in the Blom/Gumperz model and by the term "sequential unmarked code-switching" in Myers-Scotton's model)
- code-switching as a social strategy (for Myers-Scotton's code-switching as a marked choice)
- code-switching as a discourse strategy (for Gumperz's conversational code-switching)
- code-switching as an overall discourse mode (for what Poplack describes by this term and Myers-Scotton as code-switching itself as the unmarked choice)

There are some correlations between functional and structural types of code-switching. Myers-Scotton (1993c: 125) observes that while situational switching usually takes the form of inter-sentential switching, code-switching as an overall discourse mode typically includes many intra-sentential switches (cf also Poplack 1980: 614), although there may of course be inter-sentential switches as well. Another structural feature which has been discussed in connection with different functional types of code-switching is "flagging" of the switches by false starts, hesitations, lengthy pauses, metalinguistic commentary etc. Poplack (1985) finds that such flagging is common when each switch has a specific function (cf also Myers-Scotton 1993c: 141f). Code-switching as an overall discourse mode, in contrast, is described by Poplack (1985) as typically "smooth", i.e. the switch points are not salient.

Finally, links between functional types of code-switching and macrosociolinguistic aspects of language use in bi- or multilingual communities have been suggested (Scotton 1986, 1988a): where there is little functional overlap between two linguistic varieties used in a community (as in classic diglossia), there will normally only be situational switching; code-switching as an overall discourse mode requires some functional overlap between different linguistic varieties, as may be found in broad diglossia (cf also Abdulaziz Mkilifi 1972: 207ff on code-switching in the Tanzanian triglossia situation).

2.4.2 Borrowing

As an aspect of language change, linguistic borrowing - the incorporation of elements from one language or language variety into another – has a tradition of study which goes back to 19th-century historical linguistics. One of the constants in research on borrowing since the 19th century have been observations on the different degrees of borrowability of different types of linguistic elements (Whitney 1881: 19f; Haugen 1950: 223f; Moravcsik 1978: 110ff; Muysken 1984: 68; Thomason & Kaufman 1988: 74ff). Romaine (1995: 64) sums up a number of such statements in the following "hierarchy of borrowing":

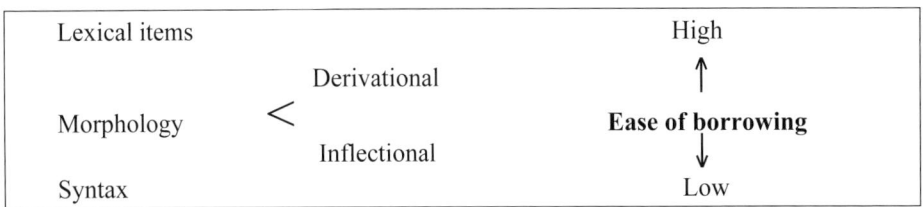

Figure 2.1 Hierarchy of borrowing
Source: Romaine (1995: 64)

This basic hierarchy can be elaborated in a number of ways. As Romaine (1995: 65) adds, nouns are often said to be more frequently borrowed than members of other lexical word classes. Some authors also mention function words. For example, in Thomason & Kaufman's (1988: 74ff) more elaborate "borrowing scale", conjunctions and adverbial particles are shown to be less susceptible to borrowing than lexical items but more than derivational morphology, while prepositions and pronouns are on the same level as derivational morphology.[21]

Most authors argue that the borrowing hierarchy reflects an inverse relation between the tightness of structural organization of a component of a language and the ease with which new elements can be incorporated into it, but other factors have been mentioned as well. For example, as Muysken (1984: 68) points out, a factor which may contribute to the high propensity of nouns to be borrowed is that the elements which are commonly taken over

---

[21] Thomason & Kaufman's scale is also more elaborate than, and somewhat different from, earlier observations on borrowability in its treatment of syntax: different aspects of syntactic borrowing are distinguished (e.g. borrowing of postpositions in an otherwise prepositional language as a minor aspect of a switch from SOV to SVO syntax is classed as more likely than extensive word order changes) and on the whole, syntax is, according to this scale, not less likely to be borrowed than morphology. Furthermore, in contrast to e.g. Romaine (1995), Thomason & Kaufman (1988) include phonology (also differentiated into various aspects) in the borrowing scale.

from one culture into another are mostly of the type encoded by nouns. It is, however, also known that in some contact situations, there may be a great deal of lexical borrowing not motivated by any actual need for new terms (see e.g. Haugen 1953: 373f; Poplack, Sankoff & Miller 1988: 61f).

While ranking linguistic elements in order of borrowability, the borrowing hierarchy as discussed so far does not indicate under what conditions borrowing will be restricted to those elements most susceptible to the process and what conditions favour a greater degree of borrowing. This aspect features prominently in Thomason & Kaufman's (1988) discussion of borrowing processes. Their basic tenet is that more than anything else it is the social nature of the contact situation which determines the degree of borrowing (p 35). Their "borrowing scale" is in fact not merely a ranking of types of linguistic elements, but the groups of linguistic elements in it are correlated with a scale of intensity of contact. In addition, they consider purely linguistic factors as relevant, though secondary to the social nature of the contact situation (p 35). The main point they make about linguistic factors is that in contact situations of low to moderate intensity a close typological fit between particular structures in the source language and the recipient language can result in a greater than expected degree of borrowing (pp 54, 97). In their discussion of such "typologically favored borrowing" (pp 97ff) they cite as typical examples borrowing between dialects of the same language or between closely related languages, where the borrowing process is facilitated by a close correspondence between the source language and the recipient language in both typological structure and lexicon. They also mention as a case that fits "at least partly" in this category borrowing into a Creole from its lexifier in "decreolization". This, as they concede, is obviously not quite the same as dialect borrowing, since a (basilectal) Creole, while sharing a high percentage of its vocabulary with the lexifier, often does not correspond to it closely from the structural point of view (they cite the example of tense/aspect systems).

A question which has become important in recent language contact research is how borrowing is to be characterized in relation to code-switching, with the crux of the matter being the description of single lexical items from one language in synchronic speech data in another. Poplack with her various associates and Myers-Scotton, who have both addressed the issue in a number of publications (e.g. Poplack & Sankoff 1984, Poplack, Westwood & Wheeler 1987, Poplack, Sankoff & Miller 1988; Myers-Scotton 1992, 1993b) hold fundamentally different views on the relationship between the two phenomena. The position of Poplack and her associates is that "borrowing as a process differs radically from code-switching" (Poplack, Westwood & Wheeler 1987: 37). Myers-Scotton, in contrast, argues that "a continuum exists between borrowing and all sorts of CS [code-switched] material so that codeswitching and borrowing are not distinct phenomena" (1992: 21). In their data analyses both distinguish borrowed from code-switched items, but on a different basis: for Poplack and her associates, the decisive criterion is linguistic integration, whereas for Myers-Scotton, it is frequency. I do not wish to contribute to the theoretical debate about the relation between the processes of borrowing and code-switching, but since the present study centres on the speech of bilinguals I inevitably have to face the question of how to distinguish borrowed from code-switched items. In the following I will therefore discuss relevant aspects of the above-mentioned studies by Poplack and her associates and Myers-Scotton in more detail.

Poplack & Sankoff (1984: 103f) abstract from the literature on borrowing the following four basic criteria for characterizing a lexical item of foreign origin as a borrowing or loanword in a language:
- frequency of use
- native-language synonym displacement
- morphophonemic and/or syntactic integration
- acceptability

In the analytical part of that study, they use a combination of some of these or similar criteria to identify English loanwords in Spanish among a data set gathered from Spanish/English bilinguals by means of direct elicitation. According to this analysis, "it is the concepts showing most English use, most phonological and morphological integration, and fewest different types for which the designations can be considered true loanwords" (Poplack & Sankoff 1984: 129). In Poplack, Westwood & Wheeler (1987), the morphological criterion of obligatory case-marking in Finnish is used, in addition to several other types of evidence, to determine the status of single English-origin nouns (by far the most frequent category of English incorporations) in a corpus of Finnish as spoken by Finnish-English bilinguals. The authors argue that those English-origin nouns which are not case-marked may be treated as single-word switches. Those which are integrated into the Finnish inflectional system are considered borrowings. However, not all English-origin nouns which are thus integrated satisfy the frequency criterion for established borrowings, and the authors therefore set up an additional category of nonce borrowings. The relationship between code-switching and the different types of borrowing is summed up in the study in the figure reproduced below.

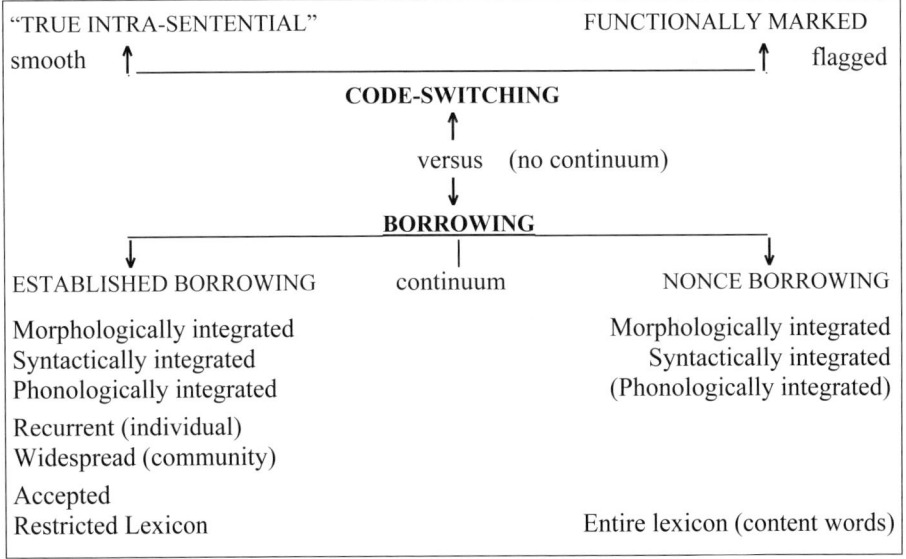

Figure 2.2 Characterization of code-switching and borrowing
Source: Poplack, Westwood & Wheeler (1987: 52)

The figure shows that morphological and syntactic integration are considered the primary distinguishing features of borrowings and that these are seen as falling along a continuum from nonce to established according to their frequency and acceptability, with phonological integration, optional for nonce borrowings, as an additional feature of established borrowings. The criteria of morphological and syntactic integration are also used by Poplack, Sankoff & Miller (1988) in their analysis of single English-origin items in a corpus of Canadian French. Poplack, Sankoff & Miller (1988: 93) admit, however, that as noun morphology is often zero in both languages (nouns again predominate among the data) and word order is similar, these criteria do not provide such clear-cut evidence as in the case of more divergent languages like the Finnish-English pair studied by Poplack, Westwood & Wheeler (1987). To the extent that this can be determined, they find that single English-origin items predominantly follow French morphological and syntactic patterns,[22] thus qualifying as borrowings according to Poplack and her associates' understanding of the term. Borrowings are categorized in that study into four basic types according to the criteria of overall frequency and number of speakers using an item:
- nonce (used only once in the corpus)
- idiosyncratic (used frequently but only by one speaker)
- recurrent (used more than ten times but not necessarily by as many speakers)
- widespread (used by more than ten speakers)

In addition, Poplack, Sankoff & Miller (1988: 59) find that acceptance as gauged by attestations in dictionaries and other French sources is a feature distinguishing different types of borrowings, as few of the nonce and idiosyncratic but most of the widespread ones are attested. Phonological integration is shown by Poplack, Sankoff & Miller (1988: 70ff) to increase as a function of spread in the community (i.e. the number of speakers using an item) and length of attestation history.

Being of the opinion that neither phonological nor morphosyntactic integration is useful as a criterion to distinguish borrowed and code-switched items, Myers-Scotton (1992, 1993b) rejects Poplack and her associates' category of nonce borrowings. She distinguishes two types of borrowings on a semantic basis: cultural borrowings, which encode objects or concepts new to the culture of the community in which the recipient language is spoken, and core borrowings, i.e. items for which an equivalent exists in the recipient language. As cultural borrowings fill lexical gaps, they are "'instant' B [borrowed] forms and unrelated to code-switching as a phenomenon" (Myers-Scotton 1992: 29). It is core borrowings which Myers-Scotton sees as related to code-switching, with the latter constituting the "gate" for the former (Myers-Scotton 1993b: 174): core lexical items from a foreign language are first used in an isolated fashion as code-switches and may then catch on. In addition to all lexical items designating objects or concepts new to the borrowing culture (irrespective of their frequency), Myers-Scotton considers core items as borrowed if they occur in three or more different samples in a fairly large corpus; otherwise they are considered code-switches. While the number of three is, as she readily acknowledges, an arbitrary cut-off point, it at least provides a clear criterion for data analyses, whereas the semantic distinction

---

[22] This applies to noun morphology, verb morphology and syntax (Poplack, Sankoff & Miller 1988: 67ff). Adjective and adverb morphology are identified by Poplack, Sankoff & Miller (1988: 69) as an area in which English-origin items resist integration into French patterns.

between cultural and core items is rather fuzzy (Myers-Scotton 1993b: 170 cites an analysis according to these criteria in which more than 30% of the data were classed as borderline cases). Myers-Scotton (1993b: 195ff) also shows in some detail that in addition to absolute frequency, relative frequency (i.e. the frequency of an item of foreign origin in relation to that of a native synonym) can be useful to consider. However, as Myers-Scotton (1993b: 204) points out as well, this criterion is not workable in all cases, as it becomes meaningless when both the item of foreign origin and its native equivalent have very low frequencies.

In the present study, semantic criteria will not be used to distinguish borrowing from code-switching. Phonological, morphological and syntactic integration will not be used either (the category of "nonce borrowings" thus becoming irrelevant) because, apart from the fact that the validity of these criteria is controversial, phonology is not an issue in the study and NigP and English are not distinct enough for morphological and syntactic integration to be always analysable. In my discussion of borrowing I will therefore rely on the criteria of absolute and, where appropriate, relative frequency (or "native synonym displacement") and acceptability.

2.4.3   *Interference*

Interference is the key concept of Weinreich's (1953) classic study of *Languages in Contact*. Weinreich's notion of interference is a broad one, encompassing synchronic as well as diachronic cross-linguistic influence ("in speech, interference is like sand carried by a stream; in language, it is the sedimented sand deposited on the bottom of the lake"; Weinreich 1953: 11).

In second language acquisition research the term *interference* (or *negative transfer*) is used in a more restricted sense to describe an aspect of imperfect second language acquisition: it refers to cross-linguistic influences in the language production of a learner of a language resulting from differences between the target language and his/her native language or any other language known to him/her (see e.g. Klein 1986: 25; Odlin 1989: 26f). As NigP is spoken mostly as a second language, this notion is relevant to the present study, and it is in this sense that the term *interference* will be understood.

2.5   Quantitative analysis of natural linguistic data: the Labovian paradigm

In 2.2.4 I mentioned the quantitative sociolinguistic approach to linguistic variation initiated by Labov (1966) as a method that has been used in analysing variation in Creole – lexifier contact situations. This method will play an important role in the present study. In this section, some of its basic principles as well as some relevant problems that have arisen in its diverse applications will be discussed.

2.5.1   *The (socio)linguistic variable*

The basic unit of variationist sociolinguistic analysis is the (socio)linguistic variable. A linguistic variable is a linguistic element with two or more semantically equivalent variant realizations. A sociolinguistic variable is a linguistic variable which is correlated with an extra-linguistic (i.e. social or situational) variable. A linguistic variable may also be correlated with another linguistic variable. While the latter is, strictly speaking, not a sociolinguistic phenomenon, the Labovian paradigm is associated with the study of both types of variation on the basis of natural linguistic data.

Labov (1966) applied the concept of the variable to the analysis of phonological variation only. Subsequently, it has been extended to other levels of linguistic analysis (see e.g. Sankoff 1973 and Weiner & Labov 1983). This has given rise to some controversy. Lavandera (1978), citing Sankoff (1973) and in particular an earlier, unpublished version of Weiner & Labov (1983), argues that contrary to the claims and proceeding of these authors, the notion of the variable as developed for phonological analysis is not directly transferable to non-phonological variables, since the variants of the latter are carriers of meaning and can therefore not be semantically equivalent in the same way as those of phonological variables.[23] She proposes that in the analysis of non-phonological variables the criterion of semantic equivalence should be replaced by "functional comparability" (p 181). Romaine (1981; revised as Romaine 1984) also cautions against a direct transfer of the Labovian notion of the variable from phonology to other levels of linguistic analysis and advocates a functionalist framework for the study of syntactic variation. She argues, however, that a distinction needs to be drawn between the less problematic "morphological or morpholexical variables" such as complementizer *que* deletion in Montreal French (one of the variables dealt with by Sankoff 1973) and the kind of variables she has in mind when she speaks of syntactic variation, namely "pure syntactic variables" like the agentless passive (the variable analysed by Weiner & Labov 1983).

Winford (1984) takes up the points raised by Lavandera (1978) and Romaine (1981) and extends the discussion to variation between a Creole and its lexifier. In this case, he argues, the problem of semantic equivalence is compounded by the embeddedness of the variants of presumed morphosyntactic and syntactic variables in different systems (p 272ff). For example, he points out that while it seems fairly unproblematic to regard basilectal, mesolectal and acrolectal pronoun forms as synonymous, the case of tense/aspect markers is much more complicated (p 275ff). This difficulty is also recognized by Bickerton (1973a, 1975b), who regards a Creole continuum as a single system and uses the implicational method of analysis: in Bickerton (1973a: 646) he explains that the choice of the copula and pronoun systems for his analyses is motivated by the fact that these are among the categories which can be studied across the whole continuum; a category like the perfect would not have been adequate, he says, because the basilect does not have a direct equivalent of the English perfect (as he notes in Bickerton 1975b: 42, completive *don* in the Guyanese basilect has some of the functions of the English perfect, but not all instances of *don* are translatable by a perfect form and vice versa).

---

[23] Another major point of criticism in her paper is that the syntactic variables that the authors cited have studied do not have social or situational correlates. She acknowledges that Weiner & Labov analyse the choice between active and agentless passive as a linguistic, not a sociolinguistic variable, but for her, the linguistic and the sociolinguistic variable can be equated since the notion of the variable was developed in Labov's early work to account for sociolinguistic variation.

2.5.2 The principle of accountability

Fundamental to quantitative linguistic analysis is the "principle of accountability" (Labov 1982: 30), which Labov (ibid.) describes as follows:

> For the section of speech being examined, all occurrences of a given variant are noted, and where it has been possible to define the variable as a closed set of variants, all non-occurrences of the variant in the relevant environments.

He adds:

> There are a number of variables that can be studied now by noting only each occurrence, but not each non-occurrence, since it has not yet been possible to close the set of possible variants. [...] Here, quantitative work is confined to tracing the relative frequency of occurrence in some globally defined section of speech, controlled for length by an independent measure like number of sentences, pages, or hours of speech. (Labov 1982: 87n10)

To give a reliable account of variability in one's data, it is also important to identify and exclude exceptions, i.e. cases where the type of variation one is studying is either absent or subject to special factors, and neutralization contexts, i.e. cases where the phonetic environment makes it impossible to determine the presence or absence of the relevant segment (see e.g. Wolfram 1993: 214f).

2.5.3 Variation and change in language

Bickerton in his early work on the Guyanese Creole continuum simply equated synchronic variation with diachronic change, arguing that "a synchronic cut across the Guyanese community is indistinguishable from a diachronic cut across a century and a half of linguistic development" (1975b: 17). The relation between linguistic variation and change is also an important aspect of work in the Labovian tradition, but the notion of an automatic relation between the two phenomena has never been accepted: "Not all variability and heterogeneity in language structure involves change; but all change involves variability and heterogeneity" (Weinreich, Labov & Herzog 1968: 188). Therefore, according to scholars working in this tradition, change cannot be directly inferred from any kind of synchronic variation that one may observe but must be studied either in "real time", i.e. on the basis of diachronic data, or in "apparent time", i.e. on the basis of synchronic age-stratified data (cf Labov 1994, 2001).

2.6 Additional methodological and terminological considerations for the present study

In the course of the general theoretical discussion in the preceding sections I have already pointed out in many cases how the concepts that have been introduced relate to the present study and which terminology I will use. This section will round off the discussion by dealing with a few points of methodology and terminological usage in the present study that remain to be clarified.

2.6.1 The linguistic relationship between Nigerian Pidgin and English

As has already been stated in Chapter 1, the variety that will be analysed in the corpus study in Chapter 5, the main part of this work, is educated NigP. This means that the focus will be on the language use of the type of speakers who, judging by their social characteristics, are unlikely to be regular users of the basilect in a P/C continuum situation (cf the discussion in 2.2.3). There are of course situations which might prompt such speakers to produce the most basilectal variety in their repertoire, but one also has to consider that in a Creole continuum, "one speaker's attempt at the broad patois may be closer to the standard end of the spectrum than another speaker's attempt at the standard" (DeCamp 1971: 350). Besides, the corpus does include situations which seem suitable for eliciting the variety of NigP that a speaker uses most naturally and unselfconsciously (in particular informal conversations), and for an educated speaker in a speech community in which there is a P/C continuum, this is most likely to be a mesolectal one. In view of these expectations, and since the question of a NigP-English continuum is a central one in the study, one of the aims of the corpus analysis will be to determine whether educated NigP has at least some of the typical morphosyntactic features of a mesolect, namely:

- forms which are intermediate between the basilectal and the standard English ones (cf the example discussed in 2.2.1)
- forms which are not intermediate in the same way as those referred to above but which nevertheless distinguish the mesolect both from the basilect and the acrolect (like the preverbal past or anterior marker *did* in mesolectal Jamaican Creole, as opposed to basilectal *bin/ben* and acrolectal *-ed*; see Patrick 1999: chapter 6)
- extensive variation between Creole and standard English forms (cf e.g. past marking in mesolectal Jamaican Creole as described by Patrick 1999: chapters 6 and 7)

A continuum depends on the existence of a mesolect. If educated NigP has typical features of such a variety, we may say that there are at least parallels between the situation in Nigeria and the one in Jamaica or Guyana. If, however, English influences in NigP are relatively unimportant and/or can be satisfactorily explained as language contact phenomena like code-switching, borrowing and interference, NigP and English can be considered discrete varieties.

The educational status of the speakers in the additional recordings that will be analysed in Chapter 6 ranges from low to medium. These data may corroborate the existence or non-existence of a spectrum of variation in NigP that may be characterized as forming part of a P/C continuum, but my aim is not to provide a comprehensive description of NigP as spoken by less educated speakers, which has already been done by other scholars (cf 1.3).

2.6.2 The analysis of linguistic variation

In the corpus study, I employ quantitative methodology and supplement it by some qualitative work.

As pointed out in 2.5.1, a fundamental aspect of the quantitative study of language use is the analysis of variation between different variants of linguistic variables, but the identification of semantically equivalent variants can be problematic outside the area of phonology, and more so if two different linguistic systems are involved. In the present study, the number of variables that can be defined as a closed set of variants is therefore limited. How this problem has been handled will be explained in the course of the discussion of the results.

The additional texts from less educated speakers, being a rather heterogeneous group and not a systematic corpus, will be described on a text-by-text basis.

2.6.3 *The analysis of linguistic change*

Since the present study focuses on educated NigP, my perspective on change will be limited to the period in which this variety can be said to have emerged, i.e. the post-independence period in which the language has gradually gained some measure of acceptability in educated circles (cf Agheyisi 1984a, 1988). We are thus dealing with a relatively short time span, and today NigP is still more popular among younger educated Nigerians than among older ones.[24] Since, besides, the very young cannot satisfy the educational criterion, the speakers in my corpus of educated NigP are inevitably concentrated in the 20-29 and 30-39 age brackets. An apparent time study is thus ruled out. A further complication is that because of their different methodology (see 1.3), most previous studies are not directly comparable to the present one. Therefore, while I can offer a perspective on change in NigP by situating my findings in the context of previous work, which, as pointed out in 1.3, deals for the most part with traditional, conservative varieties of the language, I do not presume to be able to arrive at the kind of precise conclusions that only a strict study in apparent or real time would permit.

2.6.4 *Situational variation*

Within the sample of educated NigP, I investigate the influence of the speech situation. As pointed out in 1.4, this aspect of the study is motivated primarily by my interest in the linguistic consequences of the increasing use of NigP in formal domains. The focus of the analysis of situational variation will therefore be on differences between face-to-face speech and NigP as used in the more formal context of radio broadcasting, but, as will become clear in chapter 5, the corpus also permits more fine-grained analyses.

Situational variation is an area of sociolinguistics where there is little agreement on terminology. For example, Trudgill (1995: 84ff) distinguishes *register* and *style,* two terms which are often used in this context,[25] by linking the former with occupations and the latter with different levels of formality. Crystal & Davy (1969), in contrast, use the term *style* to describe variation along a wide range of situational parameters, and Biber (1995) uses the term *register* in a similarly general way. The present study follows Biber's (1995) usage of *register* as "a cover term for any variety associated with particular situational contexts or purposes" (p 1).

---

[24] Agheyisi's (1988: 230) observation on "older educated and conservative members of society", that they "invariably neither speak NPE [Nigerian Pidgin English] nor encourage its use" is now of course slightly dated, but Mann (2000: 468) still alludes to the age factor when he describes NigP as "*the* more likely language of interethnic sociocommunication for the generations between 15-40 years in urban centres in the south and abroad" (emphasis in the original).

[25] There are also several other terms (e.g. *genre*) which have been used in the study of contextually determined variation in language; see the discussion in Biber (1995: 7ff).

3

Nigerian Pidgin in its sociolinguistic context

3.1 Introduction

This chapter describes the sociolinguistic context of Pidgin use in Nigeria at large and in Lagos. The discussion of this topic begins with a general description of the language situation in Nigeria (Section 3.2). The following sections elaborate on the use of NigP and on specific aspects of the language situation in Lagos.

I draw on the work of previous authors but I also use data from my own work on the status and functions of NigP. One source of my data is the results of a survey of the use of, and attitudes towards, NigP ("language survey") which I conducted by means of a questionnaire ("language questionnaire", see Appendix A).[1] A total of 161 informants participated in this survey. The population group from which the sample was drawn is that which is also the focus of the microsociolinguistic part of the present study: younger, educated urban residents in southern Nigeria, in particular students in tertiary education. While the sample is not representative in the technical sense, I tried to achieve a certain balance within this restricted group by distributing the questionnaires at several different locations (mostly higher education institutions in Lagos and Calabar) and, within these locations, among different groups (e.g. an undergraduate and a postgraduate class).[2] In addition to these data, I take into account relevant parts of the interviews in Appendix C. These interviews were designed to complement the data elicited by the above-mentioned as well as my other questionnaires with more detailed information. They are therefore not formal interviews with a standardized set of questions, as in the questionnaires, but represent various types of the informal interview (cf Moser & Kalton 1971: 296ff). Interviews 1-3 and 5-7 are the most informal. Interview 1 is a non-directive interview, in which the informants were asked

---

[1] The results of this survey are documented in full in Deuber (1998).
[2] The details of the sample are as follows: 70% of the 161 completed questionnaires are from Lagos, 19% are from Calabar, and 12% were completed by participants of a national teachers' conference in Owerri (percentages do not always add up to 100 due to rounding). All informants had a secondary education or higher. The majority (66%) were students at one the following tertiary institutions: University of Lagos, Yaba College of Technology (Lagos), University of Calabar, Calabar Polytechnic. The remaining informants were teachers (20%) or had diverse other occupations (14%). 57% were male and 39% female (4% omitted to indicate their sex). The distribution across age groups was: 17-19, 12%; 20-29, 32%; 30-39, 29%; 40-50, 6% (21% did not specify their age). As their mother tongue 39% claimed Yoruba, 31% Igbo, 27% a minor Nigerian language, and 1% each Hausa and a non-Nigerian African language (1% gave no answer to this question).

to talk freely about the topic in question, Interview 5 is a conversational interview, i.e. I asked language-related questions casually in the course of a conversation with the informants, and interviews 2-3 and 6-7 developed out of interactions which were not even intended as interviews at the outset. Interviews 4 and 8-11 are closer than these to formal ones. They are guided interviews, i.e. I inquired about a range of topics I had worked out before the interview, but in a flexible manner and not according to a standardized questionnaire. A number of the interviews are group interviews. The language is in most cases English but I used NigP when this was the more natural choice. This was the case in the conversational interview (5) as well as in Interview 10, where I interviewed a person with whom I had habitually interacted in NigP over a period of time.

3.2   The language situation in Nigeria

3.2.1   The languages of Nigeria

Nigeria is a highly multilingual country, with a total of about 450-500 indigenous languages belonging to three different phyla (Crozier & Blench 1992, Grimes 2000) spoken by an estimated population of about 134 million (Central Intelligence Agency 2003). Among these languages, three are dominant: Hausa in the north, Yoruba in the southwest, and Igbo in the southeast (cf Map 2). Each of these has at least 18-19 million first language speakers but, unlike the other two, Hausa is also widely spoken as a second language (Grimes 2000). The other indigenous languages may be grouped into two or three categories according to their demographic and functional characteristics (cf Adekunle 1972; Agheyisi 1984b; Akinnaso 1990, 1991; Brann 1989, 1990); there are several languages including Kanuri, Fulfulde, Efik, Edo, Ijo[3] and Tiv which are recognized as having considerable regional importance, but most of the others are truly minority languages with no significance beyond their immediate locality.

About 20% of Nigerians speak English (Bamgbose 1996: 366). The majority of these are second language users. NigP is estimated by Faraclas (1996: 1) to have more than 40 million second language speakers and more than 1 million first language speakers, both of which numbers, he adds, are increasing rapidly. This amounts to a total number of speakers that only Hausa can come close to, but NigP may be more extensively spoken than even that language: Elugbe (1995: 288) and Faraclas (1996: 2) describe NigP as the most widely spoken language in the country.[4]

---

[3]   Ijo is a cluster of related languages spoken in an area along the coast which stretches from Ondo State in the west to Rivers State in the east (Crozier & Blench 1992). The language with the highest number of speakers is Izon (cf Map 2).

[4]   In the language survey 76% of the informants agreed with this view.

3.2.2 Language acquisition

In Nigeria monolingualism is widespread only in linguistically homogeneous rural areas. Bi- or multilingualism is the more usual phenomenon. For example, it is common for an educated urban resident in southern Nigeria to speak one or more indigenous languages and NigP, in addition to English. In many cases such a speaker acquired an indigenous language at home and NigP informally outside the home (often in the school environment outside the classroom) and learned English through formal schooling.

Although access to formal education is increasing, English remains to some extent an elite language. (In connection with the social connotations of English in Nigeria, it is interesting to compare the two family planning posters at the end of this chapter.) In elite families it is even possible that a child may acquire English at home. This is usual when the parents do not share an indigenous language, but there are also couples who share an indigenous language but prefer their children to acquire English and therefore use English as the language of the home (Bamgbose 1996: 367; see also Interview 1, ll 216-220; Interview 4, ll 10-27). Depending on their backgrounds, NigP is another option when a couple do not share an indigenous language, and their children may then acquire it as their first language.[5] NigP may also come to be used in the home even if the parents share an indigenous language: in multilingual urban compounds and neighbourhoods where children are exposed to NigP from an early age it may be introduced into the home by the children. Several scholars who have commented on the acquisition of NigP by children (Mafeni 1971, Shnukal & Marchese 1983, Donwa-Ifode 1984) have also pointed out that in many cases, NigP is acquired alongside and not instead of an indigenous language.[6] It is on this ground that it has been denied that NigP is creolizing in the traditional sense (Donwa-Ifode 1984; cf also Mann 1996: 169), but what is in fact in question is the definition of terms like *first language*, *mother tongue* and *creolization*, and not the fact that some NigP speakers acquired the language in early childhood.

3.2.3 Legal provisions

Nigeria does not have an explicitly formulated language policy as such, but there are two documents which contain language policy statements, the *National Policy on Education* (Federal Republic of Nigeria 1998; earlier editions in 1977 and 1981) and the Constitution (Federal Republic of Nigeria 1999; earlier editions in 1979 and 1989).

The *National Policy on Education* echoes the colonial policy with regard to language use in the education system (cf Akinnaso 1990: 342) by stipulating that the medium of instruction should be the "language of the environment" for the first three years of primary education, while from the fourth year English should progressively be used as the medium of instruction (Section 17). In addition, the government is to ensure that the medium of instruction at the pre-primary level is "principally the mother-tongue or the language of the immediate community" (Section 14). Furthermore, the policy states that it is "in the interest

---

[5] As Bamgbose (1996: 367) notes, the couple may also decide to restrict NigP to communication among themselves and speak English to the children. Cf also Shnukal & Marchese (1983: 20).

[6] However, Elugbe & Omamor (1991: 49) say that "the assumption that every speaker of a pidgin also has *another* language, at least his 'native language' is certainly not supported by the situation in the areas around Warri and Sapele" (emphasis in the original).

of national unity" that every child should be required to learn either Hausa, Igbo or Yoruba (Section 10). A "major Nigerian language" other than the language of the environment is therefore a compulsory subject in junior secondary school (Section 22).[7] Finally, the 1998 revised version makes the teaching of French compulsory in primary school from the fourth year and throughout secondary school (Sections 10, 17, 22, 23). This is the only major change compared to earlier versions of the document.[8]

The Constitution contains the following two provisions regulating language use in the National Assembly and the state Houses of Assembly, respectively:

> The business of the National Assembly shall be conducted in English, and in Hausa, Ibo and Yoruba when adequate arrangements have been made therefor. (Section 55)

> The business of a House of Assembly shall be conducted in English, but the House may in addition to English conduct the business of the House in one or more other languages spoken in the State as the House may by resolution approve. (Section 97)

Both of these provisions have been retained unchanged from earlier versions of the Constitution (cf Bamgbose 1996: 358).

3.2.4 Language functions

English is *de facto* Nigeria's official language. The provision for the use of Hausa, Yoruba and Igbo in the National Assembly has remained unimplemented (Bamgbose 1996: 364). In several of the highly multilingual states, English also remains the sole language of the state Houses of Assembly; other state legislatures have approved either Hausa, Yoruba or Igbo as an additional language for the conduct of their business,[9] but such approval does not always translate into practice (Akinnaso 1991: 49ff). Furthermore, all written communication in government and administration is in English (Bamgbose 1996: 364).

English also retains a dominant position in the education system. In spite of the policy stipulation for the use of indigenous languages, pre-primary schooling is in English because such schools are privately owned and those who can afford them want their children to be taught in English (Bamgbose 1996: 363). Elite parents often also send their children to English-medium private primary schools (Akinnaso 1990: 353). In government-owned primary schools, the major and some of the minor indigenous languages function as media of instruction. However, while indigenous languages are used in more or less monolingual (typically rural) schools, the medium of instruction in multilingual (typically urban) schools is often English from the first year (Akinnaso 1990: 353f; cf also Interview 1, ll 240-261 and Interview 4). This at least is the case officially; unofficially, NigP is sometimes used as the medium of instruction in multilingual schools in southern Nigeria (Obilade 1980; Shnukal & Marchese 1983: 19; see also Interview 2, ll 96-101). As regards the teaching of an additional Nigerian language as a subject at the secondary level, this is a provision of the

---

[7] The language of the environment is to be taught as a subject as well, as is also the case at the upper primary level. In senior secondary school students are required to study only one "major Nigerian language" (Section 23).

[8] Earlier versions of the *National Policy on Education* are discussed e.g. in Akere (1995), Akinnaso (1990) and Bamgbose (1996).

[9] Only in one case was an indigenous language other than Hausa, Yoruba or Igbo also selected: In Borno State, Hausa as well as Kanuri were approved as languages of legislation in addition to English.

National Policy on Education which has proven difficult to implement (Akinnaso 1990: 350ff; Bamgbose 1996: 365).

In the mass media, English has a dominant position as well. Since literacy in Nigeria still means primarily literacy in English, this dominance is overwhelming in the print media. While there are a few weeklies in indigenous languages, all the major newspapers and quality magazines are in English (Bamgbose 1996: 365; cf also "Nigeria" 2003: 847ff). When NigP is used – typically in newspaper columns and popular magazines – it is most often associated with light entertainment or bawdy subjects, although a few of the major English language newspapers also feature political cartoons in NigP (see Ofuani 1981b).[10] In the electronic media, indigenous languages and NigP have a more important role. However, as in sub-Saharan Africa generally (Bourgault 1995: 103), television tends to be an urban and something of an elitist medium because of the lack of electricity in many rural areas and the relatively high cost of television sets (Interview 8, ll 55-63). Therefore it is on the radio, which also caters to a grass roots audience, that indigenous languages and NigP are most widely used. News is broadcast in indigenous languages and in some cases in NigP both on radio and on television (Osaji 1991, Jibril 1995). Such news broadcasts are invariably translations of the English version (Osaji 1991; Bamgbose 1996: 365).

There is some literary production in indigenous languages, but Nigeria's famous writers like Achebe and Soyinka write in English. NigP occurs in some novels by these and other authors, where (with the exception of Ken Saro-Wiwa's *Sozaboy*[11]) it is confined to the direct speech of some of the characters, and there is some drama and poetry in the language.[12]

English is also an important language of Christian religious practice, but this is one of the formal domains where indigenous languages and NigP have been able to make significant inroads (Bamgbose 1996: 364; Mann 1993b: 174; Oloruntoba 1992: 94). Another formal context in which indigenous languages and NigP are used is information transmission by government and non-government agencies (Agheyisi 1984a: 212; Modigie 1997; see also Interview 1, ll 69-79, Interview 6, Text D 2 in Appendix D, and the family planning posters at the end of this chapter).

The primary domains of use of indigenous languages and NigP are, however, not formal but informal ones. Members of the elite can resort to English as a lingua franca, but since many Nigerians are not competent in the language, one can say that the most common lingua francas in public informal communication are NigP (in the south and to some extent in the north) and Hausa (in the north); Yoruba and Igbo are demographically major languages but not major lingua francas.[13] Also, it is not impossible for English to be used in private informal communication between family members, friends etc. who share an

---

[10] The critical column *Popular Side* in the *Sporting Champion* (see Appendix D, Text D 3) is also in a somewhat different vein from the typical uses of NigP in the print media.

[11] In this novel, what the author describes as 'rotten English', a mixture of Nigerian pidgin English, broken English and occasional flashes of good, even idiomatic English" ("Author's Note", n p) is the medium of first-person narration.

[12] The topic of NigP in literature is beyond the scope of the present study. For discussions of literary uses of NigP (from a linguistic and/or literary perspective) see e.g. Obilade (1978), Barbag-Stoll (1983: chapter IV), Mair (1992), Zabus (1992), Omamor (1997), Nitzl (1999).

[13] On the extent to which NigP and indigenous languages are used as lingua francas see e.g. Agheyisi (1984b: 237ff), Akinnaso (1991: 33f) and Jowitt (1995: 47).

indigenous language, but in most cases the indigenous language is preferred (cf also Bamgbose 1996: 368). NigP is a common alternative when there is no shared indigenous language, also among educated speakers, and is sometimes even used among speakers who share an indigenous language. It is especially popular among university students:

> Nigerian University campuses have become a primary locale for communication in A N P [Anglo-Nigerian Pidgin]. And it is not enough to say, in this case, that the ethnic mixture of the student population is wholly responsible for this state of affairs. A N P has become a trendy code for the young generation, in which they discuss their lectures, social life, politics, and love affairs. (Mann 1993b: 171f)

3.2.5 *Language attitudes*

English is the one highly prestigious language in Nigeria in terms of overt prestige. However, attitudes to English are not wholly favourable. For some, it is ruled out as a candidate for a national language because it is viewed as a foreign language and its colonial associations still loom large (Jowitt 1995: 36). On the individual level, its elitist and formal connotations make it less suitable than NigP and indigenous languages for informal communication: its use in this context may create a social barrier and imply arrogance or unfriendliness (see Interview 1, ll 309-319, 350-362; Interview 2, ll 369-385, 449-460, 582-586; Interview 4, ll 93-122).

The indigenous languages are symbols of Nigerian cultures, but on the national level their identificational and integrative value is undermined by the fact that language is bound up with ethnic group membership. Ethnic rivalry and resentment are potent forces in Nigerian life and politics, and they are also an important factor in language policies and their implementation or lack thereof. For example, according to Dada (1985: 292), a bill for the implementation of the constitutional provision that Hausa, Yoruba, and Igbo may be used in the National Assembly failed due to protest from minority groups. Similarly, it was suggested that in the revised version of the 1979 Constitution, Hausa, Yoruba, and Igbo should be designated as Nigeria's national languages and the teaching of these languages in all primary and secondary schools should be made mandatory, but the motion had to be withdrawn after speakers of minor languages walked out of the Constituent Assembly in protest (Bamgbose 1996: 361). Ethnolinguistic rivalry is, in addition to lack of resources, also one of the reasons why the provision in the *National Policy on Education* for the teaching of the three major languages has proven difficult to implement. As Akinnaso (1990: 350ff) points out, the provision is resented by the minorities and the states are generally reluctant to promote a language not spoken within their borders. (Akinnaso also observes (ibid. p 353) that the southern multilingual states have an additional reason to be hostile to the policy, namely that NigP as a vital language in these states is not included in the policy.) In individual language use, too, ethnicity is an important factor. On the one hand, the covert prestige of the indigenous languages as markers of ethnic identity can be exploited in certain situations to establish solidarity (cf e.g. Nwoye 1993: 373). On the other hand, the use of an ethnic language is likely to be viewed with suspicion and hostility in a multilingual public setting (Scotton 1975).

NigP has been described as "neither foreign nor indigenous to Nigeria" (Agheyisi 1984b: 237), but it has also been argued that it can be considered indigenous because it originated and has been expanded in Nigeria (Elugbe 1995: 291). One of my informants contrasted attitudes to English and NigP in the following way:

> Pidgin is important for two reasons that come to me immediately. The first one, because it is spoken across the country, and the second thing is that, for maybe what I can call "patriotic reasons" or "emotionally gratifying reasons". Unlike English, if you speak English, the problem we have, or at least it's at the back of your mind, is that you are speaking somebody else's language, a language which is probably the strongest symbol that at one point in time, you were under his governance, you were colonized by him, and you still speak his language. That is what happens if you speak English. But if you speak Pidgin, Pidgin is that language that you have taken from the colonizer and you have made it your own. (Interview 1, ll 22-30)[14]

The great asset of NigP is that it is the most neutral language in Nigeria: it has neither the elitist connotations of English nor the ethnic connotations of the indigenous languages (see also Interview 1, ll 44-49, 128-130). However, it still suffers to some extent from the prejudice going back to the colonial era that it is a corrupt form of English used by the lowly and ignorant. This prejudice is still held by some conservative members of the elite (cf e.g. Interview 7), in particular among the older generation (Agheyisi 1988: 230). Coupled with the perception by some that it is not fully a Nigerian language, such views are probably in large measure responsible for the fact that in spite of its acknowledged usefulness (cf e.g. Interview 6, ll 3-9), NigP has so far not been given any official recognition.[15] However, it is also clear that attitudes towards NigP are changing. This was already observed by Agheyisi (1984a: 212, 231) almost 20 years ago, and it is also quite apparent in my data. In the language survey, the number of those who agreed that NigP is a corrupt form of English was equalled by those who disagreed (22% each), and the majority (53%) opted for the compromise answer ("Pidgin is similar to English, but it does have its own grammatical rules"; cf the language questionnaire in Appendix A).[16] For the younger generation, to be ashamed of speaking NigP is associated with a colonial mentality (see Interview 1, ll 390-395). Among this group, the language has a high degree of covert prestige. As two of my informants put it: "it brings endearment", "it's a symbol of familiarity, a sign of friendship" (Interview 1, ll 438-439).

While NigP and the indigenous languages play a pivotal role in Nigerian life, they lack the socioeconomic prestige associated with English. Therefore, parents and students alike often consider education in an indigenous language or NigP a disadvantage (see Interview 2, ll 118-124; Interview 3, ll 66-84). And whereas the person who uses NigP in an informal context meets with friendly reactions, the one who uses it where English is expected is looked down upon (see Interview 1, ll 289-294; Interview 3, ll 32-36).

---

[14] See also Interview 5, ll 168-179 for a similar view.
[15] Cf also Akinnaso (1991: 59), who observes that the former Bendel, Rivers and Cross River States were not able to adopt a legislative language in addition to English because NigP as the lingua franca in these linguistically highly fragmented states could not be chosen, "partly because of its stigmatization and partly because it is not viewed as a Nigerian language *per se*".
[16] 3% of the informants did not answer this question.

3.2.6 Language development

Language development (cf Ferguson 1968) is roughly equivalent to standardization in the broad sense. Ferguson (1968) describes three aspects of language development: graphization (development of a standardized orthography), standardization (in the narrow sense of the development of a norm which overrides the different regional and social varieties of the language and codification of the norm) and modernization (development of vocabulary and forms of discourse necessary for the language to function in a modern society). According to these and other criteria, Hausa, Yoruba and Igbo are, not surprisingly, the most highly developed indigenous languages in Nigeria (Brann 1975, Jowitt 1995), although there is still some controversy about the Igbo standard.[17] These are followed by "major minor" languages like Efik, Edo, Ijo and Tiv and other indigenous languages with varying degrees of development (Brann 1975), but many of the smaller languages remain undeveloped. According to Williamson (1990: 142), at least 117 of Nigeria's languages can claim to be written languages in the sense that there is at least one publication in the language, but not all of these have a standardized orthography; the number of languages whose orthography has been standardized is about 60 (Emenanjo 1991: 160). NigP is among the languages that do not have a standardized orthography. There is no codified standard variety of the language, nor have there been any systematic efforts to expand its lexicon.

3.2.7 Conclusion: the sociolinguistic status of Nigerian Pidgin vis-à-vis English and the indigenous languages

When the foregoing description of the language situation in Nigeria is compared to Ferguson's (1959) sociolinguistic criteria for diglossia (see 2.3.2), it becomes clear that from a sociolinguistic point of view, the relationship between NigP and English can broadly though not strictly speaking be described as a case of diglossia. English dominates in all H domains, is highly prestigious, has an important literary heritage, is typically learned through formal education and has a high degree of standardization or language development. NigP is typically used in L domains, does not have overt prestige, is acquired informally and lacks language development. There is, however, a greater functional overlap between the two languages than in Ferguson's classic diglossia model, since among the Nigerian elite English may also be used informally while NigP has some limited functions in formal domains.

When the indigenous languages are taken into consideration the picture becomes more complicated. It is clear that English, NigP and the indigenous languages represent in many ways three different language types, and their relationship can therefore be characterized as triglossia: English as the official language is primarily associated with the modern formal sector; NigP as a neutral lingua franca is the linguistic medium par excellence of the "neo-African society" (Gilman 1979), i.e. the informal aspects of the modern, urban way of life; the indigenous languages are markers of ethnic identity and particularly representative of,

---

[17] Whereas Yoruba and Hausa have well-established standard varieties based on the Oyo and Kano dialects, respectively, the problematic history of the standardization of Igbo has been characterized by controversy over the base dialect and attempts to find a compromise solution (see Ndukwe 1982: 142f; also Emenanjo 1975 and Nwoga 1994 on the special case of Igbo).

though by no means restricted to, a traditional, rural way of life. However, the Nigerian situation is more complicated than the Tanzanian case as described by Abdulaziz Mkilifi (1972; see the discussion in 2.3.3). This is due mainly to two factors. First, Nigeria does not have one but two major local lingua francas, Hausa and NigP, with a geographical division regarding their use, and in addition two other demographically major languages, Yoruba and Igbo. Second, only one of the lingua francas, Hausa, and in addition the other two demographically major languages have official recognition as the major languages of the country and a relatively high degree of linguistic development, whereas the second major lingua franca, NigP, lacks these. This points to a gap between language policy and sociolinguistic realities.

3.3 Nigerian Pidgin in the media

The use of NigP in the media has a considerable tradition. The humorous *Wakabout* column in the weekly *Lagos Weekend* first appeared in 1969 (Ofuani 1981b: 335). The use of NigP in electronic media was pioneered in the radio drama serial *Safe Journey*, a comedy serial which was launched in 1959 and continued for 14 years (Uwabor 1995: 1ff). The variety of NigP employed in *Safe Journey* was "highly exaggerated – designed to reflect the characteristic juxtaposition of features of the pidgin and those of 'bad English' found in the speech of a large proportion of uneducated adults in urban Nigeria" (Agheyisi 1971: 4n1). The definitive breakthrough for NigP in drama came with *Gandu Street* (Uwabor 1995: 5). Created by Tunde Aiyegbusi, one of Nigeria's most renowned writers of radio drama, in 1975, this radio drama serial became very popular and was broadcast for almost two decades (ibid. pp 3ff, 295). The drama brought together a diverse set of characters representing the different parts of the country in the community of "Gandu Street" with the objective of contributing to nation-building and was also used to spread information on various development programmes (ibid.). It is thus a prime example of informational or educative drama, a thriving genre on Nigerian radio. Another of several popular drama serials in which NigP has been used (cf Agheyisi 1984a: 213; Elugbe 1995: 294) is *Masquerade*, a satirical comedy serial (cf Oreh 1985). While some of the characters in *Masquerade* employ regular NigP, the television and radio serial is most famous for the mixture of ungrammatical English expressions, distorted English words and NigP elements in the speech of its main character, Chief Zebrudaya, which contributes much to its humour (cf Elugbe & Omamor 1991: 63ff; Oreh 1985: 111f). Apart from drama, advertisements and music in NigP have long been prominent features of the programme of Nigerian radio stations (Agheyisi 1984a: 213), and there are advertisements in NigP on television as well. News broadcasts in NigP were introduced in the 1980s (cf Agheyisi 1988: 240n2; Elugbe & Omamor 1991: 151n3).

NigP in the media is definitely quite popular,[18] but not all types of media uses of NigP have the same popularity among all sections of the population. Informational broadcasts

---

[18] Mann (1998: 140) describes NigP as "the language of the most popular radio and TV adverts, jingles, public service announcements, record requests, local political debates and drama sketches". See also Interview 9, ll 102-112 on the popularity of the request programme *I Salute Una* on Radio Nigeria 2 and Interview 5, ll 147-156 for an individual view.

such as news are designed for those who do not have enough formal education to be able to follow English language programmes, and therefore do not usually attract the interest of educated audiences. The only text type that seems capable of bridging the gap evident in the results from the language survey summarized in the figure below seems to be radio drama which combines entertainment with an educative message.

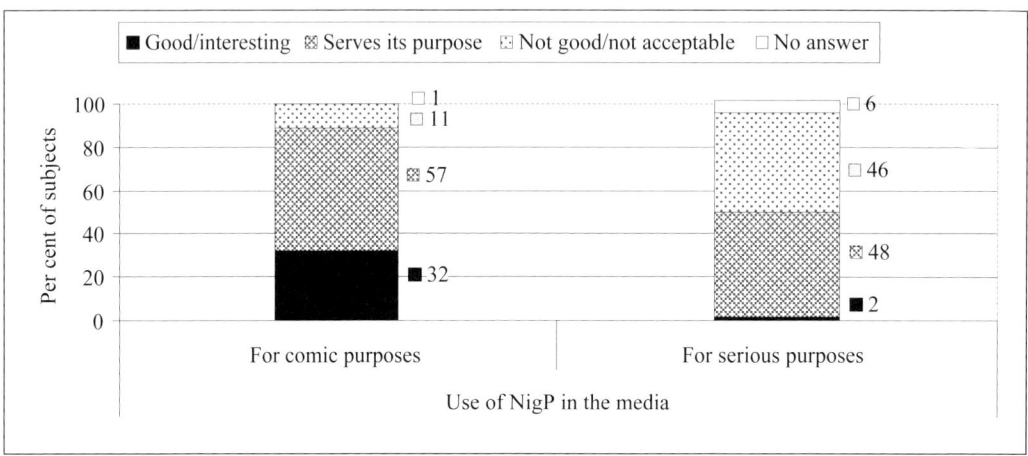

Figure 3.1 Opinions on the use of NigP in the media according to the language survey

3.4 Nigerian Pidgin in Lagos

The main function of NigP in Lagos is that of a lingua franca in the streets, markets, "motor parks" (road transport terminals), and buses of the city, and as such, it has a vital importance. One of my informants remarked that the language a stranger is most likely to pick up in Lagos is NigP, not any of the other two major languages of the city, Yoruba and English (see interview 1, ll 276-279; interview 2, ll 271-273). This may appear surprising, given that the Yoruba are numerically dominant, but the disproportionately high use of NigP in public settings in Lagos can be explained by the ethnic connotations of Yoruba. This could not be better expressed than in the following quotation from one of the interviews (the speaker is Yoruba):

> [...] I, for example, whenever I'm in a bus or whatever, I usually use either Pidgin or standard English, because I have learned to my embarrassment that the person I address in Yoruba will always say "I don't understand what you are saying". And in Nigeria, we have to do with the problem of language and status in this country. If you use Yoruba to a person who does not speak Yoruba, he will sometimes be angry. The question is, why should you assume that he is Yoruba? So, most people use English or Pidgin with a person they do not know. So if you know the person and you know that he's Yoruba, yes, you may use it. (Interview 2, ll 323-330)

Scotton's (1975) quantitative study of language use in Lagos confirms this view. Her findings show that it is not uncommon for the dominant Yoruba to privately converse in their language with non-Yoruba friends if these speak it (p 85). In any public situation, however, they normally communicate with members of other ethnic groups either in English or in NigP, because speaking Yoruba would mean using a symbol of ethnicity that would not be tolerated in public (p 83f). The choice between English and NigP depends on social considerations and the context. In informal situations, as the informant already quoted above also points out, NigP is more common:

> Supposing you are in a bus, and you ask somebody to please create more space by moving along the bench for you, and the person is refusing to do so, supposing that person is wearing a suit and a tie, you will speak to that person in the bus in standard English. But supposing the person is dressed like a mechanic or somebody who has gone to sell bread or who is not dressed in a particularly formal way, you will use, or you are most likely to use Pidgin English. Because if you use standard English, people will think that maybe you are trying to show off your knowledge of the language. But in most informal situations Nigerians in fact use Pidgin English. (Interview 2, ll 425-432)

As in other parts of the country, NigP is also used in Lagos by the educated for informal communication among themselves. It is commonly heard in the student hostels, canteens, and other places where students gather informally on the University of Lagos campus and in other educational institutions, as well as in offices, banks etc. (cf e.g. Interview 1, ll 421-432).

A further aspect of NigP use in Lagos worth mentioning is that there is a special community in which NigP is clearly a Creole: the suburb of Ajegunle on the southern mainland (cf Map 3). Ajegunle is the only part of Lagos in which the Yoruba are not in the majority (Peil 1991: 44). As the nearest housing area for low income workers, it started to grow rapidly when the port and industrial area at Apapa were developed in the 1950s (ibid. p 21). Many migrants from the Delta area as well as Igbos settled there (Interview 2, ll 7-27; on the Igbo settlement cf also Peil 1991: 38). NigP has established itself as the language of this community. While the older generation (roughly, those above 40) speak it as a second language, NigP is, according to the interviews I conducted with residents of the area, the first language of the majority of Ajegunle's younger inhabitants; many apparently have only a passive competence in their parents' first language or speak it less fluently than NigP, which often becomes the language of the home (see Interview 2, ll 32-59, 156-159; Interview 3, ll 40-65; interview 4, ll 50-58, 89-107; Interview 5, ll 1-29). Of course, there are also children in other parts of Lagos who learn NigP at an early age, but Ajegunle is unique in that NigP is the dominant language throughout the community.

NigP is also used in Lagos as a language of radio broadcasting, although, as elsewhere, English predominates. The Federal Radio Corporation of Nigeria is represented in Lagos with three stations. The national Radio Nigeria 1 broadcasts exclusively in English. The local Radio Nigeria 2 broadcasts mainly in English but has a few programmes in NigP as well (phone-in and record request programmes – see Interview 9, ll 48-77 – and drama). Radio Nigeria 3 is an additional local station that was set up in 1987 to complement the other two stations with broadcasts exclusively in Yoruba, Hausa, Igbo and NigP (see Interview 10, ll 1-58). During the research period in 2000, the station had five hours of NigP programmes daily on its programme schedule, including news, public enlightenment and entertainment. Lagosians can also tune in to the public stations of Lagos State and the neighbouring Ogun State, both of which have some programmes in NigP and Yoruba, in addition to English. A relatively recent addition to the scene are a few private stations.

These broadcast mainly in English, but there are a few NigP programmes on private stations as well. NigP programmes produced by state-owned and private stations tend to be of the same type as those on Radio Nigeria 2, i.e. phone-in shows and entertainment. In addition, a notable feature of the programme of Lagos local radio stations during the time of the research were two educative drama serials, *Rainbow City* and *One Thing at a Time*, the former mainly and the latter wholly in NigP. Produced by independent organizations, the weekly episodes were broadcast by several public and private stations at different times.

3.5 Nigerian Pidgin and gender

Gender differentiation has never been claimed to be a very prominent aspect of Pidgin use in Nigeria, but Dadzie (1985: 119) and Huber (1999: 147ff) report in their studies of Ghanaian Pidgin that among educated Ghanaians, the use of Pidgin is a predominantly male phenomenon.[19] This situation corresponds to the well-known "sociolinguistic gender pattern" (Fasold 1990: 92), according to which men are more influenced by covert prestige, whereas women display a stronger orientation towards high-status varieties.[20] Trudgill (1995: 72) describes gender differentiation of this type as "the single most consistent finding to emerge from sociolinguistic work around the world in the past thirty years". Most of the studies in question were conducted in western societies and Fasold (1990: 93) points out that the pattern may not be transferable to other parts of the world, especially those where women traditionally have only limited access to formal education, but there are indications that it does obtain at least in some African societies.[21]

The few remarks that have been made in previous studies about gender aspects of NigP use appear at first sight to contradict the conventional gender pattern. For example, Marchese & Shnukal (1983: 20) report in their study of the creolization of NigP that it is usually the father who is most resistant to the introduction of the language into the home. Donwa-Ifode (1984: 202) also observes that children are more likely to speak NigP with their mothers than their fathers. The mothers, she points out, normally have less formal education than their husbands. In such cases, it appears that the variable education overrides the variable gender. The variable occupation has to be taken into consideration as well. For example, Mann (1993b: 174) argues that while gender does not seem to be a major determinant of NigP use, "women might seem more socially constrained to use A N P [Anglo-Nigerian Pidgin], for example for shopping in public markets and petty trading". On the basis of my own informal observations as well as the formal questionnaire data, I would argue that among young well-educated Nigerians such as university students, the use of NigP is to some extent subject to the conventional gender pattern,[22] with women

---

[19] According to Huber (1999: 151), there are, however, indications that the situation is now changing.

[20] A difference between the classic cases of the gender pattern reported in the sociolinguistic literature (see e.g. Trudgill 1972) and the Ghanaian case is that in the former it applies to the choice between variants of linguistic variables within one linguistic system, whereas in the latter it affects the choice between entire linguistic systems.

[21] In addition to the above-quoted observations on Ghanaian Pidgin, cf also Schmied (1991: 49) and Swigart (1994: 180).

[22] For some interesting observations on female attitudes towards, and use of, NigP, see also Interview 2, ll 278-294.

somewhat more conservative in their language use and attitudes than men. Consider especially the following results of the language survey:[23]

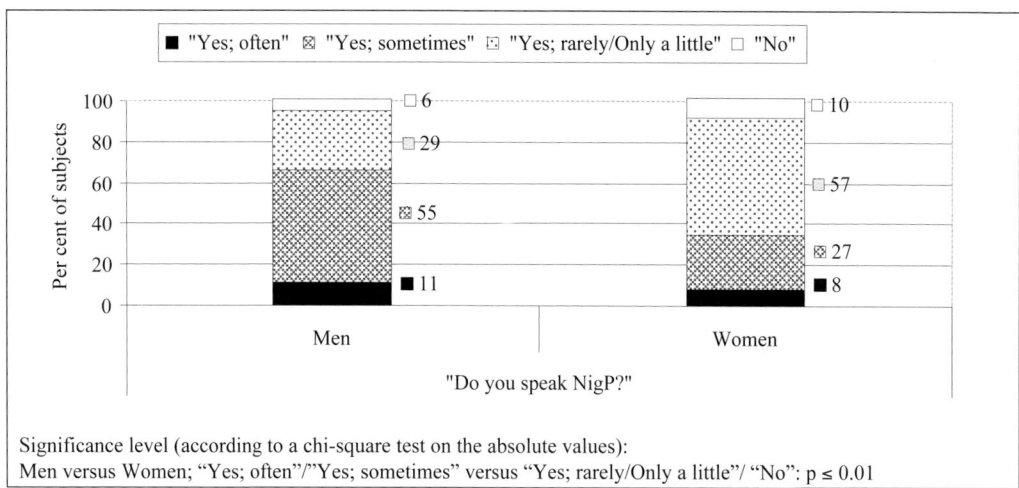

Figure 3.2 Knowledge/use of NigP reported in the language survey by sex

However, the gender pattern is certainly not as pronounced as it is in the case of Ghanaian Pidgin. This ties in with Huber's (1999: 156f) observations that Ghanaian Pidgin cannot (yet?) claim the widespread use and positive values that NigP has acquired in the last few decades.

---

[23] Of course, self-reports such as those summarized in Figure 3.2 do not always correspond to the informants' actual language use, but the data show at least that the women in the sample were more reluctant to describe themselves as regular users of NigP than the men.

Family Planning posters in English and NigP

4

Aspects of language variation and change in Nigeria

4.1 Code choice and code-switching

In the preceding chapter, the language situation in Nigeria was characterized as, to some extent, triglossia with English, NigP and the indigenous languages as three different language types, and within this overall configuration, diglossia (in the broad sense) between English and NigP. It was shown that there is a clear functional differentiation between the three language types but also some overlap. Therefore, there is not always a one-to-one correspondence between types of communicative events and code choice. This is particularly evident in oral, face-to-face communication. Code choice in this domain is determined by a complex interaction of several situational factors, the most important of which seem to be the setting of the communicative event, its purpose, the degree of formality, the topic and the participants (their social status, ethnicity, language abilities, sex, attitudes and behaviour, and the relationship between them). For example, English is not the language of choice in an informal conversation between friends in a private setting, but if technical issues are discussed, the factor topic may override all other factors in code choice and lead to the use of English. The interviews in Appendix C provide ample reports by the informants on how the different situational factors influence the choice between English and NigP, and to some extent the indigenous languages (see especially Interview 1, ll 149-153, 320-325; 421-465; Interview 2, ll 147-382, 401-498; Interview 3, ll 5-27; 85-92; 123-139; Interview 5, ll 203-259; Interview 8, ll 64-69). If one of the relevant factors changes, the result is likely to be situational code-switching (see also Interview 1, ll 320-322; Interview 2, ll 166-168, 311-317).

There have been a number of studies on code-switching (or what is considered as such in the present study, see 2.4.1) in Nigeria (e.g. Amuda 1986, 1994; Essien 1995; Goke-Pariola 1983; Madaki 1983; Nwoye 1993; Uzoezie 1986), and more general studies of language contact phenomena in Nigeria naturally address the issue as well (see e.g. Akere 1983, Banjo 1986). All of the studies cited are concerned with indigenous language/English code-switching. That the language situation in Nigeria inevitably gives rise to some situational code-switching has already become clear, and some of these studies show that Nigerians also commonly exploit code-switching as a social or discourse strategy (see especially Amuda 1994; Madaki 1983: chapter 3; Nwoye 1993). The following example (from Nwoye 1993: 374) illustrates what I refer to as code-switching as a social strategy (on code-switching terminology see 2.4.1):[1]

(1) **Inspector:** *I would like to see your vehicle registration, your driving license and your insurance papers, please.*
O: *I'm sorry, I don't have them here. They're at home.*
Inspector: *In that case you will park the car here and go and get them.*
(At this point, O overheard another policeman address the Inspector in Igbo.)
O: Enyi, bịa kam kowalụ gị. Kedụ ka isi emezi etua? ('Friend, come let me explain to you. Why are you acting like that?')
Inspector: *I have told you what to do. This is not a matter for speaking Igbo.*[2]

Nwoye (ibid.) interprets this example as follows:

> In the above episode English was the unmarked code at the onset of the interaction and was adopted until O, realizing that the inspector was from the same language group as himself, switched into Igbo, their common language. In doing so, he was signalling ethnic solidarity. The inspector, however, interpreted the situation as one in which his duty as a police officer had a higher value than ethnic group membership and so continued in English, at the time telling O that he quite understood his strategy but did not intend to fall for it.

In example (2), which is taken from Amuda (1994: 123), the indigenous language is Yoruba. This example illustrates one of the uses of code-switching as a discourse strategy, marking of quotations (as well as the use of single nouns from English in Yoruba discourse):

(2) Mo lọ sọ́dọ̀ - *man* - kan ní àárọ̀ yìí. Bi mo ti dé ọ̀dọ̀ - *man* - yẹn, ó kó - *file* - lọ́wọ́, mo ní *"I am a lecturer in the Department of Geography"*. - Ó rò pé - *Doctor* - kan ni mí ni. Ó ní - *"I am Dr. X"* - Mo ní - *"I am Akin"*.

'I went to see a man this morning. When I got to his office he had a couple of files with him. I told him "I am a lecturer in the Department of Geography". He thought I had a doctoral degree, so he said "I am Dr. X". I simply told him "I am Akin".'

Furthermore, it has been pointed out, for example by Amuda (1986: 296), that code-switching also functions as an overall discourse mode in informal conversations among educated Nigerians who share an indigenous language. As an example of this phenomenon one may take the extract from Igbo/English bilingual discourse in example (3), which is quoted from Uzoezie (1986: 79). (Uzoezie (ibid. p 78) explains that this is part of a conversation between "two young lecturers, one telling the other of a potential fiancée who turned out to be a flirt, and how she involved him in an ugly quarrel with a rival".)

(3) *I can't forget that insult* o nyelum *that day.* Na ọ ga-e*deal with me.* Na-ekwu noọ *nonsense.* I mago. *Totally confused.* The girl na onwe ya nọkwọ n'ụnọ *feel*ie na ya raputalụ m. *Conspiracy* ... mụnwa *put*ulu ya *December. I am not getting her to Jos. I will have a lot of problems. In December I am coming to X; to the people* ga-eti ya ife. O *believe*-ue na ... ọ ga-*explain why* o ji-eme yabụ omume.

'I can't forget that insult which he gave me that day. That he would deal with me. Talking nonsense, you know. Totally confused. The girl herself was in the house

---

[1] For the sake of consistency, the format of the examples of code-switching quoted from the various sources cited has been adapted. Note in particular that English segments always appear in italics, regardless of their role in the example and the respective author's convention.
[2] This conversation, as Nwoye (1993: 373) says, is a reconstruction, not a recorded one.

> feeling that she had betrayed me. Conspiracy ... I leave it for December. I am not getting her to Jos. I will have a lot of problems. In December I am coming to X; to the people who would beat her up. If she believed that ... she has to explain why she behaved as she did.'

Uzoezie (ibid. pp 79f) comments:

> The extract was taken from a longer speech. In it, the speaker maintained communicative fluency all through and the occurrences of the switch did not at any point destroy the internal unity of the exchanges in which they occurred. The passage contained almost an even number of words in Igbo and English, with switches occurring both intra- and inter-sententially. There was an even flow of speech form one sentence to another, without hesitations between switches.

As this example in particular already indicates, and as is to be expected in a situation where all functional types of code-switching, including code-switching as an overall discourse mode, occur, code-switching between indigenous languages and English in Nigeria manifests itself in all structural types, i.e. one finds inter-sentential and tag-switching as well as intra-sentential switching (or code-mixing). Amuda (1986: chapter 7) and Madaki (1983: chapter 5) have shown in detailed corpus-based studies that English insertions in indigenous language discourse may include whole clauses or sentences, constituents and other sentence chunks as well as single words. Among single word switches, nouns are found by both authors to be the most frequently switched category, followed by verbs in Amuda's and adverbs in Madaki's study, with relatively few adjectives. As regards function words, Amuda (1986: 248) as well as Essien (1995: 276) report that conjunctions can be singly switched. Amuda's examples include the following Yoruba sentence with the English conjunction *so that* (ibid. p 249):

(4)   Won máa ń gbee mì - *so that* - ẹ ò ní gbọ́ ohun tí wọ́n ń pè gaan.

   'They usually swallow their words, so that you won't really understand what they are saying.'

Essien (1995: 276) gives a similar example of the use of an English conjunction (*but*), in Ibibio in this case, and he also has an example with an English preposition (*according to*) in an otherwise Ibibio sentence. However, not all classes of function words allow the free substitution of English items for native ones. Amuda (1986: 220) in his study of Yoruba/English mixed discourse identifies personal pronouns as a class which resists single-word switching into English. The tense/aspect/modality system is also highly resistant to English influence: for Yoruba and to some extent other Nigerian languages belonging to the Niger-Congo phylum (Igbo, Ibibio) it has been shown that single English verbs in indigenous language discourse are generally in the base form and modified by the appropriate tense/aspect/modality markers of the indigenous language (Akere 1983: 293; Amuda 1986: 227ff; Banjo 1986: 541; Essien 1995: 277f; Goke-Pariola 1983: 42f).[3] Consider, for instance, the following Yoruba sentences containing English lexical verbs from Banjo (1986: 541) (*ti* and *ń* are the Yoruba markers for perfective and continuous aspect, respectively):

---

[3]   In Hausa/English code-switched discourse, single English verbs are, according to Madaki (1983: 85ff), usually in the *-ing* form, but this is also part of a Hausa structural pattern.

(5)   Mo ti *send* ẹ̀.
      'I have sent it.'

(6)   A ti ń *count* wọn.
      'We have been counting them/We have started counting them.'

Several authors (Amuda 1986: 231; Banjo 1986: 542; Essien 1995: 278f) also mention that verb negation generally follows the pattern of the indigenous language. The following example, with an English verb and the Yoruba negator *ò*, is from Amuda (1986: 231):

(7)   ... won ò *arrest a single person*
      '... they did not arrest a single person'

The noun phrase is quite a different case from that of the verb phrase, at least according to studies of Yoruba/English language contact. Banjo (1986: 542) observes that "plurality is regularly morphologically marked in the English elements in language-mixing, though it is also, in addition, lexically marked as in the Yoruba system" (cf also Amuda 1986: 215), and he gives the following two examples (*àwọn* indicates plurality;[4] *yen* is a demonstrative):

(8)   Àwọn *men* yen ti dé.
      'Those men have arrived.'

(9)   Àwọn *buildings* yen *look nice*.
      'Those buildings look nice.'

Besides the studies which have so far been discussed, Agheyisi (1977) also deals with indigenous language/English contact phenomena that fall under the present study's definition of code-switching (as well as with what may be considered borrowing, see 4.2), albeit under a different heading, namely "language interlarding". What Agheyisi describes as interlarded speech (which she distinguishes from code-switching) is indigenous language speech interspersed with English words and expressions. This pattern, according to her, is a typically urban speech style of the indigenous languages in Nigeria. She distinguishes three types of interlarded speech (which, she says (p 105), are not mutually exclusive but clearly manifest particular tendencies). Type A will be discussed in 4.2. Type B is largely restricted to educated speakers and characterized by the use of a very wide range of English words; these, as Agheyisi (1977: 106) observes, can be of different grammatical categories, but nouns and verbs tend to be most frequent. (Many of these items would probably best be characterized as single-word switches or nonce borrowings in a framework with such categories.) In type C English elements are restricted semantically to mainly technical words and expressions. Examples (10) and (11) are from conversation transcripts in Agheyisi (1977: 102f) illustrating types B and C of interlarded speech (in these particular cases in Yoruba). In the conversation from which example (10) is taken the English words are of the kind available to all educated speakers (type B of interlarded speech), while in the one from which I quote example (11) some technical – in this case linguistic – vocabulary is used (type C of interlarded speech):

---

[4]   *Àwọn* is the third person plural free/emphatic personal pronoun (a category also found in NigP, see 5.5.4.4) or "pronominal" (Banjo 1967: 19). It can also be preposed to a noun to indicate plurality.

(10)   *Lectures* wa ò tíẹ̀ *stable* l' ókè l' ọ́hun yẹn, *especially Part Two; timetable* wa kan wa *scattered* ní [...].

'Our lectures are not even stable over there, especially Part Two; our timetable is simply scattered [...].'

(11)   [...] "ó" kò jẹ *separate morpheme* nigbati o ba sọọrọ *agentive*. "Oní-" naa l' o wa ninu "alaṣọ" yẹn. T' o ba jẹ pe *noun* l' o pari ẹ l' ọ́un, k' o ti mọ wipe "oní-" yẹn l' o maa *separate*; nitoripe "oní-" *is always joining with ... noun* l' o maa ri "oní-" mọ́ *in all cases*.

'[...] that "ó" is not a separate morpheme when you are talking about agentive. It is the "oní-" that is in that "alaṣọ". If it is a noun that ends it over there, then you will know that it is the "oní-" that you will separate; because "oní-" is always joining with ... it is with a noun that you will always find "oní-" in all cases.'

Little work has so far been done on code-switching between NigP and English. In studies of code-switching between an indigenous languages and English, NigP occasionally comes up as a third code that speakers may switch into (Amuda 1994; Madaki 1983: 78ff; Nwoye 1993). Agheyisi (1984a: 218ff) mentions the free use of English words (what she describes as "language interlarding" in Agheyisi 1977; cf also Agheyisi 1984a: 232n11) and code-switching into English as common features of the NigP speech of educated speakers and illustrates these phenomena by extracts from recorded conversations between students. Oloruntoba (1992: 127ff) describes a campus variety of NigP "characterized by switching back and forth between Nigerian Pidgin and English" (p 128f), which she labels "student talk".

4.2   Changes in indigenous languages due to the contact with English

Loanwords from English (primarily nouns) are widespread in indigenous languages (cf Akere 1981: 288ff; Banjo 1986: 536f). Banjo (1986: 537) observes with reference to Yoruba that while the internal resources of the language have been used to some extent, the contact with the foreign culture represented by English has in a large number of cases led to the adoption of the English designation for a new object or concept. As mentioned above in the discussion of code-switching, grammatical word classes (except conjunctions) have, as expected, proven more resistant to English influence than lexical ones. However, the relatively well-studied case of Yoruba/English language contact shows that the indigenous language grammar is not necessarily exempt from English influence. Banjo (1986: 543) mentions a case of English syntactic influence in Yoruba, namely copula use in equative constructions. In Yoruba, as the following example from Banjo (ibid.) shows, such constructions do not have a copula (*ó* translates as 'it' in this case and *kúrú* as 'short'):[5]

(12)   ó kúrú

'it is/was short'

---

[5] In fact, constructions of this type consisting of a subject and a Yoruba predicate corresponding to an English adjective can be considered subject-verb clauses, which means that they naturally do not require a copula, since in Yoruba, as in NigP (see 5.5.6), lexical items corresponding to English adjectives function as stative verbs when they are used predicatively (cf e.g. Bamgbose 1967: 35).

Another of Banjo's examples (ibid. p 542) demonstrates that it is possible for English adjectives to enter this Yoruba construction:

(13)   ó *late*
       'he/she is/was late'

However, as Banjo (ibid. p 543) reports, there is also an alternative construction, which has developed under the influence of English. In this construction, which occurs only with English adjectives, the Yoruba existential copula *wà* is used in equative function in analogy to the English copula. Thus, Yoruba speakers may also say "ó wà *late*" instead of "ó *late*".

A final point that remains to be dealt with here is Agheyisi's (1977) "interlarded speech" of type A. In the summary of Agheyisi's study in the preceding section the discussion of this aspect has been deferred to the present one. This was done because it may be argued that the English words which characterize this type of interlarded speech represent items which have been borrowed into certain varieties of the indigenous languages. Agheyisi (1977: 105) writes about this kind of English words:

> These are what may be described as the set of English words which have undergone diffusion so completely into the other languages coexisting with English in the urban environment, that they have practically come to be perceived primarily as urban rather than English designates for whatever they stand for, by urban dwellers. The result is that these words are used quite spontaneously in both English and the indigenous languages, by practically everybody.

She distinguishes two categories of such words: those which are in general use and those which are specific to a particular group or domain. The general items, according to Agheyisi (1977: 105), include link words (*so, but, and, then, because* etc.), address terms such as *sir* and *madam,* and a large variety of nouns. As examples of specific vocabulary sets she gives a "schoolchildren's list", which includes words like *pen, pencil, uniform, class, lesson,* and an "undergraduates' list" containing the words *lecturer, lecturer, campus, class, hostel,* among others (pp 105f).

4.3   Variation in Nigerian English: the competence factor

Since a speaker's degree of competence in English, which, as has already become clear, depends to a great extent on his/her educational level, plays a central role in the present study as a factor influencing NigP use, a brief consideration of variation in Nigerian English along this parameter will be useful for the analyses.

In one of several classifications that have been proposed to account for variation in Nigerian English due to speakers' competence level, Banjo (1971, 1986, 1993) distinguishes four varieties.[6] Variety I is associated with speakers who have acquired a knowledge of English outside the formal education system. This variety is characterized by a very limited grammar and vocabulary and massive mother tongue interference. Variety II is the type of English used by those who have had a limited formal exposure to the language (typically in

---

[6]   Other studies in which variation in Nigerian English due to competence is discussed include Bamgbose (1982), Awonusi (1987) and Jowitt (1991: chapter 3).

the form of a primary school education). Mother tongue interference is more restricted in this variety. The vocabulary is larger and the grammar is less deviant from standard usage than in variety I, but it is still marked by "common errors" (of concord, tense, prepositional usage etc.). Variety III, in contrast, largely conforms to the "world standard" syntactically. Its distinguishing features are a Nigerian accent and local vocabulary items. While warning against a simple equation of varieties of English and educational levels, Banjo (1986: 49) states that variety III is normally attainable only by education at least up to the secondary level and that this variety may therefore be described as educated Nigerian English (or standard Nigerian English, as he proposes). Variety IV, lastly, is associated with exposure to native speaker English and distinguished from variety III mainly by a non-Nigerian accent.

Since it has already been pointed out at the very beginning of this study that scholars generally recognize NigP as a language in its own right, it hardly needs saying that NigP is not part of the spectrum of variation in Nigerian English outlined above. In an early study addressing variation in English specifically in southern Nigeria, Brosnahan (1958) did in fact include NigP as the lowest level of English, but Banjo in the above-mentioned studies as well as other scholars (e.g. Awonusi 1987: 53; Jowitt 1991: 54) make it clear that NigP is distinct from all varieties of English in Nigeria. As Banjo introduces the description of variety I in one of his studies:

> Brosnahan is correct in his observation that there is a clear difference between those who have picked up the language [English] outside the educational system and the rest. Such speakers – *excluding speakers of Pidgin,* unless at the same time they also speak some variety of English picked up outside the educational system – belong to Variety I in Banjo's classification. (Banjo 1993: 265; emphasis added)

4.4 Variation in Nigerian Pidgin: the competence and education factors

Two major factors in variation in NigP are competence in the language itself and competence in English, as a correlate mainly of a speaker's educational level (see 4.3). On the basis of the first factor, Agheyisi (1984a) distinguishes two main varieties of NigP, NigP "proper" and "interlanguage" NigP. If in addition the second factor, also a major aspect in Agheyisi's (1984a) analysis, is taken into consideration, one arrives at a four-way distinction between NigP-proper as spoken by the educated and as spoken by the less educated, and interlanguage NigP as spoken by the educated and as spoken by the less educated. I found that a basic division of this type is an adequate way of approaching variation in NigP, but the question is of course where to draw the line, as both of the relevant distinctions are matters of degree. To distinguish educated from less educated speakers of the language, I have used the criterion of a completed secondary education (at least). A speaker of educated NigP as defined in the present study is thus a speaker who is likely to also speak Banjo's variety III of English in Nigeria or educated Nigerian English (see 4.3), although it is clear that some speakers' performance in English may be below the expected level. As regards competence in NigP, I found that the most practicable distinction is one between those whose knowledge of the language is only rudimentary and those who have a medium to high degree of competence. I thus distinguish four basic varieties of NigP as follows: educated NigP, rudimentary and non-rudimentary, and NigP as spoken by less educated speakers, also rudimentary and non-rudimentary. The study deals mainly with the non-rudimentary varieties, and if in subsequent chapters reference is made to the educated or less educated variety of NigP, this will imply that I am speaking of the non-rudimentary variety unless the rudimentary variety is explicitly referred to. Before I go on to discuss the non-rudimentary varieties (Chapters 5 and 6), however, I will illustrate the rudimentary varieties by one text sample each. I begin with rudimentary NigP as spoken by the less educated. The speech of M in Text 4.1 is a good example of this variety.

Text 4.1 Bargaining

Place and date: Market in Lagos, 15 July 1997
Speakers: M, market woman; M2, another market woman; C, customer (research assistant)

[original version]   [translation]

    C: how much be dis one [[SET OF PEARS]]?   **C:** How much is this?
    M: twenty// ten//   **M:** Twenty. Ten.
    C: twenty and ten//   **C:** Twenty and ten.
    M: en//   **M:** Yes.
5 **C:** you no go reduce price for us[7]?   **C:** Won't you reduce the price for us?
    M: uh how many? how many you go buy?   **M:** How many? How many are you going to buy?

    C: we no go buy-- we no get money/ we no get money to buy plenty//   **C:** We aren't going to buy-- we don't have money, we don't have the money to buy many.

    M: how much you go--   **M:** How much are you going to--
10 **C:** eh? how much? make we give you ten naira now?   **C:** What? How much? Can we give you ten naira?
    M: eh?   **M:** What?
    C: make we give you ten naira now//   **C:** We could give you ten naira.
    M: ten ten naira last// if you buy dis one/ fifteen naira//   **M:** Ten naira each [is the] last [price]. If you buy this one, fifteen naira.
15 **C:** ah/ if we pay fifteen naira you go give us? ah// what about dis one here?   **C:** Ah. If we pay fifteen naira you'll give [it] to us? What about this one here?
    M: which one?   **M:** Which one?
    C: pineapple//   **C:** The pineapple.
20 **M2:** fifty naira// fifty naira//   **M2:** Fifty naira. Fifty naira.
    C: fifty naira// but no be you dey sell dis one now//   **C:** Fifty naira. But you aren't the one who's selling it.
    M: how much you dey pay?   **M:** How much are you going to pay?
    C: uh// [~] [EXAMINES FRUIT] e don rotten//   **C:** Uh ... it's gone rotten.
25 **M:** no ah-ah// e no rotten// nothing do am//   **M:** No, not at all. It's not rotten. There's nothing wrong with it.

    C: dis one don old well well// you no get one wey fresh?   **C:** This one isn't fresh at all. Don't you have one that's fresh?
    M: dis one nko? fresh now//   **M:** What about this one? [This one is] really fresh.

---

[7]   C was accompanied by the author.

	C: so how much go be di last price?	**C:** So what's the last price going to be?
30	**M:** forty naira//	**M:** Forty naira.
	C: forty naira//	**C:** Forty naira.
	M: forty naira// e too cost now//	**M:** Forty naira. It's [an] expensive [fruit].
	C: e too cost eh?	**C:** It's expensive, you said?
	M: en//	**M:** Yes.
35	**C:** we no get money//	**C:** We don't have money.
	M: you no get-- hah [LAUGHTER]	**M:** You don't have-- ...
	C: money no dey//	**C:** There's no money.
	M: ah money dey o//	**M:** Ah, the money is there.
	C: oya make you give us dis one [[SET OF PEARS]]//	**C:** All right, give us this one.
40	**M:** you no buy again?	**M:** Aren't you going to buy [the pineapple] any more?
	C: e too cost//	**C:** It's too expensive.
	M: pay thirty-five// pay thirty-five//	**M:** Pay thirty-five. Pay thirty-five.
	C: di money too plenty// [...]	**C:** The price is too high.
	M: how much you go pay?	**M:** How much are you going to pay?
45	**C:** We go give you twenty-five now//	**C:** We'll give you twenty-five.
	M: eh?	**M:** What?
	C: twenty-five//	**C:** Twenty-five.
	M: thirty naira//	**M:** Thirty naira.
	C: twenty-five/ you hear? abeg// [...]	**C:** Twenty-five, all right? Please.
50	**M:** thirty naira last//	**M:** Thirty naira [is the] last [price].
	C: thirty naira last? make you take twenty-five now/ make we buy am with dis one [[SET OF PEARS]]// abeg abeg//	**C:** Thirty naira [is the] last [price]? Take twenty-five and we'll buy it together with this one. Please, please.
	M: thirty naira/ thirty naira//	**M:** Thirty naira, thirty naira.
55	**C:** make we just give you forty naira with dis one// eh?	**C:** We'll give you forty naira with this one. Okay?
	M: eh?	**M:** What?
	C: I say make we give you forty naira with one of dis// you hear?	**C:** I said we'll give you forty naira and take one of these as well. Do you understand?
60	**M2:** [[TO M IN YORUBA]] ó fẹ́ kó ọjà ẹyọ kan pẹ̀lú eléyìí ó jẹ́ forty naira//	**M2:** He wants to buy one of those and one of these for forty naira.
	C: Oya make you break di head of dis one [[PINEAPPLE]] for us.	**C:** Now please break off the top of this one for us.

It is obvious in the text that M's NigP is very limited in terms of both lexis and grammar. She uses mainly numerals and a set of words and expressions that constitute the characteristic vocabulary of market transactions, e.g. *buy, pay, how many, how much* and the conventionalized expression *last* meaning 'is the last price'. Many of her utterances consist only of phrases made up of an isolated numeral, a numeral combined with the currency name *naira,* or an expression of this type naming a price accompanied by a single word like *pay* or *last* (see e.g. ll 2, 44, 50, 52). Negotiating a price with such simple expressions is apparently the only type of interaction she can carry out confidently in NigP. There are several instances where she has difficulties understanding her customer, a fluent speaker of NigP, when he offers a price in a more elaborate way (cf ll 10ff, 47ff, 57ff), and some of her replies to him are elliptical expressions that could be described either as "broken NigP" or as "broken English" (cf "if you buy dis one/ fifteen naira" (ll 14f); "fresh now" (l 29)). In addition to these expressions, there are some complete sentences in what is recognizably NigP (ll 6, 23, 26, 33, 38, 46), but these are also very short and simple and often of the type that are stock phrases in the context of trading (cf ll 6, 23, 46).

Rudimentary NigP as spoken by educated speakers is distinguished from the uneducated variety by the fact that educated speakers, having English at their disposal, operate with a large vocabulary, but the grammar is also limited. This variety is illustrated by Text 4.2. This text is an extract from an interview which was recorded by one of my research assistants in the course of the data collection for the face-to-face speech section of the corpus (see 5.1). The text was not included in the corpus because the speaker had indicated on the "background information sheet for research contributors" (see Appendix A) that she had only a rudimentary knowledge of NigP (cf the discussion of text selection procedures in 5.1.2.1).

Text 4.2 A teacher on people's claims that the standard of education in Nigeria is falling

Place and date: Lagos, May 2000
Speaker: teacher, female, aged between 30 and 39; highest educational qualification: master's degree; first language: Igbo

[original version]

people dey talk about falling standard/ falling standard of education// and oders go talk say "[+there is nothing like falling standard+]"// how do we know wheder
5   education don fall/ or wheder e never fall? oders go talk say/ "wetin we go take measure am?" some oders go still talk say/ "if we look at di society/ we go see say/ education don fall"// now as we dey discuss about dis
10 falling standard/ [+we want parents to also pay attention+]/ and see wheder dem go fit gain anything from what we are discussing// [+how do we know that education has fallen? how do we even begin to measure
15 it?+] if we go schools dese days/ we go see a lot of people sitting on di ground/ no chairs/ di buildings (dipla#) diplated/ di physical structure not good/ one teacher go teach twenty-eight periods/ one teacher go teach
20 J.S.S. one/ J.S.S. two/ through S.S.S. three// how we go even measure her own efficiency? [+how can she be capable and efficient going through the various arms? not to talk of the students//+] where di textbooks
25 wey dem dey read? [+the library/ how equipped are the libraries?+] students demself self/ dem no dey read again// na to join one society or di oder/ to join one cult or

[translation]

People talk about the falling standard, the falling standard of education. And others will say ...
How do we know whether education has declined or whether it hasn't declined? Others will say: "How are we going to measure it?" Some others will say: "If we look at the society we'll see that education has declined". Now as we're discussing about this falling standard, ... and see whether they can gain anything from what we are discussing. ...

If we go to schools these days we'll see a lot of people sitting on the ground, no chairs, the buildings dilapidated, the physical structure not good; one teacher will teach twenty-eight periods, one teacher will teach J.S.S. [Junior Secondary School] one, J.S.S. two through S.S.S. [Senior Secondary School] three. How are we even going to measure her own efficiency? ... Where are the textbooks to study? ...

Even the students themselves, they don't study any more. [What they do] is to join one society or the other, to join one cult or

	di oder/ to talk about one fashion or di oder//	the other, to talk about one fashion or the
30	when we look at all dese things/ we go see say education/ wheder we believe am or we no believe am/ we go see say education don fall// wheder we say e get measurement or e no get measurement/ [+we will notice that	other. When we look at all these things, we'll see that education, whether we believe it or not, we'll see that education has declined. Whether we say that there's a measurement or that there's no measurement, ...
35	those who read standard six then can speak better English today than those who have finished university+]// you go see say students do all sorts of things/ all manner of things/ to get admission// so make we no try	You'll see that students do all sorts of things, all manner of things to get admission. So we shouldn't try to deceive ourselves by saying
40	to dey deceive ourself say education never fall/ education never fall// yes we go agree say no measurement/ [+but at least what you see/ what you experience every day as you go about/ is one way of measuring it// [...]+]	that education hasn't declined, education hasn't declined. Yes, we'll agree that there's no measurement, ...

One of the most striking features of this text are the many parts entirely in English which are marked as non-NigP speech (ll 3, 9f, 11ff, 19ff, 22f, 30ff, 37ff). In the corpus, as will be explained in detail in Chapter 5 (Section 5.3.1), I have used marking as non-NigP speech to deal with major English elements, and these are defined by four criteria: conformity with standard English grammar, a clausal structure, separation from the surrounding discourse by intonation (or by virtue of being a quotation), and identification as an English element in the questionnaire study. In Text 4.2 I have transcribed as non-NigP speech the elements which fulfil the first three criteria (the fourth does not apply since only the corpus texts were included in the questionnaire study; see 5.2). This feature of the transcription highlights the fact that the speaker frequently falls back on English. One might explain this as code-switching as an overall discourse mode; as will become clear in the discussion of the corpus data, such switching occurs in the speech of fluent speakers as well. However, my data also bear out the observation made by code-switching researchers that this is an informal mode of discourse (see 2.4.1): It is characteristic mainly of some of the conversations that were recorded in the course of the fieldwork, and not generally of interviews and other more formal types of discourse (see 5.6.1.1). In the whole interview section of the corpus, with about 10,000 words, there are only 15 English elements marked as non-NigP speech (see table 5.15 in 5.6.1.1), while the short extract above alone, with only 445 words, contains 7 of these. The figures are of course not directly comparable because in the corpus marking as non-NigP speech is subject to the additional criterion of identification in the questionnaire study. Nevertheless, it is clear that the speaker in Text 4.2 shows a very high rate of English use, and the main reason for this is probably that she is simply not able to speak NigP without recourse to a language she is more familiar with. The parts of the text which are not marked as non-NigP speech also contain several whole constituents and clauses entirely in English (e.g. *how do we know* (l 3f), *gain anything from what we are discussing* (l 10f), *measure her own efficiency* (l 19), *students do all sorts of things/ all manner of things/ to get admission* (l 33ff)).[8] On the whole, the language in this text can be described as more

---

[8] In one instance (*di physical structure not good* (l 16)) the speaker produces what amounts to broken English in her attempt to speak NigP (the grammatical NigP version would be *di physical structure no good*).

English than NigP; a certain NigP flavour is achieved mainly by the use of a few salient NigP function words in the place of English ones, especially the auxiliaries *go, dey,* and *don* as well as the latter's negative equivalent *never*, the complementizer *say* and the pronouns *e* and *am*. One may point out that the topic is one that favours the use of English, but topics of this sort are discussed in the corpus texts as well. It thus seems fair to say that the NigP speech of this educated speaker displays strong interference from English. This is of course to be expected in a bilingual situation when a speaker has only limited competence in a second language. As Agheyisi (1984a: 226) also observes, speakers of interlanguage NigP who predominantly use English or indigenous languages "tend to have limited fluency in NPE [Nigerian Pidgin English], with their stronger language(s) exerting a lot of grammatical influence on their NPE speech, especially when the former is English".

5

Educated Nigerian Pidgin in face-to-face speech and radio broadcasts: the corpus study[1]

5.1 The corpus

5.1.1 Size, structure and composition of the corpus

The NigP corpus compiled for the study has a total size of about 80,000 words and is made up of 40 texts of approximately 2,000 words. Face-to-face speech and radio broadcasts are the two major text categories, with 20 texts each. Both of these categories have three subcategories (see Table 5.1).

Table 5.1 The NigP corpus

	Text categories	Number of texts	Text codes
Face-to-face speech	Interviews	5	V01-05
	Discussions	5	D01-05
	Conversations	10	C01-10
Radio broadcasts	News	5	N01-05
	Advice	5	A01-05
	Drama	10	R01-10

The composition of the corpus is determined by sociolinguistic realities, the research aims and practical constraints. Of the types of radio texts available in NigP (see 3.3-4) the following had to be excluded for different reasons: phone-in shows, because in this type of programme the distinction between the domain of broadcasting and ordinary language use is blurred by the participation of speakers who are not broadcasting professionals; entertainment programmes, because these often consist of more music than speech; and

---

[1] I would like to thank all my research assistants, colleagues and friends who contributed to one or more of the different stages of the fieldwork for the corpus study (recording, transcription, questionnaire study), and at the same time those who helped in recording and/or transcribing the additional samples analysed in Chapters 4 and 6. Those of them who agreed to have their names mentioned are: Remi Adedibu, Emmanuel Adedun, Rasheed Adegbesan, Chris Anyokwu, David Aworawo, Michael Dibie, Ejiro Diejomaoh, Evelyn Ebhomien, Anya Egwu, Presley Ifukor, Anthonia Makwemoisa, Emmanuel Mbah, Clara Modigie, Ejiroghene Noserime, Austin Nwagbara, Apollonia Nwankpa, Atinuke Obakoya, Charles Ogbulogo, Kolade Ogunsanya, Esther Ohali, Nkechi Okoroanyanwu, Patrick Oloko, Harry Olufunwa, Joseph Osoba, Mojisola Shodipe, Laura Uduma, Raphael Uzoezie, Uduopegeme Yakubu.

advertisements, because these are usually short and a limited number tends to get repeated over a period of time, which makes it difficult to obtain sufficient data. The radio text types that were found to be both suited to the purposes of the study and available in sufficient quantities and were therefore selected for the broadcast section of the corpus are news, public enlightenment programmes ("advice") and drama (of the educative type). The latter category contains twice as many texts as the other two because of its prominence in the programme of Lagos radio stations at the time of the research.

As has been shown in 3.3, NigP broadcasts of the types included in the corpus have the less educated sections of the population as their prime target audience. In the texts of the category "face-to-face speech", by contrast, educated speakers communicate among themselves. A further difference is that the broadcasts are usually scripted, while the speech recorded in the face-to-face context is spontaneous. In order to facilitate the comparative analysis of language use in these two different contexts, the three subcategories of face-to-face speech not only have the same number of texts as the radio subcategories but were also designed so as to have some similarities with the latter in terms of discourse format and topics. The interviews are in large part monologues with thematic parallels to the news. The discussions, like the advice texts, centre on problems of daily living. Although not monologues, they are oriented more towards the exposition of problems and ideas and less towards dialogue than the conversations, which parallel the drama format.

5.1.2 Data collection, text selection and transcription

5.1.2.1 Face-to-face speech

The sample of NigP in face-to-face speech included in the corpus is based on a combination of a social network approach to data collection and judgment sampling of speakers (cf Milroy 1987: 35ff, 26f). A number of local research assistants were asked to record members of their social networks (friends, fellow students, colleagues, relatives, neighbours etc.). For the research assistants the choice of speakers was at first entirely free except for the requirement of a completed secondary education (cf 4.4), but I had more recordings made than actually needed, and in the compilation of the corpus texts from the recorded material I observed several quotas for speaker groups. When I was not able to fill a certain quota I obtained additional recordings of this particular group of speakers. The quotas had been defined on the basis of the speaker variables I had identified as relevant in my research on the macrosociolinguistic aspects of NigP use (see Chapter 3). For two variables, age and occupation, no quotas were set up. I accepted a strong bias towards younger speakers and students because this is consistent with sociolinguistic realities. I also expected that the material would be biased towards male speakers. This was partly because of the tendency for educated men to use NigP more than educated women, but the tendency was likely to be reinforced by the fact that most of my fieldworkers happened to be male, and in order to avoid a too strong bias I set up a quota of at least one third of the sample for women. A quota of at least one third was also fixed for the Yoruba as the majority in Lagos but generally the less typical NigP speakers. Speakers from any single ethnic group or region were, however, not allowed to constitute more than half of the sample. As my aim was to take advantage of the diversity of the city while investigating NigP use in Lagos, I also determined that about one third of the speakers were to have come to Lagos only as adolescents or adults, while another one third were to be Lagosians by birth. In addition, a one-third quota was fixed for speakers who had acquired NigP from birth or at least pre-school age; speakers who had first come into contact with the language as older children, adolescents or adults, who were expected to be in the majority, were allowed to constitute up to two thirds of the sample. It should be noted, however, that the amount of speech per speaker varies so that the quotas are only a rough method of structuring the sample.

The recordings were made non-surreptitiously. After the recording each speaker filled in a "background information sheet for research contributors" (see Appendix A) with questions on his/her social and linguistic background and a statement of permission for the use of the recording in linguistic research. The research assistants completed background information sheets for the tapes, in which they indicated the place and date of the recordings and listed the speakers in the order in which they appeared on the tape, so that the speaker background information sheets could later be matched with the corresponding voices.

The speakers were asked to give their names but were given the option of remaining anonymous in publications resulting from the research. I had decided not to automatically leave out the names because I had discovered in the course of the 1997 fieldwork that such an approach did not necessarily do justice to the speakers' wishes: some were concerned not about anonymity but about having the fact that they had made a contribution to the research acknowledged. In the fieldwork for the corpus it turned out that speakers who wished to remain anonymous were a minority. A list of speakers is therefore included on the CD (in the texts, the speakers are not identified by name).

During my earlier fieldwork, I had also noticed that some of those who made recordings for me encouraged the informants to speak "proper" NigP. For the corpus study it was of course important that the speakers' linguistic behaviour should not be directed in such a way. I therefore specifically instructed the research assistants to refrain from such comments, and also, not to interrupt the speakers in case they should switch to English. This meant that code-switching was one of the factors that had to be taken into consideration in the process of text selection. I recognize code-switching as a factor in NigP use, but the present study is not a study of code-switching per se. If a speaker switched and continued in English for more than about five intonation units, this part of the recording was not used, and recordings marked by extremely frequent switching were excluded.

Another factor in the selection of texts, besides code-switching and the speaker group quotas, was the speakers' competence in NigP. Since the corpus is supposed to represent the non-rudimentary variety of educated NigP, recordings were considered for inclusion if the speakers had rated their knowledge of NigP on the background information sheets as "very good", "good" or at least "moderate", but not "rudimentary"; in addition, in doubtful cases, a competent speaker was asked for his/her judgment on the recording.[2]

My initial intention had been that each text in the category "face-to-face speech" should be from a different recording and consist of a single unit of 2,000 words.[3] Ideally, a

---

[2] In one case (Text D05) I decided to include a speaker who claimed a "moderate" knowledge of NigP but whose performance was clearly below that level (which explains the comment on extract D05/1 in Table B 2) because he played only a relatively minor role in an otherwise suitable recording.

[3] 2,000 words is a text size that has been used in several major corpora, e.g. the Lancaster-Oslo/Bergen Corpus of British English (LOB) and the Brown Corpus of American English as well as their Freiburg updates (LOB and Frown, respectively), and the International Corpus of English (ICE).

recording was therefore supposed to have a duration of at least 20 minutes, which corresponds to well above 2,000 words. However, some of the recordings I obtained were too short and others were suitable only in parts, while there were also some high-quality recordings long enough for more than one 2,000-word units. Since the nature of some of the radio texts and the limited number of sources for these also dictated a similar approach in the broadcast section, I finally decided to allow, on the one hand, texts put together out of subtexts from different recordings, and on the other, more than one text from the same source.

The recordings were transcribed by a few of my research assistants who were particularly competent in NigP. I checked the transcriptions and adapted them to the orthographic and transcription conventions adopted in the corpus. Whenever I was uncertain about the transcription, I consulted a third person, i.e. a competent speaker of NigP other than the one who had produced the initial transcript.

5.1.2.2 *Radio broadcasts*

Since I was able to gain access to sources of more and higher quality data, much of the material from which I have compiled the broadcast sample in the corpus was actually not recorded from the radio. Rather, I often recorded programmes directly in the studio if the broadcast was live, or, in the case of recorded programmes, copied the material from the original recording. In addition to the recordings, I was able to obtain copies of the script of some news broadcasts and a large number of drama episodes.

In the selection of the texts for the broadcast section of the corpus, the choice was of course rather limited, especially since news and public enlightenment programmes were available only from one station, Radio Nigeria 3, which, moreover, broadcast only irregularly during the time of the research due to technical problems. However, I tried to achieve at least a certain balance between texts by different speakers or scriptwriters. In the category "news", each of the four broadcasters at Radio Nigeria 3 who read NigP news at the time of the research[4] is represented with one full 2,000-word text and one subtext of about 500 words. For the category "advice", I had recordings of only two suitable programmes, and I included three texts from one and two from the other. In the category "drama", there are five texts each from the two serials already mentioned in 3.4, *Rainbow City* and *One Thing at a Time*. I chose episodes of the serials consisting mostly of dialogue representing informal conversations or used parts of episodes which were of this type so that the texts would be comparable to the face-to-face conversations. Scenes representing more formal language use were largely excluded.[5] Also excluded were scenes in which an English-speaking character appears.

Since radio broadcasters working with NigP can be expected to meet the criteria I had set up for the speakers in the corpus regarding education and competence in the language, they were automatically included by virtue of their professional status. Nevertheless, I also

---

[4] A fifth newscaster, whom I mention in Deuber (2002: 198), was on leave for a considerable period.
[5] In a few cases a brief scene of this type was included in order to keep an episode complete. A comment on one of these scenes obtained in the questionnaire study (see Table B 2 in Appendix B, extract R07/9, comment (c)) shows how important it is that situational variation within the drama subcategory is kept to a minimum.

obtained background information on the speakers in the categories "news" and "advice"[6] (as well as a number of other NigP-using professionals in the radio field in Lagos, see 7.3.1), and this confirmed that such speakers usually have the expected characteristics.

The texts were transcribed according to the procedure outlined above for the recordings of face-to-face speech except that when a script was available this replaced the initial transcript by a research assistant.

5.1.3   The texts and speakers in the corpus

Some general characteristics of the texts are described in the following paragraphs, and an overview of the characteristics of the speakers is given in Table 5.2 (overleaf). Detailed background information on each text and speaker is found on the CD.

The texts in the category "face-to-face speech" were recorded on the campus of the University of Lagos and in other parts of the Lagos mainland (Surulere, Ilupeju, Ikeja, Ketu) in May and June 2000. The broadcasts date from February 1995 to August 2000.

As a result of my approach to data collection, the face-to-face situations were all relatively relaxed, but the subcategories of face-to-face speech still differ to a certain extent in formality or the amount of attention the speakers paid to their speech because of the different discourse formats. The interviews represent the most formal type. In these, a single speaker was asked to give his/her opinion on a number of current issues chosen by the research assistant. The contribution of the research assistant was usually limited to stating the topics, and the speaker was then free to expound on them. In the corpus, these texts have been arranged as more or less a series of monologues by the interviewee on the different topics (in a few cases, a question or remark by the interviewer is interpolated), with each topic as a different subtext.

The discussions represent a format which is intermediate between the interviews and the conversations. Like the conversations, they have two or three participants, but they are more structured. Turn-taking is more organized and the turns are usually longer. The topics – mostly aspects of daily living although there is also a discussion about political and economic issues (Text D05) – were chosen either by the research assistant or by the speakers themselves.

The conversations were supposed to be as informal as possible and there were no constraints on the topics, but the research assistants were told that the number of speakers should be limited to a maximum of three, or exceptionally, four, because conversations with more speakers are often very difficult to transcribe.[7] Most of the texts in this category (C03-10) are conversations between students at the University of Lagos recorded in student hostels and other informal settings on the campus (Texts C01 and C02 are from a recording of a conversation in a private home). The students converse about aspects of student life or about general issues of interest to them (e.g. politics).

---

[6] The drama texts are a more complicated case. I was able to contact one of the scriptwriters (cf also 7.3.1), but the script is often adapted considerably in the production of the recording so that speech in a drama recording is essentially the result of a process in which more than one person is involved.

[7] Cf also Nelson (1996: 34) on the recording of conversations for the British component of the International Corpus of English (ICE).

Table 5.2 Sociolinguistic profile of speakers in the NigP corpus

The first number indicates the number of speakers in the face-to-face speech section; the second number (after the slash) indicates the number of speakers in the broadcast subcategories "news" and "advice".

Total number of speakers: 34 / 6					
Sex					
Male			Female		
23 / 4			11 / 2		
Age group					
16-19	20-29		30-39		40-49
2 / –	24 / 1		7 / 3		1 / 2
Occupation					
Student		Broadcaster		Other	
26 / –		– / 6		8 / –	
Highest educational qualification					
Secondary school certificate	O.N.D.[a]	First degree/ H.N.D.[b]	Master's degree		No answer
18 / 1	5 / 2	9 / 2	2 / –		– / 1
Ethnic affiliation					
Yoruba	Igbo	Delta/Edo State ethnic groups (Urhobo, Edo, Esan etc.)	Cross River/Akwa Ibom State ethnic groups (Efik, Ibibio etc.)		No answer
15 / 1	8 / 3	6 / 2	3 / –		2 / –
Place of birth					
Lagos	Yoruba-speaking states	Igbo-speaking states	Delta/Edo	Cross River/ Akwa Ibom	Other/no answer
13 / 1	6 / –	2 / 2	9 / 2	1 / –	2 / 1
In Lagos since age					
	0-5	6-11	12-17	18 or over	No answer
	3 / –	5 / –	7 / 2	5 / 2	1 / 1
First language[c]					
NigP	English	Yoruba	Igbo	Minor language of Delta/Edo State	Minor language of Cross River/ Akwa Ibom	No answer
3 / 3	11 / 1	12 / 1	6 / 2	3 / –	2 / –	3 / –
Age of first contact with NigP					
	0-5		6-11	12-17	18 or over
	9 / 1		9 / 1	12 / –	1 / 1
Knowledge of NigP					
Very good		Good	Moderate		No answer
7 / 5		13 / –	13 / 1		1 / –
Speaker uses NigP					
Often		Sometimes	Occasionally		Rarely
11 / 5		15 / –	7 / 1		1 / –

[a] Ordinary National Diploma, obtained after two years of higher education at a polytechnic.
[b] Higher National Diploma, obtained after four years of higher education at a polytechnic.
[c] Six of the speakers in the face-to-face speech section gave two first languages (five English and an indigenous language and one NigP and an indigenous language). One of the broadcasters gave English and Igbo as first languages.

Turning now to the radio subcategories, it has already been mentioned that the texts in the subcategory "news" were compiled from news broadcasts by Radio Nigeria 3 in Lagos. These consist of four to six news items, usually a mixture of national and local news. The basis of Radio Nigeria 3 news broadcasts is a typewritten English script, which is given out to the station's different sections (Pidgin, Hausa, Yoruba, Igbo) for translation and reading. In the Pidgin Section, a common practice is that the newscaster whose turn it is to read the news will produce a handwritten translation before reading,[8] using his/her idiosyncratic version of an English-based spelling (an illustration is provided in Appendix D). However, I also observed in the course of my internship in the station that due to lack of time and other constraints (such as the unpredictability of broadcast times due to the technical situation), the newscasters sometimes go to the studio with the English script and translate it orally. This is of course likely to negatively affect the quality of the broadcasts, since the delivery will be less fluent and the newscaster will be more prone to take over English expressions.

The "advice" Texts A01-03 were compiled from recordings of *Make We Think Small* ('let's have a moment of reflection'), a programme which was broadcast by Radio Nigeria 3 in 1995 and described in the programme schedule for that year as "exhortative talk". Many of the 3-6 minute talks deal with everyday problems in the country's big cities, in particular Lagos, e.g. housing, transport, crime, but the programme also comments on events in areas like sports and politics. Texts A04 and A05 are from *Woman Corner*, a women's magazine programme on Radio Nigeria 3 which deals with issues like child rearing and cooking.

The texts coded as R01-05 are from the drama serial *Rainbow City*. *Rainbow City* is written by Tunde Aiyegbusi (cf also 3.3) and produced by the African Radio Drama Association. The 15-minute episodes deal with various social issues, in particular citizens' rights and duties in a democratic society. Most of the characters use NigP but there are a few English-speaking characters as well. The texts coded as R06-10 are from *One Thing at a Time*. This drama serial is about AIDS and other problems in the area of reproductive health. The episodes, also of a duration of 15 minutes, are written and produced by Kola Ogunjobi with support from the Society for Family Health and funding from the Department for International Development. The characters represent members of the different ethnic groups of southern Nigeria; all of them use NigP.[9]

5.2 The questionnaire study

5.2.1 *The questionnaire*

After the corpus had been compiled, the next step in my work during the field trip in 2000 was to obtain an initial analysis of the entire corpus and judgments on the texts from Nigerian informants. For this purpose, I designed a "text evaluation sheet" (see Appendix

---

[8] The same practice has been observed by Simpson (1985: 139) and Bamgbose (1992: 2) for Yoruba news translations.
[9] *One Thing at a Time*, of which there is also a Yoruba and an Igbo version, is written specifically for the southern part of the country. For the North, there is a similar programme in Hausa, which is adapted to Islamic religious and cultural sensibilities (Kola Ogunjobi, p c).

A) in the format of a questionnaire, to be combined with a text sheet containing an extract from the corpus (see 5.2.2).

The questionnaire has two sections. In the first, the informants were asked to assess the frequency of what they considered English lexical and, separately, grammatical elements in the extract in question on a four-point scale ranging from "very frequently" to "not at all". They were also asked to give examples of such elements (if applicable) and to suggest NigP equivalents for them. In the second section the informants were asked for an overall assessment of the language used in the extract (also on a scale) with regard to two criteria: how satisfactory they found the language of the extract as a form of NigP, and how intelligible they thought it would be to a speaker of NigP with little or no formal education. In addition, space was provided for further observations and for comments. (Some of the informants also took part in a final group interview, where they had the chance to elaborate on their comments; see Appendix C, Interview 11.)

5.2.2 The corpus extracts

In preparing the text sheets, I split up the texts in the corpus into shorter units. I aimed at an average length of 250 words, which means that there were supposed to be eight extracts for the analyses per text. In order to obtain meaningful units, I had to allow some variation in the length of the extracts, and in a few exceptional cases a text has one extract more or less than eight, but such deviations are always evened out within the same text subcategory. The number of extracts is therefore 40 and 80 for subcategories with 5 and 10 texts, respectively, and 320 in total. The extracts received a code consisting of the text code and the extract number (separated by a slash). In addition to the corpus extract, the text sheet included brief information on text type and context (e.g. "conversation between students").

5.2.3 The informants

The extracts were distributed among 22 educated speakers of NigP (first language speakers and competent second language speakers). Most of these informants were students or members of staff of the Department of English and other departments of the Arts Faculty of the University of Lagos.

5.3 English elements in the corpus according to the questionnaire study

5.3.1 Categories of English elements

A total of almost 900 English elements (types) were cited in the sections of the questionnaire for examples of English elements in lexis and grammar. About two thirds of these are single lexical or grammatical items. The remaining one third are discourse chunks of varying size and a few idiomatic expressions (these items were often entered in the section for lexis as well as the one for grammar). In addition, some informants marked code-switching for mostly longer stretches of discourse on the text sheet. One such case – which is of course particularly obvious because the switch is flagged by metalinguistic commentary – is the part the following example transcribed in standard English orthography in the final version of the corpus:

(1)   okay/ make I give di best solution for refuse disposal for Lagos// make I speak small English// [+there should be designated specific areas for refuse disposals// now for individuals// individuals should be advised to pack their refuse in front of their house/+] if dem fence deir house// (V02 70ff)[10]

'Okay, let me give the best solution for refuse disposal in Lagos. Let me speak English for a moment. ...'

I had decided to handle cases like the one in example (1) by adding marking for "non-NigP speech" to the transcription and change the spelling accordingly once the questionnaire study had been completed. I intended to apply this type of marking only to the major English elements[11] among those that had not been excluded from the corpus (cf 5.1.2.1), but the problem was where to draw the line. In code-switching studies, as mentioned in 2.4.1, a distinction is often made between inter- and intra-sentential switching. The first type is generally acknowledged to be "code-switching" while the second type is described by some authors as "code-mixing" (see 2.4.1). It therefore seemed reasonable to treat at least whole sentences entirely in English as separate entities in the transcription. However, most of the longer stretches of discourse cited as English elements in the questionnaires or marked as code-switches on the text sheets are in the texts of the category "face-to-face speech". Distinguishing between inter- and intra-sentential switches would thus have meant having to identify sentences in transcriptions of spontaneous discourse. This is rather problematic, and I had therefore not imposed such divisions onto these transcriptions but had marked different types of intonation units instead, which I had identified on the basis of pitch contour and pauses.[12] (In the scripted texts, I had found it adequate to use punctuation as in written language.) An intonation unit boundary suggesting finality can often be taken as indicating a sentence boundary, while an intonation unit boundary suggesting non-finality may correspond to a clause boundary, but this need not be the case. Besides, the distinction between these two types of intonation unit boundaries, although often helpful, is not always clear-cut. In view of this, I finally decided to take into account both structure and intonation and set up the following set of criteria, which all have to apply in order for a part of the corpus in which a speaker uses English to be marked as non-NigP speech:

- The part of the corpus was cited as an English element in the questionnaire for the extract in question or marked as a code-switch on the text sheet[13] (and/or it is an extraneous element such as a quotation from an English text),
- it conforms entirely to standard English grammar,
- it consists of at least one clause,

---

[10] References to the corpus consist of the text code (see Table 5.1) and the line number(s).
[11] The same convention (square brackets combined with a plus sign) is also used to mark indigenous language elements. In the present context, however, only its use to mark English elements will be discussed.
[12] The intonation unit and its use in systems of discourse transcription is discussed e.g. in Du Bois et al. (1993) and in more detail in Chafe (1993). Cf also Cruttenden's (1986) "intonation groups" or Gumperz & Berenz's (1993) "informational phrases" and the discussion of various other approaches to identifying units of intonation and their different terminologies in Couper-Kuhlen (1986: 73ff).
[13] If an element that at least once had been cited in a questionnaire or marked on a text sheet recurred in the corpus (cf Table B 1 in Appendix B, items 15-1-1, 15-1-2, 15-1-3), the other occurrences were also marked as non-NigP speech.

- it is separated from the surrounding discourse by intonation unit boundaries (in scripted texts, by punctuation marks) and/or by virtue of being a quotation.

According to the above criteria, most, though not all, of the clauses and larger segments in English that were cited in the questionnaires fall into the category of major English elements marked as non-NigP speech. After I had identified these elements, I separated the remaining discourse chunks and idiomatic expressions from single lexical or grammatical items. This meant that I had to take a decision on how to deal with the fluid boundaries between single lexemes consisting of more than one orthographic word and free combinations of two or more words. I decided to include in the category of single items established phrasal or prepositional verbs, complex prepositions or conjunctions, and compound nouns, as well as a number of other nominal expressions, mostly noun-noun combinations, which seemed to form to a certain extent a semantic unit (the distinction between noun compounds and noun phrases was the most problematic). The items that remain for the category of English multi-word elements neither marked as non-NigP speech nor classified as single units are mostly discourse chunks that can be interpreted as the result of code-switching at the intra-clausal level.

I thus distinguish three major categories of English elements in the corpus on the basis of structure, degree of integration into the surrounding discourse and semantic cohesiveness: stretches of discourse marked as non-NigP speech, other discourse chunks or idiomatic expressions, and single lexical or grammatical items.

5.3.2 *Discourse chunks or idiomatic expressions in English and quantitative analyses of the corpus data*

Stretches of discourse entirely in English can present a problem in quantitative analyses of the corpus data. For example, a simple count of the frequency of the English modal *should* as part of an analysis of tense/aspect/modality marking in educated NigP would be misleading if most of the occurrences of *should* were in parts of the corpus in which the speaker did not intend to speak NigP at all, as in the case of the two instances of *should* in example (1) above. Code-switching is therefore a factor which has to be taken into consideration in the analyses. Idiomatic expressions from English, whether they are best analysed as code-switches or as borrowings, have to be considered as well, since an item may have been borrowed only as part of idiomatic expressions and may not be freely combinable. As a basis for an approximate assessment of the role of these factors, I will use the results of the questionnaire study: in the analyses of lexis and grammar, I will take into account the extent to which the items in question are used as part of non-NigP speech and other discourse chunks or idiomatic expressions in English which were cited. A high proportion of occurrences in these elements (non-NigP speech and other discourse chunks or idiomatic expressions together make up less than 3% of the corpus) can be taken as an indication that in spite of a certain frequency in discourse, an item may not be part of the NigP system.

5.3.3 English elements according to the questionnaire study: the detailed list

A full list of the English elements that were cited in the questionnaires is given in Table B 1 in Appendix B (elements which were marked only on the text sheet are not included). The elements are listed along with their NigP equivalents, if any was suggested.[14]

In some cases part of the context of an item is also included. The item itself is then underlined. If an item was cited more than once it was sometimes necessary to distinguish different contexts or meanings. Contexts, specifications of meaning and NigP equivalents for items which were cited only once apply to the instance cited but not necessarily to other occurrences of the item in the corpus.

Single lexical or grammatical items are listed in Sections 1 to 14 of the table according to word class or grammatical category. Section 15 contains the discourse chunks and idiomatic expressions. This section is further subdivided into a section for clauses and larger segments, including those marked as non-NigP speech, and six other sections in which the remaining elements are, to the extent possible, classified according to phrase type.

The items in each section are arranged in descending order of their frequency in the corpus, which is indicated.[15] If a component of a multi-word element also occurs on its own in the same section of the table, the entry for the larger element follows the entry for this component, irrespective of its frequency. Items with the same frequency are ordered alphabetically.

The column for overall frequency also indicates the number of occurrences in parts of the corpus marked as non-NigP speech as well as in other multi-word elements. In addition, the table shows the number of texts in which the item occurs, and the number of citations in questionnaires. The number of citations includes "direct" and "indirect" citations. By direct citations I mean those where the item alone was entered into a questionnaire. For these citations extract references are given in brackets. Indirect citations are those in which the item forms part of a larger element that was cited.[16]

The numbers included in the table can give a certain indication of the extent to which items from English which are not considered part of NigP's English-derived core have become established in educated NigP. The best candidates for the status of borrowed forms are of course those which are frequent in the corpus outside non-NigP speech and other discourse chunks or idiomatic expressions in English and occur in many different texts. A borrowed form also has to be relatively acceptable, and to gauge acceptability, one may consider the number of citations in relation to occurrences, taking a low number of citations to suggest a relatively high degree of acceptability. However, as the questionnaire analysis of the corpus extracts was not meant to be exhaustive and there is the possibility of multiple occurrences in the same extract, this can provide only a very rough measure.

---

[14] In a few of the more difficult cases an informant gave a rough equivalent but put it into brackets or put a question mark. I have used brackets in all of these cases.

[15] Note that occurrences in parts of the corpus where the transcription is marked as uncertain have been disregarded in all quantitative analyses of the corpus data.

[16] If an item was cited as part of a larger element but retained in a NigP equivalent provided for that element, the citation is not counted.

5.3.4 *English elements according to the questionnaire study: overview*

Figure 5.1 gives an overview of the English elements in the corpus which takes into account both the questionnaire citations and other elements marked as non-NigP speech. The classification is the same as in Table B 1 except that parts of the corpus marked as non-NigP speech are a separate category. The figure shows the number of types in each class of items as well as the number of tokens of the items in each class in the corpus.[17]

One can see in the figure that single nouns are the category of English elements with the highest number of types as well as tokens. There are also many lexical verbs but far fewer adjectives[18] and adverbs. In the other categories of single items, there are, predictably, few types, but several of them have remarkably high token counts: prepositions, conjunctions, pronouns, the particle *to* and noun inflections. This points to some borrowing of free as well as bound grammatical morphemes. The token count for verb inflections and auxiliaries is far lower than that for noun inflections, which is a striking result in view of the high frequency of lexical verbs. In the category of discourse chunks and idiomatic expressions, the distribution of the items across phrase types is similar to the distribution of the single items across word classes, with noun phrases, verb phrases and prepositional phrases as the predominant categories.

The results of the questionnaire study for nouns, lexical verbs, adjectives and adverbs will be discussed in more detail in the section on lexis (5.4). The elements with grammatical function (prepositions, conjunctions, pronouns, determiners, noun inflections, verb inflections, auxiliaries, *to* as particle, adjective/adverb comparison and negation) will be dealt with in 5.5. (The category of interjections is so marginal that it need not be considered further.) While elements marked as non-NigP speech and other discourse chunks or idiomatic expressions in English will be taken into account as a factor in the lexical and grammatical analyses, the use of these elements will also be discussed as a subject in its own right in the section on discourse features (5.6).

---

[17] Tokens of an item which are part of a token of a larger element are not included in the token count for the item alone.

[18] I have classified the items cited as English elements according to the word class system of (traditional descriptions of) English. Note, however, that lexical items which in English are adjectives may function like verbs in NigP (see 5.5.6).

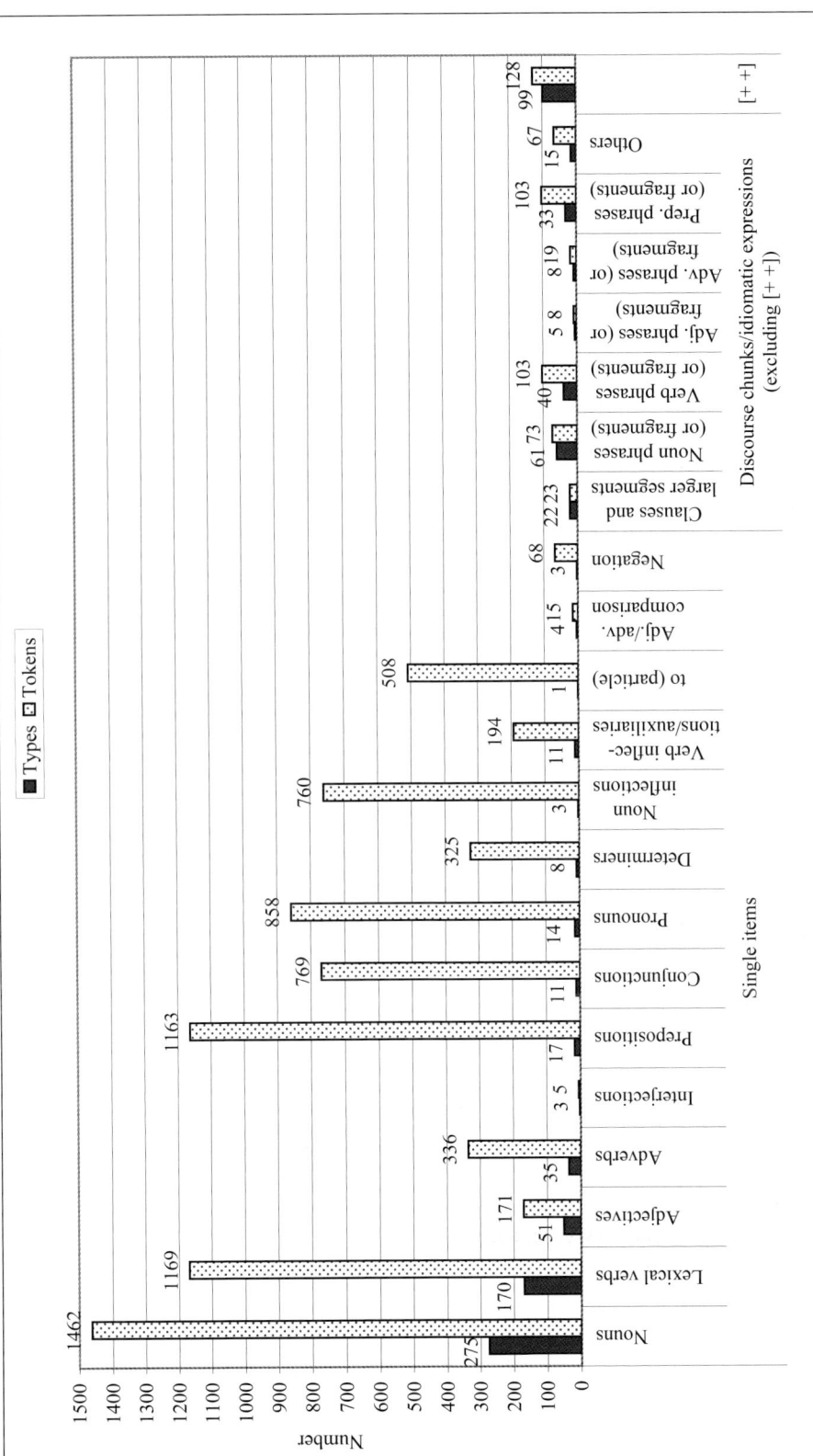

Figure 5.1 English elements in the NigP corpus according to the questionnaire study

5.4 Lexis

5.4.1 *Results of the questionnaire study*

5.4.1.1 Nouns

At the top of the list of nouns in Table B 1 is *government*. With over 160 occurrences spread over more than half of the texts in the corpus, not counting *federal government* and *local government*, this item is very common, and there is no other word for it in NigP. It is included because of the three direct citations but it can in fact be considered part of the established English-derived lexicon of the language; even Agheyisi (1971: 174) mentions it as a NigP word. *Local government* and *federal government*, with over 20 occurrences and only one citation each, are clearly acceptable as well.

Government is followed in the frequency ranking by four items with between 80 and 40 occurrences: *guy, problem, union, programme*. Unlike *government*, these items cannot be described as very well-established words, but they are common enough to be considered newer borrowings. However, if a classification of borrowings similar to the one in Poplack, Sankoff & Miller (1988; see the discussion in 2.4.2) is adopted, two of the items in this group, *union* and *guy*, are of the recurrent but not widespread type, as they occur in fewer than ten texts. Most of the occurrences of *union* are in the *Rainbow City* texts (R01-05), where social organisations are an important topic. *Guy* occurs only in the student conversations (Texts C03-10) and a discussion between students (Text D05). It may be a peculiarity of the student vocabulary, but the fact that it occurs mainly in conversations also shows that as in English, it is a rather informal expression; in the other texts, the neutral *man* is used.[19] The two other items in this group, *problem* and *programme*, occur in 23 and 19 texts of 6 and 5 categories, respectively, and are thus clearly widespread. However, *problem*, with a total of 69 occurrences, has not displaced the Hausa-derived *wahala*, although it is somewhat more frequent: *wahala* occurs 53 times and is also represented in all 6 text categories.[20] *Programme* has no generally accepted NigP equivalent. The suggested *talk-talk* fits only in the context of radio/television programmes. There is one occurrence of *talk-talk* in this sense in the corpus, but *programme* seems to be the normal term (11 occurrences in this sense in 7 texts of 4 categories).

After the few very frequent words follows a group of 28 items (items 1-11 to 1-42 excluding compounds) with below 40 but more than 10 occurrences. A few of these items can, on the basis of the present data, not be described as integrated into NigP in spite of a relatively high absolute frequency. For example, *refuse* is, with 22 occurrences, much less frequent than its NigP equivalent *dirty*, which is used 55 times in this sense, and it is restricted to only two texts (other items which are restricted to one or two texts are *World Cup* and *progress*). Some at least of the remaining items do, however, qualify as borrowings. Many are not translated, or the suggested NigP equivalent is a word with a much more general meaning. The items in question include a number of words which occur only or mainly in the student conversations and may be considered borrowings in the student vocabulary, in analogy to Agheyisi's (1977) "undergraduate list" of borrowings in the indigenous languages (see 4.2): *test, lecturer, textbook, semester, result, faculty*.

---

[19] The suggested NigP equivalent for *guy*, *bobo*, occurs only once in the corpus, in a radio text.
[20] The other NigP equivalent for *problem* that was suggested, *palaver*, occurs only 4 times.

Another important semantic field is politics and social organisations: *president, member, chairman, democracy, election, committee*. For *president*, the Yoruba loanword *oga kpatakpata* ('highest chief') may also be used, but it occurs only 15 times in the corpus and is not in all instances equivalent to *president*, while *president* occurs 38 times. *Democracy* has more citations in questionnaires than other items of comparable frequency, but it also occurs in more texts. One informant suggested *government of talk make I talk* 'government of speak-and-let-me-speak' as a NigP equivalent, but an expression similar to this one occurs only once in the corpus.

The remaining items – those from 1-43 and most compounds – have 10 or fewer occurrences. 10 occurrences in an 80,000-word corpus is of course as arbitrary a cut-off point as other frequency criteria that have been used in corpus-based language contact research, but I will consider lexical items with 10 or fewer occurrences infrequent. Of the 241 infrequent items in the list, 71 occur more than once and in more than one text, 63 occur more than once but in only one text and will be considered "idiosyncratic", and 107 occur only once. In a framework without categories like "nonce borrowings" or "cultural borrowings" (see the discussion in 2.4.2), most of these infrequent items, in particular the idiosyncratic and nonce ones, are best analysed as single-word switches in their respective discourse contexts, if they are not part of larger English elements. It is of course clear that some items which may be candidates for loanword status will be infrequent due to the limitations of the corpus. On the other hand, there are also highly specialized or learned words which an educated speaker may take over spontaneously in a specific context but which are unlikely to become generalized, and idiosyncratic and nonce items would certainly have figured prominently even in a list based on a much larger corpus.[21] There are also items which are infrequent because they compete with an established word which remains the normal designation for the concept in question: the 7 instances of *car* may be compared to 64 occurrences of *motor*[22]; *electricity* is, with 4 occurrences, much less frequent than *light*, which is used 43 times in this sense; *pregnancy* occurs 5 times, while *belle* is used in this sense in 23 instances.[23]

Examples such as *car, electricity* and *pregnancy* show that educated speakers sometimes use anglicisms in place of other English-derived nouns which are established in NigP, but it has also become apparent in the discussion so far that "cultural" items such as terms related to education or political vocabulary play an important role. If the whole list of nouns is examined from a semantic point of view, one finds that about half of the items can be grouped into the following semantic fields reflecting the modern, formal and Western-influenced domains in which English predominates:

- politics, government, social organisations, official procedures (e.g. *election, constituency, impeachment, Constitution, House of Assembly, chairman, treasurer, conference, motion, notice of increment*)
- (higher) education (e.g. *lecturer, faculty, degree, graduate, assignment*)

---

[21] Cf also Poplack, Sankoff & Miller (1988), whose study of English-origin words in Canadian French is based on a corpus of over 2 million words.

[22] These, though, include instances of *motor* in the more general sense of 'motor vehicle'. Also included in the count are occurrences in compounds like *motor people* 'motorists'.

[23] This includes instances of *get belle* 'be pregnant'. *Pregnant* (cf item 3-23 in Table B 1) is, with only three occurrences, also infrequent.

- law and law enforcement (e.g. *curfew, accused, allegation, criminal, capital offence*)
- technology and modern agriculture (e.g. *public address system, recycling, incinerator, grain silo, transformer*)
- finance (e.g. *budget, allowance, excise duties, levy, subvention*)
- economy and industry (e.g. *resources, distributor, brewery*)
- (non-traditional) medicine (e.g. *blood pressure, cerebral meningitis, venereal disease*)
- mathematics and science (e.g. *calculation, quadratic equation, diagram*)
- media (e.g. *programme, interview*)
- Christian religion (e.g. *salvation, commandment*)

Most of the remaining items cannot be assigned to specialized semantic fields, but one aspect that may be noted is that there are many abstract nouns (e.g. *condition, solution, effect, analysis, habit*), which are rare in the established NigP lexicon (Agheyisi 1988: 233).

In view of the above, it is not surprising that NigP equivalents were provided for little more than half of the items in the list. Moreover, more than one third of the NigP equivalents that were provided are circumlocutions or words with a more general meaning than the English ones. The circumlocutions often consist of a generic noun postmodified by a relative clause, e.g. *law wey dey say make people no waka for outside* 'law which says that people should not go out' (for *curfew*), *place wey dem dey burn dirty* 'place where refuse is burned' (for *incinerator*), or *di people wey dey make law* 'the people who make laws' (for *legislative house*); for a number of mostly abstract nouns a verbal periphrasis was offered, e.g. *dem don comot am* 'he has been removed' for *impeachment*, or *dem join hand* 'they have joined hands' for *partnership*. Among the general words which were given as equivalents for more specific English terms are *talk/talk-talk*, which has to serve as an equivalent not only for *programme* but also for five other items in the list (*seminar, address, workshop, conference, interview*), and *people*, which was suggested as an equivalent for *members, committee, staff, constituency, organisation, community* and *subjects*.

It is clear that not all of the items in the list fill gaps in the NigP lexicon, but one can conclude that lexical need is an important motivation for the borrowing of English nouns or their use in discourse as code-switched elements by educated NigP speakers.

5.4.1.2 Verbs

The list of verbs is headed by a highly frequent item: *know*, with 431 occurrences, of which only 11 in parts of the corpus marked as non-NigP speech and other discourse chunks or idiomatic expressions in English. There is no single text in the corpus in which this item does not occur. Only few of the informants chose it as an example of an English element: 15 of the 20 citations are by the same informant. When *know* was cited, *sabi* was given as its NigP equivalent. *Sabi* occurs only 38 times in the corpus, but a closer examination of the data shows that it is also not entirely equivalent to *know* and that different meanings have to be distinguished. Like *know*, *sabi* can mean 'have information about', 'be familiar with', but in 21 instances it refers to skill, experience or ability, as in the following examples:

(2) If you no *sabi* slice, dose women wey dey sell for market dem go help you slice am. But women dem e good make we *sabi* do everything o, so far na cooking o. (A05 124ff)

'If you don't know how to slice, those women who sell in the market will help you slice it. But it is good for us women to be able to do everything, as long as it has to do with cooking.'

(3)   According to dose wey *sabi* doctor work well well, dem say na inside hot weader plenty different different disease dey waka pass [...]. (A01 7f)

'According to medical experts, it is in hot weather that diseases are particularly rampant'

(4)   if God bless woman/ woman *sabi* take care of family well well// (D04 42f)

'If God blesses a woman, a woman can take care of the family very well.'

When the complement is a verb, as in the two instances in (2) and the one in (4), *sabi* can be analysed as a modal. There are 14 instances of the modal use of *sabi*. *Know,* in contrast, takes only nominal complements and is used mainly in the sense of 'have information about', 'be familiar with' (I found only three occurrences of *know* in the context of skill or experience). The following are typical examples of the use of *know* in the corpus:

(5)   ah e be like say una no *know* wetin dey happen// (C08 11)

'Ah, it seems you don't know what's happening.'

(6)   Na somebody wey *know* dem well well [...], na im tell me. (R03 42f)

'It was somebody who knew them very well who told me.'

The literature suggests that a certain differentiation between *know* and *sabi* can be found in some, but not all, dialects or idiolects. Agheyisi (1971: 133) gives *know* as an example of a NigP stative verb, without restricting it to any particular variety. *Sabi* is mentioned in her study (p 138) as an abilitative modal as well as a main verb. In her translations of *Wakabout* articles into "proper" NigP (in Huber & Görlach 1996), Agheyisi replaces *sabi* by *know* when the author of *Wakabout* uses the former in the sense of 'have information about', 'be familiar with'. Faraclas (1996), in contrast, has *sabi* throughout in the examples in his grammar based on the Port Harcourt dialect, even in the sense 'have information about', 'be familiar with'. In his NigP vocabulary list, *know* is mentioned but marked as an "acrolectal" item (p 288). The only conclusion one can draw is thus that at whatever stage English *know* may have been taken over into NigP, it has led to differentiation in the lexicon but has not totally displaced the Portuguese-derived *sabi* even in the educated variety.

Know as well as *sabi* were also suggested as equivalents for the second item in the list, *understand* (depending on the context, *hear* is another possibility). With 68 occurrences, this item is not nearly as frequent as *know* but still common. However, 25 of the 68 occurrences are in *you understand (me) (now)* used as a discourse marker. Several instances of this were cited in questionnaires as a unit and a tag-switching analysis was proposed in the comments section (cf item 15-1-1 in Table B 1 and the comments on extracts C05/7, C05/8 and C10/5 in Table B 2). The total number of citations is also relatively high. *Understand* thus appears to be common in educated NigP but not yet fully integrated.

Items 2-3 to 2-21 can be grouped together as items which are not highly frequent but occur more than 10 times. Like the comparable group of nouns, this group of verbs contains a number of items which qualify as borrowings. Again, however, some items are not as good candidates as others. For example, *eat* (25 occurrences, 2 citations) and *look for* (17 occurrences, 1 citation) appear quite acceptable, but one also has to take into consideration 87 occurrences of NigP *chop* 'eat' and 39 of *find* in the sense of 'look for'. More established seems to be *live,* which Faraclas (1996: 288) also mentions as an "acrolectal" NigP item. With 26 occurrences, *live* is more common than its NigP equivalent *stay* (11 occurrences in this sense). Other items which one might want to consider borrowings include *collect, spend, complain, organise, solve* and *advise*.

What is noticeable about the relatively frequent verbs is the total absence of specialized words. If the infrequent ones (146, of which 20 idiosyncratic and 65 nonce items) are also considered, one does find items related to the specialized semantic fields identified in the analysis of the list of nouns (*campaign, elect, impeach; educate, graduate, lecture* etc.), but they are few. This is of course to be expected, as nouns always predominate among cultural terms. Looking at the aspect of lexical need from the converse perspective, one finds that the proportion of items with NigP equivalents (about four fifth) is also much higher than in the list of nouns. A number of these equivalents are of course circumlocutions, e.g. *use am make anoder* 'use it to make another' for *recycle,* or *say I go do am anoder time* 'say I will do it another time' for *postpone*. Again, there is also a small set of very general words which serve as translations for several items each, e.g. *talk* (for *complain, discuss, interview* and *campaign*), *comot* (for *remove, impeach, evacuate* and *withdraw*), or *look* (for *investigate, view* and *consider*). However, on the whole, the list of verbs clearly has a higher degree of translatability than that of nouns. Thus, while verbs are also an important category among the English elements in the corpus, their use is motivated to a lesser extent by lexical need than that of nouns.

5.4.1.3 Adjectives and adverbs

Since adjectives and adverbs are few in the data from the questionnaire study compared to nouns and verbs, I will consider them only briefly and confine myself to those with more than ten occurrences in the corpus.

Among the adjectives (Section 3 in Table B 1), there are only three items which occur more than ten times. One of these, *national,* is frequent only because it occurs as part of names of official institutions and organizations. The remaining two items are *serious* and *important*. Agheyisi (1971: 187) lists both of these as English lexical items without surface reflexes in NigP. The present data indicate that in the educated variety at least, these items are now common usage. *Serious* also has few citations in relation to occurrences, while *important* does not seem to be quite so acceptable.

With the category of adverbs (Section 4 in Table B 1) we have reached the transitional zone between lexical and grammatical items. The list of adverbs includes a number of closed-class items and is also headed by such an item: the adverbial question word *why*. *Why* is mentioned by Agheyisi (1971: 129) as a question word in NigP, but she adds that this and a number of other question words which are direct reflexes of English ones "tend to feature more in the speech of people who also speak Standard English fairly well". Faraclas (1996: 11) also mentions *why* as a NigP question word, and he does not even restrict it to the "acrolectal variety". It is therefore not surprising that the corpus data show *why* to be a normal feature of the variety of NigP under investigation.[24] The second adverb in the list, *very*, may be described as a common but not fully established item (like the verb *understand*), as the proportion of occurrences in non-NigP speech and other discourse chunks or idiomatic expressions in English is considerable. The third item, *maybe*, is also mentioned by Faraclas (1996: 23) as occurring in "acrolectal varieties". This item and the following three in the list (*really, about, especially*) may be considered borrowings in educated NigP.

5.4.2 *Anglicisms versus pidginization strategies*

The discussion of the questionnaire data has shown that in the category of nouns at least, an important motivation for the use of anglicisms in educated NigP is lexical need. It was observed that anglicisms filling lexical gaps were often left untranslated in the questionnaires, but that the informants sometimes tried to render them in NigP by using the resources of the language to create equivalents. In the present section, I will take a closer look at such pidginization strategies and discuss their use in the corpus texts in relation to the use of anglicisms. I will confine myself to nouns and noun phrases, and I will focus on one text category, the news (5.4.2.1-3); as these texts are direct translations from English aimed at a not very well-educated target audience and reference has to be made in them to many concepts which have not traditionally found expression in NigP, it is in this category that there is the greatest need for pidginization strategies. Lexical usage in the other text categories will be considered more briefly in 5.4.2.4.

5.4.2.1 *Pidginization strategies in the news texts*

One of the strategies employed in the news texts to render English nouns and noun phrases in NigP is circumlocution, as in the NigP translations in the questionnaire study. One can distinguish two different types of circumlocutions. Semantically, these could be described as "neutral" and "imaginative". Circumlocutions of the neutral type involve straightforward explanation, whereas the imaginative circumlocutions also add colour to an expression. These are, of course, tendencies and not absolute categories. Structurally, many of the neutral circumlocutions follow the pattern of a generic noun postmodified by a relative clause. The imaginative circumlocutions often involve nominalization of a clause. Similar types of circumlocutions have been found by Bamgbose (1992) in Yoruba news translations. The two types I distinguish are in many ways comparable to the translation strategies referred to in Bamgbose's study as "explication" and "idiomatization", respectively. Bamgbose illustrates these strategies by the examples which I have taken over as (7), for explication, and (8), for idiomatization, among several others:

(7) àwọn orílẹ̀ èdè gbogbo wọ̀n-ọnnì tí wọ́n ti gbòmìnira kúrò lábẹ́ ìjoba Gẹ̀ẹ́sí

 'those nations that have gained their independence from under the British government', i.e. Commonwealth

---

[24] The alternative question element in NigP, *wetin make*, occurs only twice (A01 138, A03 22), and in these instances it could also be translated into English as 'what made'.

(8)   owó gbà má. bínú
        'money of take-and-don't-be-angry', i.e. compensation

Circumlocutions in the NigP news texts which are of the neutral, explanatory type include the following:

(9)   people o wey dey do dirty carry-carry work[25] (N04 54)
        'people who do the work of carrying waste away', i.e. waste disposal companies

(10)   money to put inside di business make e dey grow well well (N01 13f)
        'money to put into the business so that it will prosper', i.e. money for investments

In the following example, the English word is cited and a circumlocution of this type is added as an explanation:

(11)   di things wey oyibo people dey call "radars" wey dem take dey look how aeroplane dey fly for air (N03 118ff)
        'the things that the white people call "radars", which are used to watch how aeroplanes fly in the air'

Circumlocutions of the imaginative type include the one for *democracy* which is similar to the one suggested in the questionnaire study (see 5.4.1):

(12)   government of make you talk your own make I talk my own (N02 142)
        'government of you-can-say-what-you-think-I-can-say-what-I-think'

Further examples are:

(13)   you-no-like-me you-no-like-me katakata (N05 86)
        'you-are-not-like-me you-are-not-like-me trouble', i.e. ethnic strife

(14)   I-no-gree I-no-gree strike strike (N05 140)
        'I-don't-agree I-don't-agree strike', i.e. protest strike

Strategies which may be used to form NigP equivalents for English nouns also include compounding and reduplication. Noun compounds are, according to Agheyisi (1971: 59) and Faraclas (1996: 243), often formed with generic nouns. Agheyisi (ibid.) mentions *man* 'man', *taim* 'time' and *ples* 'ples' as the most common generic nouns used in compounds. Her examples of compounds with these items include *kontriman* 'native', *monitaim* 'morning' and *chopples* 'restaurant' (p 60). Such noun-noun combinations are described by her as the dominant pattern (p 59), but adjective-noun combinations like *kresman* 'madman' are mentioned as well (p 61). Faraclas (1996: 243) cites *ples* 'place' and *pesin* 'person' as generic nouns commonly used in compounds. His example of a compound with a generic noun is *moto-man*. A plural form of this compound, with *people* (15), is often used in the news texts, as is another *man/people* compound (16):

(15)   motor people (N01/02, 9 occurrences)[26]
        'motorists'

---

[25] This circumlocution also illustrates the processes of reduplication (*carry-carry*) and compounding (*dirty carry-carry work*); see below.

[26] If an item occurs more than three times in the corpus, only the text(s) and the number of occurrences are indicated.

(16)   new(s)tory man/people (N01/N03/N04, 13 occurrences)
       'reporter(s)'

The news texts show in addition that the nouns *work* and *matter* can be used in similar noun-noun combinations. Of course, the distinction between compounds and what Faraclas (1996; see especially p 67) refers to as the "associative/possessive construction" is not clear-cut (see also Faraclas 1996: 252), but one can observe that noun-noun combinations with *work* or *matter* as the second element sometimes replace English abstract nouns:

(17)   farm work (N01 138, 139)
       'agriculture'
(18)   minister for works and *house matter* (N05 9f)
       'Minister of Works and Housing'

By reduplication – as by conversion without reduplication – nouns can be derived from verbs (cf also Faraclas 1996: 243). This strategy is not as important as circumlocution and compounding, but there are a few examples of reduplicated nouns derived from verbs in the news texts. These include the following:

(19)   suffer-suffer (N01 61)
       'suffering'
(20)   gader-gader (N03 95)
       'gathering'
(21)   call-call (N03 103)
       'appeal'

A final remark that has to be made about compounding and reduplication is that both work well in examples like those cited above, but that there are also cases of superficial pidginization, where these word formation processes are applied to words which are not part of the NigP vocabulary, like *aviation* and *launch* in the examples below:

(22)   minister of *aviation matter* (N03 121)
       'Minister of Aviation'
(23)   launch-launch (N05 81)
       'launch' (n.)/launching'

5.4.2.2   Anglicisms in the news texts

Circumlocution is in many cases the only way to render an English expression in NigP. However, as circumlocutions are long and often imprecise, it may sometimes appear preferable to use the English word – which is of course what is often done. For example, the anglicisms cited from the news texts in the questionnaire study include items like the following:

(24)   brewery (N01, 4 occurrences; cf Table B 1, item 1-81)
(25)   laboratory (N03 20; cf Table B 1, item 1-231)
(26)   minimum wage (N01/05, 5 occurrences; cf Table B 1, item 1-56)

In these cases, it is hard to think of a NigP equivalent other than a circumlocution. In the questionnaire study, *brewery* was translated as *place wey dem dey make beer* 'place where beer is produced', while the other two items were left untranslated. Whether the absence of a straightforward, long-established equivalent in NigP justifies the retention of the English word in a news translation of course depends on whether the latter is common enough to be considered a borrowing, or, at least, has gained a certain currency in a particular situation. For example, one informant who cited *minimum wage* as an English expression in an interview extract (V01/7) commented in the questionnaire that as this was a "burning issue" (there was at the time a strike of Lagos State workers over their minimum wage), "[the] extract's technical terms (*minimum wage*, especially) appear through popular usage, to have passed into the Pidgin vocabulary" (cf Table B 2).

There are also cases where a motivation for the use of an anglicism is more difficult to perceive than in the case of the items cited in (24) to (26) above. In (27) and (28), for example, an English abstract noun could easily have been replaced by a verb or verbal periphrasis; in (28), this would also have eliminated the preposition *of*, which was cited in the questionnaire study as an English element along with the noun:

(27)   *construction* work [...] go [...] start (N05 52f) → (NigP:) dem go start dey build 'they will start to build' (cf Table B 1, item 1-111)

(28)   *harassment of* motor people (N02 92) → (NigP:) wahala wey dem dey give motor people 'trouble that they give motorists' (cf Table B 1, item 15-2-30)

In (29), the whole noun phrase is a blatant anglicism:

(29)   poor electricity supply (N01 62) → (NigP:) light wey no dey steady 'electricity which is not steady' (cf Table B 1, item 15-2-49)

In the following case, a derived noun in NigP could have replaced the English noun:

(30)   request (N02 28) → (NigP:) beg/beg-beg (cf Table B 1, item 1-259)

Anglicisms like those in (27) to (30) fit into the type that one informant described as "undiscriminating carry-overs from standard English" in an evaluation of a news extract (N02/2; cf Table B 2). Such carry-overs are, one may assume, particularly likely to occur in the course of spontaneous oral translations of English scripts.

One can also observe variation between an English expression and a possible NigP equivalent in texts by different newscasters (or even within the same text):

(31)   vice president (N02 4f; N05 77, 80) - di number two oga kpatakpata for our country 'the second highest chief in our country' (N04 40)

(32)   conference (N01 133, N03 132) - talk-talk 'conference' (N01 119)

Such variation contrasts with Bamgbose's (1992: 3) observation on Yoruba news translations that there is a high degree of consistency in the handling of specific concepts.

5.4.2.3 *Pidginization strategies versus anglicisms in the news texts: analysis of text extracts*

Having discussed both pidginization strategies and anglicisms in isolation, I will now analyse how the translation problem of pidginization versus anglicisms is handled in two extracts from the texts. The first of these, Text 5.1 below (from subtext N04-1 in the corpus; also available on the CD as a sound sample) is the broadcast transcription which corresponds to the script extract in Appendix D (Text D 1). Note that the English version is a re-translation, not the original one (it was unfortunately not possible for me to take copies of the English scripts with me).

Text 5.1 News broadcast (extract)

[broadcast version]

Check your time dere you go see na five minutes e take dodge two o'clock, e don reach di time for our Pidgin news for today wey be number seventeen day for di month
5 of May wey be number five month for di year two thousand. But before I go chook leg for di news proper, I go tell una di ones wey carry kanda for inside. [~] Dem don retire some people for Petroleum Ministry. One
10 ogbonge oga wan look for money to repair F.R.C.N. and N.T.A. Dem don set task force o wey go follow put eye for dirty matter for Lagos Mainland Local Government. Igbo people wan celebrate Igbo Day for on di
15 twenty-ninth of May for di year two thousand. My name na God'swill Adheke Joseph. Make una listen to how di news e berekete reach. [~] Na feader wey no good, na im e go dey pluck throway for im body o.
20 Na im make di Department of Petroleum Resources wey be people wey tanda on top petroleum matter don retire some people wey dey work with dem. Dem retire dem o to make di department dey kamkpe pass as
25 before. Na di mouth of di special adviser on top petroleum matter and energy matter dis order fall comot. E say dis retirement o go continue until dem see say petroleum don dey contribute dem own part well well for
30 our economic matter. [~] I no bellefull o, na im make Oliver Twist ask for more o. Di oga on top ofofo and talk-talk matter Professor Jerry Gana say e go soon write anoder give-me-money paper go meet National Assembly
35 so dat dem fit bring money wey im go take buy things and repair Federal Radio Corporation of Nigeria and N.T.A. property dem. Di oga talk dis word o by di time wey im carry waka come look di working
40 property wey dey for F.R.C.N. compound for Lagos here.

[translation]

Check your time, you'll see it's five minutes past two, time for our Pidgin news for today, the seventeenth of May two thousand. But before I enter into the news proper, I'll give you the headlines.

The Petroleum Ministry has retired some of its staff. A top government official is going to seek funds to overhaul F.R.C.N. [Federal Radio Corporation of Nigeria] and N.T.A. [National Television Authority]. A task force has been set up to help supervise waste disposal in Lagos Mainland Local Government. The Igbo will celebrate Igbo Day on the twenty-ninth of May two thousand. My name is God'swill Adheke Joseph. You'll now hear the news in detail. If a feather is bad, it will be shed. In the same way, the Department of Petroleum Resources has retired some of its staff in order to increase efficiency. The step was made public by the Special Adviser on Petroleum and Energy. He added that there will be further reductions in the workforce until the petroleum sector will have become more economically viable.

Oliver Twist didn't have enough, that's why he asked for more. The Minister of Information, Professor Jerry Gana, has announced that he will make a request to the National Assembly for more funds for the purchase and repair of equipment at the Federal Radio Corporation of Nigeria and N.T.A. He announced this intention during an inspection of the F.R.C.N. station here in Lagos.

By di time wey our newtory man o Chika Emerenwah dey take question dey jam di oga body, e say e go change all di F.R.C.N. equipment dem to chabe one wey dem dey use nowadays for town, wey dem dey call "latest". [~] Na for dry season, ant dey gader dem food dey put for inside hole o. Na im make di government of Benue State don bring out fifty-nine million naira to buy fertilizer to divide for di farmers wey dey dem state for dis farming season. Na di oga madam on top agriculture matter for Benue State Mrs. Elizabeth Shuluwa tell our newtory people for Makurdi say dem go use new style to dey divide fertilizer give farmers for di state as from now, so dat dem go make sure say di fertilizer e reach many farmers dem hand. (N04 1-37)

In an interview with our reporter Chika Emerenwah, the minister said he intends to have all the F.R.C.N. equipment replaced with the latest type.

In the dry season, ants gather food and store it in holes. Similarly, the government of Benue State has made fifty-nine million naira available for the distribution of fertilizer to farmers in the state during this farming season. The Benue State Commissioner for Agriculture, Mrs. Elizabeth Shuluwa, told our reporters in Makurdi that a new strategy would be adopted in the distribution of the fertilizer to ensure that it would reach a large number of farmers.

Dagmar Deuber with God'swill Adheke Joseph in the studio at Radio Nigeria 3

One obvious question in the news translations is how to refer to government and other institutions and government posts, as the official designations for these are in English. In Text 5.1, the newscaster has taken a mixed approach. *National Assembly* (l 34) and *Federal*

Radio Corporation of Nigeria (ll 36f) are retained. The newscaster also takes over *Department of Petroleum Resources* (ll 20f) but adds an explanation in NigP (*wey be people wey tanda on top petroleum matter* 'which is the people who stand on top of petroleum matters', i.e. the people who are in charge of petroleum matters). The terms for government posts show various degrees of pidginization. *Oga on top ofofo*[27] *and talk-talk matter* 'Minister of Information' (ll 31f) is a case of full translation. In *oga madam on top agriculture matter* 'Commissioner for Agriculture' (ll 52f) the term for the post is again translated by *oga*, here in combination with *madam*; the term for the department is only superficially pidginized by the addition of *matter* to the anglicism *agriculture* – which the newscaster quoted in example (17) above translates as *farm work* (cf also Table B 1, item 1-108). In *special adviser on top petroleum matter and energy matter* 'Special Adviser on Petroleum and Energy' (ll 25f), the preposition *on* is expanded to *on top*[28] and *matter* is added to both *petroleum* and *energy*, but otherwise the term remains as in English.

A mixed approach can also be observed in the handling of the general vocabulary. Among examples of full translation by strategies described in 5.4.2.1 are the already cited compound *newtory man/people* 'reporter(s)' (ll 42, 55), the compound *dirty matter* 'waste disposal' (l 12), the circumlocution *people wey dey work with dem* 'people who work with them' (ll 22f) for *staff* (cf also Table B 1, item 1-78) and a rather imaginative circumlocution for *headlines*: *di ones wey carry kanda for inside* 'the ones that have skin among [the news]', i.e. the ones which are "thick" or important (ll 7f). What must have been *economy* or a derivative thereof in the original English script is superficially pidginized as *economic matter* (l 30). In the third news item (ll 47ff) the newscaster seems confident that the key word *fertilizer* will be understood, as he makes no attempt to translate or explain it.

For further illustration, I will use one news item from a different text in the corpus (N01-1), which is printed below as Text 5.2. In this news item, the newscaster seems unsure how to handle one of the key words, *education* (cf also Table B 1, item 1-25). *Get ... education* is rendered as *read ... bookuru* in l 6, whereas in l 12 the English expression is used; in l 14f, the English and NigP expressions are combined: *education tabi bookuru matter* (*tabi* means 'or'). The second key word, *committee* (cf also Table B 1, item 1-36), is treated as a borrowing which requires no translation or explanation (ll 1, 9, 20, 24), like *fertilizer* in Text 5.1. This newscaster also uses the term *democracy* (l 18) and does not attempt a circumlocution. *Activity* (l 25) could have been replaced by the general *thing*, which was suggested in the questionnaire study as an equivalent (cf Table B 1, item 1-107), as its meaning is already specified by the relative clause *wey de dey do* 'which they do'.

In conclusion, it is possible to point out words which seem to have been taken over directly from the English scripts although they could have been rendered in NigP, but it is also clear that not every lexical item in an English news script can be translated by a core NigP word or paraphrased by such words. To translate news from English into NigP is in essence a tightrope walk between anglicisms and pidginization.

---

[27] *Ofofo* is a word of Yoruba origin meaning 'gossip'.
[28] Mann (1993a: 62) cites *(fɔ̀) ọntọp (of)* as a NigP complex preposition. *On* on its own is not a normal feature of NigP (cf also Agheyisi 1971: 190), although it does occur in educated usage.

Text 5.2 News broadcast (extract)

[broadcast version]

One committee o don tanda for Shomolu Local Government Area inside Lagos State and di committee o we hear say get plan to help all di poor students wey dey for di
5   local government for di money wey dem go take read all di bookuru dem wan read. When di oga kpatakpata for di council wey be Prince Sesan Olanrewaju dey standa di committee for last Thursday, di oga o come
10 talk say de start dat kind scholarship award to help all di poor people wey dey for dat local government get better education. E come dey talk o say im council put eye well well as e concern education tabi bookuru
15 matter, because e dey important mkpa to help all di students plus di people wey dey dere to know wetin government dey talk about democracy. Prince Olanrewaju o dey say na better challenge e be for di five people
20 wey dey inside di committee, especially especially dem oga wey be Dr Idowu Sobowale, to make sure say de do di work well well as e go sweet people for belle. Di committee o we hear say de set am up to join
25 hand for many many activity wey de dey do to remember say Prince Olanrewaju don dey one hundred days for dat office. [~] (N01 38-55)

[translation]

A committee has been set up in Shomolu Local Government Area in Lagos State. The committee, we're told, has plans for giving poor students in the local government the necessary financial assistance to enable them to get the education they desire. During the inaugural session of the committee last Thursday, the council chairman Prince Sesan Olanrewaju said that this scholarship was introduced in order to help poor people in the local government to get a good education. He further explained that his council placed great value on education because of its key role in the effort to make students as well as the population at large aware of the government's pronouncements concerning democracy. Prince Olanrewaju said that it was a great challenge for the five members of the committee and especially the chairman, Dr Idowu Sobowale, to ensure that they perform their duties as they are expected to. The committee, we're told, was set up as part of a number of activities to mark Prince Olanrewaju's first one hundred days in office.

5.4.2.4 *Lexical usage in the other text categories*

In the radio text categories "advice" and "drama", the question of anglicisms versus pidginization is not such a problematic issue as in the news texts. Firstly, the texts in these categories are not translations. Secondly, the topics of the advice texts are not generally as demanding as those of the news, and the fictional everyday conversations which predominate in the drama texts reflect a traditional domain of NigP. However, the question of how to render or explain in the language English terms which might not be familiar to all listeners sometimes arises in these texts as well, especially in some of the texts from *Make We Think Small* (A01-03) - the *Woman Corner* texts (A04–05) are of a very practical nature – and in scenes in the drama texts in which technical terms occur.

In *Make We Think Small*, a great effort is made to stick to the core NigP vocabulary. Such words as are taken over from English (often technical terms or proper names) are usually explained. In the following examples, circumlocutions are used for what in English could have been expressed more succinctly:

(33)   Inside all di machine dem wey oyibo do for person to dey take move from one place to di oder, na motor people dey use pass. (A01 54f)

'Among all the machines that the white people have made for people to move from one place to the other [i.e. means of transport], it is the motor vehicle that people use most.'

(34) [...] armed robber no be spirit, na *person like you and me wey get blood for body.* (A02 142ff)

'an armed robber is not a spirit but a person like you and me who has blood in his body [i.e. a human being].'

(35) But nobody do anything to stop *all dese people wey dey lef village, lef farm work come town come work.* (A02 15f)

'But nothing was done to stop all these people who left their villages and gave up agriculture to go and work in the towns [i.e. rural-urban migration].'

In (36) and (37), an English common noun and an international acronym, respectively, are introduced into the text accompanied by an explanation in NigP:

(36) Na when rain fall like dis, we dey see di secret of town dem wey no get *good gutter, wey rain water fit pass go under*, abi better "*drainage*" as oyibo people go call am. (A01 15ff)

'When rain has fallen like this, we can see the secrets of towns that don't have good gutters where rain water can flow under the ground, or proper "drainage" as the white people would call it.'

(37) *FIFA wey be di oga kpatakpata for anything wey concern football matter for di world*, dem don do Nigeria bad bad o [...]. (A03 5f)

'FIFA, which is the international governing body of football, has dealt very badly with Nigeria'

There are also examples of compounds similar to the ones employed by the newscasters:

(38) doctor work (A01 7; cf also example (3) above)

'medicine'[29]

(39) soldier work (A02 105)

'military'

(40) armi robber matter (A02 87, 89f)

'armed robbery'

The technical terms which occur in the drama texts are mainly terminology related to social organisations (*Rainbow City*) and medical vocabulary (*One Thing at a Time*). The aim is probably for the listener to become familiar with these terms, so they cannot be avoided. They are also not normally clarified by direct explanations, but some dialogues are constructed in such a way that the listener can gather information about concepts referred to by technical terms from the context. In (41), for instance, the context makes it clear that treasurer and financial secretary are the elected officers who are in charge of a union's financial affairs:

---

[29] In the concrete sense, *melecine*, i.e. a phonetic adaptation of the English word, is used (A03 128).

(41) **Chairman:** When you don register, una go take all your union money go bank.
Asabe: Mmh.
Chairman: If una wan spend any money, wheder na one naira or na one thousand naira, na *di person you vote for treasurer and di one you vote for financial secretary go dey know everything about di money.*
Asabe: So nobody go fit do magomago with di union money?
Chairman: No way! (R03 138ff)[30]

'**Chairman:** Once your union is registered, you'll take all the union's money to the bank.
Asabe: Mhm.
Chairman: If you want to spend any money, whether it's one naira or one thousand naira, the person you've voted treasurer and the one you've voted financial secretary will know everything about the money.
Asabe: So nobody will be able to cheat us?
Chairman: No way!'

In (42), Saratou, a doctor, asks her patient Evaristus what he knows about HIV. His reply contains essential information for the listener:

(42) **Saratou:** Wetin you know about *H.I.V*?
Evaristus: Uh sister, I just dey hear say *person fit catch am through sex if person no dey use condom.* Uh and say *e no get cure.* (R06 112ff)

'**Saratou:** What do you know about H I V?
Evaristus: Uh sister, I've only been hearing that one can get it through sex if one doesn't use a condom. Uh and that it's incurable.'

The texts in the category "face-to-face speech" are quite a different case from the radio texts. In spontaneous speech directed at educated peers, educated speakers obviously have little motivation to attempt translations or explanations of English words for which NigP has no straightforward equivalent. One therefore does not find instances of the replacement of such words by circumlocutions. However, in the interviews and discussions, a speaker occasionally adds an explanation in NigP when he/she uses what he/she perceives as an English expression:

(43) dirty suppose dey Lagos State because dis *urban drift* wey dem dey talk about/ [...] *di urban drift na whereby say people dey comot from villages//* (V02 16ff)

'There must be refuse in Lagos State because this urban drift that people talk about [...] the urban drift is whereby people leave their villages.'

(44) because federal government talk say/ okay o dem go dey pay *minimum wage* of seven thousand five hundred// *minimum wage na im be say/ di person wey dey bottom of government/ when e start for bottom/ e go dey earn wetin? seven thousand five hundred//* (V01 118ff)[31]

'Because the federal government said they'd pay a minimum wage of seven thousand five hundred [naira]. Minimum wage means that the lowest government worker, when he/she starts at the bottom, he/she will earn what? Seven thousand five hundred.'

---

[30] The full dialogue between Chairman and Asabe about the union issue (R03 71-173) is one of the sound samples on the CD.
[31] The full interview subtext about the minimum wage issue (V01-3) is one of the sound samples on the CD.

(45) [...] dis issue of uhm-- (dem dey call am for) uh oyibo man dey call am "*brain drain*"// like *all di brains wey we get for dis country for instance/ every one of dem wan go America Germany London/ all dis advanced country/* (D05 172ff)

'this issue of uhm-- (they call it in) uh the white man calls it "brain drain". Like all the brains that we have in this country, for instance, every one of them wants to go to America, Germany, London, all these advanced countries'

In the only instance of such an explanation in the conversations, the speaker recounts how he explained an English word to an apparently less educated person:

(46) **B:** dat fight last for more dan one month o// maybe everything go-- so dem come introduce *curfew*//
A: for dat area?
B: for dat area now//
A: I hear dat {I hear dat story//}
B: {some people} come dey think say na coffee na im government wan give// [LAUGHTER] (me I come tell) I come tell di man say no be coffee o// na *curfew* be dis one o// *say within dis time nobody go waka for road//* (C09 40ff)

'**B:** That fight lasted for more than one month. Maybe everything would-- then they introduced a curfew.
A: In that area?
B: Yes, in that area.
A: I've heard about that.
B: And some people thought the government was going to distribute coffee. I then told the man that it's not coffee. That this is curfew. That within this time nobody is allowed to be on the road.'

The role of compounding as a strategy for speakers to create NigP equivalents for English lexical items is more difficult to assess than that of circumlocution. While circumlocutions are usually ad-hoc solutions, compounds form a gradient from ad-hoc creations to established ones. What one could say is that items like *craze man* (V02 127) or *motor people* (D03 120) (cf the discussion in 5.4.2.1) occur in the texts in the category "face-to-face speech" but that the speakers do not normally try to form new NigP words by compounding (or any other word formation strategy). For educated speakers of NigP, their knowledge of English is, in the context of face-to-face communication with educated peers, the one important resource for lexical enrichment.

5.5 Grammar

In this section, I will discuss the use of English function words and inflections in the corpus, continuing the analysis of the questionnaire data where it was left off in 5.4.1.3.

5.5.1 *Note on methodology*

The frequency of function words and inflections is often more difficult to assess than that of lexical items on the basis of the number of occurrences in relation to the corpus size alone because such items may have a high potential number of occurrences even in a small corpus. To use the number of occurrences in relation to that of a NigP equivalent is not always a viable option, either, especially when, as is the case with some prepositions and conjunctions in particular, both English and NigP have several alternative ways of expressing the meaning(s) associated with the item in question. In some cases I will therefore use an additional method to assess whether an item cited as an English element can be considered frequent in the NigP corpus or not: I will compare its frequency in the NigP corpus to that in an English corpus. For this purpose, I will, in the absence of a Nigerian English corpus, use a corpus of spoken British English consisting of selected text categories from ICE-GB, the British component of the International Corpus of English (see Greenbaum 1996). The composition of this corpus, which will henceforth be referred to as the ICE-GB subcorpus, can be seen in Table 5.3.

Table 5.3 The ICE-GB subcorpus

Text categories	Number of texts (total = 160)
Direct conversations	90
Broadcast discussions	20
Broadcast interviews	10
Broadcast news	20
Broadcast talks	20

As the table shows, the ICE-GB subcorpus is not exactly parallel to the NigP corpus, but there are many similarities. Like the NigP corpus, the ICE-GB subcorpus contains direct (i.e. face-to-face) speech and broadcasts, dialogues and monologues, scripted and unscripted speech and informal as well as more formal text types. The number of words per text in ICE is about 2,000, as in the NigP corpus, so that with 160 texts, the ICE-GB subcorpus is exactly four times as large as the NigP corpus. In the comparative analyses, the numbers of occurrences of the items in question in the ICE-GB subcorpus[32] will therefore be divided by four in order to make them comparable to those in the NigP corpus (unless the counts are normed to another basis).

5.5.2 *Prepositions*

NigP traditionally has few prepositions. The most common one is *for,* which expresses a wide range of spatial, temporal and other meanings (Agheyisi 1971: 70; Mann 1993a; Faraclas 1996: 60, 141ff). Faraclas (1996) refers to *for* as the "general preposition" and to other prepositions as "minor" ones. Examples (47) to (49) illustrate some of the uses of *for*:

(47)　how person go dey *for* e village/ [...] and e come to hear say *for* Lagos/ money dey Lagos nyafunyafu/ say if you come Lagos you don make money// e go run comot *for* village// (V02 23ff)

　　'How can somebody be in his village, and he/she comes to hear that there's a lot of money in Lagos, that if you've come to Lagos you've made money? He/she will run away from the village.'

---

[32] In counting the numbers of occurrences of the items in the ICE-GB subcorpus, I have made use of the ICE word class tags. Due in particular to the handling of certain multi-word elements in ICE, this leads to some minor differences between the items included in my manual analyses of the NigP corpus and the automatic analyses of the ICE-GB subcorpus, but as only very rough comparisons are intended, these do not detract from the usefulness of the ICE tags.

(48) Na only God know how many people don die *for* our bridge and road dem o, especially on top I.B.B. Bridge, sake of say dem no dey see sign well well *for* night, because light no dey *for* di bridge too. (A01 145ff)

'Only God knows how many people have died on our bridges and roads, especially on I.B.B. Bridge, because they can't see the signs well at night, because there are also no lights on the bridges.'

(49) see if you go *for* north na sharia// (C09 83)

'See, if you go to the north it's sharia.'

In addition, all authors agree that *with* (*witi, wìt*) is part of the NigP set of prepositions (Agheyisi 1971: 67; Mann 1993a: 63; Faraclas 1996: 61). Agheyisi (1971: 67) also mentions *abaot* 'about' as a preposition in NigP but adds that "it is highly restricted to the speech of people who speak standard English well". *To* 'to' may, according to Agheyisi (ibid.), be used in NigP as well, but "only in construction with *giv* 'give' (and a few other verbs)". About *fron* 'from', Agheyisi (1971: 68) says that it "occurs only as a bound affix in the word *fronkom* 'originate'". Faraclas (1996: 61), however, mentions *fròm* as a preposition in NigP. He finds that *fòr* does not commonly express motion away from a location, *fròm* being used instead (p 152). Faraclas (1996: 61) also observes that "in acrolectal speech, several other prepositions such as *tìl* 'until' and *òf* 'of' may occur as well". Mann (1993a: 63) cites *frọm, sins, til, àftà, bifọ, amọng, bitwin* and *nia* as examples of prepositions that may be used in NigP in addition to *for* and *with*.

Alternative ways of expressing prepositional meanings in NigP[33] include the use of locational or motion verbs followed by a place name or other noun without a preposition (cf e.g. *dey Lagos* and *come Lagos* in example (47) above) and serial verb constructions (Agheyisi 1971: 102ff; Faraclas 1996: 75ff), e.g. with *go* or *come* (directional) or with *take* (instrument/means/manner and other meanings):

(50) Where you wan make I take am *go*, Madam Asabe? Carry am *go* our room? (R02 205f)

'Where do you want me to take it to, Madam Asabe? To our room?'

(51) Now wetin carry you *come* hospital? (R06 101)

'Now what has brought you to the hospital?'

(52) dem just *take* di hanky rub di woman leg e just pray// (C02 33)

'They just rubbed the woman's leg with the hanky [and] he just prayed.'

(53) [...] dis country sha (na na) na di grace of God na im we go *take* survive sha// (C04 112f)

'It's by the grace of God that we'll survive in this country.'

The list of prepositions in Section 6 of Table B 1 begins with four items which have all been mentioned by previous authors as prepositions in NigP, if only in the educated or "acrolectal" variety: *of, to, from* and *about*. These seem relatively well-established, although *of* is somewhat problematic because of its tendency to occur in English discourse chunks or idiomatic expressions. *In* and *at*, which follow these items in frequency, do not appear to be established, as more than half of their occurrences are in parts of the corpus marked as non-NigP speech and other discourse chunks or idiomatic expressions in English.

---

[33] Cf also the NigP translations in Section 6 of Table B 1.

The next frequent item, *by,* has, like *in* and *at,* so far not been cited in any study as a NigP preposition, but its occurrence is not restricted in the same way as that of *in* and *at*. The remaining items in the list are considerably less frequent than those mentioned so far and cannot all be discussed. *According by* (item 6-10) is apparently derived from the distorted English/NigP of Chief Zebrudaya in the comedy serial *Masquerade*[34] (cf the comment on extract N01/6 in Table B 2), and *during by* (cf note 11 to Table B 1) may be an extension of this usage. The use of *according* and *during* with *by* is restricted to the news texts. Given the origin of *according by,* it is of course rather ironic that such usages should occur only in the news, of all text categories.

In Figure 5.2, the frequency in the NigP corpus of each of the more frequent prepositions among those cited in the questionnaire study, and in addition *for* and *with,* is compared to its frequency in the ICE-GB subcorpus.

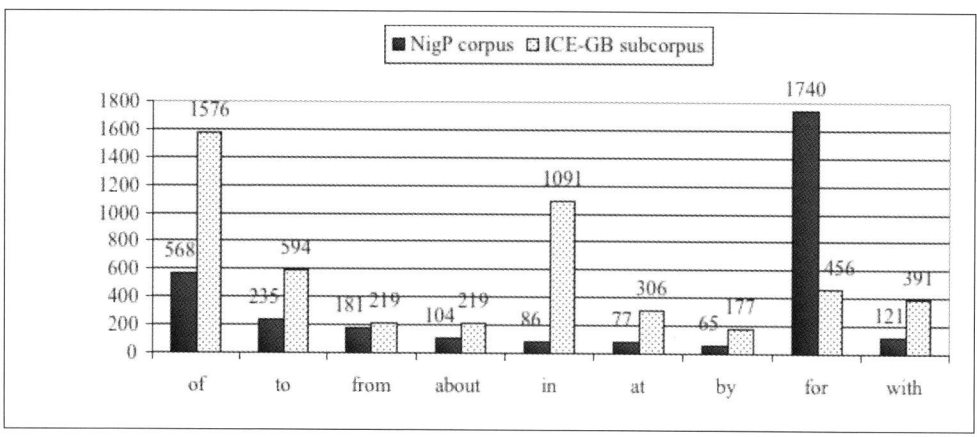

Figure 5.2 Frequency of selected prepositions in the NigP corpus and the ICE-GB subcorpus

The figure shows that all of these prepositions except *for* and *from*[35] are considerably less frequent in the NigP corpus than in the ICE-GB subcorpus, and *in* very much so. This result is of course due to the widespread use of *for,* which, as can also be seen in the figure, is much more frequent in the NigP corpus than in the ICE-GB subcorpus, but also to alternative expressions in NigP such as those mentioned above. For example, there are 78 occurrences of the locative copula *dey* + NP, 94 occurrences of non-serial *go/come* + NP, 37 occurrences of serial *go/come* + NP and 210 occurrences of serial *take* + NP. Thus, educated speakers may use more prepositions than is traditionally the case in NigP, but basically the system remains unchanged, with one general preposition, *for,* and some minor ones, as well as various alternative ways of expressing prepositional meanings.

---

[34] Cf also the section on NigP in the media, 3.3.
[35] Although *from* is a common preposition in the corpus, *for* is also used to indicate motion away from a location (cf e.g. example (48) above). After the verb *come,* only *from* is used, but after *comot* 'come out, go away' (also transitive 'take out, take away' and as serial verb 'out, away'), *for* is actually preferred (43 occurrences, as compared to 13 of *from*).

5.5.3 Conjunctions

In contrast to what was observed above for some of the prepositions, none of the conjunctions in Table B 1 (Section 7) has many occurrences in parts of the corpus marked as non-NigP speech or other discourse chunks or idiomatic expressions in English, and all of them also have very low numbers of citations. For low-frequency items, this obviously does not say much, but for the more frequent items, the data in Table B 1 suggest that they are well-established, and this is corroborated by the comparative data provided in Figure 5.3.

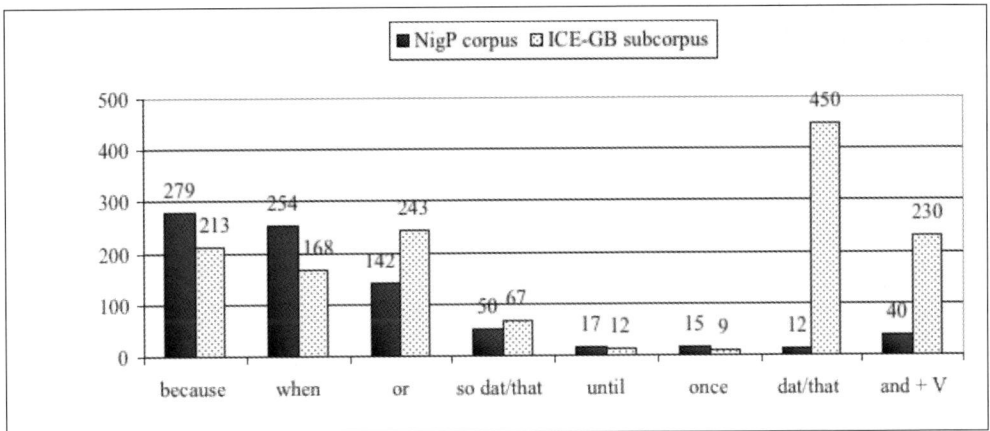

Figure 5.3 Frequency of selected conjunctions in the NigP corpus and the ICE-GB subcorpus

As can be seen in the figure, the two most frequent conjunctions in the NigP corpus of those cited in the questionnaires, *because* and *when*, are even more frequent than in the ICE-GB subcorpus. *Because* is probably a case of recent borrowing. In Agheyisi's (1971) English-NigP word list, it appears as an English item without a surface reflex in NigP (p 191), with *sekof* as its semantic equivalent in the language. (In the present corpus, there is only one occurrence of *sake of say* as a conjunction,[36] the one in the sentence cited as example (48) above, where it is probably used in order to avoid repetition of *because*.) Eze (1980: 125) observes that "for literate pidgin speakers 'because' may be used frequently", while Faraclas (1996: 43) states that *bìkôs* 'because' may be used "in most lects of Nigerian Pidgin". Elugbe & Omamor (1991: 131) cite *because* as an element that may be considered an English intrusion in a story in NigP from a popular magazine they have analyzed, but they qualify this analysis by saying that "the use of 'because' [...] is not particularly unusual nowadays". *When* (*wẹn*) is mentioned by Elugbe & Omamor (1991: 109) as a NigP subordinating conjunction, without any restrictions. According to Faraclas (1996: 42), however, it is an "acrolectal" item.

That *or* was cited in the questionnaire study may have to do with dialectal or idiolectal differences. Agheyisi (1971: 191) lists *or* as another English conjunction without a surface reflex in NigP and gives *abi* and *tabi* (both from Yoruba) as semantic equivalents in the

---

[36] In addition, there are three occurrences of *for sake of* as a preposition.

language. Eze (1980: 97f) mentions *or* and *abi*. He observes that the two are often interchangeable, but that in cases where one or both of the coordinated elements is an interrogative clause, most speakers would prefer *abi*. According to Faraclas (1996: 75), the coordinator generally used in NigP to denote an alternative is *òr*,[37] and *àbi* may be used only in alternative questions. In my NigP corpus, both *or* and *abi* are quite common, and their distribution is to a certain extent complementary, which explains why *or,* in spite of seeming to be well-established, is considerably less frequent than in the ICE-GB subcorpus (see Figure 5.3): *abi* is often (in about 46 of 72 occurrences as a conjunction[38]) used when one or both of the coordinated elements is an interrogative clause/sentence, as in examples (54) and (55) below; only one informant suggested it as a replacement for *or* in coordinate structures involving non-interrogative clauses/sentences or NPs (cf Table B 1, item 7-3), and only some speakers in the corpus use it in such structures ((56) and (57) are two examples).[39]

(54) If you look for dis our Jigida Local Government, na special place e be o, *abi* no be special place? (R06 217ff)

'If you look at our Jigida Local Government, it's a special place, or is it not a special place?'

(55) you say till now *abi* na before you dey talk about? (C10 25)

'Did you say till now, or is it before you were talking about?'

(56) all dem know be say when month end *abi* when year end dem must collect deir money// (D01 100f)

'All they know is that at the end of the month or at the end of the year, they must collect their money.'

(57) you go see one old woman *abi* one old man/ you no know where e from come out// (D01 146f)

'You'll see an old woman or an old man, you don't know where he/she has come from.'

Or is also used in constructions like those in (54) and (55), but not as commonly as *abi* (17 of 142 occurrences).

So dat/that, which follows *or* in the frequency ranking for the NigP corpus, is, as Figure 5.3 shows, not much less frequent in the NigP corpus than in the ICE-GB subcorpus. The following two items, *until* and *once,* are infrequent in both corpora. The complementizer *dat/that,* whose equivalent in NigP is *say,* occurs several hundreds of times per 80,000 words in the ICE-GB subcorpus, as is to be expected, but in the NigP corpus, it is, with only 12 occurrences, an extremely marginal element.

In addition to the conjunctions cited in the questionnaire study (excepting the very infrequent adverbial subordinators, items 7-8 to 7-11 in Table B 1), the data in Figure 5.3

---

[37] He also mentions the use of *ayda* 'either' between two coordinated elements; this usage is not attested in my corpus.

[38] *Abi* is also occurs as a sentence-initial or sentence-final yes-no question marker (cf Faraclas 1996: 8). There are a few instances of sentence-initial *abi* where both an analysis as a conjunction and an analysis as a question marker are possible.

[39] *Tabi* also occurs in the corpus, but it is much less frequent than *abi* (18 occurrences) and restricted to two text categories (news and advice). Very much unlike *abi,* it coordinates in all instances non-interrogative clauses/sentences or NPs.

also include *and* + VERB. I have included this construction because according to Todd's (1994: 3181) NigP "continuum" (see 2.2.7), *and*-coordination of VPs (in addition to English verb and pronoun forms, which are discussed in 5.5.5 and 5.5.4.4, respectively) is apparently supposed to be a feature of a variety that one could describe as "upper mesolectal" if such a continuum existed. In NigP (as also shown by Todd's examples for the lower range of the supposed continuum; see 2.2.7), coordinated VPs typically appear in serial constructions:

(58)   e bring paper bag of dirty come outside put am for middle of road enter motor drive comot// (V01 9ff)

'He brought out a paper bag of refuse, put it in the middle of the road, entered the car and drove away.'

Eze (1980: 93ff) observes that *and* is used in NigP to coordinate NPs and, to a lesser extent, sentences, but not VPs. Faraclas (1996: 74) has an example of *and*-coordination of VPs, but he points out that the serial construction is much more common. Figure 5.3 shows that verbs are in some cases preceded by *and* in the present corpus, but that in comparison to the extent of its use in English, the construction is not common.[40]

To summarize, NigP seems to have borrowed *because* from English in recent times and educated speakers also use a number of other adverbial subordinators which are not traditionally part of the NigP system, but *that*-complementization remains alien to the language and coordination of VPs by *and* has not become common, either.

5.5.4   The noun phrase

5.5.4.1   Determiners

The list of determiners in Section 8 of Table B 1 contains eight items, four with frequencies below ten, which will not be discussed here, and four more frequent ones: the quantifiers *some*,[41] *every*, and *many*, and the indefinite article, *a(n)*. According to Agheyisi (1971: 160f), none of these four items is part of NigP. Faraclas (1996: 71, 233), however, mentions *sọm* 'some' and *ẹvri* 'every' as quantifiers in NigP; *mẹni* is mentioned by him (p 71, p 235) as a stative verb ('be many'), and Elugbe & Omamor (1991: 97) cite *mẹni* 'many' as a determiner. The present data confirm for the educated variety that *some, every,* and *many* are well-established determiners in NigP. They have very low numbers of citations and do not occur mainly in parts of the corpus marked as non-NigP speech or other English discourse chunks or idiomatic expressions (see Table B 1, items 8-1, 8-3 and 8-4, respectively), and, as Figure 5.4 shows, they are all about as frequent or even more frequent than in the ICE-GB subcorpus. The case of the indefinite article is different. Faraclas (1996: 70, 173) is here in agreement with Agheyisi (1971: 160f) that singular indefinite

---

[40]   The 40 instances of *and* + VERB in the NigP corpus (cf Figure 5.3) are concentrated in two text categories, "drama" (23 occurrences) and "news" (9 occurrences). In all other text categories, the construction is very rare (3 occurrences each in the categories "interviews" and "conversations", 2 in the category "advice", and none in the category "discussions").

[41]   As in English, *some* can also be used in NigP as a determiner for singular count nouns with the meaning 'a certain', but, in contrast to Ghanaian Pidgin (see Huber 1999: 192f), it does not function as indefinite article.

nouns in NigP take either the numeral *one* (*wan/w<u>o</u>n*) as article (cf e.g. *one old woman* or *one old man* in example (57) above) or no article, as in example (59) below, but not *a(n)*.

(59) I don dey pass for *road* one day when I see *man* with *motor*/ e put *tie* for neck/ wetin e do? (V01 7f)

'I was passing along a road one day when I saw a man with a car, he was wearing a tie, [and] what did he do?'

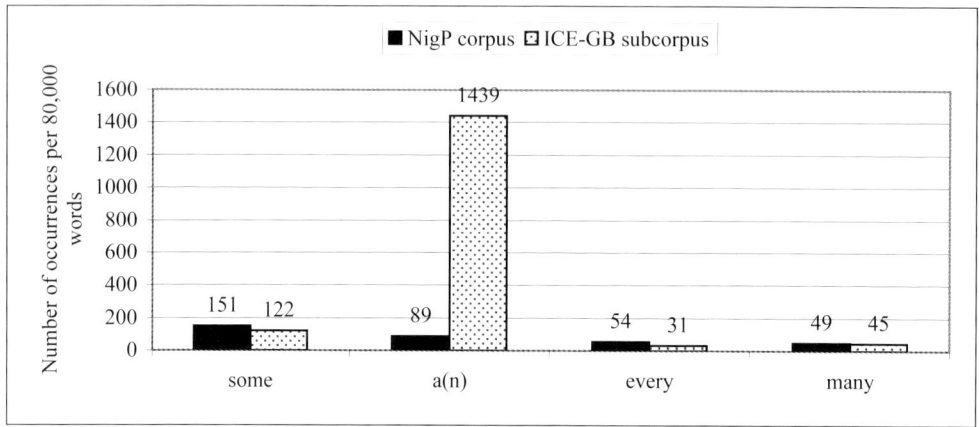

Figure 5.4 Frequency of selected determiners in the NigP corpus and the ICE-GB subcorpus

While *a(n)* does occur in the present corpus, it is clear from Figure 5.4 that its frequency is very low in comparison to the ICE-GB subcorpus. Moreover, more than half of its occurrences in the NigP corpus are accounted for by parts of the corpus marked as non-NigP speech and other discourse chunks or idiomatic expressions in English (see Table 1, item 8-2). Thus, while some of the quantifiers now in common usage may not have been established a few decades ago, the questionnaire and corpus data do not provide any indication that determiner usage in educated NigP differs substantially from what Faraclas (1996) observes in his description of the NigP core system.

5.5.4.2 *Plural marking*

In most Atlantic Creoles, the plural of nouns is optionally marked by a free morpheme homophonous with the third person plural pronoun (Holm 1988: 193). NigP also has a pluralizer of this type, postnominal *dem*. This is illustrated below by examples from the corpus:

(60) Di thing wey we go talk put today, na how to train our *pikin dem* [...]. (A04 4f)

'What we're going to talk about today is how to educate our children'

(61) [...] Kwara State and Lagos State Government don kneel down dey beg all dem *worker dem* make dem quench dat minimum wage war o go back to work. (N01 122ff)

'the Kwara and Lagos State Governments have appealed to their workers to stop that minimum wage war and go back to work.'

(62) Na di vice chancellor of di university Professor Roger Makanjuola na im talk dis one for Osun State for one papa and mama talk-talk meeting to discuss how life go take better for *student dem*. (N03 165 ff)

'It was the vice chancellor of the university, Professor Roger Makanjuola, who said this in Osun State at a meeting for parents to discuss how the life of students can be improved.'

(63) Make we try see say all our *street dem* dey clean. (A03 138f)[42]
'We should try to see to it that all our streets are clean.'

In the early studies by Mafeni (1971: 110) and Agheyisi (1971: 54), postnominal *dem* is the only plural marker mentioned. Elugbe & Omamor (1991: 97f) also mention only postnominal *dem* as a plural marker in NigP (apart from quantifiers like *plẹnti/mẹni* 'many'), adding that definite nouns (cf also examples (60), (61) and (63) above) are "commonly" marked for plurality in this way, and indefinite ones (cf example (62) above) "sometimes". A definite/indefinite distinction with regard to plural marking is a widely attested feature in Atlantic Creoles (Holm 1988: 193; Alleyne 1980: 100), but there seem to be differences among the English-based varieties as to whether the distinction is absolute or, as adumbrated by Elugbe & Omamor for NigP, merely a tendency. Mufwene (1986b) writes that in Jamaican Creole the pluralizer *dem* occurs only when a possessive or a definite article is present in the NP (p 40), and that in Gullah, too, pluralization with *dem* presupposes definiteness (p 45). By contrast, Jones (1990: 314) observes that in Krio some, though not all, indefinite NPs allow pluralization by a reflex of English *them*.[43] The two varieties analysed by Mufwene and Krio also seem to differ with respect to another factor which is often said to affect plural marking in English-based Atlantic Creoles, the presence of a numeral or quantifier in the NP. According to Mufwene (1986b: 40, 44), post- and prenominal *dem* in Jamaican Creole and Gullah, respectively, do not co-occur with numerals or quantifiers, whereas in Krio, according to Jones (1990: 313), the postnominal pluralizer is often used redundantly in NPs with number-transparent determiners. For NigP, no author has so far claimed that postnominal *dem* and other means of plural marking in the NP are mutually exclusive (cf also my examples (61) and (63), with the quantifier *all*), although it has also not been said explicitly that they may co-occur. A third factor that is known to affect plural marking in Atlantic and other P/Cs, though not specifically the use of *dem* in NigP, is semantic and concerns the feature [±animate] or [±human]. Holm (1988: 193) notes that the pluralizer in Atlantic Creoles in general is most frequently used with animate nouns, adding, however, that this is not always the case (he cites an example from NigP in which *dem* is combined with an inanimate noun; cf also example (63) above). Sebba (1996: 209) observes for Jamaican Creole that postnominal *dem* is used especially with human nouns. In Tok Pisin, which has *ol* (< *all*) preposed to the noun as a pluralizer, the development of plural marking in the stabilization phase is reported by Mühlhäusler (1981: 44) to have been subject to an animacy hierarchy (among other constraints), with overt marking favoured for animate and especially human nouns.

A number of studies (e.g. Rickford 1986, Mufwene 1986b, Jones 1990, Mühlhäusler 1981, 1986) have shown that in English-based P/Cs co-existing with the lexifier, plurality can be marked not only by the P/C independent morphemes but also by the English *-s*

---

[42] In constructions like this one, where NOUN *dem* is in subject position and not followed by any postmodification such as a prepositional phrase or a relative clause, the plural construction is distinguished from left dislocation only by intonation. I have checked such cases against the recording.

[43] Jones does not specify under what conditions indefinite NPs allow the use of this morpheme.

suffix, in particular in "mesolectal/acrolectal" or "anglicized" varieties. The -s plural is described as a development in "decreolization" (Rickford 1986) or the "post-pidgin" phase (Mühlhäusler 1981, 1986). According to the Bickertonian theory of decreolization, new forms from English always appear first in Creole functions (see especially Bickerton 1980), and one might therefore expect the -s suffix to be used in the same environments as the P/C plural markers, but some, though not all, studies contradict this prediction. Mühlhäusler (1981: 60) concludes from his findings that "the emergence of -s does not follow any of the hierarchies that determine pluralization in non-anglicized dialects of Tok Pisin", and on this basis he disputes Bickerton's new form – old function model of change in decreolization (1986: 563). Romaine (1992: 235), in contrast, does find some evidence for an influence of animacy as well as of another factor which Mühlhäusler found to be relevant to the development of the *ol* plural (the syntactic function of the noun) on the use of the -s suffix in Tok Pisin.[44] Mufwene (1986b) observes that in Gullah, -s – unlike the Gullah pluralizer – co-occurs with numerals and quantifiers (p 44), but he also argues, contra Rickford (1986), that an individuated/non-individuated distinction, corresponding to Gullah grammar, is relevant to the -s plural (pp 49ff). For Krio the -s suffix is described by Jones (1990: 319) as being often redundant, which, as noted above, he says applies to the Krio plural marker as well, but Jones also points out that -s is sometimes complementary to the Krio plural marker, being used precisely in those indefinite NPs in which the latter cannot occur.

The use of -s has also been reported for NigP. Faraclas (1996) claims that postnominal *dem* is the most common plural marker in NigP (p 169) but mentions the use of -s in "acrolectal varieties", "especially", he adds, "with items recently borrowed from English" (p 171). Jibril (1995: 237) cites English plural forms from one of his sample texts (a news broadcast) and remarks that the use of -s instead of postnominal *dem* "is becoming increasingly common". Elugbe (1995: 289f) finds that pluralization is always by means of -s in the Bendel Television news broadcast transcribed in Elugbe & Omamor (1991: 168ff), which he criticizes as a violation of the NigP plural formation "rule" as described by himself and his co-author in that book (see the discussion above). Tagliamonte, Poplack & Eze (1997: 109) report that 59% of the plural nouns they have extracted from their corpus have the -s suffix; zero accounts for 39% of their data, while the percentages given for postnominal *dem* as well as double marking (i.e. -s + *dem*) are lower than 1.

The influence of semantic and syntactic factors on the -s plural in NigP has so far been investigated only by Tagliamonte, Poplack & Eze (1997).[45] One of their findings is that nouns of weight, measure, and monetary denomination favour the -s plural, in contrast to what obtains in English (p 110). Furthermore, [+human] nouns strongly favour overt marking (p 117). The authors also report that number-neutral determination structures, including possessives, definite articles, and undetermined nouns, favour zero, while number-transparent determiners such as numerals and quantifiers tend to lead to overt

---

[44] Smith (2002: 72f) confirms Romaine's observation on the relevance of animacy in that several human nouns top the list of nouns commonly occurring with -s plurals in his corpus. However, he also points out that in some cases the common occurrence of -s may be attributable to the circumstances of the adoption of a word, as some words (e.g. *perents* 'parents') were certainly heard mainly in the plural.

[45] In addition to semantic and syntactic factors, the authors analyse two phonological ones, preceding and following phonological segment. They find that these factors do not have a significant effect on plural marking (p 110).

marking by -s (p 114). This, they go on to point out, runs counter to the "received wisdom" that plural markers in English-based Creoles are used only where number needs to be disambiguated and that they co-occur with definite determiners. As regards determination or reference, they also find, however, that it is the undetermined or generic nouns which show the greatest propensity to remain bare, and that generic nouns differ significantly from non-generic ones (pp 116f).[46] Tagliamonte, Poplack & Eze conclude (pp 125f) that plural marking in NigP is conditioned by animacy and nominal reference (generic versus non-generic), which, they suggest, are substratal features, as they are attested in Igbo (the first language of eight of their twelve informants) and other West African languages; thus, they argue, educated NigP speakers use the English plural *form*, but its *use* is subject to factors alien to the grammar of plural marking in any variety of English.

Table 5.4 Distribution of plural markers in the NigP corpus

Plural marker[a]	Number	%
Ø	498	38
-s	600	46
dem	184	14
-s dem	34	3
TOTAL	1316[b]	101[c]

[a] In addition to the plural forms in the table, there are three instances of reduplication of a noun to indicate plurality, a strategy also noted by Faraclas (1996: 169). (In one of these cases, *dem* is used in addition to reduplication.) Because of their extreme marginality, the reduplicated plurals have not been included in the table and will not be taken into account in subsequent analyses, either.

[b] That the total number is the same as in Tagliamonte, Poplack & Eze (1997) – they also analyse exactly 1316 plural nouns – is a coincidence.

[c] Percentages do not always add up to 100 due to rounding.

My data on the -s suffix in Appendix B (Table B 1, item 9-1) also suggest that the -s plural has become a very common form in educated NigP,[47] but its use needs to be compared to that of *dem* and zero. I have therefore analysed marking on all nouns with plural reference in the corpus except irregular ones.[48] The results are displayed in Table 5.4. Apart from irregular nouns, these data exclude non-NigP speech, neutralization contexts and a number of cases in which plural marking is strongly favoured or disfavoured, including proper names such as *United Nations*, nouns which in English occur only in the plural (in a given

---

[46] The authors emphasize the generic factor but concede that the effects of generic reference and undetermined status cannot be disentangled, as these two categories are strongly correlated (pp 113, 118n3).

[47] If it is taken into account that of the 37 direct citations, 19 are due to one informant whose judgment is very likely to have been influenced by the linguistic literature (cf note 13 to Table B 1), it also appears quite acceptable.

[48] In addition to nouns, regular plural marking also concerns *one* and *oder* in their pronominal uses. These cases are included in the analysis.

sense), e.g. *goods*, *arms*, and fixed expressions, e.g. *at times* (categorically marked by *-s*) or *join hand* 'join hands [fig.]' (categorically bare).[49]

The table shows that the proportion of zero is about the same as in Tagliamonte, Poplack & Eze's results, but *-s*, although the most common marker, is considerably less frequent than in their data, and the *dem* plural is, with 14%, not a negligible category. An analysis of plural marking according to text category (Figure 5.5) reveals that the differences between Tagliamonte, Poplack & Eze's results and mine with respect to the choice of overt markers are due to the inclusion in my corpus of text types which are not part of their study. The figure shows that as far as plural marking is concerned, the six text categories in my corpus fall into two major groups, which I will call the "*s*-group" and the "*dem*-group". In the *s*-group, which comprises the three subcategories of face-to-face speech and the broadcast subcategory "drama", the *-s* suffix is the preferred plural marker; postnominal *dem* is virtually not used. One may further note that within this group, the category "conversations" stands out as the one with the highest proportion of *-s* plurals.

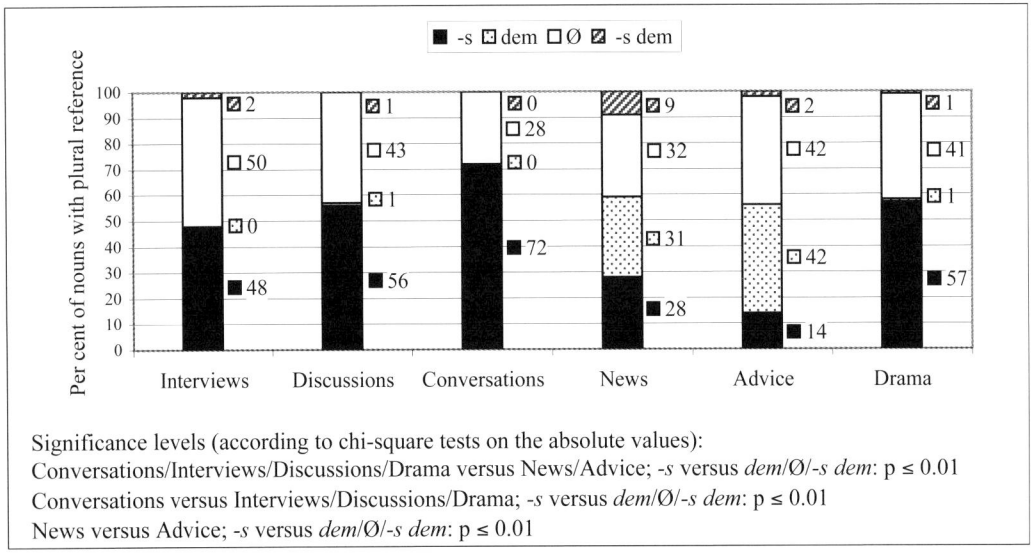

Significance levels (according to chi-square tests on the absolute values):
Conversations/Interviews/Discussions/Drama versus News/Advice; *-s* versus *dem*/Ø/*-s dem*: p ≤ 0.01
Conversations versus Interviews/Discussions/Drama; *-s* versus *dem*/Ø/*-s dem*: p ≤ 0.01
News versus Advice; *-s* versus *dem*/Ø/*-s dem*: p ≤ 0.01

Figure 5.5 Distribution of plural markers in the NigP corpus by text category

The broadcast subcategories "news" and "advice" – the *dem*-group – have a very significantly lower proportion of *-s* plurals than the remainder of the corpus, and it is these texts which account for the 14% of *dem* plurals in the results for the whole corpus. The reason for the frequent use of *dem* in the news and advice texts is apparently not only accommodation to a target audience which (actually or supposedly) uses this form, but also a perception that it is the correct or "standard" form appropriate to language use in a formal context. When I asked one of the newscasters who had explained to me that *-s* plurals should be rendered by *dem* in the news translations whether *-s* was not a possible form in NigP as well, I was told that no, the correct form was *dem*. In spite of this, the newscasters

---

[49] The number of occurrences of *-s* given in Table B 1 includes *-s* plurals not counted in the present analysis and *-s dem* plurals.

use -s significantly more often than the speakers in the advice texts, and the news texts are also the only ones in the corpus in which doubly marked nouns, i.e. those with -s dem, are not an insignificant category. This probably reflects the conflicting pressures of an English script (particularly in on-air translations) and conscious pidginization.

The results presented so far are clear evidence that postnominal dem is a form which has virtually disappeared from the speech of the average educated NigP speaker and is used only by some broadcasters as a conscious pidginization strategy, and that the -s suffix has become the norm. -s plurals are found not only with nouns in the corpus that could be characterized as new borrowings or single-word switches, but also with established NigP words like *thing* or *place,* although they are rare with nouns of non-English origin.[50] One can thus say that the -s suffix has been borrowed into educated NigP. Its use is, like that of postnominal dem, optional, and the question that remains now is what factors govern variability in plural marking in the present corpus.

I have analysed the influence on plural marking of the semantic factor groups measure/non-measure and [±human], and the syntactic aspect of determination structure. The latter is operationalized as two separate factor groups, presence/absence of a definite determiner and presence/absence of a number-transparent determiner. For the analysis of the factor group [±human] and the two syntactic factor groups, I have used VARBRUL. The factor group measure/non-measure had to be excluded from the variable rule analyses. As can be seen in Table 5.5, measure nouns never take dem or -s dem as plural marker,[51] which means that VARBRUL would have rejected the factor measure as a "knockout factor" in the analysis of dem and -s dem.

Table 5.5 Distribution of plural markers in the NigP corpus: measure nouns versus non-measure nouns

Plural marker	Measure nouns[a]		Non-measure nouns	
	Number	%	Number	%
Ø	7	9	491	40
-s	69	91	531	43
dem	0	0	184	15
-s dem	0	0	34	3
TOTAL	76	100	1240	101

[a] Most of these nouns are temporal nouns in measure phrases (*for two months, for four years* etc.). Monetary denomination is not included because the name of the Nigerian currency, *naira,* is an invariant noun which never takes -s or dem as plural marker.

Table 5.5 shows in addition that zero plurals are also rare and that marking by -s is almost categorical for measure nouns. Since they are comparatively few and clearly exceptional with regard to plural marking, these nouns have been excluded from the variable rule

---

[50] Conversely, postnominal dem is by no means restricted to established NigP words; cf e.g. *Federal Information Centre dem* (N02 17), *pension and gratuity dem* (N03 140), *cooperative organisation dem* (N01 136).
[51] The non-occurrence of dem and -s dem with measure nouns is not due to non-occurrence of such nouns in the dem-group: 23 of the 76 measure nouns are in texts in this group.

analyses. Variable rule analyses have been carried out for the whole corpus as well as for the *s*-group and the *dem*-group separately. In preliminary analyses of all four categories of plural marking, I found that *-s dem* always patterns with *dem*, and I have therefore collapsed this rather minor category with *dem*. Table 5.6a gives the results for the whole corpus.

Table 5.6a   Contribution of syntactic and semantic factors to the probability of selection of plural markers in the NigP corpus, according to separate binomial variable rule analyses for each category of plural marking[a]

Factors analysed		Ø	-s	(-s) dem
Definite determiner	*present*	0.50	0.47	0.55*
	absent	0.50	0.52	0.46*
Number-transparent determiner	*present*	0.47	0.50	0.55
	absent	0.52	0.50	0.48
[human]	+	0.42*	0.54*	0.56*
	−	0.55*	0.48*	0.46*

[a]   The results for factor groups selected as significant in the stepwise selection procedure included in IVARB, the binomial analysis tool in the VARBRUL package, are marked by an asterisk.

Table 5.6a shows, firstly, that the factor group presence/absence of a definite determiner does not have any effect whatsoever on whether a noun remains bare or is overtly marked for plurality. The probability that zero will be selected is exactly the same for nouns with definite determiners as for those without. However, the factor group has an influence on the choice of overt marker: *(-s) dem* has a significantly higher probability of occurrence in definite than in indefinite NPs, while *-s* has a slightly higher probability of occurrence in indefinite NPs, although for *-s* the tendency is not statistically significant. Secondly, the table shows that the factor group presence/absence of a number-transparent determiner does not have a significant effect on plural marking. *-s* seems to be totally indifferent to this factor group; *(-s) dem* has a higher probability of occurrence in number-transparent NPs, but this is not a statistically significant result. Thirdly, it is apparent from this table that it is the factor group [±human] that has the strongest effect on plural marking in the corpus. This factor group was selected as significant for all three categories of plural marking. The probabilities indicate that [+human] nouns disfavour zero and tend to be overtly marked for plurality by either *-s* or *(-s) dem*. However, in the analysis of the *s*-group alone (see Table 5.6b, opposite), the tendency for [+human] nouns to attract overt marking fails to reach statistical significance. Table 5.6b also shows that the factor group presence/absence of a definite determiner does not yield a significant result for what are virtually the only plural markers in this group of texts, zero and *-s,* as was also the case in the analyses of these markers for the whole corpus, but the factor group presence/absence of a number-transparent determiner has a significant influence: marking by *-s* is more likely in environments which are not number-transparent. That this was not apparent in the results for the whole corpus is due to a different behaviour of *-s* in the *dem*-group (see Table 5.6c, opposite).

Table 5.6b Contribution of syntactic and semantic factors to the probability of selection of plural markers in the text categories "interviews", "discussions", "conversations" and "drama" in the NigP corpus, according to separate binomial variable rule analyses for each category of plural marking[a]

Factors analysed		Ø	-s
Definite determiner	present	0.53	0.47
	absent	0.48	0.52
Number-transparent determiner	present	0.54	0.45*
	absent	0.48	0.52*
[human]	+	0.47	0.52
	−	0.52	0.49

[a] The results for factor groups selected as significant in the stepwise selection procedure included in IVARB, the binomial analysis tool in the VARBRUL package, are marked by an asterisk.

Table 5.6c Contribution of syntactic and semantic factors to the probability of selection of plural markers in the text categories "news" and "advice" in the NigP corpus, according to separate binomial variable rule analyses for each category of plural marking[a]

Factors analysed		Ø	-s	(-s) dem
Definite determiner	present	0.44	0.46*	0.58*
	absent	0.54	0.53*	0.44*
Number-transparent determiner	present	0.32*	0.63*	0.58
	absent	0.59*	0.44*	0.46
[human]	+	0.29*	0.44	0.72*
	−	0.59*	0.53	0.40*

[a] The results for factor groups selected as significant in the stepwise selection procedure included in IVARB, the binomial analysis tool in the VARBRUL package, are marked by an asterisk.

Table 5.6c shows that *-s* has a significant tendency to occur in number-transparent environments. In addition, the tendency for *-s* to function complementarily to *(-s) dem* with respect to the factor group presence/absence of a definite determiner is significant in the *dem*-group. Table 5.6c also shows that *-s* is significantly more likely to occur when no definite determiner is present in the NP. *-s dem* is favoured when there is a definite determiner, as could already be seen in Table 5.6a. The other significant tendency that has already been observed for *(-s) dem* in the analysis of the whole corpus, that it is more likely to be used with [+human] nouns, becomes very pronounced if the analysis is restricted to the *dem*-group, while *-s* does not display the same tendency in this group of texts. The variable rule analyses show, thus, that two of the three factor groups, presence/absence of a definite determiner and [±human], have a significant effect on plural marking by *dem* in the corpus. The observation that *dem* has a significant tendency to co-occur with definite determiners is in line with what previous authors have observed for NigP and other Atlantic Creoles. Although this has not previously been reported for NigP, plural marking by *dem* is in the present corpus also significantly more likely for nouns with the feature [+human] than for those with the feature [−human]. For -s, however, the evidence for an influence of the factor group [±human] is not so clear. In the s-group, -s is, like *dem* in the *dem*-group, more likely to be used with [+human] nouns, but the tendency was selected as significant only in the analysis of the whole corpus, and not in the separate analysis of the s-group. As regards the factor group presence/absence of a definite determiner, not only does -s consistently not follow the behaviour of *dem,* a contrary tendency for -s to appear in indefinite NPs was even selected as significant in one analysis, that of the *dem*-group. I would therefore argue that plural marking by -s in educated NigP is not generally conditioned by an underlying Creole or substrate grammar. It seems, rather, that the introduction of -s has also affected the grammar of plural marking in educated NigP and that we are not dealing with a new form – old function type of change.

5.5.4.3 *Nigerian Pidgin possessive constructions and the s-genitive*

NigP expresses possessive relations in the noun phrase by an "associative/possessive construction" (Faraclas 1996: 67ff) in which the possessor and the possessed are juxtaposed (64), or a variant thereof with an intervening third person possessive pronoun (65):

(64) how person (go) go cook for house/ e go pack all di dirty for house go throway for *anoder man land/* because say dem never build house for dere// (V02 65ff)

'How can somebody cook in his house, and then clear away all the rubbish in the house and go and throw it onto somebody else's land because no house has been built there?'

(65) But na for *Papa Vero e hand* di money dey. (R05 193f)

'But it is in Papa Vero's hand that the money is', i.e. 'but it is Papa Vero who has the money'.

When *dem* occurs between two nouns, the construction is ambiguous between an associative/possessive construction without possessive pronoun, in which case *dem* would function as plural marker, and a construction with *dem* as third person plural possessive pronoun:

(66) E come explain say if dem deal with dem well well as im talk am, e go bring respect to Nigeria, especial especial as e be say *taxpayer dem money* dey inside dis money wey e dey talk so. (N03 159ff)

'He [president of the Nigeria Labour Congress] explained that if they deal with them [corrupt public officers] properly as suggested by him, it'll bring respect to Nigeria, especially since taxpayers' money is among the money in question.'

In contrast to the -s plural, the -s genitive (Table B 1, item 9-3) has not been integrated into educated NigP. Table 5.7 makes it clear that it is the exception in contexts where English would require or favour the s-genitive and that the NigP associative/possessive construction (without or, occasionally, with an intervening possessive pronoun) is much more common.[52]

---

[52] Possessive constructions with the preposition *of* are not taken into account in the present analysis, as prepositions have already been discussed in 5.5.2.

Table 5.7 Possessive constructions in the NigP corpus (NPs taking -'s in English[a])

Construction		Number of occurrences
s-genitive		16 (of which 10 in proper names or fixed expressions[b])
NigP associative/ possessive construction	without possessive pronoun	115[c]
	with possessive pronoun	4
	ambiguous	8
	TOTAL	143

[a] The analysis is based on the categories of nouns cited in Quirk et al. (1985: 324) as taking the s-genitive (except for the rather vague category of "other nouns 'of special relevance to human activity'").

[b] See note 14 to Table B 1; another 2 of the 16 occurrences of the s-genitive are in whole noun phrases/noun phrase fragments in English cited in the questionnaires (see Table B 1, items 15-2-28, 15-2-36).

[c] Excluding occurrences in neutralization contexts.

5.5.4.4 *Pronouns*

The list of pronouns in Table B 1 (Section 10) contains some personal and possessive pronouns (*our, deir/their, de/they, she, you* [pl.]*, your* [pl.]*, her*), several indefinite pronouns (*everybody, nobody, anybody, somebody, everywhere*[53]*, everyone*) and one *wh*-pronoun form occurring in interrogative and nominal relative clauses (*what*). I will first discuss personal and possessive pronouns in the corpus in some detail, and then briefly some indefinite pronouns and the pronoun *what*.

NigP has two types of personal pronouns, bound (or non-emphatic) and free (or emphatic) pronouns, with a subject-object distinction in some persons, and a single set of possessive pronouns (Agheyisi 1971: 122ff; Elugbe & Omamor 1991: 89ff; Faraclas 1986, 1996: 174ff). Bound pronouns occur in non-emphatic non-contrastive contexts (67), while free pronouns are used in emphatic or contrastive contexts, e.g. as the focussed element in a cleft sentence (68):

(67)   make *I* tell una something o/ (C03 196)
       'Let me tell you something'

(68)   Oga abeg o, no tell am say na *me* tell you o. (R10 214)
       'Sir, please don't tell him that it was me who told you.'

The set of possessive pronouns is used in determinative function. Independent possessives are formed by combining the determinative forms with *own*:[54]

(69)   But you see, dis your boot [...] e different from *my own*. (R06 161f)
       'But you see, your boots are different from mine.'

---

[53] In pronominal use, e.g. *everywhere quiet* 'everywhere is quiet' (A02 132).

[54] This pattern is very stable in the corpus. There is only a single occurrence of an English independent possessive pronoun, *mine* (R06 236), and this is in a sentence marked as non-NigP speech.

Table 5.8 gives an overview of the NigP personal/possessive pronoun forms based on three previous studies (Agheyisi 1971: 122, Elugbe & Omamor 1991: 90f, Faraclas 1996: 179).

Table 5.8   NigP personal and possessive pronouns according to previous studies

Pronoun category	According to	Personal pronouns				Possessive pronouns
		Bound		Free[a]		
		Subject	Object	Subject	Object	
1st pers. sing.	Agheyisi (1971)	a	mi	mi		mi/ma
	Elugbe/Omamor (1991)	a	mi	mi		mai
	Faraclas (1996)	à	mì	mi	mi	mà
2nd pers. sing.	Agheyisi (1971)	yu	yu	yu		yu/yuo
	Elugbe/Omamor (1991)	yu	yu	yu		yọ
	Faraclas (1996)	yù	yù	yu	yu	yọ̀
3rd pers. sing.	Agheyisi (1971)	i	am	im		im
	Elugbe/Omamor (1991)	i	am	in		in
	Faraclas (1996)	ìm	-àm	im	am	ìm
1st pers. pl.	Agheyisi (1971)	wi	wi	wi		wi
	Elugbe/Omamor (1991)	wi	wi/ọs	wi		wi/awa
	Faraclas (1996)	wì	ọ̀s	wi	ọs	àwa
2nd pers. pl.	Agheyisi (1971)	una	una	una		una
	Elugbe/Omamor (1991)	una	una	una		una
	Faraclas (1996)	ùnà	ùnà	ùnà	ùnà	ùnà
3rd pers. pl.	Agheyisi (1971)	dem	dem	dem		dem
	Elugbe/Omamor (1991)	dẹm	dẹm	dẹm		dẹm
	Faraclas (1996)	dèm	dèm	dem	dem	dèm

[a]   Whereas Agheyisi (1971) and Elugbe & Omamor (1991) do not distinguish subject and object forms of the free pronouns, Faraclas (1996) does. According to Faraclas (1996), free object pronouns are used e.g. when a pronoun in object function is postmodified by a relative clause (cf his example (786), p 176) or when it is the object in a comparative construction with *pass* (cf his examples (511) to (515), p 109). I adhere to Faraclas's distinction. Free object pronouns are, however, rare in the data in comparison to free subject pronouns because in what is the most common function of free pronouns, that of the focussed constituent in cleft sentences, subject forms are, it seems, generally used in NigP, irrespective of whether the focussed constituent functions as subject or object in the underlying sentence – contrary to the situation in English. Cf the following example from Elugbe & Omamor (1991: 91; emphasis added): "*No-bi in a de fain, na yu* 'It is not him I am looking for, it is you'". In my corpus, *im* is used consistently in such cases (a total of 53), and these pronouns are included in the count for subject pronouns in Tables 5.9 and 5.12. (The only other category of pronoun apart from *im/am* for the third person singular (occasionally also plural, see Table 5.12) where free subject and object forms are distinct, the first person plural pronoun, does not occur in this type of construction in the corpus.)

In the first and second person singular, there is, in the present corpus, variation only between monophthongal and diphthongal pronunciations of the first person bound subject pronoun *I* ([a/ai][55]) and the two possessive pronouns *my* and *your* ([ma/mai] and [jɔ/juɔ], respectively); *me* and *you* do not occur as possessive pronouns. The third person singular forms are shown in Table 5.9.

---

[55]   In his detailed study of pronoun usage in a subsample from his full sample, Faraclas (1986: 7) found that all speakers, regardless of their social status, vary in their pronunciation of the first person singular bound subject pronoun between the monophthongal and the diphthongal form.

Table 5.9 Third person singular personal and possessive pronouns in the NigP corpus

Pronoun forms			As personal pronoun			As possessive pronoun
			Subject		Object	
		Pronoun type	Number of occurrences[a]	Pronoun type	Number of occurrences[a]	Number of occurrences[a]
Masc.[b]	e[c]	bound	528	-	-	21
	im[d]	bound/free	271	bound	2	125
	am	bound/free	2	bound	181	-
	him	bound/free	23 {15}	bound	2 [1]	9 {8}
	he	bound/free	11 [5] (1) {4}	-	-	-
	his	-	-	-	-	9 [2] (3)
Fem.	e[c]	bound	93	-	-	6
	im[d]	bound/free	16	-	-	33
	am	-	-	bound	71	-
	him	free	1 {1}	-	-	4 {4}
	she	bound/free	73 [3]	-	-	-
	her	-	-	-	1 [1]	7
Neuter	e[c]	bound	586	-	-	1
	im[d]	bound/free	150	-	-	12
	am	-	-	bound	563	-
	him	-	-	-	-	-
	it	bound	24 [13] (9)	bound	19 [8] (4)	-
	its	-	-	-	-	-

[a] Of which number indicated in square brackets in parts of the corpus marked as non-NigP speech, number indicated in round brackets in other discourse chunks or idiomatic expressions in English cited in the questionnaire study, and number indicated in braces in drama texts.
[b] Pronouns referring to persons of undetermined sex are counted as masculine.
[c] Pronounced [i].
[d] Pronounced [im/in/ĩ].

One can see in the table that there is some variation between the gender-neutral NigP forms – *e* (bound subject and occasionally possessive), *im* (free and bound subject, possessive) and *am* (bound object) – and the gender-differentiated English forms *he/she/it*, *him/her/it* and *his/her* for subject, object and possessive, respectively. However, with the exception of *she*, all of the English forms are very infrequent compared to the NigP ones and tend to occur mainly in parts of the corpus marked as non-NigP speech and other discourse chunks or idiomatic expressions in English. *Him* is exceptional among the English forms in that it also occurs in non-English functions, namely as masculine or feminine subject or possessive pronoun, but these usages are not common. Besides, most occurrences of *him* in these functions, as well as some of the occurrences of *he* outside non-NigP speech, are in the drama texts, and these very likely reflect the influence of the script rather than the speakers' natural speech habits. Pronoun forms with an initial *h* are sometimes used in NigP texts written in English-based orthography, without the writer necessarily intending the *h* to be pronounced. For example, I found the spellings *he* and *him* in one of the news scripts, that from which Text N03-4 was read, yet there are no pronoun forms with an initial *h* in this text. As they read their own scripts, the newscasters will of course not be misled by the spelling, but the drama texts are a different case because they are not read by the writers themselves. For example, in the *Rainbow City* script, third person singular pronoun forms with an initial *h,* especially *him*, are quite frequent, and although the *h* is usually not pronounced, it has in a few cases apparently been carried over into the recorded version (see Table 5.10).[56] The use of the form *him* instead of *im* in several of the latter's functions is thus largely an idiosyncrasy of the drama texts which could be explained as a spelling pronunciation, although the drama texts are also idiosyncratic with respect to another feature which cannot be attributed to the spelling system: as demonstrated in Figure 5.6, the frequent use of *she* as the third person singular feminine subject pronoun is characteristic only of the drama texts. In all other text categories, the gender-neutral NigP forms are clearly preferred.

Table 5.10 Third person singular pronoun forms with and without initial *h* in *Rainbow City* texts

Pronoun forms	Script for Texts R01-05		Texts R01-05	
	Functions	Number of occurrences	Functions	Number of occurrences
him	- masc. free/bound subject - fem./neuter free subject - masc. bound object - masc./fem. possessive	57[a]	- masc. free/bound subject - fem. free subject - masc./fem. possessive	23[a]
im	- masc. bound subject - fem. free subject - masc./fem. possessive	9[a]	- masc./fem. free/bound subject - masc./neuter free subject - masc. bound object - masc./fem. possessive	55[a]
he	masc./fem./neuter bound subject	24	masc. bound subject	4
e	masc./fem./neuter bound subject	72	masc./fem./neuter bound subject	92

[a] Occurrences of *him* and *im* in the script and in the corpus texts do not add up to same total due to deviations from the script in the recorded version.

Figure 5.6 Third person singular feminine subject personal pronouns in the NigP corpus by text category (excluding non-NigP speech)

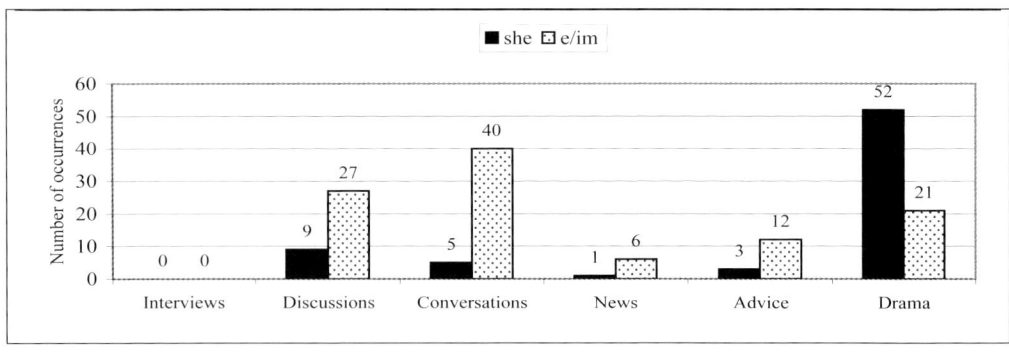

[56] 3rd person singular pronoun forms with an initial *h* also occur in the *One Thing at a Time* script. I have used *Rainbow City* for the detailed comparison of script and recorded version because an electronic version of this script was made available to me by the producers, which facilitated the analysis.

One can thus conclude that apart from a few idiosyncrasies of specific texts and generally the sporadic use of some English pronoun forms, educated NigP speakers adhere to what one would describe as the basilectal third person singular pronoun system if there was a continuum situation, and this contrasts sharply with what can be observed in such a situation. In the Guyanese continuum, for example, according to Bickerton (1973a; see Table 5.11), the use of acrolectal forms like *shi* as feminine subject pronoun and *it* as neuter object and subject pronoun extends to a greater or lesser degree into the mesolectal range, and this area of the continuum is in addition characterized by several usages which are shared neither with the basilect nor with the acrolect, namely *i* as masculine and feminine object pronoun and *shi* as feminine object and possessive pronoun. Bickerton also argues (1973a: 658) that because the number of variants in the different pronoun categories ranges from only one to as many as four, it would not make sense to try to divide the continuum into even three discrete systems (basilect-mesolect-acrolect), since many forms cannot be assigned to a single lect. In NigP, by contrast, not only do speakers who one would expect to produce mesolectal forms if such existed mostly use "basilectal" third person singular pronouns, what variation there is can generally be explained as alternation between two discrete systems, NigP and English.

Table 5.11 Third person singular personal and possessive pronouns in the Guyanese Creole continuum from basilect (I) to acrolect (IX)

Isolect	Personal pronouns						Possessive pronouns	
	Subject			Object				
	Masc.	Fem.	Neuter	Masc.	Fem.	Neuter	Masc.	Fem.
I	*i*	*i*	*i*	*am*	*am*	*am*	*i*	*i*
II	*i*	*shi*	*i*	*am*	*am*	*am*	*i*	*i*
III	*i*	*shi*	*i*	*am*	*am*	*it*	*i*	*i*
IV	*i*	*shi*	*i*	*i*	*i*	*it*	*i*	*i*
V	*i*	*shi*	*i*	*i*	*shi*	*it*	*i*	*i*
VI	*i*	*shi*	*i*	*i*	*shi*	*it*	*i*	*shi*
VII	*i*	*shi*	*it*	*i*	*shi*	*it*	*i*	*shi*
VIII	*i*	*shi*	*it*	*im*	*or*	*it*	*i*	*shi*
IX	*i*	*shi*	*it*	*im*	*or*	*it*	*iz*	*or*

Source: Adapted from Bickerton (1973a: 659f)

While the third person singular pronouns are one of those aspects of NigP grammar where the contact situation with English has not had a significant impact, the plural pronouns are an area where some borrowing seems to have taken place. The pronoun forms as given by previous authors (see Table 5.7) suggest that in the first person plural, the system has changed in recent times from one with only one form, *we*, as subject, object and possessive pronoun, to one with the three forms *we*, *us* and *our*, as in English. In the present corpus, the three-way distinction is generally made (see Table 5.12). *We* as object and as possessive pronoun appear to be usages which are on the verge of dying out, as they hardly occur even in the often more conservative radio texts.[57] In the second person, there is, as Table 5.12 shows, some variation between *una* and *you/your*, and in the third person between *dem* and *de/deir*. *You/your* as second person pronouns and *de* as third person subject pronoun do not seem to be very frequent in comparison to *una* and *dem*, respectively (but cf notes c and e to Table 5.12). *Deir*, however, is more commonly used than *dem* as third person possessive pronoun. The distribution of the forms *deir* and *dem* across the text categories in the corpus (see Figure 5.7) is similar to that of the plural markers *-s* and *dem*: in the three subcategories of face-to-face speech, *deir* is the normal form, and *dem* is virtually non-existent; in the radio subcategories "news" and "advice", *dem* is the preferred form, but whereas in the advice texts, *deir* hardly occurs, it is used a considerable number of times in the category "news" (in the drama texts, the numbers are, obviously, too low to be conclusive). The third person plural possessive pronoun is thus apparently another case of borrowing of an English grammatical form into (educated) NigP and retention (or an attempt to retain) the older NigP form in the advice and news texts.

Table 5.12   Plural personal and possessive pronouns in the NigP corpus

Pronoun forms	As personal pronoun				As possessive pronoun
	Subject		Object		
	Pronoun type	Number of occurrences[a]	Pronoun type	Number of occurrences[a]	Number of occurrences[a]
1 *we*	bound/free	570	bound	2[b]	4[b]
us	free	2	bound/free	5	-
our	-	-	-	-	230
2 *una*	bound/free	176	bound	72	34
you	bound/free	43[c] [1]	bound	13[c] [1]	-
your	-	-	-	-	14[d]
3 *dem*[d]	bound/free	1854	bound	289	80
de[e]/*they*[f]	bound/free	114 [13] (2)	-	-	-
e[g]	bound	26	-	-	1
im	bound/free	16	-	-	1
am[g]	-	-	bound	52	-
deir/their[f]	-	-	-	-	174 [5] (2)

[a]   Of which number indicated in square brackets in parts of the corpus marked as non-NigP speech and number indicated in round brackets in other discourse chunks or idiomatic expressions in English cited in the questionnaire study.
[b]   In radio texts.
[c]   Uses of *you* and *your* as second person plural pronouns can be difficult to identify because there are cases where it is either not clear whether a speaker is addressing all or only one of several interlocutors, or whether the interlocutors/audience are being addressed or *you/your* is being used impersonally (cf Faraclas 1996: 191). The counts given in the table are conservative, including only clear cases.
[d]   Pronounced [dem/den/dẽ], as object pronoun generally [dem].
[e]   Pronounced [de]. The form is sometimes difficult to distinguish from reduced forms of *dem*. The count includes only clear cases.
[f]   In non-NigP speech.
[g]   Faraclas (1986: 5) also mentions the use of *i* and *àm* with plural reference.

---

[57]   Note in this connection also Faraclas's observation in his detailed study of pronoun usage (1986: 5) that in the subsample studied, the first person plural object pronoun is always <u>os</u>, but that *wi* occurs in the speech of some other, "elderly" speakers.

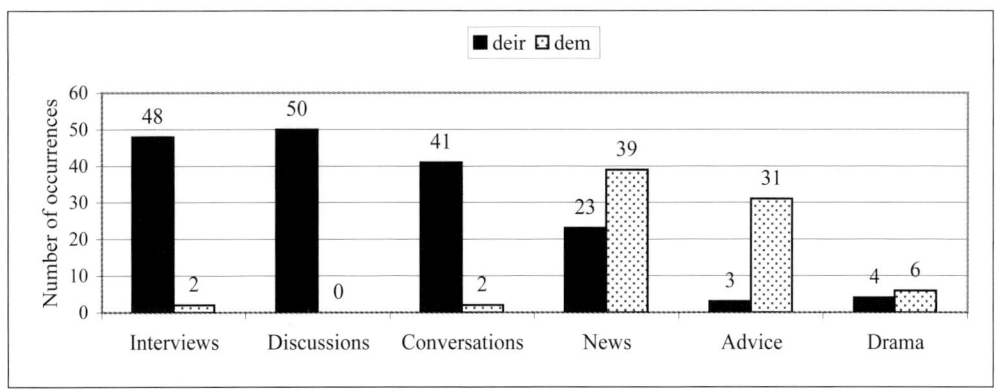

Figure 5.7 Third person plural possessive pronoun forms in the NigP corpus by text category (excluding non-NigP speech)

Indefinite pronouns are cited by Agheyisi (1984: 220f) as an area in which English forms are gradually being taken over into educated NigP. According to the data in Table B 1 and Figure 5.8, the *-body* series of compound indefinite pronouns with personal reference (but not the *-one* series), is now well established in this variety of the language.[58] Faraclas (1996: 251) also mentions compound pronouns with *-body* (*-bɔ̀di*) for NigP generally.[59]

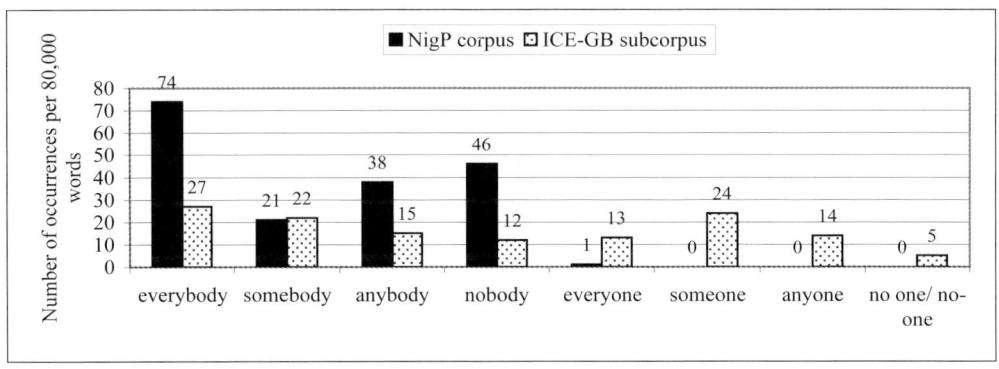

Figure 5.8 Frequency of compound indefinite pronouns with personal reference in the NigP corpus and the ICE-GB subcorpus

---

[58] Agheyisi (1984: 220f) cites the whole *-body* (*-bɔdi*) series as well as *ɛvriwan* 'everyone' and *sɔŋwan* 'someone'. As "Pidgin proper" equivalents she gives *ɔl pɛsin* (for *ɛvribɔdi* and *ɛvriwan*), *pɛsin* (for *sɔmbɔdi*, *sɔŋwan* and *ɛnibɔdi*) and *pɛsinnɔ* (i.e. syntactic negation of *pɛsin*, for *nobɔdi*). In my corpus, pronominal uses of *person* are common, but only in the generic sense ('one', 'you'; e.g. *di one wey dey happen for Lagos now dey fear person too much* 'what is happening in Lagos now makes one very afraid' (A02 113f)) and in the sense of 'somebody' (cf e.g. example (64) above). This explains why, in contrast to the other forms in the *-body* series, *somebody* is not more frequent in the NigP corpus than in the ICE-GB subcorpus in spite of the non-occurrence of *someone* (see Figure 5.8). *All person* does not occur in my corpus, and I found only one instance of *person no* translatable as 'nobody' and two of *person* translatable as 'anybody' (as well as 5 of *any person*). In addition to the compound indefinite pronouns with personal reference, Agheyisi mentions *ɛvritiŋ* 'everything' and *ɛnitiŋ* 'anything', which occur in the present corpus but were not cited in the questionnaire study.

[59] The *-one* (*-wɔn*) forms, which are virtually not used in my corpus, are mentioned by him as well (ibid.).

The pronoun *what* is one of those forms which are sporadically used in the corpus but which are clearly not integrated into the NigP system. *What* may be used in NigP in the expression *what of* (see Faraclas 1996: 27), but otherwise the NigP form is *wetin*. In the corpus, *what* occurs only 46 times, while *wetin* is used in 430 instances, and 10 of the 46 occurrences of *what* are in *what of* and another 18 in parts of the corpus marked as non-NigP speech and other discourse chunks or idiomatic expressions in English (cf Table B 1, item 10-8).

5.5.5 *The verb phrase: tense, aspect and modality*

NigP has a set of preverbal tense/aspect markers which, according to Agheyisi (1971: 133ff) and Faraclas (1996: 195ff), includes the following: *dey* (*de, dè*) for imperfective aspect (progressive and habitual), *don* (*dọn*) for perfective aspect, *been* (*bin, bìn*) for past tense, and *go* (*gò*) for future tense. Elugbe & Omamor (1991: 99ff) mention primarily *de, dọn* and *go* (*bin* is referred to only in a note, p 112). *Go* may be more appropriately characterized as a marker of irrealis modality than as a tense marker, but since, like in English the modal *will*, it serves as the primary means of expression of future time (see also Ofuani 1981a), it is described by Agheyisi (1971: 134) and Elugbe & Omamor (1991: 100) as a tense marker, and by Faraclas (1996: 195) as a tense marker "borrowed" from the modality system. Faraclas (ibid.) also observes that the future is "the most consistently marked tense". He emphasizes, however, that neither *gò* nor any other tense/aspect marker is obligatory and that it is common for tense and aspect not to be formally marked, although aspect is, he says, marked more often than tense (1996: 195, 197). Where time reference is not indicated by preverbal markers or by time adverbials or other contextual cues, the verb is said to receive a non-past reading if it is stative, and a past reading if it is non-stative (Agheyisi 1971: 133f; Faraclas 1996: 177). If a non-stative verb also has the past tense marker *been*, the verb phrase may be interpreted as referring to anterior past (Faraclas 1996: 197) or remote past (Agheyisi 1971: 134).[60]

In addition to the preverbal markers for past, future/irrealis, and imperfective and perfective aspect, NigP has a negator which combines the meanings of negation and perfective aspect, *never* (cf Agheyisi 1971: 148f; Faraclas 1996: 89). Faraclas (1987, 1996: 208f) also reports an auxiliary use of *come* (*kọm*). Poplack & Tagliamonte (1996) and Tagliamonte (2000) confirm this analysis, but the meaning of preverbal *come* is controversial. Faraclas (1987: 50; 1996: 208) describes it as a marker of "realis modality" and explicitly asserts (1987: 49) that it indicates neither location in time nor temporal sequence. Poplack & Tagliamonte (1996; cf also Tagliamonte 2000), however, found in a study of past marking in their NigP corpus that *come* (*kɔm*) has a significant tendency to occur with verbs which are in a sequential temporal relationship with the preceding verb, and they therefore interpret it as a marker of "sequential past" (1996: 86). In my data, a sequential analysis of preverbal *come* is possible in many cases, but the time reference of VPs with *come* is not always to the past. Rather, *come* can also combine with *go* to express sequentiality in non-past contexts. This usage can be seen in (73) in the series of examples

---

[60] Agheyisi (1971: 134n1) points out that *bin* before non-stative verbs may also "redundantly mark simple past". (Note, however, that while Todd 1994: 3181 seems to want to suggest as much in her example of variation in the Nigerian "continuum" (see 2.2.7), it has never been claimed in the literature on NigP that *been* (*bin*) is the regular marker of past tense for non-stative verbs.)

given below to illustrate the use of the tense/aspect markers that have been discussed so far (for examples of preverbal *come* in a past reference context see example (46) above).

(70) In di next election wey *go* come eh/ in fact none of dem *go* come back o// [...] because plenty people *go don* learn deir lesson// (C04 93ff)

'In the next election that will come, in fact none of them will come back. Because many people will have learned their lesson.'

(71) As we *dey* talk now self, e fit be say dem *don dey* work for some place dem. And na every day dem *dey* change dem style too. (A02 56ff)

'Even as we're talking now, they [armed robbers] might have started working in some places. And also, they change their method every day.'

(72) Na because you *never* chop since morning [...]. (R01 171f)

'It's because you haven't eaten since morning'

(73) You *go* pound your crayfish, you *go* pound your pepper keep. You *go come* wash your meat, and stockfish, and dry fish. [...]. Den you *go come* put di fish, di stockfish and everything on top fire, with kpomo o. (A05 15ff)

'You pound your crayfish, you pound your pepper and put it aside. Then you wash your meat, stockfish and dry fish. Then you put the fish, stockfish and everything on the fire, with cow hide.'

(74) wetin I *been* hear be say/ dem talk say Obasanjo *been* wan come// (C04 124)

'What I heard was, they said Obasanjo was going to come.'

Preverbal *wan* (cf *wan come* in (74) above) may be interpreted as a tense/aspect marker in NigP as well, a marker of prospective aspect or immediate future (cf also Agheyisi: 1971: 137; Faraclas 1996: 198, 204f). Its basic meaning is, however, a modal one, volition or intention, and the aspectual or temporal meaning is often difficult to separate from the modal one except when the subject is inanimate, as in the following two examples:

(75) Plenty tenant dem dey wey be say when rain *wan* begin fall like dis, na fear dem go just dey fear o [...]. (A01 40ff)

'There're many tenants who'll be afraid when rain is about to start falling like this'

(76) and na di time wey exam *wan* nearly start/ (C06 14)

'And it was when the exams were almost about to start'

The English semi-auxiliaries *be going to* and *be about to* (cf the translations of *wan* in examples (74)-(76)) do not occur in the corpus. Items that do occur are the auxiliaries and regular inflections used in English for tense/aspect marking (*be, have, -ing, -ed*), irregular past tense/past participle forms,[61] the past habitual marker *used to* and the modals *will* and *shall* (cf also the data in Table B 1, Section 11). In Table 5.13, the number of verbs marked by each of these items, or combinations of markers where they occur, is compared to the number of verbs marked by NigP *dey, don, go, been* or *come* as well as combinations of

---

[61] Note that there are a few cases where NigP has adopted an English irregular past tense/past participle form as its invariant form (*lef* 'leave', *loss/lost* 'lose', *broke* 'break', *born* 'give birth to'). These forms therefore do not count as inflected forms.

these,[62] and in addition the number of unmarked verbs in past reference contexts. Note that while *will* often translates as preverbal *go* in NigP, English perfect forms as *don/never* + VERB etc., there is no one-to-one correspondence between any two categories in the table. These data therefore do not represent variable analyses – as was pointed out in 2.5.1, analyses of morphosyntactic variables are problematic when possible variant realizations are part of widely divergent systems – but an analysis of the extent to which non-NigP forms are used in the corpus in comparison to NigP marking options, without claims of direct equivalence. Not included in these data are a number of cases in which the options for tense/aspect marking are restricted: VPs in imperative clauses, *make*-subjunctive clauses (see 5.5.7), *to*-infinitive clauses and *-ing* clauses, non-initial members of serial constructions and VPs introduced by modal verbs (except for the combinations with *go* listed in the table). Non-NigP tense/aspect forms in these contexts are limited to a number of occurrences of V*ing* in nonfinite clauses, most of them in parts of the corpus marked as non-NigP speech and other discourse chunks or idiomatic expressions in English (cf Table B 1, item 11-4[63]). Also not included are copular verbs. These will be discussed separately below (5.5.6).

The data in Table 5.13 (opposite) make it clear that all of the English forms are extremely marginal. Among the NigP markers, *dey* and *go* are the most frequent. Also frequent is *don,* and not quite so frequent but still relatively common, *come. Been,* by contrast, is used only very sporadically. A similar finding for *been* (*bin*) is made by Poplack & Tagliamonte (1997: 79). Whether the infrequency of *been* reflects a change vis-à-vis an earlier stage at which it was more widely used is impossible to tell, as no comparable quantitative data are available in the literature.[64] But even if this should be the case, *been* has not been replaced by English inflectional past marking, so that one can at least safely conclude that the NigP tense/aspect system has so far been immune to borrowing of English forms. Another important finding is that the forms which appear in the corpus are either part of the core NigP system or fully grammatical according to the English system. Neither is there a special mesolectal past marker like *did* in Jamaican and Guyanese Creole (Patrick 1999: chapter 6 (see also 2.6.1); Bickerton 1975b: 69ff), nor do the data include any intermediate forms for progressive aspect like V*ing* or invariant *is* + V*ing* (cf 2.2.1), forms which have not been reported in any previous study of NigP, either. This means that what

---

[62] Cases where the verb following the tense/aspect markers is not the main verb but a modal (e.g. *go fit* 'will be able to') are included in the counts but are not listed as separate combinations of preverbal markers.

[63] The example of V*ing* in a nonfinite VP cited in Table B 1 (*dey* + V*ing* in a *to*-infinitive clause) is exceptional. All other occurrences of V*ing* are in *-ing* clauses, and there is no other instance of V*ing* preceded by a NigP tense/aspect marker.

[64] Fayer (1990) provides quantitative data on tense/aspect/modality marking in the *Diary of Antera Duke*, a trader in 18th-century Old Calabar (cf Forde 1956), and letters written by traders from the same area in the 19th century. She considers the language of these texts an early variety of NigP, but this analysis is queried by Görlach (1994: 249; 1998: 122f), who points out the need to distinguish "jargon English" or "broken English" from Pidgin. For auxiliary *been,* Fayer (1990) reports an increase from only 2 occurrences in the *Diary of Antera Duke*, in which she counts a total of 783 past reference verbs, to 49 occurrences in late 19th-century letters with a total of 420 verbs eligible for past marking. However, for the same late 19th-century texts, she also reports 140 inflected past forms, as well as almost consistent marking of future time reference by *shall/will* and the use of several other English forms, which shows that whatever the exact nature of the language used in these early written texts, it is indeed very different from present-day spoken NigP.

little variation can be observed in educated NigP in the forms used for tense/aspect marking – an area often cited in studies of Caribbean Creoles as evidence of the existence of a mesolectal zone linking the basilect and the acrolect – does not call for any other explanation than alternation between two discrete systems.

Table 5.13 *Tense/aspect marking and modals go and will/shall in the NigP corpus*

Forms	Number of occurrences[a]
inflected *be* + V*ing*	12 [8] (1)
(inflected) *have* + past participle	1 [1]
used to + V	1
V*ed* (regular inflected past)	8 [5]
irregular inflected past	7 [1][b]
will/'ll/won't	13 [5] (4)
shall	4 [1][c]
dey + V	1468
don + V	648
don dey + V	55
don come + V	6
never + V	113
go + V	1520
go dey + V	133
go don + V	12
go come + V	54
go come dey + V	4
been + V	7
been dey + V	4
come + V	233
come dey + V	75
zero past[d]	1112
TOTAL	5487

[a] Of which number indicated in square brackets in parts of the corpus marked as non-NigP speech and number indicated in round brackets in other discourse chunks or idiomatic expressions in English cited in the questionnaire study.

[b] Of the six occurrences outside non-NigP speech, two are in self-correction contexts (cf e.g. *([?he?] brought) e bring di person from anoder place* 'he brought the person from somewhere else' (C10 112f)).

[c] The three occurrences outside non-NigP speech are all in R06 212ff, where one sentence containing *shall* is repeated three times.

[d] Excluding regular verbs in neutralization contexts, verbs with identical present and past tense forms, modal verbs and lexical items corresponding to English adjectives used as verbs.

In addition to *go* and *wan,* preverbal markers of modality in NigP are *sabi, fit* and *for*.[65] The modal use of *sabi* has already been discussed in 5.4.1.2. *Fit*, which is very common in the

---

[65] Another item that occasionally functions as a preverbal marker of modality is *gree*. In the sense of 'allow', *gree* is used with a following *make*-subjunctive clause (e.g. *I gree make him marry my daughter* 'I allow him to marry my daughter' (R01 157)) or as part of a serial verb construction in which the object of *gree* functions at the same time as the subject of the following verb (e.g. *fear no dey gree me tell person* 'fear didn't allow me to tell anybody', or 'I was too afraid to tell anybody' (R08

corpus (353 occurrences as a modal verb[66]), expresses ability and possibility (also permission):

(76)   see dis aunty wey dem say e no go *fit* get up again/ (C02 60)

'look at this woman who they said wouldn't be able to get up again'

(77)   My God! Dis girl *fit* die. (R10 191)

'My God! This girl could die.'

For (44 occurrences in the corpus as a modal verb) is used to indicate obligation or necessity, as well as irrealis modality in main clauses of unreal conditional constructions:

(78)   una *for* go meet authority for science say okay una need public address system/ (C06 143f)

'You should go to the authorities of [the Faculty of] Science and tell them you need a public address system'

(79)   E say im do dis thing because im mama no train am, if to say e train am, e *for* no enter gang wey e enter. (A04 84ff)

'He said he did this thing because his mother didn't bring him up properly, if she'd brought him up properly, he wouldn't have entered the gang that he entered.'

Faraclas (1996: 211) observes that in "acrolectal varieties", *must* (m$\underline{o}$s) may be used in place of *for* (f$\underline{o}$) to express obligation. According to the data in Table B 1 (item 11-3), *must* is relatively common in the corpus[67] and also appears to be quite acceptable. Even more common and also quite acceptable is another item whose use as a preverbal marker of modality in NigP has so far not been reported by any author, namely *suppose* (cf Table B 1, item 11-2). Except for one occurrence of the full English form in a part of the corpus marked as non-NigP speech (*is not supposed to* (C09 167f)), *suppose* is not preceded by (a form of) *be*, nor does it have a final alveolar plosive (at least not outside neutralization contexts), while *to* is variably used:

(80)   diploma students wey *suppose to* write exam uh uh June June twelve wey dem *suppose* start/ dem never even start to dey teach dem well well// (C03 68ff)

'The diploma students who're supposed to write exams, June twelve [is] when they're supposed to start, they haven't even started to teach them properly.'

Apart from *must* and *suppose,* the use of modal verbs which are not part of the traditional set of NigP preverbal markers is very restricted. The data in Table B 1 show that *can* is attested in the corpus (item 11-6 in the table) but that it is mainly a feature of non-NigP speech. In addition, *should* occurs but is also clearly not a normal feature of NigP speech (of 15 occurrences, 11 are in parts of the corpus marked as non-NigP speech and 3 in self-correction contexts). *Could* occurs only once. The remaining three English central modals, *would, may* and *might,* do not occur at all. An English semi-auxiliary which occurs – but only sporadically – is *be able to* (see Table B 1, item 11-11). In addition, one finds in the

---

150f)). These are the only two uses of *gree* mentioned by Faraclas (1996: 211). In my corpus, there are also a few instances of *gree* used preverbally in the sense of 'be willing to' (e.g. *dat time NITEL no <u>gree</u> connect dem* 'at that time NITEL wasn't willing to connect them' (V03 136)).

[66] *Fit* also occurs as a main verb (e.g. *e fit you well well* 'it [dress] fits you very well' (R05 171)).

[67] In most cases, *must* is used in the deontic sense, but the epistimic use also occurs.

corpus 7 instances of *need to*.[68] There are also 3 occurrences of *have to*,[69] and one speaker once uses *got to*.[70] Other English marginal modals, modal idioms and semi-auxiliaries with modal meanings (or adaptations thereof) do not occur. One can therefore conclude that the system of preverbal markers of modality has not been as immune to borrowing as the tense/aspect system, but that English influence is largely restricted to the expression of obligation and necessity and that most of the English modal verbs remain alien to educated NigP.

5.5.6 The English copula be *and its Nigerian Pidgin equivalents*

In addition to the tense/aspect forms and modal verbs discussed above, the data for verb inflections and auxiliaries in Table B 1 include three inflected forms of *be* as copula (items 11-1, 11-5, 11-10). NigP, as some of the translations in Table B 1 also show, has uninflected *be* as a copular verb. However, this is only one of several items and constructions which in NigP fill the semantic space occupied in English by the copula *be*. *Be* is used in NigP when the complement is a noun phrase or a clause and does not have a locative meaning (81), but a different item, *dey,* is employed as locative copula (82, 83) and in existential sentences (84):[71]

(81) no *be* say I *be* anyhow nurse I *be* qualified nurse// (D01 51f)
      'It's not that I'm just any kind of nurse, I'm a qualified nurse.'

(82) You see, na only me *dey* for house [...]. (R10 224f)
      'You see, it's only me who's at home.'

(83) Stand where you *dey*! (R08 124)
      'Stand where you are!'

(84) If light no *dey* you go complain say light no *dey*// (C07 169)
      'If there's no electricity you'll complain that there's no electricity.'

Impersonal *e get* also has an existential meaning:

(85) *E get* one fish wey dem dey call mangala, if you no use mangala o, e no go sweet. (A05 17f)
      'There's a fish that's called mangala, if you don't use mangala, it won't be tasty.'

In addition to *be* and *dey*, NigP has a third element which has certain functions in common with English *be,* namely *na*. *Na*, which Faraclas (1996: 50) describes as an "emphatic introducer", introduces the focussed constituent in cleft sentences (cf e.g. *na only me* in (82) above). Its negative equivalent in this function is *(e) no be*:[72]

(86) *No be* me do am eh, *no be* me do am. (R10 195)
      'It wasn't me who did it, it wasn't me who did it.'

---

[68] One of these is in non-NigP speech.
[69] Including one instance of *has to,* with a third person singular subject, in non-NigP speech.
[70] There is also a speaker (the one in text V01) who uses the NigP verb *get* 'have' combined with *to* in the sense of 'have to'.
[71] In contrast to *dey* as imperfective aspect marker, which is low-toned, locative/existential *dey* bears high tone.
[72] The dummy subject *e* is often omitted before the negator *no* (cf also Faraclas 1996: 55).

When the complement is a noun phrase or clause and does not have a locative meaning, *na* can also function as a non-emphatic copula (cf also Faraclas 1996: 51):

(87) nobody perfect// if to say everybody perfect/ ehen we for talk say okay o Omotola *na* perfect man/ (C03 57f)

'Nobody's perfect. If everybody was perfect, we would say Omotola is a perfect man'

(88) [...] and di next thing *na* to break leg// (D03 127f)

'and the next thing is to break a leg.'

Example (87) above also illustrates an additional construction in NigP which is equivalent to certain English copula constructions: the use of predicates corresponding to English adjectives – in this case *perfect* in *nobody perfect* and *everybody perfect* – as verbs (cf Agheyisi 1971: 139ff; Faraclas 1996: 221ff; also Holm 1988: 85f, 176f on the syntactic behaviour of lexifier adjectives in Atlantic Creoles generally). Predicates corresponding to English quantifiers exhibit the same syntactic pattern (cf e.g. *di breeze too much* in example (90) below). As verbal elements, these items are not preceded by a copula, and they can take preverbal tense/aspect/modality markers (cf e.g. *go sweet* in example (85) above). Even transitive uses are possible:

(89) e no *sweet* my belle when I dey hear (dis kind) dis kind stories// (C08 98f)

'I'm not pleased when I hear this kind of stories.'

However, the verbal character of these items in predicative function does not preclude them from being used as noun premodifiers. Elugbe & Omamor (1991: 93, 96) therefore have a category of attributive adjectives in their grammatical description of NigP. Faraclas (1996: 222ff), in order to be able to do away with the category "adjective" entirely, proposes an analysis of lexical items corresponding to English adjectives in attributive function as deverbal modifier nouns in associative/possessive constructions. Furthermore, he mentions that these items may also be used in copula constructions with *dey* (*de*) or *be* (*bi*) and argues that in these cases, they can be analysed as pronominalized deverbal modifier nouns.[73] The following examples from my corpus illustrate these two constructions:

(90) **A:** hah you dey enjoy o// dis lagoon front e be like say e *dey* very very cosy {and cool//}
      B: {man di breeze} too much o// (C05 4f)

'**A:** Hah, you're enjoying yourself. This lagoon front, it's as if it's [i.e. it seems to be] very very cosy and cool.
B: Man, the breeze is too much.'

(91) di fact say di pikin *(be) be* male no mean say e go do better for life// (D04 20f)

'The fact that the child is male doesn't mean he'll do well in life.'

The construction with *be* does not seem to be well-established. In my corpus, there are 43 adjectives or quantifiers preceded by inflected or non-finite *be*, of which 22 in parts of the corpus marked as non-NigP speech and other discourse chunks or idiomatic expressions in

---

[73] According to Faraclas (1996: 224), pronominalized deverbal modifier nouns in copular constructions with *dey* (*de*) refer to relatively temporal qualities, while pronominalized deverbal modifier nouns in copular constructions with *be* (*bi*) refer to relatively permanent qualities.

English, and only 9 examples like the one in (91), with uninflected *be*.[74] The construction with *dey* is quite common (139 occurrences in the corpus), but the most common construction for predicates corresponding to English adjectives and quantifiers is the verbal one without a copula (246 occurrences; cf also Table 5.14 below).

In Table 5.14, the number of occurrences of inflected forms of *be* is compared to the number of occurrences of the NigP items and constructions that have been discussed. There are of course, on the one hand, instances of the NigP items and constructions where one might not use the copula *be* in an English translation (cf e.g. the case of *e be like say* in example (90) above), and, on the other, NigP verbs not included in the analysis which, depending on the context, may be translated into English by a construction with a form of *be*:

(92)   Doctor uh e don tay small. (R08 150)
       'Doctor, uh it's been quite some time.'

(93)   en na because time never reach midnight/ (V01 70)
       'yes, it's because it's not yet midnight'

This analysis is therefore again not a strict variable analysis, but an analysis of the extent to which two sets of comparable but not necessarily always equivalent forms or constructions are used in the corpus, as in 5.5.5.

Table 5.14   The English copula be *and its NigP equivalents in the NigP corpus*

Forms/constructions		Number of occurrences[a]
Inflected *be* (copula)[b]	*is/'s*	121 [37] (41)
	are/'re	20 [7] (8)
	was	8 [3][c]
	'm	1
na (emphatic introducer and copula)		1648
uninflected *be* (copula)		870
dey (copula and existential verb)		499
Lexical items corresponding to English adjectives and quantifiers in verbal constructions (no copula)		246
impersonal *e get*		60
TOTAL		3473

[a]   Of which number indicated in square brackets in parts of the corpus marked as non-NigP speech and number indicated in round brackets in other discourse chunks or idiomatic expressions in English cited in the questionnaire study.
[b]   Inflected forms of copular *be* other than those listed do not occur.
[c]   Of the five occurrences outside non-NigP speech, two are in a self-correction context: *(di result was-- di result was-- e dey) e dey okay sha//* (C06 21).

---

[74]   Not counted are occurrences of *be small* in the expression *no be small*, glossed by Faraclas (1996: 55) as 'it is not a small matter'. The same expression exists in Ghanaian Pidgin, and Huber (1999: 323n19)

One can see in the table that there is a not quite negligible number of occurrences of *is/'s*, but a very considerable proportion of these are in parts of the corpus marked as non-NigP speech and other discourse chunks or idiomatic expressions cited in the questionnaire study, and on the whole, the NigP forms clearly predominate. An additional finding is that whenever non-NigP forms are used, they are fully grammatical according to the English system, i.e. person/number concord is always observed. There is no form like generalized *is* without person/number concord, as in the mesolects of English-based Caribbean Creoles (cf Bickerton 1973a: 651; Holm 1988: 176). Furthermore, one does not find zero before noun phrases and locative complements; copula use in these environments is obligatory. This contrasts with the situation in the Guyanese continuum as described by Bickerton (1973: 652ff): according to Bickerton, zero copula in these environments is typical of the mesolect, while the basilect has the equative copula *a* and the locative copula *de*, and the acrolect in both cases inflected *be*.

5.5.7 The particle to

The particle *to* (in clauses modelled on English infinitive clauses) was cited several times in the questionnaire study (cf Table B 1, Section 12). The NigP translations vary according to the syntactic environment. In the case of object clauses, the informants gave zero as the NigP equivalent of *to*. The *wh*-infinitive clauses were rephrased as finite interrogative clauses with modal verbs, and two of the examples of infinitive clauses postmodifying nouns as relative clauses with modal verbs. The *to*-infinitival subject clauses and adverbial clauses of purpose and one of the examples of infinitive clauses postmodifying nouns were translated into NigP as clauses introduced by *make*, which in this function is described by Faraclas (1996: passim) as a "subjunctive clause introducer". Note that *make*-subjunctive clauses are different from causative constructions with *make*: in causative constructions, *make* is followed by object pronouns, whereas in *make*-subjunctive clauses, subject pronouns are used. Compare, for example, the causative construction in (94) and the *make*-subjunctive clauses in (95) and (96):

(94) Wetin come dey *make am* cry? (R10 127)
'What has made him cry?'

(95) even na doormouth you wan *make e* drop you e go drop you dere/ (D03 107f)
'Even [if] it's at your door that you want it [motorcycle taxi] to drop you, it'll drop you there'

(96) e be like man wey dey sell coffin/ e go dey pray make people die/ *make im* for sell im coffin// (V03 44ff)
'It's like a man who sells coffins, he'll pray that people will die so that he'll sell his coffins.'

All of the constructions cited by the informants are used in the corpus,[75] but as the figures in Table B 1 show, *to*-infinitive constructions are a viable alternative in educated NigP, and one may consider the particle *to* one of the function words that have been borrowed. It

---

[75] argues that it is elliptical for *(i) no bi smɔ tin!* and therefore not an instance of adjectival predication.
A construction which does not occur is the one with *for (fo)* instead of *to* cited by Agheyisi (1971: 97): "*Meri foget fo giv Jon im moni* 'Mary forgot to give John his money'".

seems to be even more integrated than plural *-s* and the possessive pronoun *deir*, for which I have shown in 5.5.4 that in spite of being quite well-established features of spontaneous speech, they are avoided in the news and advice texts: as demonstrated in Figure 5.9, the distribution of *to* as particle across text categories in the NigP corpus is similar to that in the ICE-GB subcorpus,[76] with consistently but not extremely lower frequencies in the NigP corpus.

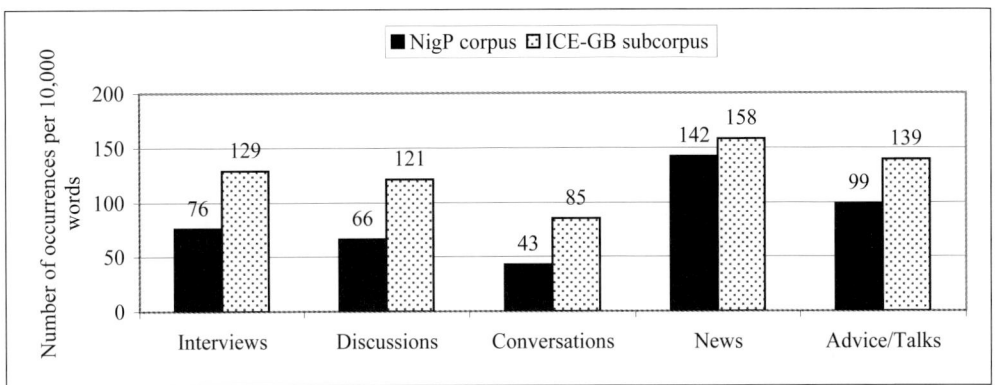

Figure 5.9 Frequency of to *as particle in the NigP corpus and the ICE-GB subcorpus by text category*

5.5.8 English adjectival and adverbial comparison and the Nigerian Pidgin serial verb construction with **pass**

The informants cited a few comparative and superlative forms of adjectives or adverbs as English elements in the corpus extracts (cf Table B 1, Section 13). The NigP equivalent of such forms (cf also the translations in Table B 1) is a serial verb construction with the verb *pass* '(sur)pass' (Agheyisi 1971: 112ff; Faraclas 1996: 109f). If *pass* is followed by an object, this construction corresponds to an English comparative construction:

(97)   [...] for my place dem dey talk parable say, okro no fit tall *pass* who plant am. (A04 71f)
'in my place they have a proverb which says that an okra tree can't grow taller than he who planted it.'

(98)   Lagos State/ for Lagos State/ house rent/ e dear *pass* anywhere for dis country// (V01 132f)
'In Lagos State house rents are higher than anywhere else in this country.'

When *pass* is used without an object, the construction usually corresponds to an English superlative construction (cf examples (99) and (100)), although, as example (101) shows, the context may sometimes suggest a comparative interpretation:

(99)   and you know (di thing wey come bad) di thing wey come bad *pass*? (C03 12)
'And do you know what was the worst thing?'

---

[76] The category "drama" in the NigP corpus is not taken into account in this analysis, as it has no direct parallel in ICE-GB. The number of occurrences of *to* as particle in the drama texts is the lowest in the NigP corpus (35 per 10,000 words).

(100) FIFA don do wetin dem sabi do *pass*, to dey spoil people work. (A03 3f)

'FIFA has done what they know best how to do, to spoil people's work.'

(101) **B:** you come make me remember (dis uh) dis uh H.N.D. and uh degree programme// na di same uh--
A: H.N.D. and degree eh?
B: en na di same wahala dey for dat place too// na so dem dey say na degree na im better *pass*// (C08 139ff)

'**B:** You've reminded me of the H.N.D. and the degree programme. It's the same--
A: H.N.D. and degree, eh?
B: Yes, it's the same problem there, too. They always say that it's the degree that's better.'

Serial *pass* expressing comparison[77] is fairly common in the corpus, with 39 occurrences spread across all text categories,[78] and there are also a few instances of non-serial *pass* translatable as English adjectives in the comparative form:

(102) As e come be say dem power don come *pass* di power of all dose wey government say make dem dey help us drive dis kind people comot, e be like say we don come dey on our own. (A02 144ff)

'As it has turned out that they [armed robbers] are stronger than all those who the government has instructed to help us drive this kind of people away, it seems we're now on our own.'

Concerning the NigP use of *better*, which in (101) above is the verbal element combined with *pass*, and that of another English comparative form, *more*, Faraclas (1996: 109) makes the following observation: "The verb *bèta* 'be very good' and the adverbial *mo* 'very much' are not normally used to show comparison, despite their resemblance to the Nigerian Standard English comparative forms *better* and *more*." He gives the following example of the use of these elements (ibid.):

(103) A no get bèta pìkîn. Dèm jost dè wàhala mo.

'I don't have very good children. They just make trouble a lot.'

Better is a common lexical item in my corpus, and it often translates as '(be) (very) good' rather than '(be) better':

(104) no be say wetin im talk (no) no *better* but you know for democracy [...] dem no dey read budget like dat// (D05 47ff)

'It's not that what he said is not good, but you know, in a democracy the budget isn't read like that.'

---

[77] There is also a directional use of serial *pass* (e.g. *you dey drive pass di place* 'you're driving past the place' (V02 13f); cf also Agheyisi (1971: 110).

[78] The construction is in almost all of these cases equivalent to an English construction with a comparative or superlative form of an adjective or adverb, as in examples (97) to (101). There are, however, also about three cases where a comparative form of a quantifier or pronoun – which are not the subject of the present analysis – would be used in an English translation (cf e.g. *you go see small boy, im with im papa go dey compete who go get girlfriend pass* 'you'll see a small boy, he and his father will compete about who'll have more girlfriends' (A04 39f)).

In three instances, *better* is combined with *pass* to express a comparison, as in (101) above. There are also cases where a translation of *better* without *pass* as '(be) better' is possible, but such examples are often ambiguous between a comparative and a non-comparative interpretation:

(105)   so dat man too prayer be say/ "God o make NEPA no *better* o/" make im dey do im work// (V03 41f)

'So that man [generator mechanic] also prays, "God, don't let NEPA [National Electric Power Authority] get better", so that he'll have work to do.' Or: '... don't let NEPA work well ...'

More as an adverb modifying verbs is not common in the corpus (four occurrences, of which one in non-NigP speech). When it occurs, it is used as a comparative form. Another English irregular comparative form which occurs in the corpus is *worse* (four occurrences, of which three in succession: *worse worse worse* 'worse and worse and worse' (V04 14)). There are also a few occurrences of superlative *best* (cf Table B 1, item 13-2) and one each of *worst* and of *most* as an adverb modifying a verb. As regards regular forms, there are, as shown in Table B 1 (item 13-1), nine instances of the synthetic comparative in *-er*, but four of these are in parts of the corpus marked as non-NigP speech and other discourse chunks or idiomatic expressions in English that were cited in the questionnaires. One can also see in Table B 1 that if occurrences in a proper name are disregarded (cf note 20 to the table), there are only two superlatives in *-est*, one forming part of a double superlative, and both were cited as English elements (cf Table B 1, items 13-3 and 13-4). In addition, there are two instances of *di* + *most* + attributive adjective (*di most important thing* (A04 19f); *di most difficult thing* (C06 19f; cf also item 15-4-5 in Table B 1)),[79] i.e. the English analytic superlative. The analytic comparative does not occur.

To summarize, the expression of comparison is an area where some English influence is observable (in all text categories), but the NigP serial verb construction with *pass* remains productive. English forms which are used are often irregular ones, and the regular English pattern of adjectival and adverbial comparison is not common and acceptable enough to be considered integrated into educated NigP.

5.5.9 *Negation*

Except in the special case of preverbal marking for completive aspect, where *don* is replaced by *never* in the negative (cf 5.5.5), verb negation is indicated in NigP by preverbal *no*:

(106)   I *no* get time. (R05 185)

'I don't have time.'

(107)   e *no* suppose dey like dat o// (D05 107)

'It ought not to be like that.'

(108)   Di committee say plenty load too dey wey dem *no* fit see di pilgrim wey get am [...]. (N03 10f)

'The committee said there are also many pieces of luggage [in the pilgrims' camp] whose owners they can't find'

---

[79]   There is also another case where, contrary to the English pattern, *most* is postposed to the adjective: *my very better most friend* 'my very best friend' (R01 78).

According to Agheyisi (1971: 145), *no* always precedes not only the main verb, but also the preverbal markers of tense, aspect and modality, if there are any in the VP. Faraclas (1996: 89) states that *no* is generally placed before the VP, but in addition he observes (p 92) that in "upper mesolectal and acrolectal speech", *no* may also occur between the preverbal auxiliaries and the main verb. As an example, he cites *a bìn no get mòto* 'I didn't have a car'. In my corpus, *no* almost always precedes the whole VP including auxiliaries, as in examples (107) and (108) above, but there are two exceptions: when a VP with the modal *fit* is negated, *no* is placed before the whole VP if, as in example (108), the meaning of the modal is the abilitative one (in which case the scope of negation includes the meaning of the modal), but between *fit* and the main verb when *fit* expresses possibility (in which case the meaning of the modal is not within the scope of negation):

(109) Person wey dem cut im head still fit *no* die o. (A03 122f)

   'Somebody whose head has been cut off might still not die.'

The second exception are VPs with the modal *for*. In all of the 9 instances of such VPs in the corpus which are negated, the position of *no* is between the modal and the rest of the VP:

(110) but I think una for *no* complain too much [...] (C06 50f)

   'But I think you shouldn't complain too much'

(111) some of dem if to say deir oga no like am/ dem for *no* dey bleach// (D03 50f)

   'Some of them, if their husband didn't like it, they wouldn't be bleaching [their skin].'

Preverbal *no* is by far the predominant negator in my corpus, with over 1500 occurrences. The English pattern consisting of operator + *not*/enclitic *n't* is vanishingly rare. Inflected *be* (in English progressives and the semi-auxiliary *be supposed to* or as copula verb) as well as the English modals cited in 5.5.5 as marginal elements in the corpus are negated according to the English pattern, but there are only 12 instances of these items in negated clauses. Almost all of these are, in any case, in parts of the corpus marked as non-NigP speech. *Must* (cf 5.5.5), in the only instance in which it is negated, is also followed by *not* instead of being preceded by *no*. In addition, *don't* is, in very few instances, used to negate VPs without auxiliaries (cf Table B 1, item 14-3). All of these are cases where *don't* could also be used in English. Other forms of *do* as negated dummy auxiliary such as past *didn't* do not occur. *Noto* (pronounced [nɔtu]; the spelling has been taken over from the drama scripts) as a substitute for *(e) no be* '(it) is not' (cf Table B 1, item 14-1) is an idiosyncrasy of the drama texts.

   The minimal intrusion of English forms into educated NigP in this area of the grammar again contrasts with the kind of variation that can be observed in the Creole continua of the Caribbean. There is no evidence of a mesolectal negator in NigP like *duon* in Jamaican Creole and *en* in Guyanese Creole, which can replace basilectal preverbal *no* and *na*, respectively, whether the time reference is past or non-past, and thus differ from forms like standard English *don't* and nonstandard English *ain't* or standard English *haven't*[80] (Patrick 1999: 199; Bickerton 1975b: 99f; Rickford 1983: 314).[81]

The pre-verb position is described by Agheyisi (1971: 146) as the only one in which the negator *no* may occur in NigP. According to Faraclas (1996: 91), *no* can also occur before noun phrases, but a special type of construction is then required: "Any noun phrase constituent within a sentence", he writes, "may also be negated by fronting it to the position of a head noun phrase, preceding it with the negative marker *no* and following it with the rest of the original sentence in the form of a relative clause". His examples of this construction include the following:

(112) No maket (we) à gò tek bay nyam (fòr-am).
'There is no market for me to buy yams (at).

(113) No pesin (we) gò bay nyam.
'Nobody will buy yams.'

The main clause is in these cases elliptical: the existential verb *dey,* which could otherwise have been negated (cf *market no dey* 'there is no market'), is omitted. When the negated NP is the subject of the underlying sentence, as in (113), and the relative clause is not introduced by *wey* (*we* in Faraclas's examples), the construction with a fronted NP negated by *no* in an elliptical clause and a relative clause postmodifying the NP is of course indistinguishable from simple negation of the subject NP in the underlying sentence.

In the present corpus, *no* is sometimes used in determiner function, and in this function it was in a few cases cited as an English element (cf Table B 1, item 14-2). Many of the constructions in which *no* + NP occurs in the corpus are similar to those cited by Faraclas. The NP negated by *no* is mostly the subject, often, though not necessarily, of an elliptical existential clause:

(114) *No* trick wey I no use, dem no gree. (R04 106)
'There was no trick I didn't use, [but] they didn't agree.' Or: 'Whatever trick I used, they didn't agree.'

(115) because wey *no* water like dis na so people go queue berekete for dat place dey buy water/ (V03 90f)
'Because when there's no water like this, people will queue up in large numbers at that place and buy water'

(116) [...] and *no* brewery self go get extra money to put inside di business make e dey grow well well. (N01 12ff)
'and no brewery will have money left for investments.'

There are also various fixed expressions from English such as *no problem, no way, no kidding,* and some constructions which do not fit into the pattern described by Faraclas (cf e.g. *I see no reason*, item 15-1-4 in Table B 1), but these are rare.

---

[80] Bickerton (1975b: 91) says about the etymology of *en* in Guyanese Creole that "it is unclear whether *en* stems from *ain't, or haven't,* or is the joint product of both".

[81] According to Bickerton (1975b: 100f), *doon* is also used in the Guyanese mesolect with both present and past reference. Rickford (1983: 314), however, argues that if forms like *don(t), doesn(t)* and *didn(t)* occur in Guyanese Creole, they almost always have the time reference associated with the corresponding English forms.

5.6 Discourse features

This section will deal with code-switching and two other discourse features that were mentioned in the questionnaires: the particle *o* and proverbs.

5.6.1 Code-switching

5.6.1.1 Clauses and larger segments

In addition to English elements fulfilling the conditions specified in 5.3.1, I also marked as non-NigP speech elements in Yoruba and Igbo[82] which met two of the conditions I had set up in the classification of the English elements for this type of marking to be applied: that the element should consist of at least one clause, and that it should be separated from the surrounding discourse by intonation unit boundaries (in scripted texts, by punctuation marks) and/or by virtue of being a quotation. Speech in minor indigenous languages was not transcribed but its occurrence and the approximate number of words was indicated in the transcription. I will now analyse the functions of these major instances of the use of codes other than NigP, focussing on the English elements but also taking into account those in indigenous languages.

Table 5.15 gives an overview of the number of units of non-NigP speech and untranscribed speech in an indigenous language in the different texts in the corpus.

Table 5.15 Non-NigP speech and untranscribed speech in indigenous languages in the NigP corpus

Type of speech	Number of units						
	Interviews	Discussions	Conversations	News	Advice	Drama: Rainbow City	Drama: One Thing at a Time
Non-NigP speech, English	15	15	53	1	4	9	20
Non-NigP speech, Yoruba	-	-	1	-	-	3	46
Non-NigP speech, Igbo	-	-	-	-	-	-	1
Untranscribed speech in indigenous language (more than two words)	-	2	-	-	-	-	7

It is clear from the table that there are more English elements marked as non-NigP speech in the three subcategories of face-to-face speech taken together than in the radio sample as a whole. The indigenous language elements are concentrated in the texts from one of the drama serials, *One Thing at a Time*, which also have more English elements than the other

---

[82] Longer stretches of discourse in Hausa, the third major indigenous language, do not occur in the data.

radio texts. I will first discuss the English elements in the face-to-face speech section of the corpus, and then the non-NigP elements in the radio texts.

A few of the English elements marked as non-NigP speech in the texts in the category "face-to-face speech" are fixed expressions like the English proverb in (117) and the biblical saying in (118):

(117) our people get proverb say/ na person wey dey stay for house na im dey do wetin? na im dey sweep di house// oyibo people dem put am in anoder way/ dem say "[+as you make your bed/ so you lie on it+]"// (V01 14ff)

'Our people have a proverb which says that he who lives in a house, it is he who does what? It is he who sweeps the house. The white people put it in another way, they say: ...'

(118) we go dey bear am first/ nothing God no fit do// [+all power belongs to God//+] na only God we put our hope for// (C01 117ff)

'We'll bear it first, there's nothing God can't do. ... It's only God we put our hope in.'

The majority, however, are cases of what I refer to as code-switching as a discourse strategy (cf 2.4.1). One common phenomenon, found mostly in the conversations, is the insertion of discourse markers in English into NigP discourse, i.e. what Poplack (1980) refers to as "tag-switching" and Gumperz (1982) as switching to mark an "interjection". This phenomenon is well described and illustrated in the comments on extracts C05/7, C05/8 and C10/5 in Table B 2 in Appendix B. One can also observe that speakers sometimes switch to English for a quotation, as in the following example:

(119) **C:** [...] I dey listen to one person for television di oder day// im talk about marginalization// e say "[+Biafra is not the solution to uh--+]"
A: our problem// (C09 184ff)

'**C:** I listened to somebody on television the other day. He/she talked about marginalization. He/she said: ...
A: Our problem.'

Particularly common is the use of code-switching for emphasis. One example is the following:

(120) **A:** [...] dem just dress like dat carry dis gun for hand eh come dey march//
B: come tie--
A: all of dem tie red tie red (for) for head eh// dem come say na O.P.C. people// as I just dey pass now I come see some house wey be say dem don damage di houses eh// [+man those people did terrible things o[83]/ real terrible things//+] (C09 10ff)

'**A:** They were just dressed like that and carried those guns in their hands and marched.
B: and tied--
A: All of them had tied something red around their head. They said they're O.P.C. [Odua Peoples' Congress, militant Yoruba group] people. As I was just passing I saw some houses that they had damaged. ...'

---

[83] The particle *o* (cf 5.6.2) is used not only in NigP but also in (southern varieties of) Nigerian English (cf Jowitt 1991: 140f).

In many cases, switching for emphasis involves reiteration, i.e. after something has been said in NigP or English the same or a similar statement is made in the other code as well:

(121) because dat first day when I come eh/ light no dey/ [+there was no light[84] there// [?1WORD?] was just terrible//+] I say me I no go fit stay// (C08 169ff)

'Because that first day when I came, there was no electricity, ... I said I wouldn't be able to stay.'

(122) Nzeribe no get anything (na--) Nzeribe na katakata/ [+that is the meaning of Nzeribe/+] katakata// (V02 149f)

'Nzeribe doesn't have anything (he's--) Nzeribe is confusion, ... confusion.'

(123) [+ [...] we ourselves Nigerians we are very dirty//+] we dirty// (V02 64f)

'... We are dirty.'

In the following example, code-switching is combined with another discourse strategy, a rhetorical question, to achieve special emphasis:

(124) di front of di house where e suppose help di community make di road to e house dere make oder people dey enjoy di road/ e no make am// na back of e house e go make am// [+that man is he a credible man?+] e no credible// na thief-thief// (V02 131ff)

'In front of the house where he ought to help the community, make the road to his house there so that other people can enjoy the road, he doesn't make it. It's at the back of his house that he'll make it. ... He's not credible. He's a thief.'

The following is an example of another discourse function of code-switching, what Gumperz (1982) refers to as "message qualification":

(125) uh Odili for Rivers State e come talk say e go pay ten thousand/ [+which is even more than what the federal government wanted to pay+]// (V05 69ff)

'Odili in Rivers State said he would pay ten thousand, ...'

There is also one good example of the code-switching function that Gumperz (1982) describes as "personalization versus objectivization". This is the switch to English quoted in example (1) in 5.3.1. The switch occurs after the speaker has given an account of personal experiences with the problem of refuse in Lagos in NigP. In the statement in English he then suggests a general solution to the problem.

Due to the mostly fairly unvarying nature of the situations in which the samples of face-to-face speech were recorded (and, in addition, my criteria for text selection, see 5.1.2.1), one does not find true situational switching or switching as a social strategy. There are, however, some cases of what may be considered topic-related switching. These occur in contexts where a speaker mentions something or somebody that is particularly likely to conjure up an association with the English language, for example a Western, English-speaking country or person. This is illustrated by the following examples (in (127), the code contrast is also exploited for emphasis):

(126) see America as e be today/ [+America (is a very big) uh is a very great country+]// (D05 180f)

'Look at America as it is today ...'

---

[84] *Light* is widely used in Nigerian English in the sense of 'electricity', as in NigP (cf Jowitt 1991: 204).

There are also some switches to which one cannot ascribe a particular function. Most of these are in the conversations. Consider, for example, the following extract from a student conversation:

Text 5.3 Conversation between two university students

[original version]

B: you see when I gader my receipt for undergraduates put togeder like dis/ [+I realised that I paid less than two hundred naira to study in the university for four
5   years//+] and di same thing happen here/ here na thirty-five naira dem dey pay//
A: now?
B: yes// in fact thirty-five naira na im undergraduates dey pay every year// [+you won't
10 believe it// I'm not talking about the G.S.T. books//+]
A: [?1WORD?]//
B: [+eh so what I'm saying is eh/+]
A: ehen//
15 **B:** [+it's not too much//+]
A: I like your argument but-- oya continue//
B: [+you finished the first degree/ you decided to come back//+] na when you don enter master's/ dem tell you say academic
20 programme/ dat is full-time educational programme&
A: yes//
B: &F.T.E.&
A: yes//
25 **B:** &dey different from non-full-time educational programme// if you dey full-time educational programme/ you're doing an academic master's/ M.A. M.Sc. {and all di oders/}
30 **A:** {yes yeah//}
B: di school fees no dey pass fourteen thousand// (C07 207-229)

[translation]

B: You see, when I gathered my undergraduate receipts together like this, ...

And the same thing happens here, here they pay thirty-five naira.
A: Now?

B: Yes. In fact, thirty-five naira is what undergraduates pay every year. ...

When you've entered a master's [programme], they tell you that an academic programme, that is a full-time educational programme,

A: Yes.

B: F.T.E.,

A: Yes.

B: is different from a non-full-time educational programme. If you're in a full-time educational programme, you're doing an academic master's, M.A., M.Sc., and all the others,

A: Yes, yeah.

B: the school fees aren't more than fourteen thousand.

Here, the speaker who dominates the conversation, B, switches back and forth between NigP and English in a way that is best explained as code-switching as an overall discourse mode. There is one longer segment in English in the speech of this speaker (ll 9-18), broken up into several units by the reactions of the interlocutor; the switches in l 9 and l 18 occur at what could be considered sentence boundaries. In ll 2-4, there is a shorter segment in English marked as non-NigP speech, with the switch in l 2 of the type that would be described as intra-sentential in a classification according to Poplack (1980). In the case of "you're doing an academic master's" (l 26), which was not cited by the informant who analysed the corresponding extract in the questionnaire study but which, according to the criteria of structure and intonation, could also have been marked as non-NigP speech, both the switch to English and the switch back to NigP could be analysed as intra-sentential. Neither in this case nor in the other cases described is it possible to pinpoint a specific reason for the switches. It is of course not unexpected to find this type of code-switched discourse, as the phenomenon has been reported in the literature for the indigenous languages in Nigeria as well as for NigP (see 4.1). That passages like the one in Text 5.3 are rather the exception in the present corpus is due to my focus on speech only or mainly in NigP. As noted in 5.1.2.1, I did not include in the corpus whole texts marked by frequent switching. Recordings excluded on this ground were mostly conversations.

The radio texts in the subcategories "news" and "advice" differ greatly from face-to-face speech with respect to the discourse feature of code-switching for whole clauses and larger segments. As can be seen in Table 5.15, there are hardly any English elements marked as non-NigP speech in these texts. The few such elements which occur are fixed expressions or quotations from English texts. In the texts from the drama serial *Rainbow City* included in the corpus, English elements marked as non-NigP speech are also relatively few. Of the nine units (cf Table 5.15), five are in the speech of the leader of a local council task force who appears in one scene (R05 1-44). The unnamed task force leader ("man") uses mainly English with his subordinates, while addressing the trader Madam Asabe, whom he accuses of selling smuggled goods, in NigP (cf Gumperz's (1982) "addressee specification" in bilingual discourse). Here is an extract from this scene:

(128) **Man:** [...] Show me receipt for di duty wey you pay on dem. Noto trader you be, abi trader no dey pay custom duty?
Asabe: I tell you say na import I import am? Na buy I buy am. I don show you people di receipt wey my customer give me. If una want custom receipt, noto im una go ask?
Man: [+Heh, boys, take the bags straight into the van. Carry all the bags straight into the van.+] (R05 17ff)

'**Man:** Show me the receipt for the duty you've paid on them. Aren't you a trader, or does a trader not pay custom duty?
Asabe: Did I tell you I imported them? I bought them. I have shown you people the receipts that my customers have given me. If you want a custom receipt, is it not them you're going to ask?
Man: ...'

Another two of the English elements marked as non-NigP speech in the *Rainbow City* texts are in the speech of Vero, a young girl, in a scene in which she is quarrelling with her father, Adolphus (R02 1-121).[85] Adolphus intends to marry Vero off to a rich old man, while she wants to continue studying for her secondary school certificate (she has already failed the examination three times). An extract from this scene is analysed in Deuber & Oloko (2003: 295f), and it is argued that "Vero invokes the connotations of English - power and knowledge - in an attempt to assert herself over her father and to prove her intellectual abilities". Her use of English in this scene can thus be interpreted as a fictional representation of code-switching as a social strategy (cf 2.4.1). A similar case is also found in one of the texts from *One Thing at a Time*. Here, the young doctor Saratou is quarrelling with Chief Omoniyi, her prospective father-in-law:

---

[85] The remaining two of the English elements marked as non-NigP speech in these texts are an instance of the idiomatic expression *God forbid* (R03 198) and a quotation (R02 30ff).

(129) **Chief:** [...] Nonsense. E wan marry Taju. [LAUGHS] (You don) you don look yourself for inside mirror?
Saratou: Chief! [+T.J. and I love and respect each other. T.J. is my man.+] (R08 83ff)

'**Chief:** Nonsense. She wants to marry Taju. Have you looked at yourself in a mirror?'
Saratou: Chief! ...'

Most of the English elements marked as non-NigP speech in these texts are, however, items like those in (130) and (131), which do not have an essential function in the situational or discourse context:

(130) **Ayi:** [...] If Chief go separate una, what of T.J.? At least you don get person wey una love each oder. My own boyfriend na every time e dey dey offshore. E no dey come see me. You fit lose T.J. o. [+And opportunity comes but once.+]
Saratou: Ayi help me! Wetin I go do, heh? I don confuse. (R07 8ff)

'**Ayi:** If Chief is going to separate you, what of T.J.? At least you have somebody where the two of you love each other. My own boyfriend is always offshore. He doesn't come to see me. You might lose T.J....
Saratou: Ayi help me! What am I going to do? I'm confused.'

(131) **Chief:** Na im go cook my food, clean di house, drive my motor, even dey run business message for me. [+In short, he's a utility man.+]
Iya Taju: Ah, so na Eva go be your wife dere abi? (R06 73ff)

'**Chief:** It's he who'll cook my food, clean the house, drive my car, even run business messages for me. ...
Iya Taju: Ah, so it's Eva [Evaristus] who'll be your wife there or what?'

Almost all of the English elements marked as non-NigP speech in the five texts from *One Thing at a Time* included in the corpus are in the speech of three characters: Saratou and her colleague Ayi, two of the most highly educated characters, and Chief Omoniyi, a character with social pretensions. One could argue that the occasional insertion of English segments into their speech is primarily a characterization strategy and adds a touch of sociolinguistic realism to the text.

The indigenous language elements in *One Thing at a Time* are deployed in a very similar way to the English ones. As already pointed out in 5.1.3, the characters in the serial are designed to be representative of the different ethnic groups of southern Nigeria. Many of them have names which identify them as members of a particular ethnic group, and in the production of the episodes, actors from the appropriate ethnic groups were chosen to read their parts (Kola Ogunjobi, p c). The indigenous language elements are evidently an additional characterization strategy. Consider, for example, Text 5.4 (overleaf). Like the English elements in examples (130) and (131) above, the short Yoruba insertions in this dialogue (ll 5, 10, 15, 19, 21, 32-33, 36-37) do not carry essential information or arguments, but the use of Yoruba is in tune with the characters and the situation.

Text 5.4 Fictional conversation between two Yoruba market women

[original version]

Market Woman 2: Mama Elewe, you no dey quick believe person.
Market Woman 1: Say wetin?
Market Woman 2: Ah.
5 **Market Woman 1:** {[+Kí ló dé?+]}
Market Woman 2: {Say na} di time wey dat girl Saratou begin work for Jigida clinic people begin stop to buy native herbs from us.
10 **Market Woman 1:** [+O sọ bẹ́ẹ̀.+]
Market Woman 2: Look as Chief Omoniyi turn back di oder day. Who for Jigida no know say di girl na Chief Omoniyi daughter-in-law?
15 **Market Woman 1:** Na true! [+O sọ bẹ́ẹ̀.+]
Market Woman 2: I no tell you?
Market Woman 1: Maybe na she dey spoil market for us.
Market Woman 2: [+N ò sọ fún ọ?+] Dat
20 girl, di oder time wey we wan go teach am lesson, [+ìwọ ni o+], no be you say make we go back?
Market Woman 1: En, dat day we hear one man voice inside di room. Di voice resemble
25 Constable Jaja own. If e catch us dey throway juju for Saratou body, na jail we for die put o.
Market Woman 2: Een een. Na our people dey talk say if lice never finish for person
30 hair, di person finger must not tire {work. No be so?}
Market Woman 1: {[+O rí yun-ùn sọ.} O rí yun-ùn sọ.+]
Market Woman 2: And if person no finish
35 di food wey e dey chop, di jaw no go rest.

Market Woman 1: Na so. Na so. {[+Òótọ́ ni.+]}
Market Woman 2: {So,} we go visit Saratou again. (R09 130-153)

[translation]

Market Woman 2: Mama Elewe, you don't quickly believe people.
Market Woman 1: What?
Market Woman 2: Ah.
Market Woman 1: What happened?
Market Woman 2: That it was when that girl Saratou started working in the Jigida clinic that people began to stop buying native herbs from us.
Market Woman 1: You said so.
Market Woman 2: Look how Chief Omoniyi turned back the other day. Who in Jigida doesn't know the girl is Chief Omoniyi's daughter-in-law?
Market Woman 1: It's true! You said so.
Market Woman 2: Didn't I tell you?
Market Woman 1: Maybe it's she who's spoiling the market for us.
Market Woman 2: Didn't I tell you? That girl, the other time when we wanted to go and teach her a lesson, it was you, wasn't it you who said we should go back?
Market Woman 1: Yes, that day we heard a man's voice in the room. The voice resembled Constable Jaja's. If he'd caught us casting a spell on Saratou, we would die in jail.
Market Woman 2: Our people say that as long as there are lice in somebody's hair, his fingers must not tire of working. Isn't it so?
Market Woman 1: You're right. You're right.
Market Woman 2: And as long as somebody hasn't finished the food he's eating, the jaw won't rest.
Market Woman 1: It's like that. It's like that. It's true.
Market Woman 2: So, we'll visit Saratou again.

5.6.1.2 *Single words or constituents*

Although it is, as shown above, fairly common for educated speakers to intersperse their spontaneous NigP discourse with clauses or larger segments in English, such switching is not a characteristic feature of all texts in the category "face-to-face speech". The extract below is taken from a conversation subtext (C04-1) from which elements marked as non-NigP speech are totally absent.

English elements in this extract are mainly nouns and noun phrases, and some verbs. The speakers employ the typical student vocabulary, e.g. *lecturer* (ll 1, 18), *lecture* (l 3), *semester* (l 15). In the analysis of the English nouns cited in the questionnaire study (Section 5.4.1.1), it was argued that these and a number of other common items may be considered borrowings in the student variety. It was also pointed out that there are many other items which are too specialized or rare to consider them integrated into NigP. Items of this type in the above extract include *course outline* (l 4), *quadratic equation* (l 17) and *quadratic formula* (l 19). These were selected as examples of English elements by the informants who analysed the two corpus extracts which contain each a part of quoted text, C04/1 and C04/2 (cf Table B 1, items 1-201, 1-115 and 1-256, respectively).

Text 5.5 Conversation between two university students

[original version]

B: [...] you go see some kind lecturers wey be say/ dem go dey give you some kind lectures wey-- imagine/ dem go give you course outline but to lecture you/ zero// and
5 dis thing na mathematics o//
A: hm//
B: just imagine when dem go tell you say/ dis na di topic wey we dey enter/ dem go just represent am by A B C//
10 **A:** ah//
B: for examination na im dem go come give you real values// [LAUGHTER] wetin you go come do? [LAUGHTER]
A: man student go confuse for exam hall o//
15 **B:** ah di thing so surprise me last semester//
A: hm?
B: just take example dis quadratic equation/ just imagine make your lecturer just go put quadratic formula for board&
20 **A:** {shoo//}
B: &{come} represent am by X I Y Z//
A: e no tell una anything?
B: just-- e no tell you anything/ e just comot// at least if e for put real digits now/
25 man for {understand}&
A: {understand//}
B: &small about am/ but man/
A: na wa o//
B: people just dey carry F anyhow now//
(C04 13-36)[86]

[translation]

B: You'll see lecturers who'll give you lectures where-- imagine, they'll give you a course outline, but to lecture you, zero. And this thing is mathematics.

A: Hm.
B: Just imagine, when they'll tell you, this is the topic we're entering, they'll just represent it by A B C.

A: Ah!
B: Then in the examination they'll give you real values. So what are you going to do then?

A: Man, students will get confused in the exam hall.
B: Ah, the thing so surprised me last semester.

A: Hm?
B: Just take for example this quadratic equation, just imagine your lecturer putting a quadratic formula on the board&

A: [exclamation]
B: &and representing it by X I Y Z.
A: He/she didn't tell you anything?
B: Just-- he/she didn't tell you anything, he/she just left. At least if he/she had put real digits one would've understood&
A: Understood.
B: &a little of it, but man,
A: [exclamation]
B: people just got F's.

The informant who analysed extract C04/2 also cited *real digits* (in the singular form), which appears in the list of noun phrases in Table B 1 (item 15-2-52). In the framework of the present study, items of this type can only be analysed as single-word or single-constituent switches (cf also the discussion in 5.4.1.1). Of the verbs in the text, *understand* (ll 25, 26) and *represent* (ll 9, 21) were cited in the questionnaires, though the former not in the one for this particular extract. For *understand,* I have shown in 5.4.1.2 that it is a fairly common but probably not fully integrated item in educated NigP, while *represent* (item 2-

---

[86] The complete subtext is one of the sound samples on the CD.

46 in Table B 1) is one of the many infrequent items in the list of English verbs. In the same way as English-origin verbs are used in indigenous language discourse (see the discussion in 4.1), these verbs are combined with NigP tense/aspect/modality markers (cf *go ... represent* (l 8f), *come represent* (l 21), *for understand* (l 25)). This is of course the expected pattern, as it has already become clear in the discussion of the questionnaire and corpus data so far that lexical verbs newly taken over from English are a common feature of educated NigP, whereas English verb morphology plays only a negligible role.

On the whole, the type of discourse illustrated in Text 5.5 fits very well into the pattern described by Agheyisi (1977) for the indigenous languages as "interlarded speech" (see the discussion in 4.1 and 4.2).

5.6.1.3 *Flagging by metalinguistic commentary*

The phenomenon of flagging of switches by metalinguistic commentary, whereby a speaker shows his/her awareness of using two different codes, has already been drawn attention to in 5.3.1. Such commentary may accompany both switches for clauses or larger segments and single-word or single-constituent switches. The phenomenon can be observed not only in the example given in 5.3.1, but also in several other examples from the corpus that have been cited in the analysis so far ((11), (36), (45), (117)). Switching flagged by metalinguistic commentary occurs a number of times in two of the interview texts (V01 and V02), and there are a few examples in the discussions as well, but none in the conversations. There are also some examples in the broadcast section of the corpus, almost all of them in the advice texts. Below, I give two more examples, one each from the interviews and the discussions:

(132) so you yourself you go carry di matter go tell dem/ wetin Bola Tinubu suppose do na "awareness programme"/ na so dem call am for oyibo// (V01 30ff)

'So you yourself will go and tell them that what Bola Tinubu ought to do is an "awareness programme", that's what they call it in English.'

(133) because some people no know (di di di) di side effect make I put am like dat/ according to oyibo people/ about bleaching// (D03 88ff)

'because some people don't know the side effect, let me put it like that, according to the white people, about bleaching [of one's skin].'

5.6.2 *The particle o*

Two informants mentioned the particle *o* in their comments in the questionnaire, criticizing the way it is used in some news texts (cf the comments on extracts N01/1 and R02/2 in Table B 2 in Appendix B). *O* has a range of pragmatic functions such as emphasis and is often added to imperatives and vocatives (Faraclas 1996: 25ff, 116). Typical examples from the conversations in the corpus are the following:

(134) ah man wahala// wahala dey *o*// (C09 144)

'Ah, man, trouble. There's real trouble.'

(135) wait *o* wait *o*/ (C10 49)

'Wait, wait'

With the functions mentioned, one would expect *o* to be most frequent in the dialogic or persuasive text categories in the corpus – conversations, drama and advice. However, Figure 5.10 reveals that while these categories do have higher frequencies of the particle than the interviews and discussions, it is in the news texts that *o* is used most often.

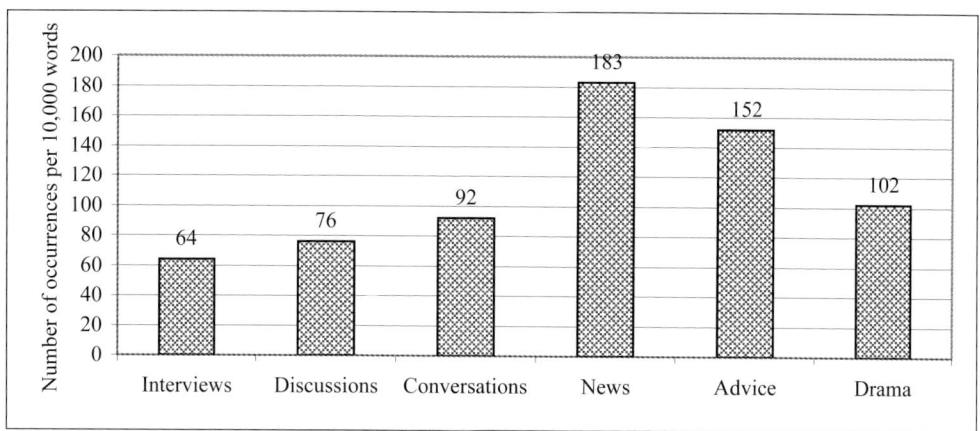

Figure 5.10 Frequency of the particle o in the NigP corpus by text category[a]

[a] The very slight discrepancy between the count of *o* in the conversations in this figure and in Figure 2 in Deuber (2002: 215) is due to a minor correction in one of the corpus texts.

Furthermore, the normal position of *o* is clause-final, but in the news texts, it often appears after or even within a (non-final) noun phrase, as in the following examples:

(136) Di Lagos State Government *o* say dem go work with Parents-Teachers Association to see say correct bookuru education show face for di state. (N05 40ff)

'The Lagos State Government said they would work together with the Parents-Teachers Association to bring good education to the state.'

(137) Na di oga kpatakpata *o* of VON, Mr. Taiwo Alemi, na im talk dis one for Yola for Adamawa State. (N04 153f)

'It was the director of VON [Voice of Nigeria], Mr. Taiwo Alemi, who said this in Yola in Adamawa State.'

The particle *o* thus seems to represent a case of the overuse of a NigP feature in the newscaster's translations.

5.6.3 *Proverbs*

Nwachukwu-Agbada (1990: 38) describes proverbs as a "common speech strategy among Nigerians". He gives examples of their role in various speech situations in Yoruba and Igbo culture and goes on to explain (ibid.):

> The examples of the Yoruba and the Igbo can be extended to all other ethnic groups in Nigeria. Speech making in Nigerian cultures is usually an effort at reaching out, at painting a picture, at shocking, at inviting the imagination and at clinching a point. This could be the case in other cultures too, but in Nigeria the use of proverbs in oral contexts is a tribute

to one's native land, a clear evidence of one who had had a rich traditional education before adulthood.

In the urban context where the indigenous languages can no longer fulfil all communicative needs, the traditional discourse strategy of the proverb has, according to Nwachukwu-Agbada (1990: 37), been carried over into the popular lingua franca, NigP.

In the present NigP corpus, the use of proverbs is particularly typical of the texts in two of the radio subcategories, namely the news and advice texts. Some informants also cited proverbs and idiomatic expressions in these texts in the section of the questionnaire for "other peculiarities" (see the responses concerning extracts N04/2, A02/3, A02/4, A03/7 and A04/7 in Table B 2). The proverbs in the news texts are particularly striking. They are not part of the original English scripts but are added by the NigP newscasters - a strategy apparently to appeal to the listener by relating the content of the news to folk culture. In the news extract cited in 5.4.2.3 as Text 5.1, each news item is introduced by a proverb. Below are two more examples.[87]

(138) Our people talk say dem no dey take empty belle dey blow fire o, but one person don do am. (N03 128f).

'Our people say that you can't blow a fire with an empty stomach, but one person has done it.' [beginning of a news item reporting that the Nigerian President had not received his salary since assuming office]

(139) If fire never spread well well, na im dem fit dey quench am o. (N04 39f)

'A fire must be put out before it can spread.' [beginning of a news item about an appeal by Nigeria's Vice President to the international community to help solve the conflict in Sierra Leone in order to stabilize the region and prevent further outbreaks of war in West Africa]

Proverbs are also quite common in the speech of some characters in the drama serial *One Thing at a Time* (for examples cf Text 5.4, ll 24-29). In the drama texts from *Rainbow City* and the texts in the category "face-to-face speech", they are used only very occasionally.

5.7 Evaluation of the texts in the questionnaire study

In the discussion of the corpus data so far I have taken into account only part of the results of the questionnaire study of corpus extracts - mainly the examples of English lexical and grammatical elements cited by the informants in Sections 1.1 and 1.2 of the questionnaire or "text evaluation sheet" (see Appendix A), and a few of the additional observations and comments they made in Sections 1.3 and 2.3. Now I will discuss the general judgments on the degree of English use and the overall evaluation with respect to the two criteria of satisfactoriness and intelligibility given by the informants in sections 1.1,2 and 2.1,2 of the questionnaire. The additional observations and comments in Sections 1.3 and 2.3, which are listed in Table B 2 (Appendix B), and the group interview in which some of the informants participated (Appendix C, Interview 11) will help to interpret the results.

---

[87] The use of proverbs in the news texts is discussed in somewhat more detail in Deuber (2002: 214ff).

5.7.1 General findings

Figures 5.11a,b display the results of the evaluation of the corpus extracts in Sections 1.1,2 and 2.1,2 of the questionnaire for the whole corpus. In Figure 5.11a one can see that English influence was found to be considerably greater in lexis than in grammar. This is in consonance with the observations made in 5.4 and 5.5, viz, that in one of the speech contexts examined, that of face-to-face speech, educated NigP speakers have a tendency to draw freely on the English lexicon, but that even in this context, the use of English grammatical elements is generally more limited. Figure 5.11b shows that the language of the great majority of the extracts - over 90% - was rated as a fully or fairly satisfactory form of NigP for the informant personally as an educated speaker, and was also thought to be fully or fairly intelligible to a NigP speaker with little or no formal education. This evaluation may appear remarkably positive, although it should not be overlooked that only about half of the extracts were found to be *fully* satisfactory and intelligible. In Deuber & Oloko (2003: 292), two factors have been put forward as possible explanations for this result. First, it seems important that over 80% of the extracts conform more or less to what the informants regard as NigP at least grammatically. With NigP having a largely English-derived vocabulary, its independent character rests primarily on its grammatical structure, and one may therefore expect grammar to have been a more important consideration in the informants' judgments than lexis. Second, it was surmised that some anglicisms may have attained a high degree of acceptability. This is confirmed by the analyses in Sections 5.4 and 5.5 of the present study, where it has been shown that some lexical and a few grammatical items which are not traditionally part of NigP are now fairly well integrated at least into the educated variety. In contrast to long-established items, they are still perceived as anglicisms to a certain extent, but they already seem common and acceptable enough to be considered borrowings. This means that their presence may be noticed in an analysis like the present one but will hardly render the language of an extract unsatisfactory as a form of NigP.

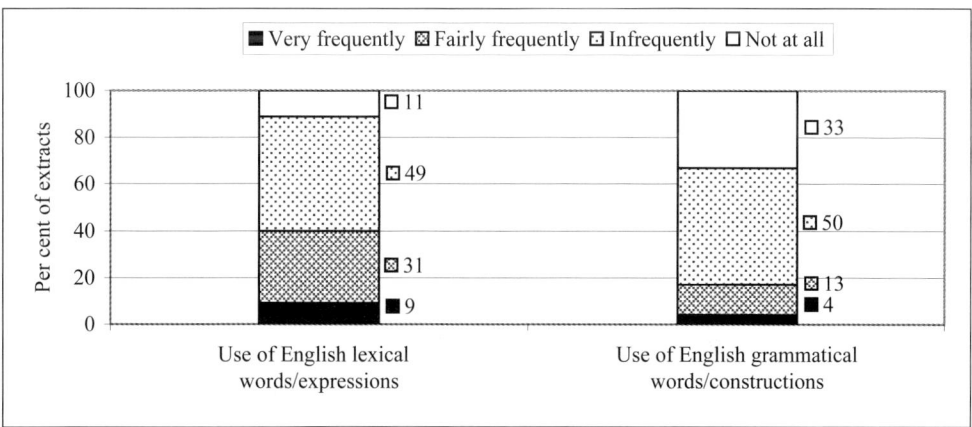

Figure 5.11a   Evaluation of extracts from the NigP corpus, whole corpus: lexis and grammar

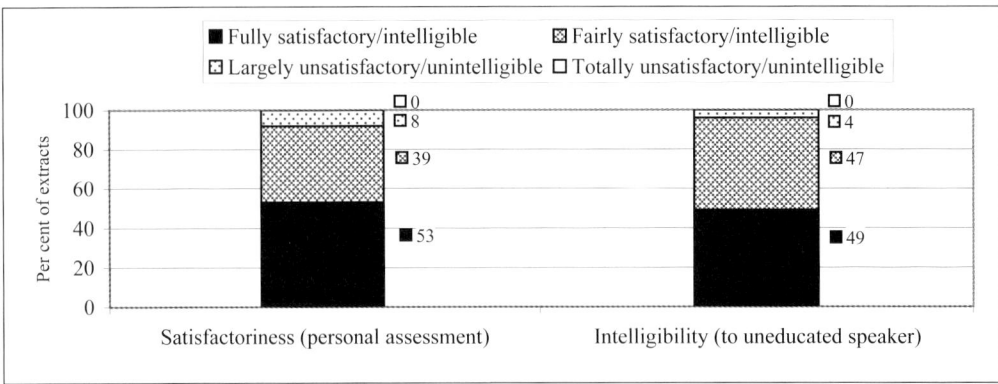

*Figure 5.11b   Evaluation of extracts from the NigP corpus, whole corpus:
overall evaluation*

That the influence of English was often found to be noticeable but not too far-reaching is underlined by some of the additional observations and comments that were made in the questionnaires. Consider, for instance, those on extracts from the student conversations (C03-C10; see Section 3 of Table B 2):[88] Their main thrust is that these texts are characterized by the use of specialized vocabulary related to the university setting and some code-switching - normal features of the student variety, as the informants point out - and that it is only or mainly the topics and the resultant lexical choice which might cause some comprehension difficulties to a less educated speaker. As one informant put it in a comment on one of these extracts (C03/4; cf Table B 2):

> Note that any non-comprehension on the part of someone with little formal education will stem from 'specialist register' and 'specialist topic'.

With lexical items from English apparently felt to be unavoidable to some extent and not a major issue, it is not too surprising that the informants should have found many of the extracts at least fairly satisfactory and intelligible; as one informant also emphasized in summarizing his assessments of news extracts in Interview 11 (ll 8-9), the difference between more and less English-influenced extracts was perceived to result mainly in fair versus full satisfactoriness and intelligibility. Regarding the latter criterion, it also has to be taken into consideration that in the urban environment of Lagos, the use of anglicisms in NigP does not necessarily make it unintelligible to a person without much schooling, at least as long as they are not too many and too specialized. As one informant pointed out in the comments section of a questionnaire in which he evaluated an extract from the discussion dealing with political and economic issues (D05/6; cf Table B 2):

> A speaker of Pidgin may have little or no formal education, but could have been so exposed to those with formal education that he/she might find the passage largely intelligible. Yet the passage appears quite distant from countryside Pidgin.

---

[88] Other relevant comments include those concerning extracts V03/7, V05/1, N04/1, A03/5 and R05/5; see Table B 2.

5.7.2   Findings by text categories

In the analyses in 5.4 to 5.6 several differences between the two major text categories, face-to-face speech and radio broadcasts, have emerged, and one will expect to see these reflected in the data from the evaluation when they are broken down into those for face-to-face speech and for radio broadcasts. This has been done in Figures 5.12a,b. The results presented in these figures make it clear that there are indeed significant differences between the assessments with regard to all four criteria. As Figure 5.12a shows, use of English elements, both lexical and grammatical, was found to be less frequent in the radio texts than in face-to-face speech. This is the expected result, since it has already become clear in the course of the analyses in the present chapter that (a) in contrast to the speakers recorded in the face-to-face context, the broadcasters try, to a greater or lesser extent, to avoid the use of English lexical items, (b) at least some of the radio texts are notably conservative with regard to certain grammatical variables, and (c) the larger segments in English marked as non-NigP speech, which account for many of the occurrences in the corpus of English grammatical elements which are clearly not integrated into NigP, are concentrated in the face-to-face speech section. In Figure 5.12b it can be seen that the radio sample as a whole also has better ratings for both satisfactoriness and intelligibility than the sample of face-to-face speech (of course, since almost all of the extracts in all categories were rated as either fully or fairly satisfactory and intelligible, a difference can be perceived only if a distinction is drawn between "fully satisfactory" and "fully intelligible", respectively, and the other answers).

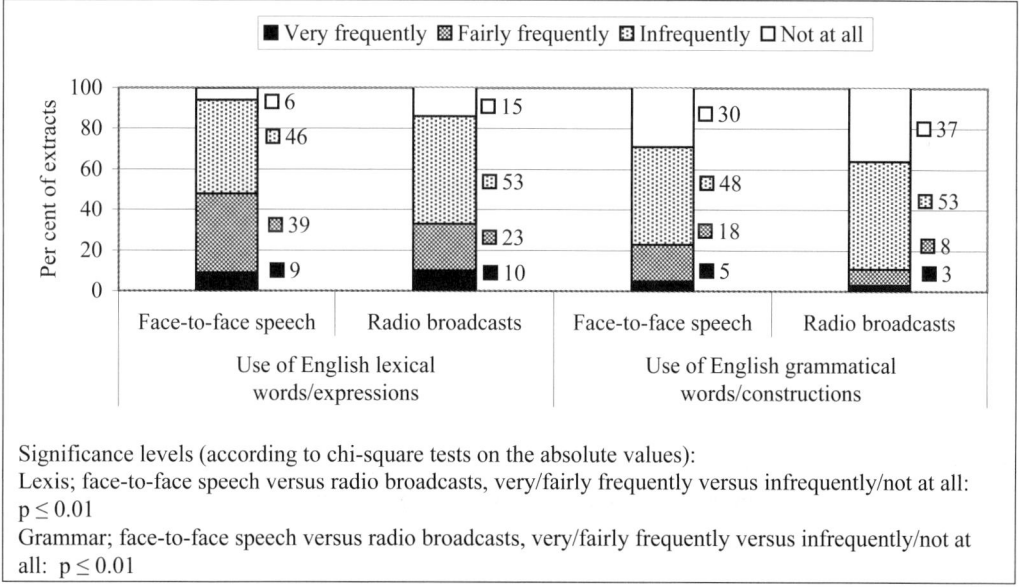

Figure 5.12a   Evaluation of extracts from the NigP corpus, comparison of major text categories: lexis and grammar

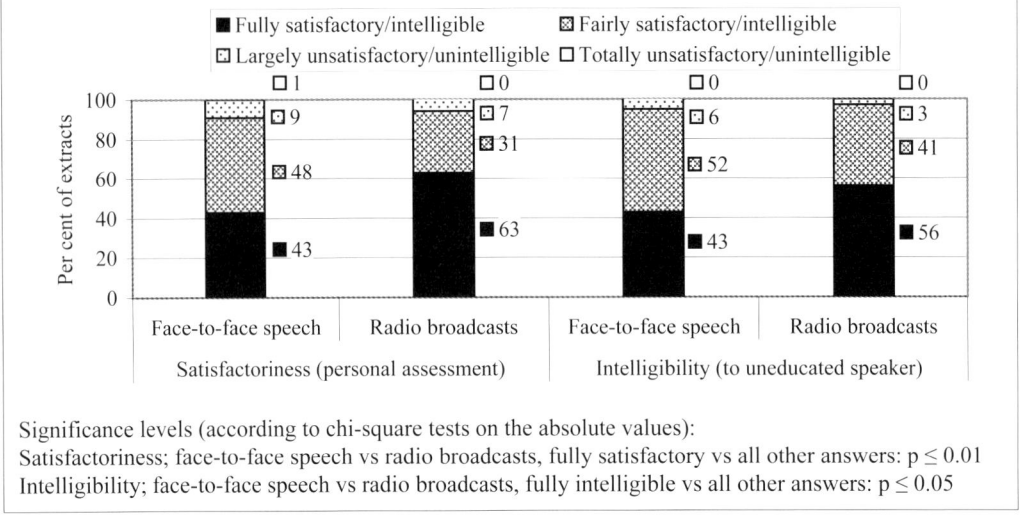

Figure 5.12b Evaluation of extracts from the NigP corpus, comparison of major text categories: overall evaluation

In Figures 5.13a,b and 5.14a,b the results for face-to-face speech and radio broadcasts, respectively, are further broken down according to subcategories. As is apparent from Figures 5.13a and 5.14a, there are in each case significant differences between certain subcategories in the degree to which the informants found lexical usage in the extracts to be influenced by English. Among the subcategories of face-to-face speech, there is an obvious difference between the discussions and the other two subcategories: while the assessments of the interviews and the conversations are very similar, the informants rated the use of English lexical words or expressions in the discussions as significantly less frequent.

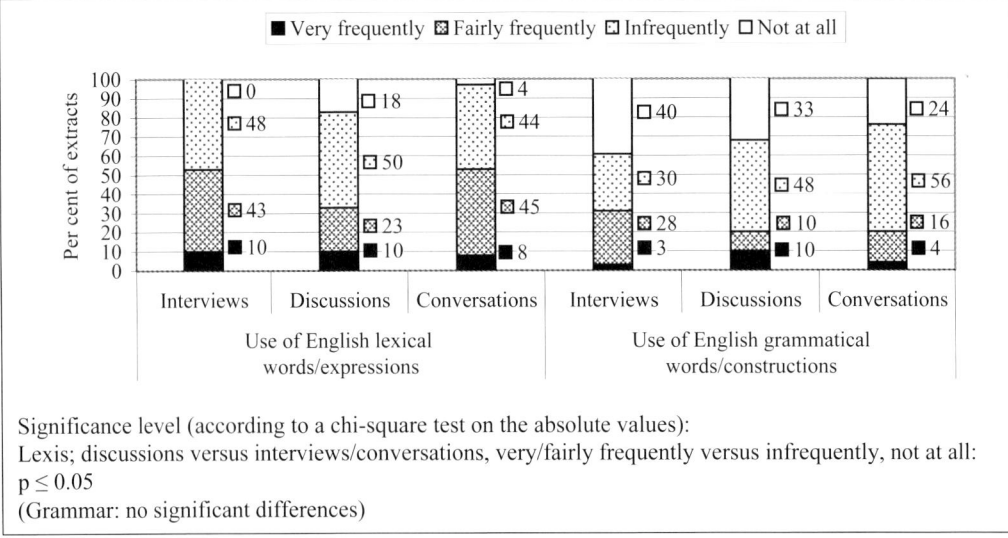

Figure 5.13a Evaluation of extracts from the NigP corpus, comparison of subcategories of face-to-face speech: lexis and grammar

In the broadcast sample, the assessments of the extent to which English lexical items are used in the texts in the subcategories "advice" and "drama" do not diverge greatly, but a significant difference emerged between the texts in these two subcategories and the news texts, in which the use of English lexical items was found to be significantly more frequent. These results are certainly attributable primarily to the nature of the topics that are most typical of the texts in the different subcategories (see, in particular, Sections 5.1.1, 5.1.3 and 5.4.2.4).

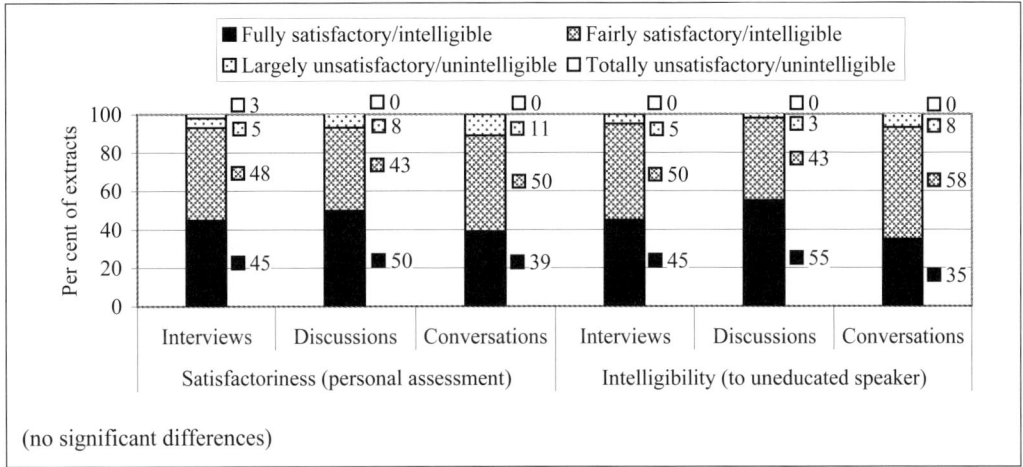

Figure 5.13b Evaluation of extracts from the NigP corpus, comparison of subcategories of face-to-face speech: overall evaluation

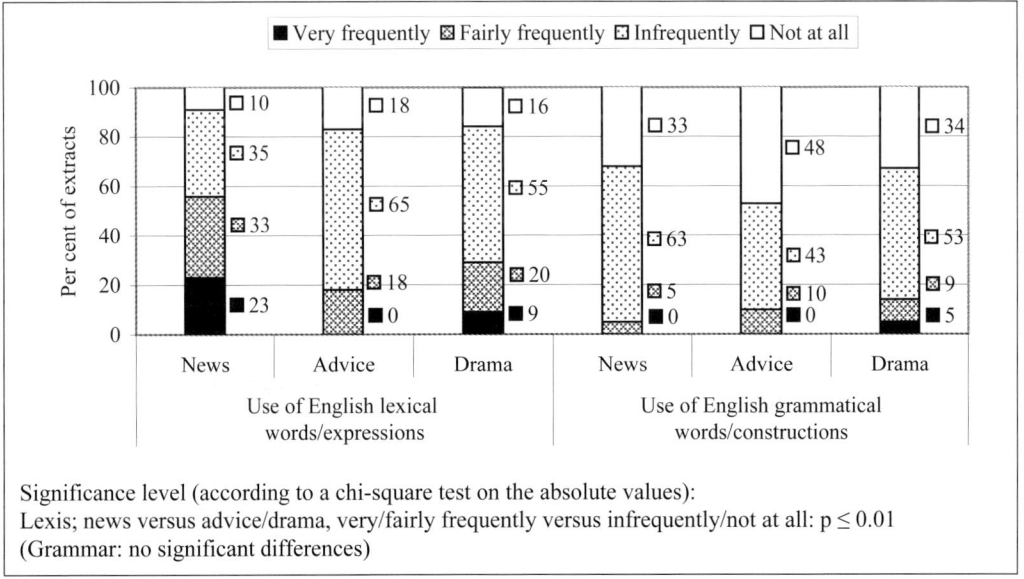

Significance level (according to a chi-square test on the absolute values):
Lexis; news versus advice/drama, very/fairly frequently versus infrequently/not at all: $p \leq 0.01$
(Grammar: no significant differences)

Figure 5.14a Evaluation of extracts from the NigP corpus, comparison of subcategories of radio broadcasts: lexis and grammar

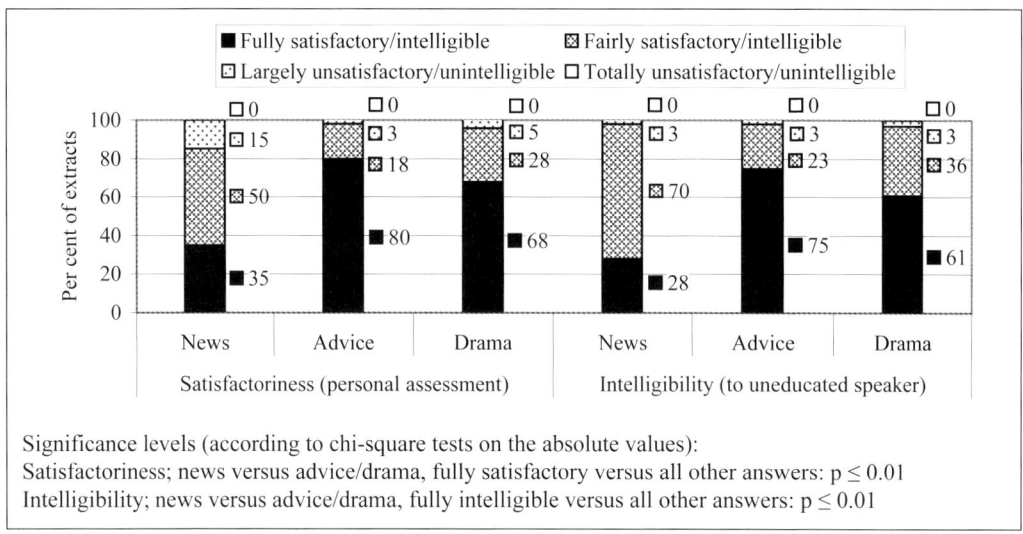

Figure 5.14b Evaluation of extracts from the NigP corpus, comparison of subcategories of radio broadcasts: overall evaluation

In the informants' assessments of the degree to which English grammatical elements are used in the texts of the different subcategories significant differences can be observed neither in the case of face-to-face speech (Figure 5.13a) nor in the case of the radio texts (Figure 5.14a). For the subcategories of face-to-face speech the results of the overall evaluation (Figure 5.13b) are also rather homogeneous. Within the results for the radio texts (Figure 5.14b), in contrast, there turns out to be a significant difference: the news broadcasts received significantly lower ratings for both satisfactoriness and intelligibility than the texts of the other two subcategories. It is of course to be expected that to some extent, the overall judgments will correlate with the degree of English influence found by the informants. However, the additional comments made in the questionnaires and the views some of the informants expressed in Interview 11 make it clear that anglicisms are not the only factor responsible for the lower ratings of the news extracts, at least as far as satisfactoriness is concerned. As can be seen in Section 4 of Table B 2, in several of the questionnaires that were completed for news extracts one finds statements to the effect that the NigP employed in these texts is artificial. This perception may of course have to do with the fact that educated Nigerians like the informants who assessed the extracts generally rely on English-medium sources of information. NigP news broadcasts may therefore easily strike them as unnatural, unlike drama texts, for instance, which, as one informant put it in Interview 11, "seem to convey Pidgin in a natural context" (l 110; cf also ll 301-303). Furthermore, it may be assumed that an educated person may not always have much understanding for, or patience with, the newscasters' attempts to frame the message in such a way that it will be understood by their less well-educated target audience (cf also Interview 11, ll 52-64, 77-88). However, an effort to get the message across to this group of listeners is made in the advice texts as well, and one of the informants also drew attention to this in one of the questionnaires (see Table B 2, extract A04/5, response (b)), yet these texts generally received very favourable comments (see Section 5 of Table B 2). Apparently it is not conscious pidginization per se that the informants disapproved of, but rather what they perceived as a misuse or overuse of pidginization strategies and typical NigP features in the news texts. The following are a few particularly revealing comments on some of the features of the news texts that have also been mentioned in the course of the discussion of the corpus data in 5.4-6:

> And the man at a point was trying to explain *democracy*. Everybody knows that, even mechanics now. You understand that. So the idea of trying to-- it makes it too simplistic. (Interview 11, ll 99-100; cf also 5.4.2.1)

> The attempt to pidginize made this newscaster resort to much creativity. The end result is Pidgin that can hardly find any basis in reality. (See for example expressions like *launch-launch* [...]). (comment on extract N05/4, see Table B 2; cf also 5.4.2.1)

> *According by* is pretentious, for no genuine speaker of Pidgin uses such. (comment on extract N01/6, see Table B 2; cf also 5.5.2)

> The Pidgin used in the extracts from the drama presentations seems to reflect standard usage more than that in the news broadcasts. The latter sound somewhat artificial, especially with the unnecessary addition of *o* at the end of many statements. (comment on extract R02/2, see Table B 2; cf also 5.6.2)

5.7.3   *Comparison of radio drama serials*

In addition to analysing the data by text categories, I have also compared the assessments of the extracts from the two radio drama serials, *Rainbow City* and *One Thing at a Time*. The results are summarized in Figures 5.15a,b. The figures reveal some significant differences between the results for the two serials: the informants found fewer English lexical items in the *Rainbow City* texts (see Figure 5.15a), and these have better overall ratings as well (see Figure 5.15b). The *Rainbow City* extracts also received favourable comments in Section 2.3 of the questionnaire wherever this section was made use of, whereas the comments on extracts from *One Thing at a Time* are mixed (see Section 6 of Table B 2). However, it has to be borne in mind in this comparison that in *Rainbow City* some characters are made to speak English (and scenes in which they appear are not included in the corpus), whereas the scriptwriter of *One Thing at a Time* has taken a different approach to the fictional representation of multilingualism. While all of the characters in this serial use NigP, it appears, as I have pointed out in 5.6.1.1, that the insertion of larger segments in English into some characters' speech (like the insertion of indigenous language segments) is used to some extent as a characterization strategy. This means that unlike in the case of the *Rainbow City* sample, scenes in which characters of the type that one informant described as "sophisticated" (see the comment on extract R07/3 in Table B 2) did not have to be cut out in compiling the corpus texts from *One Thing at a Time*, and this factor may be in part responsible for the results of the evaluation and the additional comments.[89]

---

[89] In connection with the critical comments that were made on two of the extracts from *One Thing at a Time*, R07/3 and R08/8 (see Table B 2), it is noteworthy that one of the two characters in R07/3 is Chief

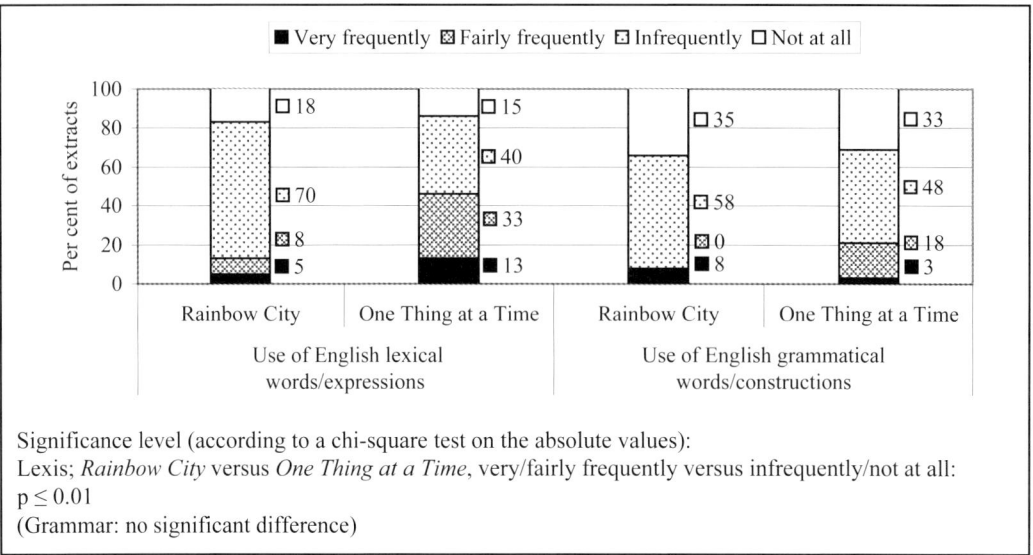

Figure 5.15a   Evaluation of extracts from the NigP corpus, comparison of radio drama serials: lexis and grammar

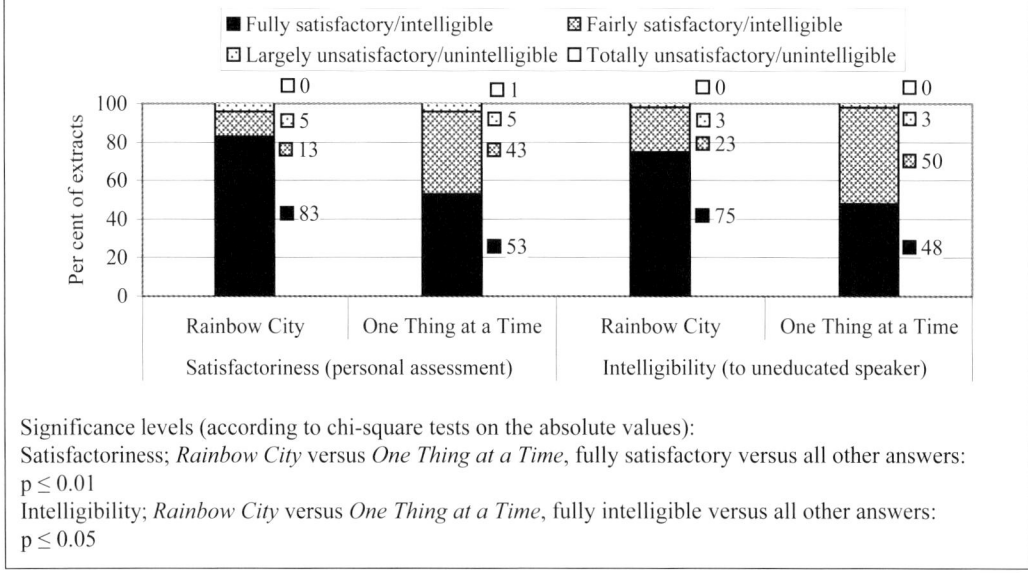

Figure 5.15b   Evaluation of extracts from the NigP corpus, comparison of radio drama serials: overall evaluation

---

Omoniyi and the two characters in R08/8 are the two young doctors (see 5.6.1.1 on these characters and their speech).

5.8 Discussion and conclusions

5.8.1 *English influence in educated Nigerian Pidgin*

The analysis of the corpus has shown that the main aspects of English influence in educated NigP are:
- code-switching for whole segments of discourse
- single-word or single-constituent switching, in particular of nouns and noun phrases and of lexical verbs
- lexical borrowing, in particular of nouns from semantic fields such as higher education or politics which NigP has not traditionally had to cope with
- some limited grammatical borrowing

All of these types of English influence are shared with educated (or, more generally, urban) varieties of indigenous languages (see the discussion in 4.1-2). The only real difference is that while in indigenous languages, according to the literature, borrowing of English grammatical forms has so far been limited to conjunctions, NigP has, as the present results indicate, borrowed not only conjunctions but also a few other grammatical forms which are on a lower level on the scale of borrowability (see 2.4.2), including one inflectional morpheme, plural *-s*.

In a theoretical framework for language contact such as that of Thomason & Kaufman (1988; see the discussion in 2.4.2), in which, in addition to the social nature of the contact situation, structural similarities between the languages involved are recognized as a relevant factor for the degree of borrowing, the greater extent of grammatical borrowing from English in NigP in comparison to indigenous languages can be explained by the high percentage of shared lexicon. For example, as has been mentioned in 4.1, the use of plural *-s* has also been reported for English-origin nouns in Yoruba discourse, and with NigP having a largely English-derived lexicon, it is clear why, in contrast to Yoruba, it should have been able to integrate *-s* to such an extent that it is not restricted to code-switched or newly borrowed nouns. It is also an important fact, however, that grammatical borrowing is the exception rather than the rule. In this connection, the caveat made by Thomason & Kaufman (1988) about borrowing into a Creole from its lexifier as a case of "typologically favored borrowing" - that, while the lexicon is shared to a great extent, there is often a structural mismatch - seems relevant. For example, the corpus data have shown that in the area of tense/aspect marking, where the structure of NigP, like that of the indigenous languages discussed in 4.1-2, diverges greatly from that of English, NigP has so far been immune to borrowing of English forms, just as the indigenous languages have also been highly resistant to English influence in this area.

In the case of tense/aspect marking and several other areas of the grammar investigated (singular personal and possessive pronouns, copula use, verbal negation), I have been able to contrast my findings on educated NigP with what has been reported in the literature for the mesolects of the Creole continua in the anglophone Caribbean. As I have pointed out in these analyses, not only is the use of English forms - those that would be described as "acrolectal" in a continuum situation - very restricted in the present data, although they do alternate to a limited extent with the "basilectal" ones, but one can also observe that none of the uniquely or typically mesolectal features found in the Caribbean are attested.

On the whole, one can say that from the point of view of its relationship with English on the one hand and the varieties of the language furthest removed from English or English influence on the other, educated NigP has more in common with educated varieties of indigenous languages of Nigeria than with the mesolects of the Creole continua in the anglophone Caribbean.

5.8.2 The question of "pseudopidgin"

The relative stability I found in many areas of the grammar when comparing my findings to descriptions of the NigP core system is all the more remarkable in view of the fact that educated NigP as investigated here is predominantly a second language spoken with varying degrees of competence (though excluding the rudimentary level). One may conclude from this that NigP has norms which are sufficiently stable for the continued spread of (primarily) second language varieties outside its core geographical area and group of users not to constitute a serious threat to its status as a full-fledged language in its own right. Thus, although the attitudes and the kind of linguistic usage she describes undoubtedly exist, statements like the following by Omamor (1997: 221f) appear somewhat exaggerated:

> [...] all the indications are that a good number of Nigerians, and more particularly the more highly literate ones who are not regular speakers of Ẹnpi [Nigerian Pidgin], appear to consider the contact-language antecedents of the language as incontrovertibly indicating that the language need not be properly learnt. The result, of course, is what seems like a never-ending process of spontaneous (or even deliberate?) creation and re-creation leading to the emergence of forms passed off as Ẹnpi which the more regular, typical speakers of the language are totally unable to identify.

As has already been mentioned in the introduction to the present study, Omamor has identified the mass media and literary works as channels for the spread of the kind of distorted NigP or "pseudopidgin" she alludes to in the quotation above, and among the present data the question of the role which this phenomenon plays in current educated NigP usage is thus particularly relevant to the broadcasts. In the analysis of the corpus it has become clear that these cannot be treated as a single class but that one needs to differentiate between the three broadcast subcategories. The advice texts may in fact be taken as a counter-example to Omamor's "pseudo-pidgin". The drama texts do have a few idiosyncrasies (see especially the observations in 5.5.4.4) and some extracts from drama texts were felt by participants in the questionnaire study to be too strongly influenced by English, but on the whole the problematic aspects do not appear to be so significant as to warrant speaking of "pseudopidgin". The text type which perhaps comes closest to this phenomenon is the news, not so much because of English influence, although this is also a problem in some cases, but because of the newscasters' tendency towards "hyper-pidginization". However, since my informants rated most of the broadcast extracts, including those from the news texts, as at least fairly satisfactory as a form of NigP, "pseudopidgin" would probably be an exaggerated description in almost all cases. It is true that the whole study, including the evaluation of the corpus extracts, was conducted outside NigP's heartland in Delta State, whose role as the home of what she describes as "regular"

NigP is much emphasized by Omamor, but it seems very significant that the informants were able to identify with the majority of the broadcasts no less than with the samples of ordinary, face-to-face language use. Furthermore, the factors mentioned by Omamor in connection with the phenomenon of "pseudopidgin" - lack of competence, an attitude of "anything goes" or deliberate distortion - are certainly not the only ones accounting for perceived deficiencies in NigP texts. In the case of the news broadcasts (as in the other texts in the corpus), the competence factor cannot be ruled out entirely,[90] and one of the informants also brought up the issue of a lack of seriousness in the newscasters' approach (see Interview 11, ll 66-67). However, in addition to these factors, it has to be taken into consideration as well that to translate news from a highly standardized language into a vernacular cannot be an easy task, so that it is not too surprising to find the NigP newscasters wavering between anglicisms and pidginization. And that the results of such efforts are not always appreciated is a fact which is not restricted to NigP. Görlach (1998: 143) makes the following remark in connection with broadcasting in NigP:

> As many experiments with semi-languages in Europe have shown (Scots, Low German, Occitan etc.) newly created formal registers impress users as artificial, and they are frequently not accepted as 'their' language by the proper native speakers of the variety.

(Seen in this light, as I have pointed out in Deuber 2002: 221, the fact that the majority of the news extracts were evaluated in the questionnaire study as at least fairly satisfactory and intelligible may even appear quite remarkable!) Besides, the quality of the news broadcasts will inevitably vary with the amount of time and care that goes into the translation. In the case studied here, the quality is indirectly affected by a problem which is not peculiar to NigP broadcasting, namely that of antiquated and faulty equipment. As daily live productions, the news broadcasts are dependent on reliable transmission. This, as has already been mentioned, was simply not guaranteed at Radio Nigeria 3 at the time of the research, and this situation did not encourage the maintenance of the time-consuming but from the point of view of quality certainly desirable practice of written translation.

In sum, one may still find traces of the phenomenon of "pseudopidgin" in current NigP radio broadcasts and there are other problems as well, but extreme deviation from ordinary language use is certainly not the norm. One can thus say that although there is room for improvement, NigP on the radio has at least more or less emancipated itself from the comic exaggeration and distortion of *Safe Journey* or *Masquerade* (see 3.3).

5.8.3   Radio broadcasts: Functional and structural expansion of Nigerian Pidgin

If one takes a puristic perspective, there is hardly a NigP text where one will not be able to detect deviations from one's ideal, but this should not blind one to the larger issues involved in actual language use. The present data show that among NigP broadcasts one can find good examples of the extension of the scope of the language beyond its typical (and stereotypical) uses as a medium for informal communication and humour in a way which is both linguistically largely appropriate and socially meaningful. Such examples are in

---

[90] As becomes clear in Interview 10, ll 84-129, the station in question has staff selection procedures which are meant to ensure the necessary level of competence among the newscasters, but these are not always applied.

particular the texts in the category "advice" and the drama texts, or at least some of them (cf also Deuber & Oloko 2003 for a discussion of the issue with regard specifically to *Rainbow City*). As concerns the news, the newscasters may not always have chosen the most felicitous compromises between anglicisms and pidginization, but these texts serve well to illustrate two important facts about the linguistic implications of the functional expansion of NigP. First, that NigP will hardly be able to cope with its expanding functions without borrowing (primarily lexical borrowing) from English. Second, that there are also a number of viable alternatives to borrowing, which make use of the resources of NigP to express modern concepts. These are important mainly for broadcasters and others who use NigP to transmit information to the segments of the population which cannot be reached with English, and, if adequately employed, they can help to enhance the usefulness of the language in such contexts.

5.8.4 Register variation in educated Nigerian Pidgin

Samarin's (1971: 122) observation that "when a person is speaking a pidgin he is limited to the use of a code with but one level or style or register" is quite plausible for a prototypical pidgin (in the sense of a reduced language with a reduced set of functions). Also, it is true to observe, as Patrick (1997: 42) does in his discussion of the topic in relation to Jamaican Creole, that style/register variation has been a rather neglected aspect in P/C linguistics, although a few studies exist. However, one would not therefore assume that a speaker of an expanded P/C such as NigP "does not have the rich variety of language styles from which to choose whatever is appropriate to the context, situation, or person (or people) to whom he is talking", as Samarin (ibid.) goes on to say about a speaker of a Pidgin.

The analyses in the present chapter have shown that the factors mentioned by Samarin in fact have an influence on educated NigP use on all of the levels that have been dealt with and that it is quite possible to distinguish situationally defined subvarieties of this variety of the language. Most obviously, radio Pidgin as it is represented in the corpus differs from the NigP use of educated speakers in the context of spontaneous, face-to-face communication with educated peers. As the results of the evaluation of the corpus extracts in the questionnaire study and my observations on the issue of anglicisms versus pidginization strategies have shown, the broadcasts generally tend to make more restricted use of anglicisms, and it is mainly in these texts that one notes that the speakers (or scriptwriters) strive to coin NigP equivalents for English lexical items or to explain their meaning. I further found in the case of two grammatical variables, plural marking of nouns and the third person plural subject personal pronoun, that in the texts in two of the broadcast subcategories, "news" and "advice", an effort is made to maintain a NigP form which apparently has been all but replaced by one newly borrowed from English in the spontaneous everyday language use of educated speakers. Furthermore, a tendency for the speakers to insert larger segments in English of a clause or more into their NigP discourse can be observed in all of the subcategories of the face-to-face speech section of the corpus, but in the broadcast section this phenomenon is practically absent from the texts in two subcategories, "news" and "advice"; only in some of the drama texts, which are in a way closer to face-to-face speech since they recreate everyday communicative situations, is this type of code alternation also quite common. In addition, it was shown that in the face-to-face context, code-switching serves a variety of discourse functions such as emphasis, whereas in the broadcasts, particularly the news and the advice texts, a different discourse strategy was found to be quite prominent: the use of proverbs, traditional in Nigerian cultures, which can serve to summarize, emphasize or comment on a point, in addition to appealing to popular taste. The differences on the lexical, grammatical and discourse levels between the broadcast and face-to-face speech data in the corpus are probably due mainly to the difference in addressee(s), and secondarily to the more formal nature of the broadcasting context. The factor of formality may also explain the differences between the texts in the subcategories "news" and "advice" and the drama texts, although, since all the texts in the former two subcategories are from Radio Nigeria 3 but this station is not responsible for the production of the drama serials from which texts are included in the corpus, a Radio Nigeria 3 "house style" may be a relevant factor as well.

As is to be expected, given that the situations in which the samples of face-to-face speech were recorded were all rather similar and differed only to some extent in formality, there are no very pronounced differences between the texts in the different subcategories of this section of the corpus. However, apart from the fact that the degree of English lexical influence naturally depends to some extent on the topics of the texts (see 5.7.2), it appears that in the somewhat more formal interviews and discussions the speakers tend to pay slightly more attention to their lexical usage (see 5.4.2.4, 5.6.1.3). Furthermore, in the analysis of one of the grammatical variables, plural marking of nouns, it was found that the variant shared with English is significantly more frequent in the conversations than in the news and advice texts. In line with what has been reported in the code-switching literature, I also found that code-switching as an overall discourse mode, of which, due to my text selection criteria, one finds only traces in the corpus, is characteristic primarily of the most informal type of interactions, the conversations. Of course, the influence of the speech situation cannot be separated unequivocally from idiolectal differences, as the texts in the different subcategories are not from the same speakers, but it does appear that the formality of the speech situation plays a role, with the tendency for bilingual speakers to mix NigP and English increasing with decreasing formality of the speech situation.

The data thus provide some evidence of educated NigP speakers accommodating to their addressee(s) and choosing between more formal and more informal registers of the language as appropriate - precisely what one would expect, but what has never been demonstrated for NigP before.

6

Nigerian Pidgin as spoken by less educated speakers: analysis of additional recordings

6.1   The speakers and recordings

This chapter will present analyses of three recordings of NigP as spoken by speakers who, like those whose speech was analysed in the corpus study in the preceding chapter, speak the language at least fairly well, but who do not have formal education up to the same level as the speakers in the corpus (if any). One of these speakers, a middle-aged taxi driver who came to Lagos from his native Kwara State in the 1960s, has never been to school. Recording A is a conversation between this speaker and a research assistant as well as the present author which took place in the taxi (due to the constraints imposed by the situation, this recording is rather short, with about 660 words in total). The other two speakers, Janet (in Recording B) and Chike (in Recording C),[1] are both teenagers and have some formal education, though in Janet's case this seems to have been rather limited. Janet is a primary school drop-out from a village in Delta State who was about twelve at the time of the recording. Apparently she spent some time with relatives living in the town of Warri before being taken to Lagos to work as a housegirl a few months before the recording was made. The recording is an interview about her life conducted by a research assistant. The research assistant reported that Janet felt somewhat intimidated and appeared rather self-conscious about her speech. This recording is much longer than Recording A (over 3,200 words, including the interviewer's questions). The speaker in Recording C, Chike, whose family is from the Igbo-speaking part of the country, has completed primary school. At the time of the recording he was about fifteen and in the second year of junior secondary school. He was recorded by one of my research assistants in his neighbourhood in Shomolu on the Lagos mainland in two separate recording sessions, in which more than 8,600 words of speech by this speaker were recorded. In contrast to Janet, Chike was apparently very much at ease in the recording situation and even enjoyed the attention. He freely related personal experiences and opinions, in addition to telling a few folktales.

In the following section (6.2) one or more extracts from the transcript of each of the three recordings will be presented and analysed. In the case of the two longer recordings this will be supplemented by additional examples and analyses of selected features across

---

[1] The names are pseudonyms.

the whole recording. In 6.3 the findings made in these analyses will be used to complete the discussion of variation in NigP as spoken in the urban environment of Lagos begun in 4.4.

6.2 Extracts and analyses

6.2.1 Recording A

Text 6.1 is an extract from the conversation with the taxi driver which comprises the greater part of this recording (the remainder does not contain any linguistic features of interest which one cannot also see in this extract).

Text 6.1 Conversation with a taxi driver

Place and date: Lagos, 25 July 1997
Speakers: T, taxi driver; R, research assistant; D, Dagmar Deuber
Context: R and D are taking a ride in T's taxi and have struck up a conversation with him.

[original version]	[translation]
R: so na Lagos here you come begin speak Pidgin?	**R:** So it was here in Lagos that you began to speak Pidgin?
T: yes/ na im/ Lagos here now//	**T:** Yes, exactly, here in Lagos.
R: but anybody teach you how to speak am?	**R:** But did anybody teach you how to speak it?
5 **T:** nobody teach me//	**T:** Nobody taught me.
R: you just begin speak am?	**R:** You just began to speak it?
T: I just dey speak am small small small small small small na im I dey hear//	**T:** I just began to speak it little by little, that's how I came to know it.
R: so you don tell me say you just come/ you 10 begin-- you no read am for book/ {you begin speak am//}	**R:** So you told me you just came, you started-- you didn't study it, you began to speak it.
T: {at all/ at all//} I no go school// [...]	**T:** Not at all, not at all. I haven't been to school.
D: na which place you come from?	**D:** Where do you come from?
T: Kwara State//	**T:** Kwara State.
15 **D:** ah Kwara State//	**D:** Ah, Kwara State.
T: di time I was small boy/ around nineteen fifty-eight/ so our fader say make I go school dat time// so I no-- because nobody go school dat time// our moder go dey dodge di 20 pikin/ say make e no carry am go// so after/ around nineteen sixty-four/ our fader die// na im I come for Lagos// so when I come start driving vehicle around nineteen sixty-nine/ start driving/ one boy one uh I dey follow I 25 dey drive one man for Ebute Metta// so after I wan comot dere I see anoder woman// I go meet am// I say (I no I no I no I no) I no read book// e say e go start me with uh fifteen pounds [?1-2words?] dat time// e don	**T:** When I was a small boy, around 1958, so at that time my father said I should go to school. So I didn't-- because nobody went to school at that time. Our mother would hide the children so that he wouldn't take them away. So then, around 1964, our father died. Then I came to Lagos. So when I started driving a vehicle around 1969, I drove for one man in Ebute Metta. So when I was going to leave there, I found another woman. I went to see her. I said I can't read. She was going to start me with 15 pounds. That was thirty years ago, thirty-something years. So as I can't read, I can't understand, read

30 reach thirty years ago now/ thirty-something years o// so as I no read/ I no understand/ read paper book/ e say make I dey go// dat time na im e go come start pain me/ di time wey my fader say make I go school/ na im I 35 no go/ dat time na im e start pain me// well well// [...]	papers, books, she sent me away. At that time I really started to regret it, that when my father wanted to send me to school, I didn't go, at that time I started to regret it. Very much.
D: di people wey dey enter for dis taxi/ dem dey talk Broken?	**D:** The people who come into this taxi, do they speak Pidgin?
T: uh yes/ some dey talk Broken/ some dey 40 speak Yoruba/ some dey speak uh Hausa// shugbo only my language and uh Broken na im I dey [LAUGHS] I dey hear/	**T:** Yes, some speak Pidgin, some speak Yoruba, some speak Hausa. But I understand only my language and Pidgin.
D: wetin be your language uhm Yoruba?	**D:** What's your language, Yoruba?
T: en Yoruba yes//	**T:** Yes, Yoruba.
45 **D:** so if di person wey dey enter for taxi talk Yoruba you go talk Yoruba?	**D:** So if the person who comes into the taxi speaks Yoruba you'll speak Yoruba?
T: yes I talk Yoruba to him//	**T:** Yes, I'll speak Yoruba to him.
D: but if di person no hear Yoruba you go talk Broken?	**D:** But if the person doesn't understand Yoruba you'll speak Pidgin?
50 **T:** I go talk Broken yes// [LAUGHS] only when e dey speak uh English/ ehen/ so I no dey understand// [LAUGHTER]	**T:** I'll speak Pidgin, yes. Only if he/she speaks English, then I won't understand.
R: so if I begin knack grammar now (you no go) you no go understand am?	**R:** So if I began to speak English now you wouldn't understand it?
55 **T:** I go just look you// [LAUGHS] I go just look you// [...]	**T:** I'd just look at you. I'd just look at you.
R: so make I ask you one question now// if government say uh everybody now for Nigeria eh/ say (na Pidgin English) na 60 Broken English na im everybody go dey speak/ how you go see am? you go like am?	**R:** So let me ask you one question now. If the government now decided that Pidgin should be the language for everybody in Nigeria, what would you think about it? Would you like it?
T: Broken? ah/ I no go like am// as my ear no hear English now/ only Broken and Yoruba I hear [?1-2WORDS?]// so if say I get 65 chance now (I want to) I want to hear English well well// shugbo if you dey knack one language or two/ ah e no good//	**T:** Pidgin? Ah, I wouldn't like it. As I don't understand English now, I understand only Pidgin and Yoruba. So if I had the chance now, I'd like to learn English very well. But if you speak [only] one language or two, that's not good.

The taxi driver, as he says himself in the conversation, does not speak or understand English. In spite of this, however, the sample of his speech contains a few English grammatical forms which I also found in the corpus study but which were so marginal in the corpus that it was clear that they have not been integrated even into the educated variety of NigP: the inflected past tense form *was* of the copula *be* (l 16), the *-ing* form of the verb *drive* in the two occurrences of *start driving* in ll 22-24, and the pronoun form *him*, which he uses in l 47 instead of the NigP third person singular (bound) object pronoun form *am*. One may say that although he may not be aware of this, the taxi driver's speech has elements of informally learned English. Of course, these are isolated features, and it is clear that what he is speaking is basically NigP (and also, that he is much more competent in the language than a speaker of rudimentary uneducated NigP like the market woman whose speech was analysed in 4.4). Note, for example, that apart from the single occurrence of *was*, there are no inflected verb forms, and that he uses no English auxiliaries but NigP *dey, go, don, come* and *wan* (though not *been*!). Also, except for the one instance of *him*, he uses NigP third person singular pronouns throughout, both in the function of object (*am*) and in the function of subject (*e*).

In addition to the English forms cited above, the taxi driver also uses a Yoruba grammatical element: the conjunction *ṣùgbọ́n* 'but' (adapted orthographically to *shugbo* in the text, as it occurs in intonation units otherwise in NigP; ll 41, 66). This does not occur in any of the samples of face-to-face speech in the corpus of educated NigP (there is one occurrence in one of the texts from the drama serial *One Thing at a Time*, where, as has been mentioned in the corpus study, indigenous language elements are used as a creative device).

Other features of the taxi driver's speech that one may note are the *-s* plurals in ll 29-31 and the particle *to* in l 65. These are features which are not traditionally recognized as part of NigP's grammar, but, in contrast to the English verb and pronoun forms in his speech mentioned above, they are, according to the analyses of the corpus in the preceding chapter, now fairly well-established at least in the educated variety.

6.2.2   Recording B

The following text comprises about the first one quarter of the interview with Janet:

Text 6.2 Interview with Janet

Place and date: Lagos, 18 August 2000
Speakers: J, Janet (see section 6.1); R, research assistant

[original version]	[translation]
R: you been go any school at all?	**R:** Did you go to any school?
J: I dey go//	**J:** I did.
R: you been go abi (you d#) you go? which school wey you go?	**R:** You did or you do? Which school did you go to?
5 **J:** [=NAME=] Primary School// [...]	**J:** ... Primary School.
R: wetin make wey you come comot now/ wey you no go again?	**R:** Why did you leave, why don't you go any more?
J: na because of my mummy//	**J:** It's because of my mummy.
R: because of your mummy?	**R:** Because of your mummy?
10 **J:** yes//	**J:** Yes.
R: wetin make-- your mummy say wetin?	**R:** Why, what did your mummy say?
J: di time when I dey go school/	**J:** When I was going to school,
R: hm//	**R:** Hm.
J: and di person say I should go and bring uh	**J:** and the person said I should go and bring
15 money for [?am?]//	money for him/her/it.
R: for?	**R:** For?
J: from di-- say I should go and bring di money for di school//	**J:** That I should go and bring the money for the school.
R: okay//	**R:** Okay.

20 **J:** as I go and meet my mummy so my mummy come told me dat say e didn't have money to give me// so I come tell my mummy dat di person say I should bring money come//
25 **R:** your mummy say wetin?
J: e say make I no go school//

R: mhm//
J: so e come take me for school// as e come take me for school so/ so (e come say) e
30 come say dat e go put me for anoder school/ say make I no worry// so as I no worry so/ my aunty mummy come go dere// as e come go dere/ come tell my mummy dat e wan carry me come Lagos/ come do housegirl
35 here// so my mummy come say make e carry me-- my grandmoder wey I dey follow dey stay// and my real mummy dat e born me/ e dey for village// and my mummy no even know dat dem carry me come//
40 **R:** your mummy no know// but as you dey here for Lagos so/ who you dey stay with?
J: [=NAME=]//
R: ah//
J: na im I dey stay// [...]
45 **R:** but uh as e be so now/ if person wan put you for school you go like to go school again?
J: I go like//
R: you go like to go// [=NAME=] (say) e say
50 im go put you for school?
J: e don say dat e go put me for school/ but I didn't know my-- my date of my birth//
R: uh you no know di date of your birth?
J: yes//
55 **R:** okay you no know/ you no sabi dat one?
J: I sabi am but (I di# I di#) I don forget di [?1WORD?]// na my mummy na im know my birth//
R: okay//
60 **J:** so dem wan carry me go school/ dem no know my birth/ na only my daddy know//

R: okay// (wey your) wey your daddy dey?
J: my daddy? my daddy and my mummy dem quarrel//
65 **R:** okay//
J: as di two quarrel so/ (so my mummy come) so my mummy come go marry anoder person// as e go marry dat person/ na im my daddy come go marry anoder person too//

J: When I went to my mummy, my mummy told me that she didn't have money to give me. So I told my mummy that the person had told me to bring money.

R: What did your mummy say?
J: She said I shouldn't go to school [any more].

R: Mhm.
J: So she took me out of the school. When she took me out of the school, she said she would put me into another school and that I shouldn't worry. So I didn't worry [about it]. Then my aunty came. When she came, she told my mummy that she wanted to take me to Lagos to work as a housegirl. So my mummy said she could take me-- [that is] my grandmother, who I was staying with. And my real mummy who gave birth to me, she's in the village. And my mummy doesn't even know that they've brought me here.

R: Your mummy doesn't know. But here in Lagos, who do you stay with?
J: ...
R: Ah.
J: That's where I stay.
R: But as it is now, if somebody was going to send you to school, would you like to go to school again?
J: I'd like to.
R: You'd like to go. Did ... say she would send you to school?
J: She said she'd send me to school but I didn't know my date of birth.
R: You don't know your date of birth?
J: No.
R: Okay, you don't know that?
J: I knew but I've forgotten. My mummy knows my [date of] birth.

R: Okay.
J: So they wanted to take me to a school, but they didn't know my [date of] birth. Only my daddy knows.

R: Okay. [And] where's your daddy?
J: My daddy? My daddy and my mummy had a quarrel.
R: Okay.
J: As the two quarrelled, my mummy married somebody else. And as she married that person, my daddy married somebody else, too.

70	**R:** okay.	**R:** Okay.
	J: but di two don settle//	**J:** But the two have settled [their quarrel].
	R: okay.	**R:** Okay.
	J: but na only me my mummy born/	**J:** But it's only me my mummy had&
	R: okay//	**R:** Okay.
75	**J:** for my daddy// but now my-- [~] but di two don settle now//	**J:** &for my daddy. But now my-- but the two have settled [their quarrel] now.
	R: your mummy and your daddy don settle?	**R:** Your mummy and daddy have settled [their quarrel]?
	J: en// dem don settle now// so my mummy come born one pikin (for) for di person wey dat e marry// so e come born three children for dat man// e born only me for my daddy//	**J:** Yes. They have settled [it] now. So my mummy had a child for the man she married. She had three children for that man. [But] for my daddy she had only me.
80		
	R: okay// I see// so na only you alone dey for your daddy now? di oder im wife no born pikin?	**R:** Okay. I see. So you're your daddy's only child now? His other wife hasn't had children?
85	**J:** no e never born pikin//	**J:** No, she hasn't had children.
	R: e never born pikin yet// but your daddy no-- [?1-2WORDS?] hear say dem dey take you come Lagos?	**R:** She hasn't had children yet. But your daddy hasn't heard that they've brought you to Lagos?
	J: no (my daddy don't know dat de) my daddy don't know dat de carry me come dis place//	**J:** No, my daddy doesn't know that they've brought me here.
90		
	R: ah//	**R:** Ah.
	J: my mummy no even know//	**J:** Even my mummy doesn't know.
	R: your mummy no even know?	**R:** Even your mummy doesn't know?
95	**J:** nobody know for di compound dat I come here// only my grandmoder//	**J:** Nobody in the compound knows that I'm here. Only my grandmother.
	R: ah// (how many-- like how many how long) how many years wey you don stay for here? [~]	**R:** Ah. How many years have you been here?
100	**J:** two week//	**J:** Two weeks.
	R: you never-- e don pass two weeks// because no be since wey I start to see you for here? two weeks na fourteen days o// eh? and me I don--	**R:** You haven't-- it's more than two weeks. Because hasn't it been quite some time since I started to see you here? Two weeks is fourteen days. And I have--
105	**J:** two days//	**J:** Two days.
	R: two days// two days (na im you don) na im you don stay for here since you come from Warri? [~] ah? e don reach two months/ or e don pass three months dey go?	**R:** Two days. You've been here for two days since you came from Warri? Is it two months, or is it more than three months already?
110	**J:** no two months//	**J:** No, two months.
	R: but dem say dem go--	**R:** But they said they--
	J: na two months I hear for my mummy mouth/	**J:** Two months is what I heard my mummy&
	R: ah//	**R:** Ah.
115	**J:** wey e dey tell somebody yesterday//	**J:** &telling somebody yesterday.

As mentioned in 6.1, Janet felt somewhat uneasy about the interview situation, and it appears that she tried to accommodate to the situation or the educated interviewer by modifying her NigP in the direction of English, although the interviewer did not address her in English. Her speech remains a form of NigP – there is no part of the recording where one could say that she has switched to what might qualify as a variety of English – but one can observe some noticeable deviations from NigP grammar in her contributions, none of which occurs in the speech of the interviewer. The most striking of these is perhaps her almost consistent use of *dat* as complementizer. In Text 6.2, this can be seen in ll 23, 30, 33, 39, 51, 89, 90, 95 (in l 21 she combines *dat* and NigP *say*). In the total of her speech in the recording, there are 34 instances of *dat* as complementizer – almost three times as many as in the whole corpus of educated NigP (see 5.5.3); only in seven instances does she use NigP *say*.[2] Another case in point is *dat* as relative pronoun. In Text 6.2, there is an example of a relative clause introduced by *dat* in Janet's speech in l 37 (with a resumptive pronoun, which are permitted in NigP syntax; see Faraclas 1996: 37). Only in the preceding intonation unit (l 36), she had used NigP *wey* to introduce a relative clause. The two forms alternate in her speech throughout the recording (with zero as a third variant; the English *wh-* relative pronouns do not occur). *Wey* is more common (17 occurrences in total) but Janet's use of *dat* in the example in Text 6.2 mentioned above is not exceptional (8 occurrences in total, of which 2 in relative clauses with resumptive pronouns).[3] That Janet's use of relative *dat* is an idiosyncratic feature becomes clear when the data from her speech in the interview are compared to the corpus data. In the corpus of educated NigP, relative *dat/that* is so rare that it did not even feature in the analyses in Chapter 5. There is only a single occurrence in the whole corpus,[4] and this is in a context where a speaker evidently begins a relative clause in English (which in addition to the relative pronoun *dat* also contains one of the very few inflected verb forms in the corpus), then breaks off and rephrases what he intended to say in NigP:

(1) like dat last semester now/ people really dey complain about dis lecturer dat came from-- (di) di lecturer come from dis uh Faculty of Science// (C06 112ff)

'Like that last semester, people were really complaining about this lecturer that came from-- the lecturer came from this Faculty of Science.'

Another interesting aspect of Janet's speech in the interview are the third person singular feminine personal and possessive pronouns (bound personal pronouns, to be precise; where NigP requires the free personal pronoun form, as in l 57 in Text 6.2, Janet always uses the NigP form, *im*). In the extract printed above as Text 6.2, third person singular pronouns referring to female persons are frequent in the function of subject (in object and possessive function they do not occur in this extract), and Janet consistently uses the NigP gender-

---

[2] The counts do not include occurrences in the combined form *dat say*, of which there is one more in the recording in addition to the one contained in Text 6.2 (see example (3) below).

[3] In addition, there is one instance of the combined use of the NigP and English forms, as in the case of the complementizer. This is contained in Text 6.2 (l 79f).

[4] Other non-NigP relative pronouns occur in the corpus as well, but none of them is common. In adnominal relative clauses (the only type of relative clause that occurs in Janet's speech in the interview), *which* and *who* are also attested in the corpus, but there is only one occurrence of *which*, in a part of the corpus marked as non-NigP speech (quoted in example (125) in Chapter 5) and six of *who*, of which one in non-NigP speech and of the remaining five, four in the same group of texts (the *Rainbow City* drama texts). (Also attested in the corpus are nominal relative clauses introduced by *what* and by *who*, and sentential relative clauses introduced by *which*.)

neutral form *e* (see ll 21, 26-37, 51, 68, 80-85, 115). However, later on in the interview, she suddenly introduces *she* (which the interviewer never uses), only to go back to *e* in the following intonation unit:

(2) [...] my aunty say make I come stay (with e) with am// I didn't know dat *e* want to carry me go anoder person// [...] *she* come say dat *she* wan carry me go her house go stay// as *e* carry me go her house/ I don stay like one week dere//

'My aunty said I should come and stay with her. I didn't know she wanted to take me to somebody else. She said she'd take me to her house to stay there. When she'd taken me to her house, I stayed there for about a week.'

Apart from the two occurrences in this example, there are two more instances of *she* in Janet's speech in the recording. The predominant form, however, is *e*, which she uses a total of 57 times in reference to female persons. Janet's sporadic use of *she* is not unusual when compared to the corpus data. As was shown in Figure 5.6 in Chapter 5, a similarly sporadic use of *she* can be observed in most of the text categories in the corpus. What appears unusual in Janet's speech is her use of the object form *her*, which, as shown in Table 5.9 in Chapter 5, is virtually absent from the speech of the educated speakers in the corpus (it occurs only once and in a part of the corpus marked as non-NigP speech, while outside non-NigP speech NigP *am* is used consistently, in a total of 71 instances). Consider, for instance, the following additional example from the interview, where the educated interviewer uses *am* (as he does throughout the recording) while Janet uses *her*:

(3) **R:** when you earn money dem dey pay to *am*?
J: en dem go come carry am go my grandmoder place// [...] so dem come tell *her* dat I want to go school/ dem come say dat-- [...] so dem come tell *her* dat say di money dem dey pay (for di) for di shop/ say make dem dey use am dey take carry me go school//
R: okay//
J: my grandmoder say no//
R: e say make dem dey carry di money give *am* dere?
J: en//

'R: When you earn money, do they pay [it] to her?
J: Yes, they'll send it to my grandmother. So they told her that I want to go to school, they said that-- they told her that the money that they pay in the shop, that they wanted to use it to send me to school.
R: Okay.
J: My grandmother said no.
R: She said they should send her the money?
J: Yes.'

The NigP form *am* occurs in Janet's speech as well (one instance is in example (2) above), but *her* is as frequent as *am*. There are four clearly intelligible instances of each in the recording (in a few other cases, the recording is not clear enough to determine with certainty which form she is using). Such a comparison is of course of limited value when the overall frequency is so low, but considering that the educated speakers in the corpus practically do not use *her* as object pronoun, it is nevertheless a noteworthy finding. As regards the third person singular feminine possessive pronoun, there are only two instances in Janet's speech in the interview, those in example (2) above, where she uses the English form *her*. It is interesting to note that like the educated speakers in the corpus, Janet uses only forms from either the NigP or the English system. Intermediate forms such as *she* in object or possessive function, which, according to Bickerton (1973a; see Table 5.11 in Chapter 5) are characteristic of some of the varieties along the Guyanese Creole continuum, do not occur in her speech, either.[5] In two other areas where she makes attempts to replace NigP forms by English ones (while, again, the interviewer uses only the NigP variants) – verbal negation and verbal morphology – one can observe in her speech a few isolated forms which are grammatical neither in NigP nor in standard English. However, these forms are restricted to this one speaker among all those recorded for the study and marginal even in her speech, so that it is clear that they are peculiarities resulting from the somewhat strained situation and the speaker's inadequate control of the language she is aiming at, and are not characteristic features of any normal variety of NigP. The forms in question are (a) *don't* with a third person singular subject in ll 89-90 of Text 6.2 (there are no other instances of *don't* with a third person singular subject in the recording), and (b) two irregular English past tense/past participle forms combined with NigP preverbal markers, *come told* in Text 6.2 (l 21) and another one, *don got*, in the remainder of the recording. About the aspect of verbal negation one can further say that the instances in the repeated *my daddy don't know* in ll 89-90 of Text 6.2 are two of a total of seven instances in the recording of the English negation pattern for VPs without auxiliaries, i.e. dummy auxiliary *do* + *not* (here always in the enclitic contracted form) + VERB.[6] While she does not observe third person singular concord in present tense forms of the dummy auxiliary *do*, Janet does distinguish present and past tense forms (cf e.g. Text 6.2, ll 21, 52 and *I didn't know* in example (2) above). The NigP pattern of verbal negation, *no* + VERB, occurs a total of 37 times in the recording (with an additional 4 verbs negated by *never*, the combined marker of perfective aspect and negation) and is thus far more common than the English one. However, in comparison to the extreme marginality of English verbal negation in the corpus of educated NigP (see 5.5.9), Janet's use of it is still extraordinary. As regards verbal morphology, apart from the two instances of English past tense/past participle forms mentioned above and two instances of the inflected form *is* of *be* as copula,[7] all the verbs in Janet's speech are in the base form. There are sporadic occurrences of two non-NigP modals, *should* (four instances in the recording, of which three in the part printed as Text 6.2 (ll 14, 17, 23)) and *can* (one instance each of *can* and the negative form *can't*), but otherwise she uses only NigP preverbal markers of tense/aspect/modality (see 5.5.5). However, as was also observed in 6.2.1 in the analysis of the speech of the taxi driver in Recording A, one item, past/past-before-past *been*, is totally absent from her speech. In fact, it is not clear whether *been* is

---

[5] There is one instance of *e* as third person singular feminine object pronoun in her speech, the one in example (2). As shown in Table 5.11, *i* is also one of the variants of the third person singular feminine object pronoun in the Guyanese Creole continuum, replacing basilectal *am* before being in turn replaced by *shi* as one moves towards the acrolect, but as Janet uses this form only in the one instance in example (2) and immediately corrects herself, it can be taken as a performance error in her speech.

[6] In addition, as will be mentioned below, there is an instance of an English modal which is negated, and, like the educated speakers in the corpus (see 5.5.9), Janet uses the English negative form in this case.

[7] In one of the two instances *is* is part of a fixed expression (*dat is* as a connective). The other instance is in a relative clause also introduced by an English relative pronoun, where it is used in a context where in NigP one would normally use the locative copula *dey*: ... *dat is here* (NigP: *wey dey here*).

part of her repertoire of auxiliaries at all, since in ll 1-3 of Text 6.2 she does not take it up when the interviewer uses it, thereby causing him some confusion.

The analysis so far has highlighted that in this interview, Janet uses a variety of English grammatical forms which are unusual in NigP even as spoken by educated speakers, which became clear in comparison with the results of the analysis of the corpus of educated NigP presented in the preceding chapter, and was also reflected in the comparison of her speech with that of the interviewer. In the preceding chapter it was shown that many English grammatical forms are only marginally present in the corpus of educated NigP, but a few cases where one may speak of grammatical borrowing were also identified, including the plural form *-s* for nouns, the third person plural possessive pronoun form *deir* and the particle *to*. In contrast to the English forms in Recording B discussed so far, all three of these forms occur in the speech of the interviewer. The particle *to* is also used spontaneously by Janet in a number of instances (a total of nine in the recording; see e.g. Text 6.2, l 22 and *how to speak* in example (4) below). The data for plural marking of nouns in Janet's speech are rather sparse. In ll 105, 110 and 112 of Text 6.2 she uses the *-s* suffix, but all of these are cases where she is responding to questions in which the interviewer had used the form. In addition to these three instances, there are two more *-s* plurals in Janet's speech in the recording, one in a context where, again, she is replying to a question by the interviewer containing an *-s* plural and one in the word *twins,* which may be known to her only in this form. In another four instances, one in Text 6.2 (l 100) and three more later on in the recording, nouns with plural reference in Janet's speech are unmarked (*dem* as plural marker does not occur).[8] For the third person plural possessive pronoun the data is even more sparse. In the only instance where Janet uses a third person plural possessive pronoun spontaneously, it appears that the form is *dem*, but the form is in a stretch of the recording which is not entirely clear (Janet's voice is at times somewhat faint). There are two more, clear instances in the recording and in these, she uses the form *deir*, but in both of these cases the form had been used by the interviewer in the immediately preceding turn:

(4) **J:** di oder one dey for Christian// I dey for Muslim// I no dey go any church// na-- (everyo#) everybody dey go Muslim/ dey go church/ and na only me go siddon for house so//
R: oh you na Muslim?
J: eh?
R: you {na Muslim?}
J: {(I no be)} I no dey-- I be Christian/ but dem no dey allow me dey go church// [...]
R: so dem go go church/ dem go (go mo# go) go *deir* own prayer/ dem no dey allow you go?
J: Me self I no even know how to speak *deir* own//
R: hm//
J: I be Christian//
R: but you dey live for *deir* house?
J: eh?
R: you dey live for *deir* house?
J: en na *deir* house I dey live//

---

[8] There is also an instance of the irregular plural form *children* (see Text 6.2, l 80). *Children* is not unusual in NigP as a suppletive plural form for *pikin* (cf Faraclas 1996: 168).

'**J:** The other one is in [a] Christian [family]. I'm in [a] Muslim [family]. I don't go to any church. Everybody goes to the Muslim place of worship, and I stay at home alone.
R: Oh you're a Muslim?
J: What?
R: You're a Muslim?
J: I'm not-- I'm a Christian, but they don't allow me to go to church// [...]
R: So they'll go to their own place of worship and they won't allow you to go?
J: I don't even know how to say theirs [i.e. their prayers].
R: Hm.
J: I'm a Christian//
R: But you live in their house?
J: What?
R: You live in their house?
J: Yes, that's where I live.'

It is thus not possible to tell from this recording to what extent Janet would use plural -*s* and the third person plural possessive pronoun form *deir* if she was speaking spontaneously and in an entirely natural situation, but at least one can say that these are forms which she seems to be familiar with.

While both Janet and the interviewer are fluent speakers of NigP, the interviewer, as has been pointed out repeatedly, has a high level of formal education and therefore speaks English fluently as well. I had observed the same speaker who here acts as interviewer code-switching extensively into English when speaking NigP with educated peers. In this interview, however, he totally refrains from inserting whole discourse chunks in English into his speech, and even single lexical items are rare. It appears that he is accommodating "downwards" while Janet is trying to accommodate "upwards", although the relative absence of non-NigP lexical items may of course also be attributed to the nature of the topic. Therefore, in spite of the huge gap between the two in terms of educational level, there are hardly any real communicative difficulties (or at least, such as are of an entirely linguistic nature – the difficulties in Text 6.2, ll 97-110 probably stem from her not sharing his clear notion of time). The only time when he has to rephrase a question in order to be understood by her is in one of the few cases where he does use an English lexical item which is clearly not part of NigP's lexicon (cf also 5.3.1.1), and which she is apparently not familiar with:

(5) **R:** una get electricity for dere?
   J: eh?
   R: una get light?
   J: yes/
   R: {NEPA light?}
   J: {we get light} dere//

'**R:** Do you have electricity there [in the village]?
J: What?
R: Do you have electricity?
J: Yes,
R: Electricity from NEPA [National Electric Power Authority]?
J: we have electricity there.'

6.2.3   Recording C

Having a level of education which is intermediate between little or none (as in the case of Janet and the taxi driver) and completed secondary schooling or higher (as in the case of the speakers in the corpus of educated NigP), the speaker in this recording, Chike, can be expected to have a tolerable though probably not a very good command of English. In the recording, it becomes clear that he is indeed capable of producing an English which is not perfect but clearly recognizable as such. The recording is largely in NigP, but like the more highly educated speakers in the corpus analysed in the preceding chapter, Chike alternates between large segments in NigP and a few shorter segments in English. In the transcription of this recording I have therefore also used marking for non-NigP speech, which is here applied to segments of at least one intonation unit with a clausal structure (as well as all quotations) which are fully grammatical in standard English or at least so to a considerable extent (as some learner errors must be expected). Two examples will make it clear that in contrast to Recordings A and B, it is quite possible in this recording to identify whole segments of discourse in English. The first, example (6) below, is one of the most obvious cases of code-switching in Recording C. Here, Chike switches from NigP to English to quote from the Bible (adding another intonation unit in English as a comment) and then switches back to NigP:

(6) so dat's why me I dey talk/ God say/ (John three) John sixteen chapter three/ e say [+"for God so loved the world/ He gave his only begotten son/ that whosoever believes in Him shall not perish but have everlasting life//"[9] yes it is true//+] although I never (receive) receive Holy Communion o/ I dey go church well well o/ I dey listen//

'So that's why I'm saying, God says, [in] (John 3) John 16, chapter 3, it says: ... Although I haven't received Holy Communion, I go to church a lot [and] I listen.'

It is most likely English language church services which Chike says in the quotation above he attends, and it therefore comes as no surprise that he switches to English in another segment where he is talking about God, although this is not a quotation:

(7) so dat's why God tell me say any time wey I dey keep make I dey pray// I go pray/ I go pray to God// [+God is almighty// He can lead me to everything that I'm doing// He can lead me to all sorts of things that I'm doing// the only God// if you don't do anything with God/ you can never survive it//+]

'So that's why God has told me that whenever I keep [goal] I should pray. I'll pray, I'll pray to God. ...'

Text 6.3 below, which consists of extracts from three different episodes of Recording C, gives a fuller picture of the kind of speech produced by Chike in this recording.

---

[9] Compare John 3:16 (King James version): "For God so loved the world, that he gave his only begotten Son, that whosoever believeth in him should not perish, but have everlasting life."

Text 6.3 Chike relating personal experiences and opinions

Place and date: Lagos (Shomolu), 3 July/20 July 2000
Speaker: Chike (see section 6.1)

[original version]

Part I (on football): [...] dat's why people just like me/ as I dey play/ I dey play play play/ ah-ah dem go dey imagine/ and I dey score goals well well// I fit score five goals
5 at a time in one first half// [...] okay you ask me which club I wan go? omo[10] I for like to play for Arsenal like Kanu o/ and I for like to play for Liverpool// I like dat club yeah Liverpool// [+Liverpool is a (correct correct)
10 correct place to play ball//+] and dem go high you well well/ yes// and di country wey me I like again/ na Holland// [+they are a very good country//+] and anoder country wey me I like again well well/ na France//
15 you no see di ball wey France play with Italy? omo dem wan kill Italy/ Italy wan kill dem/ but dem charge/ I say na lie/ France must qualify dis goal// so France come charge immediately// na so France just dey
20 give dem kpa kpa kpa// ah-ah two goals enter net// so me I come dey say "hallelujah"// [...] so wetin I come talk be [?1WORD?] say as I come do for dere/ everybody come dey tell me say "eh you dey play/ you dey play//
25 wetin be your name self?" I say "my name na Chike [[NAME CHANGED]]"// e say which class me I dey// I say I dey J.S.S. two A// e say "J.S.S. two A/ yes I know dat class//" e say "any time wey we wan play I go come
30 call you"// and (we dey) we go dey pray for you say make you dey play (for for) for big country"/ wey dem go dey (pay) pay me na dollars/ and I go dey give am for people well well// so people like me/ no be lie o// I dey
35 also like to dey play/ play like Amokachi// so I go buy plane o like Amokachi//
Part II (on an incident of armed robbery and its consequences): [...] so wetin I just dey tell una/ e get one man wey dem dey call Okolie
40 here// dat man (he dey) he dey do dustbin work// e dey pack all things anyhow// so dis man e dey get money o no be small// so as one day we come dey here/ (as we dey) as

[translation]

That's why people just like me, the way I play; I play and play and play, they'll be amazed, and I score a lot of goals. I can score five goals at a time in one first half.
Okay, you ask me which club I'd like to go to? Man, I'd like to play for Arsenal like Kanu, and I'd like to play for Liverpool. I like that club, Liverpool. ...

And you'll really get ahead there. And the country that I also like is Holland. ...

And another country that I like a lot is France. Didn't you see the match that France played against Italy? Man, they were going to kill Italy, Italy was going to kill them, but they charged, and I said no, France must score this goal. So France charged immediately. So France just kept attacking them. Two goals entered the net. I said, "Hallelujah!" So what I was saying is that, after what I did there, everybody was telling me, "You play [very well], you play [very well]. What's your name?" I said, "My name is Chike". He asked me which class I'm in. I said I'm in J.S.S. [Junior Secondary School] 2 A. He said, "J.S.S. 2 A, yes, I know that class". He said, "Any time when we're going to play [foot]ball I'll come and call you. And we'll pray for you that you'll play for a big country", where they'll pay me dollars and I'll give a lot of it to people. So people really like me. I'd also like to play like Amokachi. Then I'd buy a plane like Amokachi.

So what I was just telling you, there used to be a man here who was called Okolie. That man was a rubbish collector. He would collect anything. The man had a lot of money. So as we were here one day, as we were watching, it just happened. We used to

---

[10] Yoruba *ọmọ*, literally 'child'.

45	we dey watch/ na so di thing just happen one day// we dey talk to Okolie o// we dey get many things from im dis thing dere// even now for dat place we get dis aluminium chair// [...] so one day/ dem say one man for dis place/ armed robber come phone for im
50	house come meet am// so dem say e be like say dis Okolie/ wey dem dey call im name/ say im dey among of di people// [...] I dey even sleep when di thing start// I come come out/ I come dey hear "hoh hoh hoh"/ I no
55	know say na boys from Olorunshogo Street// so I come come out/ I come see all of dem/ dem [?1WORD?] carry dagger/ gun/ all knivees// I no know wetin I go even call dis one self/ I no know wheder na war// so even
60	soldiers pass self give dem hand/ dem just dey shout "hoh" dey continue deir movement// na so dem catch dis Okolie man tell am say make im come find truck comot dis im property here oderwise dem go burn
65	am// na so dem tell dis man o// (na dis) na so dis man use jejejejeje comot/ go im own/ dis man no put head here again// hah I come dey imagine// so dem come tell dis man make im come comot im things wey dey here/ dis man
70	wallahi dis man no gree come comot am// so one day-- so dis man don run go// [...] so na so we just dey/ dey look look look look look look/ ah we no see Okolie/ e no come// people come dey talk say why dem leave dis
75	man wey dem dey call Okolie make e run/ why dem leave dis man// [...] so as dem still dey do deir dis thing// so di Okolie man dem no see// di woman come wey come buy some things from Okolie// di woman come come
80	dey cry say dem don burn/ as I know myself/ omo/ dem don burn everything finish/ fire don dey burn// as I just dey see/ wetin di next thing wey happen/ I don dey see say dem don dey buy Omo// eh? wetin dem dey do
85	Omo/ pour sand inside bucket from gutter water dey quench di fire again// na so di fire begin again/ na so dem quench am finish fire off// na so di woman come dey cry/ some things wey im buy from Okolie// na so di
90	woman dey cry o/ dey cry dey cry/ dey cry/ dey cry/ say im no know wetin im go do/ im no know wetin im go do o/ say im no know wetin im go do// so dem come give am

talk to Okolie. We have many things from his place there. Even this aluminium chair is from there.

So one day, they said of one man here that armed robbers phoned his house and then they came to him. They said it seemed that Okolie, as he was called, was among the robbers. I was even sleeping when it started. I went out and heard shouting. I didn't know it came from the boys from Olorunshogo Street [attacking the armed robbers]. So I went out and saw all of them, they were carrying daggers, guns and all sorts of knives. I don't know what I'm going to call this, I don't know whether it was a war. So even soldiers passed and gave them a hand, they just shouted, then they continued their movement. So they caught the Okolie man and told him to look for a truck and remove his property from here, otherwise they'd burn it. That's what they told this man. So this man stole off and went his way, he hasn't set foot here again. Hah, I was surprised. So they told this man to remove his things that were here, he just didn't remove them. So one day-- so this man has run away. So we were just there, we looked and looked and looked, [but] we didn't find Okolie, he didn't come. People were asking why they had allowed this man called Okolie to run away.

So what they were doing then. So they didn't find the Okolie man. The woman came who'd bought some things from Okolie. The woman cried that they'd started a fire; as I know myself, man, they'd set everything on fire, the fire was burning. What I saw, the next thing that happened, I saw that they'd bought detergent. What they did with the detergent, they poured [it and] sand into buckets with water from the gutter and quenched the fire. When the fire started again, they poured more water onto it until it was out. So the woman was crying [that there were] some things that she'd bought from Okolie. So the woman kept crying that she didn't know what to do. So they allowed her to take all these things that were here with anything else that she liked. The woman power/ come tell am say/ all dis thing wey dey here/ dem give am authority make im carry am with anything wey im like go// di woman come go charter taxi/ abi na gwongworo/ me I no know di one wey I go call am abeg// so as una dey listen my country people// so na so e carry dat gwongworo come// na so e pack everything wey dey here/ nothing remain// di woman pack everything/ both di one wey be her own/ di one wey no be her own// e pack all of dem go for her house// e pack all of dem go sell//

<u>Part III (on electricity problems):</u> so as una dey see us for Shomolu now/ we no get light for just five days// but wetin we go do all dis NEPA sha? (person) person go dey for im house/ dem go bring bill/ person go pay// NEPA/ dem go come/ "wey your money?" if you no pay/ dem go go cut light// you go put something for fridge (e go s#) e go still dey spoil dey dey dere// NEPA dey sotay dem no go bring light for you// even many things wey NEPA dey do/ me I no even like am at all// we wan watch television/ no light// we wan chop/ no light// we wan do everything/ no light// so wetin we go come do NEPA? [BREAK IN RECORDING] so NEPA people (as I) as me I dey talk my own sha// any time wey dem wan play ball/ na so NEPA no go bring light// ah-ah any time wey dem wan play ball/ even when dem wan do important thing/ NEPA no go give us light// [+if I'm the one doing the work/+] (if n# n#) if na me dey do di work/ I go tell NEPA dat is I go show people di appreciation/ wey be say na me dey do di work// why NEPA go dey play [?1WORD?] play rubbish wayo for people? at di end of di time dem go bring bill/ person go pay/ person go pay// wetin you go do/ if you no pay/ dem cut off your light// [...] if you no wan work your work make you better find your way/ because some people dey find work/ wey dem go work/ dem no see// but you wey dem put dere still dey do yeye wey no-- (you no) you no serious for your work// [...] so as NEPA no give us light now/ wetin we go do dem/ nothing// when NEPA no give you light/ wetin you go do/ you no go do dem anything// [...] so God/ na only God

went and hired a taxi, or a lorry, I don't know what to call it. So as you've been hearing. So she brought that lorry. She packed everything that was here, nothing remained. The woman packed everything, both what was hers and what wasn't hers. She packed everything and took it to her house. She packed everything to go and sell it.

So as you see us in Shomolu now, we haven't had electricity for five days. But what are we going to do about NEPA? You're in your house, they'll bring a bill, you'll pay. NEPA, they'll come, "Where's your money?" If you don't pay, they'll cut off the electricity. You'll put something in the fridge, it'll get spoiled there. NEPA won't give you electricity. Many things that NEPA does, I don't like them at all. We want to watch television, no electricity. We want to eat, no electricity. We want to do everything, no electricity. So what are we going to do to NEPA?

So I was telling you my opinion about the NEPA people. Each time they're going to play [foot]ball, NEPA won't give us electricity. Each time they're going to play [foot]ball, even when there's going to be an important match, NEPA won't give us electricity. If I was the one doing the work, I'd tell NEPA, that is, I'd show people my appreciation, that I'm the one doing the work. Why should NEPA cheat people? In the end they'll bring a bill, you'll pay, you'll pay. What are you going to do, if you don't pay, they'll cut off your electricity.

If you don't want to do your work, you should leave, because some people are looking for work to do, they don't find any. But you that they've put there, you still do nonsense which is not-- you're not serious with your work. So as NEPA doesn't give us electricity now, what are we going to do to them, nothing. When NEPA doesn't give you electricity, what are you going to do, you can't do anything to them. So God, only

go save us for dis Nigeria// make NEPA dey 145 hear our voice// if dem no wan hear our voice/ wetin we go do [?wey be say?]-- do dem/ nothing now// [...] so God E go bless us sha/ for dis Nigeria/ and e go bless all dose NEPA people/ NITEL/ all of dem/ at di end 150 of di time// na so dem go dey do wayo wayo// e no good/ Nigeria don spoil// [...] [+okay look at last Sunday// we bought-- (my) my brother my daddy my brother went to market// he bought many turkeys// he put 155 it in the freezer// we eat meat because we want to celebrate (my) one of my aunties' birthday// okay look at that turkey now and the meat that he bought from the market/+] all of dem don spoil kpatakpata/ no one 160 remain// de carry am throway go buy anoder one// no be NEPA cause am? if to say we see light put better thing for freezer/ dis thing no fit be like dis now// [...] but dese things wey NEPA dey do/ so okay small time/ light go 165 trip off// small time/ light go trip off// [...] I just imagine/ [+I left Shomolu/ I just say let me go and see how (FET#) FESTAC is// that is how I went to FESTAC// there was no light// there was no single light in FESTAC// 170 they told me that (since) since last week/ that the light has been tripping off/ tripping off/ that it was only yesterday that they got light/ but today they have not seen NEPA's miracle//+]	God can save us in this Nigeria. NEPA should listen to us. If they don't want to listen to us, what are we going to do to them, nothing. So God will bless us in this Nigeria, and He'll bless all those NEPA people, NITEL, all of them, in the end. They just keep cheating us. It's not good. Nigeria is rotten. ... all of it was totally spoiled, nothing remained. They threw it away and bought new one. Isn't that NEPA's fault? If we had electricity to put things in the freezer, something like this couldn't have happened. But these things that NEPA does, after a short time, the current will trip off. After a short time, the current will trip off. I just wondered - ...

In this text there are five segments marked as non-NigP speech, three shorter ones (ll 9f, 12f, 126f) and two longer ones (ll 152ff, 166ff). The two shorter segments in ll 9f and ll 12f can be explained as the result of topic-related switching of a type that has already been described in the analysis of the corpus of educated NigP: as shown in 5.6.1.1, speakers sometimes switch to English, if only briefly, when they mention countries they associate with the English language – Western English-speaking countries or Western countries generally – or anything or anybody connected with these countries.[11] The third shorter segment (l 126) seems to be a case where, as can also occasionally be observed in the corpus (cf e.g. the example from the corpus quoted above in connection with the analysis of Recording B, example (1)), the speaker starts off in English but on realising this decides to go back to NigP. In the case of the two longer segments the code contrast is particularly clear; the motivation for the use of English may not be so obvious in these cases, but note how the switch from English back to NigP in l 159 nicely underlines the contrast between the anticipated feast and the spoiled meat,[12] and that the switch in l 166 coincides with a

---

[11] Compare in particular ll 12f in Text 6.3 and the very similar example (126) in Chapter 5.
[12] The part of the transcript immediately preceding the switch in l 152 (a part in which the speaker was more or less repeating what he had already said about NEPA problems) were omitted because there were quite a number of

shift in the topic, from the situation in Shomolu, where the speaker lives, to that in another part of Lagos, FESTAC Town.[13]

That English and NigP segments are clearly distinguishable in Chike's speech is not only because of his comparatively good grasp of English grammar but also because his NigP does not show the kind of deviations from NigP grammar unusual for fluent speakers that were found in the analysis of Janet's speech. Outside the parts of the recording marked as non-NigP speech – about 570 words, or about 7% of this rather long recording – the complementizer is either *say* or zero, and relative clauses are introduced either by zero or by *wey*, never by any of the English overt relative pronouns (cf the observations on Janet's use of complementizer and relative *dat* in 6.2.2). English third person singular personal /possessive pronoun forms are very infrequent. Outside non-NigP speech, the only ones are: the repeated *he* in l 40 of Text 6.3; the three instances of *her* in ll 103ff of the text; and, in other parts of the recording, one instance each of *him* and *it* in the function of masculine and neuter object pronoun, respectively, and two instances of *his* as masculine possessive pronoun. (Note that, again, all of these forms are used in accordance with the standard English system.) In the overwhelming majority of cases, Chike uses the appropriate one of the NigP gender-neutral third person singular personal/possessive pronoun forms (*e/im/am*). Verbal negation according to the standard English pattern does not occur at all outside non-NigP speech, and non-NigP verb forms are exceedingly rare. Apart from sporadic occurrences of inflected forms of the copula *be* (almost always third person singular *'s/is* and almost always in one of the expressions *dat's why* (see e.g. Text 6.3, l 1 and examples (6) and (7) above) and *dat is* (see e.g. Text 6.3, l 128)), the only inflected verb form in the recording outside non-NigP speech is the one instance of V*ing* in the following context:

(8) all dose boys just dey jubilate/ dey talk dey talk dey do do do// dem come catch one/ naked am/ almost *burning* (di boy) di guy self// dem wan kill di guy/ dem come dey beg for di guy say (make) make dem leave di guy//

'All those boys were just jubilating, talking and making a commotion. Then they caught one [and] tore off his clothes, even almost burning the guy. They were going to kill the guy, [but] people pleaded for the guy, that they should leave him.'

All other verbs in the recording apart from those in the few segments marked as non-NigP speech are in the base form. If they are overtly marked for tense/aspect/modality, it is always by means of one (or more) of the following preverbal markers: *dey, don/never, go, come, wan, fit, for, must, suppose*.[14]

Been as preverbal tense marker, which was found to be very rare in the corpus of educated NigP (see 5.5.5) and of which there were no instances in the speech samples from the taxi driver and Janet, does not occur in this recording, either. Nor does Chike use *dem* as third person plural possessive pronoun or as plural marker for nouns – two other forms which were found to be notably rare in the (spontaneous, face-to-face) speech of the speakers in the corpus (see 5.5.4.4 and 5.5.4.2, respectively). The third person plural possessive pronoun is *deir* throughout; there are a total of 19 instances of this pronoun in the

---

acoustically unclear segments, which appeared to result from the speaker having moved away from the microphone for a moment.

[13] Originally constructed to provide accommodation for the 1977 Festival of African Arts and Culture.
[14] On NigP preverbal markers of tense/aspect/modality and on the status of *must* and *suppose*, see 5.5.5.

recording, all of them outside non-NigP speech (two examples are in Text 6.3, ll 61, 77). Nouns with plural reference are, as expected in a recording of this length, quite frequent: I counted a total of 102. Of these, 60 (including 6 in non-NigP speech) have the -*s* suffix as plural marker and 41 zero (the remaining one is a very unusual case, with double -*s* suffix: *kniveses* (see Text 6.3, l 58)). This gives a rate of -*s* pluralization outside non-NigP speech of 57%, which is very similar to the rate in the face-to-face speech section of the corpus of educated NigP (see 5.5.4.2.).[15] In fact, there seems to be little in the way of grammar which distinguishes Chike's NigP from that of competent speakers with more formal education than he has had so far. In addition to the aspects of his grammatical usage discussed so far, one may mention in connection with this observation that, like the speakers in the corpus (and the taxi driver and Janet as well), he uses the particle *to* (19 occurrences outside non-NigP speech, of a total of 30 in the recording; see e.g. Text 6.3, ll 6, 7, 35). One may further mention the conjunction *because*, which is quite common in the recording, with 16 occurrences outside non-NigP speech (of a total of 19 in the recording; one example is in Text 6.3, l 136);[16] as shown in 5.5.3, this is another item which seems to have come into NigP relatively recently but, according to the corpus data, is now very widespread at least in the educated variety. Like the speakers in the corpus, Chike also uses a few prepositions which are not traditionally part of the language, e.g. *in* or *at*, but as is also the case in the corpus (see 5.5.2), he uses them only infrequently outside non-NigP speech and mainly in fixed expressions (e.g. *in short, at least*).

As regards lexis, one may note a number of lexical items which reflect Chike's exposure to English, e.g. in Text 6.3 *qualify* (l 18), *immediately* (l 19), *continue* (l 61), *movement* (l 62), *authority* (l 95), *appreciation* (l 129).[17]

What distinguishes Chike's language use from that of the speakers in the corpus analysed in Chapter 5 is, one may say, not his NigP but his English, insofar as this comes through in the recording. While it is clear that he is fairly competent in the latter language as well, the parts of the recording marked as non-NigP speech and, occasionally, English influences in the NigP parts reveal some problems in the areas of lexical usage, grammar and idiomatic expressions. Examples from Text 6.3 include: the rather odd use of *qualify* in l 18; the combined use of the prepositions *among* and *of* in l 52; the expression *at di end of di time* (ll 131f, 149f); the non-use of the article in *went to market* and the uninflected verb

---

[15] As shown in Figure 5.5 in Section 5.5.4.2, the rate of -*s* plural marking in the face-to-face speech section of the corpus ranges from 48% in the interviews to 72% in the conversations. Since the discourse type in recording C, free monologue, has no direct parallel in the corpus, it is perhaps best to take the whole face-to-face speech section for comparison, for which the rate of -*s* plural marking is 61%.

[16] The conjunction *because* is not confined to Chike among the three less educated speakers whose speech is analysed in the present chapter, but the data from this recording are of course again more conclusive than those from the two shorter recordings. The taxi driver uses it once (see Text 6.1, l 18) and Janet uses it twice and in both cases spontaneously, without the research assistant having used it in the immediately preceding discourse (none of these two instances of the conjunction *because* is in the part of the recording printed as Text 6.2, but in Text 6.2 there is an instance of the preposition *because of* used spontaneously by Janet (l 8)). Note also that *sake of say* 'because' (cf 5.5.3) occurs in none of the three recordings discussed in this chapter.

[17] Other lexical items of this type in the recording are the nouns *opportunity* as well as (not surprisingly, given the speaker's exposure to Christian religious discourse) *forgiveness* and *salvation*, and the verbs *jubilate* (see example (8)), *support, remove, ensure, perform* and *contest*.

forms *eat* and *want* ('were going to eat', 'wanted') in the first of the two longer segments in English (l 153-156), and in the second of these, the lack of past tense inflection on the verb *say* (l 166). These kinds of deviations from standard English usage mark Chike as a speaker of a variety of English which, according to the classification proposed by Banjo (see the discussion in 4.3), can be described as variety II of Nigerian English, rather than the variety used by those with full competence in the language, variety III.

6.3 Discussion and conclusion

In summarizing the findings I made in the corpus study on English influence in educated NigP (section 5.8.1), I have stated that one finds, in particular, larger segments of discourse and recently borrowed or singly-switched lexical items. Grammatical borrowing, as I have pointed out, can be observed as well but is limited. The most striking among the cases where one could speak of grammatical borrowing were probably the plural marker *-s* for nouns and the third person plural possessive pronoun form *deir* (see 5.5.4.2 and 5.5.4.4, respectively). In both of these cases, I found (as, for the *-s* suffix, also Tagliamonte, Poplack & Eze 1997) that the form had virtually displaced a NigP one, *dem* (postnominally as plural marker, prenominally as possessive pronoun), in spontaneous, face-to-face speech. (It has to be remembered, though, that in the case of plural marking, another possibility that has always existed in NigP, zero, remains a viable option.) This is a finding which, in the light of previous studies up to Faraclas (1996), one would hardly have expected. The extent to which these forms are used in varieties of present-day NigP other than the educated one is therefore a matter which would merit more empirical investigation than has been possible within the framework of the present study. However, the indications from the three additional recordings analysed in this chapter are that the variables of plural marking of nouns and the third person plural possessive pronoun do not systematically distinguish the NigP use of educated and less educated speakers, at least not in the urban environment of Lagos.

In addition to the variant *dem* of the plural marker and the third person plural possessive pronoun, there was another item mentioned in most previous grammatical descriptions of NigP which I found to be very rare in the corpus, and in this case not only in the face-to-face speech section: *been* as preverbal tense marker (see 5.5.5). In the three recordings analysed in the present chapter, the only instances of this item were in the speech of the educated interviewer in Recording B. I have thus no evidence that *been* is a feature which distinguishes varieties along a NigP-English continuum in the way Todd (1994; see her example quoted in 2.2.7) suggests.

There was also another grammatical element besides the variants *-s* and *deir* of the plural marker and the third person plural possessive pronoun, respectively, which I found to be surprisingly well-established in the variety of NigP investigated in the corpus study, namely the particle *to* (see 5.5.7). The data presented in this chapter indicate that this is by no means confined to educated speech, either, as there were instances of it in all three of the additional recordings analysed.[18]

Other cases of what appeared to be relatively recent grammatical borrowing from English that were identified in the corpus study include the conjunction *because* and the *-body* series of compound indefinite pronouns (see 5.5.3 and 5.5.4.4, respectively). However, in these cases, some previous studies (Faraclas 1996 for both, for the former also Elugbe & Omamor 1991; see the discussion in the respective sections) already suggest that the forms are not uncommon in NigP. It is therefore not contrary to expectation that the three less educated speakers whose speech has been analysed in the present chapter should use them as well.[19]

Apart from the few that could be considered borrowings, quite a number of other English grammatical forms were present in the corpus of educated NigP as well, but only marginally. This kind of sporadic use of English forms occurred in the speech of the three less educated speakers in the recordings analysed in the present chapter as well. In addition to that, one of the least educated speakers, Janet, showed a striking tendency to use some English grammatical forms which were very rare in the corpus of educated NigP. I interpreted this as an attempt to accommodate to the educated interviewer in which, however, she overshot the mark, one might say, considering especially that the interviewer did not use any of these forms during the interview with her. (This phenomenon is perhaps not dissimilar from the tendency observed in the corpus study for Radio Nigeria 3 broadcasters to use *dem* as the plural marker for nouns and the third person plural possessive pronoun. The data presented in this chapter are of course not sufficient proof, but one may suspect that this tendency reflects more a stereotype than actual language use among their target audience, in particular as far as plural marking is concerned.)

In 5.8.1, I have concluded that educated NigP is not a variety comparable to the mesolects of the Creole continua in the anglophone Caribbean, with traditional varieties as described in the literature as the "basilect" and English as the "acrolect". My central argument for this conclusion was that contrary to what one would expect in a continuum situation, many important aspects of the "basilectal" grammatical system are fairly stable in the NigP of even the most educated speakers. The data from less educated speakers has been much more limited, but it can be taken as confirmatory evidence for my observation that the wide range of grammatical variation correlatable with social factors which characterizes Creole continua has no equivalent in the language contact situation under investigation here.

More apparent than grammatical differences between the NigP use of educated speakers like those in the corpus and that of less educated ones like those in the additional recordings analysed in the present chapter are differences on the lexical and discourse levels. In

---

[18] Of course, as is the case in the corpus as well, English-influenced constructions with *to* coexist in the data with the corresponding NigP alternative constructions. Note, however, that the construction with *for* instead of *to* (cf 5.5.7, note 75) does not occur in these data, either.

[19] *Because* has been mentioned in 6.2.3. For examples of indefinite pronoun forms with *-body* in the texts and additional quotations from the recordings in Sections 6.2.1-3, see Text 6.1, ll 5, 18; Text 6.2, ll 95, 115; example (4), l 2; Text 6.3, l 23. In Janet's speech in the parts of recording B not printed in Section 6.2.2 there are two further instances (one each of *somebody* and *nobody*). In recording C, there are ten further instances of *everybody* apart from the one in Text 6.3, l 23 (including one in non-NigP speech), as well as one of *somebody*, six of *anybody* (including one in non-NigP speech) and four of *nobody*.

Chapter 5, it has become clear that in addition to some words which are probably now available to most (urban) NigP speakers, educated users of the language have borrowed some specialized vocabulary items such as higher education terminology, and any English lexical item may be used by them spontaneously in discourse; as a result, their NigP may, depending on the speech situation and the topic, be heavily interspersed with lexical items that a speaker with little formal education would be likely to have difficulties with (see in particular 5.3.1, 5.6.1.2, 5.7.1). It has also become clear that speakers who are fluent in both languages switch with ease between NigP and English segments of discourse (see 5.6.1.1), a strategy which is obviously not available to NigP speakers whose knowledge of English is very limited. Particularly instructive in connection with these differences is a comparison between the face-to-face speech section of the corpus of educated NigP and the two longer ones of the recordings analysed in this chapter, B and C. It can be assumed that Janet in Recording B would have had difficulties with many of the lexical items used by the speakers in the corpus, and even some of those used by Chike in Recording C, just as the interviewer had to replace *electricity* by *light* in order for her to be able to understand what he was referring to. Furthermore, in spite of what appeared to be attempts to accommodate to the educated interviewer, there were no longer segments in her speech that could be described as code-switches into a variety that was recognizably English. This was quite different in the case of Chike in Recording C. In the extracts from the recording in 6.2.3 one could see that he was able to insert English into his NigP much in the same way as more highly educated speakers do – but it was an English marked by some learner errors.

If, in order to complete the picture, the observations made in Section 4.4 on rudimentary varieties of NigP are taken into consideration as well, one discovers an unexpected parallel between two very different speakers, namely Janet in the interview analysed in Section 6.2.2 and the teacher in Text 4.1 in Section 4.4. In their different ways, both of them used English to an extent which, in comparison to the corpus data, could only be described as unusual. Janet and the teacher are indeed two very different speakers, representing opposite poles of the educational spectrum, but they also have one thing in common: in contrast to the speakers in the corpus, they are competent in only one of the two languages whose interaction is studied here, NigP and English, and in the recordings in question they were aiming at the other (at least, in the case of Janet, to some extent).

If viewed in its entirety, the picture of variation in NigP use that emerges from the analyses in 4.4 to 6.2.3 is thus quite different from variation in a P/C continuum. The general conclusion that can be drawn from the analyses is that NigP and English remain separate languages. English influence in NigP can generally be attributed to borrowing, the code-switching behaviour of bilinguals or incomplete second language acquisition, all phenomena which also occur in language contact situations not involving a P/C language. Differences between individuals in the kind of language contact phenomena which can be observed in their speech result mainly from different degrees of bilingual competence.

7

Language planning for Nigerian Pidgin: problems and prospects

7.1 Introduction

In the discussion of the sociolinguistic context of Pidgin use in Nigeria (Chapter 3), it became apparent that there is gap between policy and reality as regards the situation of NigP. Although a major lingua franca, it has no official recognition; even without any policy statements, it performs a growing range of functions, including, for example, that of a medium of public broadcasting, but no efforts have been made to develop it in order for it to be able to cope with these functions, as has been done for the major and to some extent also for minor indigenous languages. The analysis of the broadcasts in the corpus in Chapter 5 has shown that although NigP's lack of linguistic development may not be such a serious obstacle to its functional expansion in this domain as might be expected, there are of course problems that can be attributed to this lack. It therefore makes sense to consider the possibilities for remedying the gap by language planning, without, however, overlooking the problems involved in such efforts. This will be done in the present chapter. Both social aspects or status planning and linguistic aspects or corpus planning will be considered (Sections 7.2 and 7.3, respectively).[1] The suggestions and data of previous authors will be discussed and complemented by findings of my own on these issues, the principal sources of which are:

- relevant aspects of the data from the language survey (cf Chapter 3)
- relevant parts of the interviews in Appendix C
- a second questionnaire survey I conducted in 1997 in addition to the language survey, the "national language survey"[2] (National language questionnaires were distributed to a similar group of informants as the language questionnaires – 167 younger, educated urban residents in southern Nigeria, mostly students in tertiary education – but the group was comprised of an entirely different set of individuals from those in the language survey.[3] The questionnaire is shown in Appendix A.)

---

[1] The distinction between status and corpus planning, introduced by Kloss (1969: 81), has become widely accepted in language planning studies.

[2] The results of this survey, like those of the language survey, have been documented in full in Deuber (1998).

[3] The details of this sample are: 67% of the completed questionnaires are from Lagos, 33% from Calabar. All informants had a secondary education or higher. 87% were students at one of the four tertiary

7.2 Status planning

7.2.1 Possibilities for status planning for Nigerian Pidgin

In view of the fact that NigP's importance and usefulness have never been officially recognized, it is not surprising that suggestions for status planning for the language abound in the scholarly literature (Shnukal & Marchese 1983: 24; Ndolo 1989; Awonusi 1990: 117; Gani-Ikilama 1990; Jibril 1990: 115; Elugbe & Omamor 1991: 148f; Faraclas 1991: 511, 1996: 2; Oladejo 1991; Elugbe 1995: 292; Mann 1996, 1998). These centre on three aspects: the use of NigP in education, its use in the media, and its official recognition as a (or *the*) national or official language of Nigeria, or at least as a (major) Nigerian language. I will quote just some of the relevant statements. Gani-Ikilama (1990), for example, addresses the educational aspect:

> My submission is that Pidgin is so important in Nigeria (where in many places it is even a creole, i.e. it has become the mother tongue of some of Nigeria's peoples), that it cannot and should not be ignored. It can and should be used, even if only orally, as a medium of instruction in the initial years of Primary school, if education is to be meaningful to our Pidgin-speaking children. This would mean, of course, incorporating 'the use of Pidgin' in the teacher-training programme so that, at least, primary school teachers are prepared for this. (p 219)

Mann (1998), who looks at the issue of NigP use in the media, expresses the view that "its use in the media should be stabilised, promoted and extended". Ndolo (1989: 684) makes a specific suggestion concerning this issue, arguing that the use of NigP in the media should be extended to include national news broadcasts. He also suggests, among other things, that "the Government should promote a decree making Nigerian pidgin an official language" (ibid.). Faraclas (1991: 511) argues that "official recognition should be extended to NP [Nigerian Pidgin] as a major Nigerian language", and in Faraclas (1996: 2) he points out that "Nigerian Pidgin is in most respects the most logical choice for a national language". Oladejo (1991) advocates "a new, pragmatic language policy which recognizes Nigerian Pidgin English as the national language of the country, and at the same time retains English particularly for higher education purposes, international communication, and diplomacy" (p 264). This proposal, as he points out (ibid.), implies "a replacement of the three major Nigerian languages in the present policy with a single neutral indigenous language, Nigerian Pidgin English". It is the national language question that the following discussion of the problems and prospects of such proposals will focus on (Section 7.2.2), though status planning for NigP in the education and media sectors will be briefly considered as well (Section 7.2.3).

---

institutions mentioned in 3.1 (note 2); the remaining 13% had diverse other occupations. 51% were male and 47% female (2% omitted to indicate their sex). The distribution across age groups was: 17-19, 11%; 20-29, 60%; 30-39, 16%; 40-50, 4% (no answer: 11%). As their mother tongue, 37% of the participants in this survey claimed Yoruba, 24% Igbo, 36% a minor Nigerian language, and 1% each Hausa, English and NigP (no answer: 1%).

7.2.2 Nigerian Pidgin and the national/official language question

As Jowitt (1995: 36) notes, "discussion of the national language question often becomes confused through the failure to define terms adequately. Thus, 'national language' is often confused with 'official language'. Conceptually, they are two different things, though, in practice, an official language may also be the national language [...]." (What may add to the confusion for those not familiar with this usage of the term is that in Nigeria, *lingua franca* is sometimes used in the sense of 'national language' or 'official language'; cf e.g. Awonusi 1985, Ebam 1990.) In the present study, the term *national language* is understood in Fishman's (1971: 32n1) sense of a means of "furthering socio-cultural integration at the nationwide [...] level".[4] A language designated as "national" therefore may but need not be identical with one in "official" use, i.e. one which, in Fishman's words, is associated with "political-operational needs" (ibid.). However, as such a distinction between the two concepts is not always made, I will, in the following discussion, also take into account the work of authors who talk about NigP as a possible "official language" (or "lingua franca", in the relevant sense), although my primary interest is in the national language question.

As has already been shown in detail in Chapter 3, the current state of language policy in Nigeria for the national level is that a trilingual approach has been embarked on, with equal roles for Hausa, Yoruba and Igbo, and with "national unity" as one of the objectives of the policy (see 3.2.3). However, there have been problems in implementation and attempts to officially designate these languages as national languages have failed, one of the major reasons being ethno-political factors (see 3.2.4-5). With the success of the present policy rather moderate and an explicit official pronouncement on the national language issue still lacking, the debate about the issue has continued, and there have also been quite a number of scholarly articles devoted to it (e.g. Rufai 1977, Cyffer 1982, Dada 1985, Ndolo 1989, Awonusi 1990, Ebam 1990, Oladejo 1991, Adegbija 1994, Jowitt 1995). The options discussed in these can be summarized as follows:

- an African but non-Nigerian language (Wole Soyinka has suggested Swahili)
- an artificial language (in particular "Guosa", based on a number of Nigerian indigenous languages)
- a minor indigenous language
- one of the major indigenous languages
- the three major indigenous languages in combination
- English
- NigP

Although they have their advocates, the first three of the options listed are mostly considered unrealistic. With regard to the major indigenous languages, a frequently expressed view is that Hausa has the best qualifications for the single language option but that its adoption as Nigeria's national language would not be acceptable to those who are

---

[4] This aspect also played an important role for the informants in my national language survey. This is clear from the reasons given by the huge majority who considered it important or at least advantageous for Nigeria to have a national language (the detailed results for question 3 in the national language questionnaire are: "very important": 68%; "rather important": 6%; "not very important, but may have certain advantages", 20%; "not important", 6%): the three principal reasons (in descending order of the frequency of mention by the informants) were that a national language will bring about national unity, that it will facilitate communication, and that it will help to create a national identity.

not Hausa speakers. Indeed, it seems justified to say that the option of only one of the major indigenous languages is completely ruled out by the acceptability criterion. "One must [...] come to grips with the grim reality", as Ndolo (1989: 680) writes, "that ethnic and linguistic identities are still very strong, and that any attempt to choose or reject one of the three main regional languages as the medium of national communication would arouse bitter and intense reactions". The option of the three major indigenous languages in combination is generally considered more realistic, although by no means ideal. English of course has one important plus in comparison to the indigenous languages, its neutrality in ethnic terms, but there are the problems of its perception as a foreign language (see 3.2.5) and of its being associated with formal education (see 3.2.2). In spite of these factors, very positive attitudes towards English as a possible national language were found in two surveys of opinions about the question, one conducted by Dada among 245 Yoruba-speaking residents of Ibadan (see Dada 1985: 291) and another one by Ofuokwu among 200 students with different linguistic backgrounds at Ahmadu Bello University, Zaria (see Ofuokwu 1990: 79). In a third survey conducted by Awonusi (1985) among members of the National Assembly, opinions about English were, however, much less favourable: of the 290 members who completed Awonusi's questionnaire, only a minority was in favour of English continuing to play the role of Nigeria's "lingua franca", the majority favouring Hausa instead.

    The reasons why NigP has been discussed as a possible national language are of course its widespread use and its neutrality as the one language which links Nigerians both across ethnic and across social lines (cf 3.2.1, 3.2.4-5). These were also the main reasons cited by those who expressed themselves in favour of NigP as a potential national language in the language survey (question 8) and the national language survey; the arguments cited in the surveys in favour of NigP clustered around four types, which may be stated as follows (in descending order of the frequency with which arguments of the type were mentioned):

- It is widespread.
- It is spoken by both the educated and the less educated.
- It is easy to learn and understand/It does not presuppose formal education.
- It is ethnically neutral.

Also mentioned, though less commonly than these arguments, was that the language originated in Nigeria. This argument of course implies a comparison with English. In comparison with the indigenous languages, NigP with its largely English-derived vocabulary is not on firm ground. In fact, its ambivalent status as a language which is neither perceived as foreign in the way English is nor unanimously recognized as an indigenous language (cf 3.2.5) was clearly reflected in the surveys: while some were in favour of NigP as a potential national language because of its Nigerian origin, others rejected it on the grounds that it is not an indigenous language. The main reasons given by those who rejected it were, however, the prejudices which, as has been argued in 3.2.5, seem to be receding but have of course not disappeared, and its lack of development. Below the arguments cited against NigP are summarized in descending order of frequency:

- It is a corrupt form of English.
- It is socially stigmatized.
- It lacks linguistic development.

- It lacks international intelligibility and acceptability.[5]
- It is not sufficiently widespread.
- It is not an indigenous language.

Most of these arguments have also been discussed in the linguistic literature. In particular, most authors mention those which were also cited most frequently in my surveys, negative attitudes resulting from the prejudice that NigP is a corrupt form of English or from its social connotations, and its lack of linguistic development. These problems are acknowledged even by the NigP's strongest advocates (see e.g. Elugbe & Omamor 1991: 148f; Oladejo 1991: 263). Adegbija (1994), in his detailed analysis of the obstacles to NigP becoming a national language (as compared to the aspects in favour of such an elevation in status), discusses these and other points against it and goes on to argue:

> Finally, and what would be considered by most as the most deadly argument against pidgin's candidature, is a factor parasitic on its stigmatisation, low status, association with the non-Western educated, etc. [...], namely, that it is very lowly evaluated or esteemed. [...] Attitudinally, therefore, Pidgin is most unlikely to be acceptable to the majority of Nigerians as a national language. (p 16)

To buttress this argument, he cites an unpublished small-scale survey among 24 Nigerians (carried out by an MA student at the University of Ilorin, Kikelomo Ajayi, in 1988) in which almost all of the informants were opposed to NigP as a national language. He also cites the survey among legislators by Awonusi (1985) which has already been mentioned above, in which approval for NigP as "the new lingua franca" (p 27) was abysmally low (4%, with 83% of the respondents opposed and 10% undecided).[6] Adegbija concedes that Ajayi's informants were far too few for his results to be conclusive and that Awonusi's were all members of the same privileged group. Nevertheless, he arrives at the conclusion that "given the general attitudinally negative disposition towards Nigerian Pidgin, it does seem that its candidature for Nigeria's national language is, for now at least, in great jeopardy" (1994: 18). However, in view of the results of a more recent, large-scale survey (1,200 informants) conducted by Mann (1996, 1998, 2001)[7] in six southern Nigerian urban centres among men and women in a variety of occupational sectors,[8] the conclusion that attitudes towards NigP are generally negative seems rather premature. Mann's informants were asked to state, among other things, their opinion on the adoption of NigP as the official

---

[5] Statements to the effect that NigP lacks international intelligibility and acceptability of course again imply a comparison with English. For a national language to be at the same time an international language was in fact an important advantage in the eyes of those who opted for English in the national language survey. (The types of arguments that were advanced in favour of English were, in descending order of frequency, that it is ethnically neutral, that it has international intelligibility and acceptability, that it is widespread, that it has an established status as the country's official language, and that it has social prestige.)

[6] In the other two studies reporting survey results from which I have quoted above, Dada (1985) and Ofuokwu (1990), NigP is not mentioned.

[7] In Mann (1996) and (1998), the results for two occupational sectors, education and the mass media, respectively, are discussed. In Mann (2001) the focus is on females (half of the sample) across all occupational groups, but the results for the complete sample, including the males, are also reported.

[8] The occupational sectors covered by Mann's survey are: secondary education, tertiary education, the media, the civil service, the private sector, the army, the police, legal professions, religious organizations, trading.

language, as the question was framed in this survey, and, according to Mann (2001), 33.5% were in favour. In discussing the findings for the sub-sample from the educational sector, in which the approval ratings for NigP were similar to those in the complete sample, Mann (1996: 105) concludes:

> The results recorded from the survey of A N P [Anglo-Nigerian Pidgin] can only be described as promising for a language that is not standardized, suffers from low social prestige, but, most importantly, enjoys no official recognition. Given its omnipresence in urban sociocommunication, it is high time A N P enjoyed more respect and appreciation from all those concerned with language planning and policy in Nigeria.

Mann's results may be taken as an indication that the restriction of Awonusi's study to one special occupational group (a very important one, admittedly, in the context of policy-making) may have had a greater influence on the results than Adegbija (1994) seems to believe. There is, however, at least one other relevant difference between the two surveys, namely that whereas Mann's was restricted to southern Nigeria, Awonusi's targeted a group in which northerners were well represented (cf 3.2.4 on Nigeria's north-south divide with regard to the use of lingua francas).

The data I obtained in my own two surveys in southern Nigeria are, like Mann's, quite different from Awonusi's. Of course, there was no majority in favour of NigP, but approval was still considerable in view of the present state of language policy in Nigeria. The responses to question 8 in the language questionnaire, in which the informants were asked whether they agreed that NigP would be the most adequate candidate for a national language, were as follows: yes, 22%; it might be, 11%; no, 64%; no response, 3%. This is a more favourable result for NigP than Awonusi's, but still, one might say, a clear vote against it. However, approval for NigP needs to be seen in relation to that for the other major options. Such a comparison is made possible by the results of the national language survey summarized in Figure 7.1.

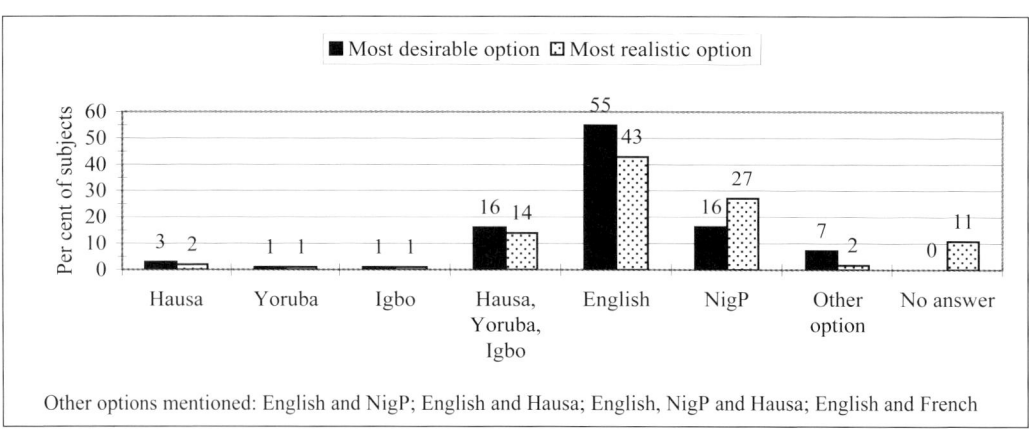

Figure 7.1 *Choice of national language according to the national language survey*

Perhaps the most noteworthy result that can be seen in the figure is that for this group of informants, NigP is as desirable a candidate for the status of a national language, and a considerably more realistic one, than the trilingual option which forms the basis of present language policies.

What is also clear from the results presented in Figure 7.1 is that it is English which attracted the most support from these informants. A word about the prospects for English in Nigeria is therefore in order. It seems reasonable to agree with Jowitt (1995: 53), who observes that whatever developments will be with regard to the national language question, English is likely to remain an official language (which concept, as the quotation at the beginning of this section has shown, he distinguishes from that of a national language) for a long time to come. That a significant change in the role of English is not likely in the foreseeable future is a view which is also shared by others who have contributed to the national/official language debate (Awonusi 1985: 29; Dada 1985: 292; Mann 1996: 104).

7.2.3 *Status planning for Nigerian Pidgin in education and the media*

In Mann's survey of attitudes towards NigP in southern, urban Nigeria which has been mentioned above in the context of the national/official language question, the informants were also asked whether, in their view, NigP should be taught in schools, as well as whether it should be used to teach in schools. In the complete sample, approval for the former was about 22% and for the latter about 28% (Mann 2001).[9] The question about NigP as an educational language was also posed in two small-scale surveys in NigP's heartland in the Delta (where in some cases it is already used unofficially as a medium of instruction, cf the discussion in 3.2.4). In one of these, Shnukal & Marchese (1983) interviewed 36 residents of Warri of ages ten to seventy. Only two of the adults, according to Shnukal & Marchese (1983: 21), as well as 7 out of 15 children under 16, were in favour of NigP as a medium of instruction in primary school. (The authors go on to point out: "It is, we think, significant that the most socially disadvantaged children, who had least control of St E [Standard English], were the most adamant in wanting to be taught in 'the good type of English'. Obviously, this represents for them a prestige acquisition, needed for social advancement.") The second of these surveys was conducted in Benin City, Sapele and Warri by Oloruntoba (1992), who reports (p 149) that out of 48 people (no further details of the sample are given), 25 were in favour of the use of NigP in schools. This seems a comparatively positive result. That support for this kind of suggestion would not be whole-hearted was only to be expected. There are, certainly, sound pedagogical and psychological arguments for providing at least initial instruction in the children's mother tongue or, as it says in the *National Policy on Education* (see 3.2.3), the "language of the environment" – which, of course, NigP is in some areas, though this provision has so far not been interpreted as being applicable to NigP. However, in a situation in which education in English is highly valued for reasons of social advancement and prestige, and education in any other language usually much less (see 3.2.5), it is clear that not all of those concerned will be easily convinced of the advantages of teaching in NigP.

That NigP can be very useful in the media (at least the oral ones) is probably the least controversial aspect of the suggestions that have been made for status planning for the

---

[9] Among the pupils/teachers and students/lecturers at the secondary and tertiary levels, respectively, for whom the results are reported in Mann (1996: 98), the approval ratings were slightly higher (about 24% for NigP as a subject and about 33% for NigP as a medium of instruction, respectively).

language. As has been shown in 3.2-3, its use in this domain has already expanded considerably over the past few decades, a development in which, it seems, policy-makers' rejection or inertia have simply been overtaken by practical considerations. Attitudes towards the use of NigP in this domain also seem to be quite positive, at least when compared to most of the findings on attitudes towards (possible) uses of the language discussed so far, although not much research has been done on this aspect. (Certainly, there have been, and are, even highly popular newspaper columns, radio programmes etc. in the language – in fact, according to Agheyisi 1984: 213, "the most effective outlet for NigP on its route to popularity have been the country's mass media"; see also 3.3 – but these have generally tended to be of a particular type: non-serious or, at most, with a serious message clothed in entertainment.) In my own language survey, as Figure 3.1 in Section 3.3 has already shown, opinions clearly differed depending on whether the issue was use of NigP for comic or for serious purposes. Not surprisingly, there was little opposition to the former. Even the latter was at least acceptable ("serves its purpose") to half of the informants, whereas real interest was very low, but this was to be expected, since, if NigP is used in the media for serious purposes, it is not with an audience composed of educated people like those who filled in the questionnaires in mind. To my knowledge, the only other survey in which opinions towards NigP in the media were elicited is the small-scale one by Shnukal & Marchese (1983). Their result was: "Although little more than half of the people we interviewed favoured increased use of NigPE [Nigerian Pidgin English] in books and magazines, all except two wanted more TV programmes in Pidgin" (p 21).

7.2.4 Conclusion

As the discussion above has shown, propositions that NigP should be given some form of official recognition and that its functions should be further expanded are certainly not unfounded. Not only are there the important arguments of its widespread use and its neutrality, but such proposals also appear to be more acceptable than some scholars have suggested. However, it is also clear that there are still obstacles to be overcome, in particular the prejudices which persist to varying degrees among different groups of the society, and at present there are no signs that a fundamental change in Nigeria's current state of linguistic policy and practice is likely to occur in the near future. Therefore, if NigP should earn official recognition, this, for now, appears more likely to take the form of an addition to, rather than a significant change of, present policies (though I would not want to commit myself to any prediction on the future course of language policy in Nigeria). The more realistic proposals among those that have been made thus seem to be the more modest ones, e.g. official recognition of NigP as a Nigerian language, official sanctioning of its use as an oral medium of instruction at the initial stages of formal education in areas where it is the predominant language,[10] and a further expansion of its use in the media.

---

[10] If NigP was approved only as an oral medium of instruction, as recommended by Gani-Ikilama (1990), the educational programme for these areas could be either one of "transitional bilingualism" or of "monoliterate bilingualism" (see Fishman & Lovas 1970; Craig 1977, 1980). In a programme of transitional bilingualism NigP would be used only to help the children to adjust to school and to learn enough English to be able to cope with English-medium instruction. In a programme of monoliterate bilingualism both languages would be developed for aural-oral skills but literacy would be limited to

7.3 Corpus planning

As was pointed out in 3.2.6, no formal steps have so far been taken for the development of NigP in any of the three respects described Ferguson (1968), viz, graphization, standardization and modernization. In this section the problems and prospects of changing this situation will be discussed. A good part of the discussion will be devoted to the basic question of graphization (Section 7.3.1), which has also received most attention in the literature so far. Section 7.3.2 will look at the issue of standardization, with modernization mentioned in passing.

7.3.1 Graphization

For the graphization of P/Cs in general, two basic approaches are available: the etymological and the phonemic one (see also the discussion in Sebba 1997: 244ff). In the etymological approach, the spelling system of the lexifier is adopted, with some adaptations where necessary. In the phonemic approach, the P/C is treated as a language in its own right independent from the lexifier; the result is a "tailor-made" orthography in which each phoneme is represented by exactly one symbol. A modified version of the phonemic approach is the "ethnophonemic" one (Hall 1966: 41). This approach is basically phonemic but digraphs and other orthographic devices are taken over from the spelling of the lexifier to represent phonemes for which no single letter is available, in order to avoid special characters.

How large the discrepancy is between an etymological and a phonemic orthography for a P/C of course depends on the extent to which the spelling of the lexifier is phonemic and the extent of phonological differences between the P/C and the lexifier. As in the case of English-based P/Cs the discrepancy between the two types of orthographies is inevitably huge due to the notorious gap between the spelling and pronunciation of the English language, the question of whether the spelling systems of these P/Cs should be etymologically or phonologically based has important ramifications. The arguments in favour of one or the other approach are obvious. People who are already literate in English usually find an English-based spelling system easier to use. In cases where literacy is to be taught initially or only in the P/C the same argument of ease of use would be a point in favour of a phonemic system (though if it is only initial literacy that the P/C is used for, it might also be argued that the orthography should be as close as possible to that of English to facilitate the transfer of the literacy acquired; cf Craig 1977: 321, 1980: 259). Furthermore, a phonemic system is likely to have a positive impact on attitudes towards the P/C, as it emphasizes its distance from English. For linguists, these arguments have usually outweighed those which, depending on the sociolinguistic situation in the area in question, may be put forward in favour of an etymological system. Baker (1997: 120) observes, "in recent decades, there has been widespread agreement among academics that the English-lexicon Creoles require substantially phonemic spelling systems, and that the inadequacies of English spelling should not be inflicted on their speakers". However, looking at the issue from a practical point of view, it seems clear that for a phonemic orthography to become generally accepted, it would need to be taught in schools, and whether it is realistic or

English. The problems and prospects of a programme which would also involve literacy in NigP are discussed in 7.3.2 below.

desirable to do so depends – at least in the view of some – on the present or envisaged sociolinguistic status of the P/C. For example, Todd (1974: 84) argues:

> While pidgin and creole speakers may spend most of their lives in a pidgin- or creole-speaking area, the majority of what they read and write will, of necessity, be in standard English [...]. Admittedly, each area must be considered separately. One might well wish to exclude Surinam, for example, and perhaps also Papua New Guinea from the above generalizations, largely because in both of these areas a form of the creole and the pidgin stands a good chance of becoming an officially used and recognized language. In such cases one can foresee a time when the majority of publications for local use will be in these languages; but until such a time and until such a policy is clearly envisaged it seems unproductive to teach reading and writing by means of pidgin or creole texts in a special orthography [...].

That initial literacy in a predominantly oral language is not worth the effort is of course not a view that all linguists or educationalists would agree with. A more common argument in fact seems to be the one which Bamgbose (1991: 82) summarizes thus:

> [...] a situation in which a child has to cope with a new system of sounds in a language while at the same time learning to represent such sounds as written symbols is most undesirable. Initial literacy should, therefore, be conducted in a language that the child already knows and, depending on other factors such as state of development of the language, size of speakers and teacher availability, this language should continue to be used as a medium of instruction for as long as possible in primary education.[11]

The problem is, as has also already become clear in the present study (see especially 3.2.4-5), that the opinions of experts and of the general public on the benefits of vernacular education do not necessarily coincide. Fasold (1997: 264f) makes the following observations with reference specifically to vernacular literacy in Nigeria:

> The point to note is the apparent disassociation between literacy and the vernaculars [...]. It appears that, for many Nigerians, whatever reading and writing skills one may acquire in the vernacular, these should not be dignified by the term literacy. Except for certain parts of the country with a strong tradition of scholarship in Arabic, to describe somebody as literate is tacitly and automatically to link their literacy to English. [...] For policy formulators, then, this dominant notion of English as the 'correct' or 'true' language of literacy has to be contended with in its various manifestations. It accounts for the 'barrier of communication' (Bamgbose 1985: 332) which exists between experts, researchers, and educators, on the one hand, and the decision-makers on the other, whereby the recommendations on vernacular literacy made by the former are not immediately obvious to the latter. It also accounts for the hypocritical attitude of the policy-maker who sends his children to English-medium private schools, whilst extolling the virtues of vernacular literacy which is to be found only in the public system.

In view of these aspects, the never officially settled question of NigP orthography (cf 1.8) is a very complex one indeed. An added complication for those who wish to change the status quo is that probably not everybody would readily agree that there is a pressing need to do so. The situation seems to be somewhat ambivalent. On the one hand, there is certainly an awareness of the issue. The informants in my surveys who were not in favour of NigP as a

---

[11] There is also a stronger, human rights-based version of the pro-vernacular argument. See the discussion in Bamgbose (1991: 81f).

potential national language for reasons which I have summarized as "it lacks linguistic development" mentioned not infrequently the specific aspect of the lack of a standardized orthography. On the other hand, some apparently have already accepted the English-based approach practised by all those who write NigP for non-scholarly purposes as a sort of *de facto* standard. Thus, I was told by Smart Esi, Head of the Pidgin Section at Radio Nigeria 3, that writing NigP needs to be properly learned, and that, while there is no codified spelling system to refer to, one can do so from those who already practise the use of NigP in writing or the texts that have so far been produced (see Interview 10, ll 371-423). In this connection, it is interesting to note that certain conventions already seem to be developing. As has been observed in 1.8, there is much variation in the spelling currently used in non-scholarly writing in NigP, but one can also identify certain common tendencies in the way the English orthography is adapted and in the way certain individual words, in particular frequent function words, are spelled. The fact that I built on such observations in constructing a spelling system for my own purposes but, for the sake of consistency, did not follow all the tendencies in the spelling of individual words that I observed in the texts available to me was not lost on the informants who analysed the extracts from the corpus of educated NigP. For example, one informant remarked in the comments section of one of the questionnaires that the orthography employed in the corresponding extract had "a high correlation with some of the supposedly accepted spellings" for NigP (see the comment on extract C01/3 in Table B.2 in Appendix B). In two other cases (see comment (b) on extract C05/6 and the comment on extract A01/3 in Table B.2) it was noted that the spelling of certain words in the extract deviated from the generally preferred spelling for these words (these were precisely among the cases where I had not followed a commonly made adaptation of a specific word for the sake of consistency). This shows just how familiar the type of spelling used in non-scholarly writing in NigP already is to some literate users of the language. By contrast, there seems to be very little awareness among the general public of the different direction that scholarly suggestions and practice have taken: linguists have for a long time argued against the etymological type of spelling and for a phonologically based system (see e.g. Mafeni 1971: 101f; Ofuani 1981b: 340ff; Agheyisi 1988: 239; Elugbe & Omamor 1991: chapter 5). The specific systems that have been proposed and used in the linguistic literature are mostly of the ethnophonemic type, with digraphs such as <sh> and <ch> for /ʃ/ and /tʃ/, respectively.[12] One example is the orthography by Faraclas shown in Table 7.1. This orthography is certainly convincing not only in terms of the systematic representation of NigP's sounds which it makes possible but also in terms of simplicity, as there are no special characters and only two diacritics, the subscript diacritics marking the mid-open vowel phonemes[13] (a device common in orthographies for Nigerian languages).[14]

---

[12] The present study is, however, not the first to go against the trend in the linguistic literature of using phonologically based and in particular ethnophonemic spelling systems. Other studies in which an English-based spelling has been used are Egbe (1980), Eze (1980) and Dadzie (1990).

[13] These diacritics usually take the form of subdots but in Faraclas (1996) underlining is used instead.

[14] A complication is that Faraclas also has superscript diacritics to mark tone. Elugbe & Omamor (1991: 117ff) argue that in the case of NigP there is not generally a necessity to mark tone and recommend it only for the few cases of lexical items distinguished solely by their tonal patterns.

Table 7.1 Ethnophonemic orthography for NigP

Phoneme	Grapheme	Phoneme	Grapheme
a	a	m	m
b	b	n	n
tʃ	ch	ŋ	ng
d	d	o	o
e	e	ɔ	o̱
ɛ	e̱	p	p
f	f	r	r
g	g	s	s
gb	gb	ʃ	sh
h	h	t	t
i	i	u	u
dʒ	j	v	v
k	k	w	w
kp	kp	j	y
l	l	z	z

(Source: Adapted from Faraclas 1996: 257)

Although the advantages of the above are obvious, there remains the problem of implementing linguists' proposals that such an orthography should be officially introduced for general use. Even Elugbe & Omamor (1991), who are among the staunchest advocates of an orthography of this type,[15] are not overly optimistic when it comes to this aspect:

> But even if an orthography were recognized for NP [Nigerian Pidgin], there would still be the problem of getting government to commit funds to the development of materials in NP, especially in the face the present financial predicament and given the fact that most of Nigeria's other myriad languages are also yet to be developed in any sense of the term. (Elugbe & Omamor 1991: 149)

A further problem, in addition to the negative attitudes towards vernacular literacy mentioned above and the practical problem of funding, is that NigP does not have the same functions in all parts of the country. In other words, what in other respects is NigP's greatest asset, its widespread use outside its core areas as a lingua franca, might make orthographic standardization on a phonological basis more difficult to implement than in a situation where the language in question has a large community of native speakers. Even if an orthography of the type recommended by linguists was approved, teaching materials developed in it and a NigP literacy programme launched in areas where NigP is the "language of the environment", those who may later on need or want to write or read in NigP are not necessarily those who would have benefited from this programme. (That NigP might be formally taught as an additional language in areas where it is not the predominant language of the environment seems a less than remote possibility.) If, however, a lingua franca closely related lexically to the dominant written language of the community is acquired only informally, one can hardly expect its users to be as motivated to learn a new orthography for it as language learners in other types of situations. Consider, for instance,

---

[15] They also explicitly oppose Todd's argument against using a P/C orthography independent of that of the lexifier for teaching initial literacy (Elugbe & Omamor 1991: 120).

the case of NigP-using professionals in the radio field – who, depending on the programme type, have a need for scripts – in Lagos. In addition to the six members of staff of Radio Nigeria 3 whose background data are included in Table 5.2, I also collected sociolinguistic background information on ten other NigP-using professionals in this field in Lagos (staff/freelancers at Radio Nigeria 3 as well as two other local stations and one of the radio drama scriptwriters of whom texts are included in the corpus of educated NigP). Relevant results for the total of sixteen persons, including the six whose data are also contained in Table 5.2, are summarized in Table 7.2.

Table 7.2 Selected sociolinguistic data on sixteen NigP-using radio professionals in Lagos

Highest educational qualification			
Secondary school certificate	O.N.D.[a]	First degree/H.N.D.[b]	No answer
6	3	3	1
Ethnic affiliation			
Yoruba	Igbo	Delta/Edo State ethnic groups (e.g. Urhobo, Esan)	
5	7	4	
Place of birth			
Lagos	Yoruba-speaking states	Igbo-speaking states	Delta/Edo State	Other
6	1	5	2	1
First language[c]			
NigP	English	Yoruba	Igbo
5	2	5	6
Age of first contact with NigP				
0-5	6-11	12-17	18 or over	No answer
1	5	1	3	1

[a] Ordinary National Diploma, obtained after two years of higher education at a polytechnic.
[b] Higher National Diploma, obtained after four years of higher education at a polytechnic.
[c] One person gave English and Yoruba as first languages and one English and Igbo.

Sixteen is admittedly a small number of persons, but with only Radio Nigeria 3 having an extensive programme in the language anyway, the data I have been able to gather mainly from staff and freelancers at this station and a few others do provide a certain insight into what kind of persons are involved in the production of NigP radio broadcasts in Lagos. One can see, first of all, that, as would be expected and as has already been pointed out in 5.1.2.2, such persons generally have a fairly high level of education. In Nigeria's current sociolinguistic set-up, this implies that English is their dominant written language by the time they have reached the end of their formal schooling, whatever their language of first literacy, if this is different from English at all. Secondly, there is a very considerable proportion of first language speakers of either Igbo or Yoruba who speak NigP as a second language,[16] and who were unlikely to have received literacy teaching in NigP even if this

---

[16] Cf also the remarks on varieties of NigP and broadcasting in 7.3.2.

was provided in certain areas.[17] One can of course point out that if a standardized orthography for NigP was to be officially introduced, the media would be another field, besides the education system, where steps would have to be taken for its implementation. This is what Ofuani (1981b) suggests; he argues that when a standardized orthography has been arrived at (like other linguists, he recommends an ethnophonemic one),

> the Nigerian Press Council, and any other body responsible for co-ordinating ideas about Nigerian languages, will then have the duty of prescribing it for Nigerian radio, television and newspaper journalists and disseminating it to them through writers' workshops, seminars and conferences in which this orthography will be practised for use. It will now be left to editors to ensure that this form is consistently adhered to in their newspapers, and in plays, novels and so on. It is hoped that with such a consistent orthography, better reading facility and enjoyment will be achieved by the reading public, irrespective of the language's relegation to only nonserious purposes: anecdotes, stories or humorous poems. (p 343)

This seems a good suggestion, but again there is the question of the chances for it to be implemented. What seems almost certain is that the introduction of a new orthography for NigP in the media would have to be part of a broader effort at raising NigP's status, augmenting its functions and implementing a new orthography, as I have hypothesized above, and that it would have to be vigorously pursued. Otherwise, it might be difficult to convince media practitioners that they ought to switch to a new orthographic system, considering the uses to which NigP is at present put in the media: as has already been mentioned in 3.2.4, if NigP is used in the print media it is usually for the amusement of an audience which the writers expect to be literate in English and which would need to be convinced of the advantages of an independent orthography for NigP (although Ofuani seems to be very optimistic about this aspect).[18] Besides, much of what is currently written in NigP by media practitioners is not intended for publication in written form at all but for oral delivery principally on the radio. Such scripts may even be read by the writers themselves, a practice which is not conducive to the enforcement of standards (see also Interview 10, ll 434-447 for a practitioner's view, and Simpson (1985: 139) and Bamgbose (1992: 2) on orthographic problems in Yoruba news scripts). Where some orthographic standardization would obviously be very useful is in cases where a script is not read by the person who wrote it (cf also the observations in 5.5.4.4). However, it does not seem likely that those involved in this kind of process would want to switch to an entirely different orthographic system, unless such a move was supported by a comprehensive language planning and implementation programme. Whether, in the absence of such a programme, they should be encouraged to at least come to an agreement on the spelling and

---

[17] There are of course individual cases where such a thing might happen. For example, one of the first language speakers of Igbo indicated that she was born in the Igbo-speaking part of the country but grew up in the former Bendel State, i.e. one of the main NigP-speaking areas.

[18] This problem is compounded in the case of creative writers with an international audience. For example, Omamor (1997) translates NigP passages from Achebe's *Anthills of the Savannah* into "regular" NigP represented in a phonemic orthography. The problem with her revised versions is, however, that for the average international reader this kind of orthographic representation is most likely to exacerbate the comprehension problems posed even by etymologically written or spoken NigP to the point of unintelligibility (cf in this connection also Mair's (1993: 224f) remark about audience reactions to a London performance of Soyinka's *The Road*).

pronunciation of certain words such as common function words that are prone to be misread is another question, since in the view of those who advocate a phonologically based system any attempt to standardize an etymological one would probably be a step in the wrong direction (cf also Hellinger 1986: 67).

I must conclude from the foregoing that the question of NigP orthography remains a problem, although not all seem to consider it such a pressing problem as some concerned linguists, and that a solution to this problem is not in sight, desirable though it may be. Linguists have put forward good arguments for a phonologically based system, in particular one of the type that has been described as "ethnophonemic", to be officially introduced. However, this would require a significant change in official attitudes towards the language and a vigorous programme of implementation. As long as there are no developments in this direction, it is most likely that, for better or for worse, NigP will continue to be spelled etymologically by those who write it for non-academic purposes.

7.3.2 Standardization and modernization

Görlach (1998: 141) observes that "older stages of the pidgins are frequently hailed as those worthy of imitation, from the Caribbean to New Guinea, especially where such conservative varieties happen to be supported by a written tradition, often introduced by missionaries", a situation which he compares to British traditional dialectologists' search for the pure forms of the dialects among older rural speakers. However, the desire to maintain conservative forms often comes into conflict with the realities of language use, and whether a possible standardization of a P/C should be based on a conservative variety may therefore be a debatable issue. For example, linguists such as Wurm (1980) – and more recently again Verhaar (1995) – have advocated a standardization of Tok Pisin on the basis of a rural, conservative variety; as Verhaar (1995: xviiif, 2f) explains, certain types of writing in Tok Pisin, in particular biblical texts, have already promoted such a variety to the status of a *de facto* standard. Romaine (1992: 320), however, argues that it has become increasingly unrealistic to stick to these conservative rural norms in any future standardization of Tok Pisin.[19]

Although NigP does not have the kind of written tradition that Tok Pisin, for example, has, conservative, puristic attitudes are in evidence in the work of some of the linguists who have written on the language (see 1.3). General attitudes among educated speakers towards English influence in NigP, according to the judgments in my questionnaire study of corpus extracts (see the discussion in 5.7), are more tolerant. However, it is noteworthy as well that the informants in the study gave particularly high ratings and favourable comments to the texts in the category "advice", which, as I found in my analyses of the corpus, display conservative grammatical features most consistently and tend to be conservative lexically as well. Similarly positive were the reactions to the extracts from the drama serial *Rainbow City* included in the corpus, although, in comparison to the advice texts, these may be described as moderately anglicized, whereas there was criticism of the tendency towards "hyper-pidginization" in some of the news texts. If the results of the questionnaire study are

---

[19] Also of interest in connection with the issue are Valdman's observations on conservative versus gallicizing tendencies in the standardization and use of Haitian Creole; see in particular Valdman (1989).

viewed in their entirety, it is, however, clear that the informants considered as the "better" type of NigP that which is relatively less influenced by English. At the same time, they belonged to the social class of NigP speakers who, when speaking the language with their peers, freely use English lexical items and may switch extensively between NigP and English segments of discourse. In view of these attitudes and the less educated target audience of NigP as used in formal functions, on the one hand, and the continued influence of English and the virtual inevitability of borrowing as one of the strategies to modernize NigP's lexicon, on the other, it seems that whoever might be interested in standardizing the language might have to seek a compromise between conservatism and anglicization. For the grammar, where I found a great deal of overlap between the educated, urban NigP of Lagos and more conservative varieties as described, for example, by Faraclas (1996), this would not even be nearly as complicated as in the case of a P/C continuum (cf Devonish 1991). In the area of lexis, however, a large number of decisions of the type that newscasters are faced with every time they translate an English script into NigP would have to be taken.

A standard variety is superimposed on social as well as on regional varieties. Regional variation in NigP is described by Agheyisi (1988: 230f) as follows. She mentions two aspects of variation, phonological and lexical. Accents are determined by the speakers' language background, so that with respect to phonology one may rather speak of "Yoruba Pidgin", "Igbo Pidgin" etc. than of regional varieties per se. In addition to phonological influence there has been lexical borrowing from indigenous languages, particularly from Yoruba and Igbo, the two major languages of southern Nigeria, and it is therefore possible to distinguish a Yoruba-influenced western dialect and an Igbo-influenced eastern dialect; these dialects are used by people with different first languages resident in the respective areas. The least accented and lexically "purest" varieties of NigP, as Agheyisi (1988: 231) writes, are those used in linguistically heterogeneous areas, such as the Delta dialect in the former Bendel and Rivers State. It is the Delta dialect which, according to Agheyisi, is the obvious choice for the basis of a standard NigP:

> In view of the extreme variation in NPE [Nigerian Pidgin English] use, there is need for the recognition of a core variety as a basis for standardization. Fortunately, the choice of variety is hardly contentious, given the fact that the Delta variety, especially as spoken in Warri and Sapele, already enjoys wide recognition among NPE speakers as the purest and most internally resourceful variety of the language. (Agheyisi 1988: 237)

Similar views were expressed by some of the NigP speakers I interviewed (see Interview 2, ll 553-567; Interview 11, ll 150-159). However, it was also pointed out in the interviews that the Delta or specifically the Warri variety has become "so advanced and so specialized" (Interview 2, l 532) that it is no longer always readily intelligible to speakers of other varieties of NigP, which apparently is due in particular to its peculiar vocabulary and idiomatic expressions (see Interview 2, ll 520-531; Interview 5, ll 54-58; Interview 10, ll 281-286). Smart Esi of Radio Nigeria 3 described Delta Pidgin, of which he is a native speaker himself, as the "standard" or "real" NigP (see Interview 10, ll 200-202, 260-261, 287), but he also distinguished a "standard" and a "slang" variety (Interview 10, ll 280-281) and mentioned differences in his own language use between the broadcasting situation and interaction with fellow Delta Pidgin speakers (see Interview 10, ll 287-321). Both he and

Ndidi Osaka of Radio Nigeria 2 also said that the informal standard for NigP use in public formal communication is a variety which is not too strongly dialectal (see Interview 10, ll 352-370; Interview 9, ll 138-158).[20] Dialect neutrality, according to Ndidi Osaka (Interview 9, ll 150-153), implies mainly the avoidance of too many indigenous language words. Accentedness, by contrast, does not seem to be considered a problem. Smart Esi argued that while NigP is spoken most "beautifully" and "cleanly" in the Delta, where it is creolizing (he drew a comparison with Sierra Leonean Krio in this connection), "correct Pidgin" can in fact be spoken with any Nigerian indigenous language or other first language accent (Interview 10, ll 204-234). Accordingly, he considers good second language competence in NigP enough of a qualification to work as a NigP broadcaster at Radio Nigeria 3 (see Interview 10, ll 145-153). It thus appears that even if NigP was standardized on the basis of the Delta variety, there would, in view of the large numbers of second language speakers, probably continue to be a high tolerance of different accents. Also, in the standardization of the lexicon a too strong regional bias may have to be avoided in order for the standard to be consistent with NigP's primary function as a neutral lingua franca (cf also Interview 1, ll 123-134). As one of my informants recommended:

> You will be talking of standardized Pidgin, which is neutral to a certain extent. It may have a base somewhere, maybe Warri or whatever. It will have a base somewhere, but from this base you draw from all the other varieties to develop it. (Interview 11, ll 265-267)

Standardization also involves codification of the norm, once one has been agreed on, in reference works such as grammars and dictionaries. This raises the question of who might be willing and able to undertake and finance such an enterprise for NigP. Agheyisi (1988), who has discussed the issue in some detail, identifies three major obstacles to the standardization[21] of NigP: the lack of official interest in the development of the language, the popular stereotype of it as a funny or inferior type of speech, leading to the promotion of deviant, exaggerated varieties in the mass media (cf Omamor's "pseudopidgin"), and the absence of the right personnel or codification agencies to carry out such a project. Therefore, she concludes, "the success of the standardization of NPE [Nigerian Pidgin English] will have to depend on the individual efforts of interested users of the language" (p 240). As official attitudes have remained essentially the same, I can only agree with this conclusion. At the same time, the gradual expansion of NigP's functions – in spite of these attitudes – is opening up more opportunities for interested users to contribute to its development. The present study has also made the points that the language has been gaining to some extent in acceptance (in particular among younger Nigerians), although there are still prejudices, and that there is a growing interest among media practitioners in communicatively viable forms of NigP, rather than in deviant ones designed for maximum comic effect. In view of these developments, the small-scale standardization and modernization projects which, in the absence of official involvement in the process, restricted groups of users might undertake out of their own initiative and for their own purposes become all the more important. To

---

[20] However, in my questionnaire study of the corpus of educated NigP, informants occasionally expressed dissatisfaction with the extent to which indigenous language words were used in news extracts; see comment (a) on extract N01/4 and the comment on extract N04/3 in Table B.2 in Appendix B.

[21] Note that Agheyisi uses the term *standardization* in the broad sense, in which it is roughly equivalent to Ferguson's (1968) "language development".

cite just one example, which has already been mentioned in Deuber (2002: 221): Simpson (1985: 145) has suggested that the quality of Yoruba news broadcasts (or broadcasts translated into Nigerian languages more generally) could be further improved if, for example, translators compiled glossaries of useful equivalent terms, and while NigP has a long way to go before it will reach the stage of development of a language like Yoruba, this type of measure could be a useful first step.

7.3.3 *Conclusion*

There have been quite a number of proposals for corpus planning measures for NigP, in particular the introduction of a phonologically based orthography. These are, however, not easy to implement. As long as there is no official interest in the development of the language, the prospects for a significant change in the status quo, in which NigP performs a broadening range of functions without any codified norms of written and spoken usage, are not particularly good. However, the individual efforts towards developing the language which might be undertaken by those most affected by this situation (e.g. NigP-using broadcasters) could certainly also make a difference in the quality of the growing number of texts produced in NigP for public consumption and should be encouraged.

8

Conclusions and future outlook

8.1 The linguistic relationship between Nigerian Pidgin and English and its theoretical implications

> *To my mind, one exciting question is whether NigE [Nigerian English] and pidgin will remain apart, or whether a continuum will develop, as it has done in much of the Caribbean. If this happens, the resulting compromise will, of course, be even further away from the International Standard than some present-day forms of NigE already are.* (Görlach 1998: 151)

To address the question of the linguistic relationship between NigP and English has been one of the primary concerns of this study. As the overview of the relevant literature provided in 2.2.7 as part of the description of the theoretical background to the study has shown, some scholars have even claimed that a continuum of the type mentioned by Görlach in the quotation above as a possibility already exists in Nigeria, whereas others have maintained that NigP and English remain separate languages. A similar controversy, as has also become evident in the theoretical discussion of the continuum issue in 2.2, has surrounded the linguistic relationship between other P/Cs and their lexifiers, notably that between Tok Pisin and English in Papua New Guinea.

In my own empirical investigation of the question I focussed on the educated variety of the NigP spoken in the urban environment of Lagos by speakers with medium to high competence in the language. In the central Chapter 5 I analysed a corpus compiled for the purpose with a view to ascertaining whether this variety represents a "mesolect" bridging the linguistic distance between the more conservative type of NigP described by several previous scholars ("basilect") and English ("acrolect"), as one would expect to find when analysing educated, urban speech in a P/C continuum situation. The result of my detailed grammatical analyses was that, according to the data assembled in the corpus, the educated NigP of Lagos does not display the kind of intermediate morphosyntactic features typical of the Caribbean mesolects and remains relatively distant from English, with central aspects of the "basilectal" grammatical system quite stable. This is one important piece of evidence showing that the linguistic relationship between NigP and English differs substantially from the kind of situation where a P/C and its lexifier are opposite poles of a continuous spectrum of varieties.

Although educated NigP as represented in my corpus cannot be described as a "mesolect" in the sense in which this term has been employed by scholars who have worked on the Creole continua in the anglophone Caribbean, the analyses revealed significant English influence in the form of code-switching – at the levels both of whole discourse chunks and of single words – and lexical borrowing. These are features which, as the discussion based on the work of specialists in the area of indigenous language-English contact in 4.1-2 has demonstrated, this variety of NigP has in common with educated or urban varieties of indigenous languages of Nigeria. The data from my corpus also indicated some grammatical borrowing, which, though limited, exceeds that which has been reported for indigenous languages. However, I am reluctant to invoke a special phenomenon of "depidginization" or "decreolization" to account for this (as has become clear, NigP, despite its name, does not fit easily into either the category of "Pidgin" or that of "Creole" as traditionally defined), for several reasons. First, I have observed grammatical borrowing but no drastic restructuring. It is possible that over time English grammatical influence in NigP will become much more pronounced, but the observations I have been able to make at the present moment do not allow the extrapolation that NigP will inevitably dissolve into a spectrum of varieties with increasing proximity to English up to the point of merging with it. This, however, is the assumption which motivated the introduction of the term *decreolization* and its extension to *depidginization*. Furthermore, while different scholars have applied these terms to all sorts of lexifier influences, one of the principal proponents of the gradual approximation theory, the early Bickerton, has linked the concept of decreolization to a certain type of change whereby forms newly borrowed from the lexifier are slotted into a space in the Creole grammar, i.e., they take on a Creole meaning, function and distribution (see especially Bickerton 1980). Bickerton argued that this mechanism, which he attributed to "faulty perceptions by the speaker and limitations on the concept 'possible change to grammatical state G_1'" (1980: 110), gives rise to the characteristically hybrid mesolectal systems. In the present case, there is mostly not even a theoretical possibility of discerning such a mechanism, as borrowing of grammatical morphemes has tended to occur mainly in those areas where there is considerable structural congruity between NigP and English anyway, i.e., apart from conjunctions, mainly in the noun phrase. The one case where it was possible to analyse this aspect, and at the same time the most notable case of what appeared to be relatively recent grammatical borrowing, namely that of plural *-s*, did not conform to Bickerton's theory of change in decreolization. (As shown in detail in 5.5.4.2, plural marking of nouns by *-s*, like marking by *dem* which apparently it supersedes, is variable, but it is not subject to the same constraints.) Bickerton (1980) concedes that at later stages, forms borrowed into a Creole from its lexifier gradually acquire lexifier functions as well, after having been used first with Creole functions, but the introduction of *-s* into NigP is probably too recent for it to have already passed along such a trajectory. Besides, in other areas of the grammar where the corpus study showed that English forms were used only sporadically, and not to such an extent that they could be considered integrated, these forms were always used according to standard English grammar (see the observations on the third person singular personal and possessive pronouns (5.5.4.4), tense/aspect marking (5.5.5), copulas and related constructions (5.5.6) and verbal negation (5.5.9)). The data therefore do not indicate any incipient decreolization process according to the Bickertonian model. Even in the speech of the less educated speakers in the additional recordings analysed in Chapter 6 – in contrast to the educated speakers in the corpus, these speakers could certainly be described as having "faulty perceptions" of English grammar – the predominant tendency was for English forms, where they occurred, to be used according to the English system; there were the expected learner errors but hardly any cases of English forms clearly functioning according to NigP grammar.[1] From this point of view, there is thus no evidence of a special language contact phenomenon which would require a special term like *decreolization* or *depidginization* to describe it. Moreover, that NigP should have borrowed more grammatical morphemes from English than indigenous languages, and such as are lower on the scale of borrowability, is consistent with its greater linguistic proximity to English, within a contact situation that is comparable from the social point of view (cf the discussion in 2.4.2 and 5.8.1). NigP's greater linguistic proximity to English is attendant on its being an English-based contact language. However, a similar outcome would be conceivable if it were a language that is closely related to English but not one of those for which the labels *Pidgin* and *Creole* have been chosen. And if the changes that one can observe in a P/C coexisting with its lexifier roughly fit into the general picture of language contact phenomena, I am entirely in agreement with Mufwene (1994; see the quotation in 2.1) that there is no need for a special term to designate them.

Additional speech samples from speakers with different social characteristics and linguistic backgrounds from the educated and moderately to highly competent NigP speakers in the corpus were examined in Chapter 6 as well as in Chapter 4, Section 4.4. These analyses revealed linguistic variation which, I argued, was most adequately explained as the result of different degrees of bilingual competence, i.e. the interaction of two competence spectra, one in English and one in NigP; the samples did not indicate the existence of a range of lects which could be analysed as part of a NigP-English continuum. At the lowest ends of the two competence spectra, where the control of grammar is inadequate and communication is based mainly on lexical items, there is of course a certain overlap between "broken English" and "broken NigP", as the lexicon of the two varieties is shared to a great extent; at higher levels there may be a great deal of interference if a speaker is not fully bilingual and particularly if he/she is only minimally so, but the more competent a speaker is in both languages, the better he/she is able to keep them apart. The conclusion on the linguistic relationship between NigP and English that I arrived at in the microsociolinguistic part of the study was therefore that for now at least, NigP and English remain separate languages (see 6.3).

Why should it be that four decades after Nigeria's independence, which, according to the theory of DeCamp and, initially, Bickerton (see 2.2.5), created the right social conditions for the development of a NigP-English continuum, I should not have been able to detect signs of the emergence of a mesolect (in the sense of "classic" continuum studies) between the two varieties? Agheyisi (1984a), who, contrary to expectations based on the DeCamp/early Bickerton theory, has argued that "the possibility of a systematic mesolectal variety emerging in the Nigerian situation is rather remote" (p 230), cites as the primary reason the heterogeneity of the NigP-speaking population. She points out, for example, that this population is made up of people who belong to various ethnolinguistic groups and

---

[1] The only case which fits fully into this pattern is the sporadic use of relative *dat* in relative clauses with resumptive pronouns by Janet in the second of the three recordings analysed in Chapter 6 (see 6.2.2).

perceive their identity as members of these groups rather than as NigP speakers (ibid.). As she further observes (p 231), depending on the speech situation, this can lead to a high degree of code-switching involving NigP and indigenous languages, and it provides a channel for the diffusion of substratal features into NigP. It is not my intention to enter into the substrate versus universals debate waged by those concerned with Creole genesis nor to go into details of structural correspondences between NigP and its various substrates, but it is probably significant that to the present day, the contact situation in which NigP is involved has included not only its lexifier but also its substrates, with which it shares important structural features (cf Faraclas 1988). In addition to this aspect, it is also pertinent that the theory of the continuum as the result of a universal process of decreolization has been increasingly questioned: as shown in detail in 2.2.5-6, there has been more and more support for the view that the Creole continua of the anglophone Caribbean have not developed out of a situation with only two polar varieties but result from a process of progressive restructuring of English which is connected with the specific sociohistory of the territories in question. Seen in this light, as I have pointed out in 2.2.7, there need not be a similar continuum in Nigeria with its very different history of Afro-European contacts; this view, I argued, can be taken whether one considers NigP as directly descended from the early trade jargons or whether one attributes a significant role in its development to Sierra Leonean Krio, as the different theories of its origin go. I also mentioned (in 2.2.8) that the same historical argument had been given by Siegel (1997) as a possible explanation for the absence, according to his analyses, of Pidgin-English continua in Papua New Guinea and other Melanesian countries. Following Siegel's lead, one might say that not only in the Melanesian case but also in the Nigerian one (and the same argument could be made for other parts of West Africa as well, see 2.2.7), it might be because no continuum developed in the early history of the contact with Europeans that there is none today. And, although the long-term consequences of the continued contact between NigP and English are difficult to predict, when the question is considered from this perspective, it is by no means certain that there will ever be one.

NigP and Tok Pisin are not the only contact languages coexisting with their lexifiers to which the continuum model as developed for the anglophone Caribbean has been transferred on the basis of a preconceived notion of decreolization/depidginization which does not always seem to have been complemented by detailed empirical investigation (cf the discussion in 2.2.7-8). Another case which has so far not been mentioned in the present study but which is also of great interest in this connection is that of Palenquero, a Spanish-based Creole spoken in the Colombian village of Palenque, as it has been described by Schwegler in his paper entitled "The myth of decreolization: the anomalous case of Palenquero" (2000). According to Schwegler, Palenquero has not undergone any significant restructuring in the last one hundred years, although all of its remaining speakers – it is gradually being abandoned – speak the regional variety of Spanish as well and code-switching is pervasive; as Schwegler emphasizes in the study (p 415), there is no continuum, no series of lects intermediate between the Creole and Spanish. Schwegler (2000: 418) explains the mischaracterization of Palenquero as a "post-Creole" variety by certain scholars (hence "the myth of decreolization") as the result of developments in the history of Creolistics: he points out that Palenquero was identified as a Creole only in the late 1960s, when Creolistics had just become firmly established as an academic discipline.

The focus on English-based Creoles of several influential scholars at that time led to the development of the continuum model tied to the concept of decreolization as a (then) assumed to be universally applicable paradigm, and, as Schwegler argues, this paradigm was extended to Palenquero without empirical data to back up the assumption that Palenquero was decreolizing. That, despite suggestions to the contrary by the supporters of the decreolization hypothesis, the structure of Palenquero has, according to Schwegler, been strongly resistant to Spanish influence is certainly very remarkable, given the intensity of the contact situation (Palenqueros have apparently been bilingual in the Creole and Spanish for well over two hundred years; see Schwegler 2000: 415). However, in view of the challenges from several corners to the Bickerton/early DeCamp theory whose extension to Palenquero gave rise to the "myth of decreolization", it does not seem so "anomalous" that a continuum of the type found in Jamaica or Guyana should not have developed in Palenque. Perhaps it is time that Creolistics freed itself of the straightjacket of the P/C continuum – particularly as linked to the controversial diachronic process of depidginization/decreolization – as the default model for all P/C-lexifier contact situations. This is in no way to diminish the validity of the continuum as a synchronic, descriptive model for those cases where data amenable to such an analysis exist, but its application should be preceded by adequate empirical research into the actual language contact phenomena to which a particular P/C-lexifier contact situation has given rise.

8.2 Register variation in educated Nigerian Pidgin and the issues of "pseudopidgin", structural expansion and corpus planning

[...] although more attention has been paid to the country's indigenous languages since independence, English still remains the country's official language, the language of the civil service, of parliament and of secondary and tertiary education. It is hardly surprising, therefore, that the Yoruba of many bilinguals is characterized by language-mixing.

There is, as one might expect, some reaction against this trend. There are purists who deprecate what they consider the corruption of the Yoruba language, and indeed the Yoruba newspapers and news broadcasts in Yoruba do show that Yoruba does have the resources to cope with contemporary demands made on it. But this has not reduced the phenomenon of language-mixing, and the prospect seems to be that while the more formal varieties of Yoruba will be characterized by purism, some informal varieties will continue to be characterized by language-mixing. (Banjo 1986: 535f)

The analysis of register variation in educated NigP integrated into the corpus study has revealed a situation which is similar to that which characterizes the use of indigenous languages, as exemplified in the quotation above by Yoruba. It was found in the analysis that the samples of radio broadcasts in the corpus differ clearly from the samples of face-to-face speech. In the broadcast samples, more use tends to be made of the resources of NigP for the expression of modern concepts and for certain discourse functions, and less of lexical items newly borrowed from English and the strategy of switching into that language; in at least two of the three broadcast subcategories one can also observe a predilection for certain conservative grammatical forms. In the conclusion to the corpus study (Section

5.8.3), these differences were attributed to the influence of two principal situational factors on the speakers' NigP use: the addressee(s) – chiefly less educated people in the case of the broadcasts, a fellow educated speaker, or fellow educated speakers, in the case of the samples of face-to-face speech – and, secondarily, the degree of formality of the speech situation. It was further argued that the latter factor is probably also at least in part responsible for the more subtle differences that were found between subcategories of texts both within the broadcast section and within the face-to-face speech section of the corpus. Generalizing, one can say that greater informality correlates with an increased tendency for bilinguals to produce mixed NigP-English discourse rather than a "pure" form of NigP speech, as also observed by Banjo in the quotation above for Yoruba.

Another factor which accounts for some of the differences in the degree of English influence in the different categories of texts in the corpus is of course the topic (see e.g. the discussion in 5.7.2). The more modern or technical concepts need to be expressed, the less NigP's traditional lexicon is adequate for the purpose, and educated speakers naturally resort to the use of English words when NigP has no equivalent for these. In the face-to-face speech section of the corpus one therefore finds, alongside relatively less English-influenced texts about everyday issues, certain samples of NigP discourse which are heavily interspersed with newly borrowed or singly switched English lexical items, e.g. when students talk about university-related issues (cf 5.6.1.2). Broadcasters, however, need to restrict their use of such items if they want to communicate effectively with their target audience. In the case of NigP news broadcasts in particular, the conflicting pressures of the nature of the topics (reinforced by the fact that the texts are translated from English), on the one hand, and the addressees and the formality of the speech situation, on the other, put the broadcasters into a situation which has been described in 5.4.2.3 as a "tightrope walk between anglicisms and pidginization". It was also noted in the corpus study that although the conflict between the inevitable English influence and the desire to pidginize – which may result in an acceptable compromise or one of the extremes of "hyper-anglicization" or "hyper-pidginization" – manifests itself mainly in the lexis of the news texts in the corpus (see 5.1.2.1-3), examples can be found on the grammatical and discourse levels as well (see especially 5.5.4.2 and 5.5.7).

In view of the fact that their nature and production circumstances make them the most problematic type of radio text in the corpus, it was not surprising to find that the news texts received significantly lower ratings in the questionnaire study than the texts in the other broadcast subcategories (see 5.7.2). Nevertheless, I argued 5.8.2, it would in most cases seem exaggerated to speak of "pseudopidgin", as Omamor (1997) has labelled certain literary and media uses of NigP, since one also has to take into consideration the inherent difficulties of all vernacular news translations and the fact that most of the extracts from these texts received at least fair ratings in the questionnaire study. On the whole, in fact, the broadcast section of the corpus can be taken as evidence that NigP on the radio is no longer just a comic, distorted variety but that NigP's usefulness as a medium of information transmission is increasingly leading broadcasters to adopt a more serious approach. However, it is also clear that problems remain, and among the factors that are responsible for these is certainly NigP's lack of development, i.e. the lack of systematic efforts to modernize its lexicon and of a standard variety of the language as well as a standardized orthography. Thus, uses of NigP like those on the radio would clearly benefit from a programme of corpus planning for the language, but in my discussion of this issue in 7.3, I could, in view of the continued official disinterest, only agree with Agheyisi (1988) that the development of NigP will probably have to depend on individual users. This makes the work of people like NigP broadcasters, who, in the absence of a language planning programme to support them, try to find their own ways of adapting the language to their needs, all the more important. In fact, in spite of the problems that have been identified in the study, one could say that the sample of radio texts in the corpus at least points the way that any standardization and modernization of NigP will most likely have to take, namely, that a compromise will have to be sought between anglicization and purism. On the one hand, a certain anglicization is inevitable, and exaggerated purism will result in forms that are likely to be perceived as artificial. On the other hand, the resources of the language ought to be developed as well, and for educated NigP speakers to limit their recourse to English in formal contexts is in keeping not only with the goal of intelligibility to those who do not understand English well but also that of acceptability for the NigP-speaking population at large. Frequent switching between NigP and English is widely practised among educated speakers but is certainly not considered the best way of speaking NigP (see the discussion in 7.3.2). In any case, whether or not formal usage will be standardized, the prospect seems to be *mutatis mutandis* that which Banjo has described in the quotation at the beginning of this section, viz, that the present register differences will continue.

8.3   Sociolinguistic aspects of the Nigerian language contact situation

It seems to me that Pidgin has this ability to coexist with standard English, because they are both strong, they are both dominant in different areas. (Interview 1, ll 303-305)

The discussion of the macrosociolinguistic context of NigP use in Chapter 3 has shown that the relationship between NigP and English can be described as a broad diglossia with English as the H ("high") and NigP as the L ("low") language. The indigenous languages, as has also become clear, can be seen as the third basic factor in Nigeria's sociolinguistic make-up, though they form a heterogeneous group with regard to their size and functions. They have in common with NigP the broadly diglossic relationship with English as H, but are differentiated from the neutral NigP by their ethnic associations. In this sense, one can speak of a triglossic language situation in Nigeria. This situation seems, at present, fairly stable. It is of course true that NigP has been gradually expanding its functions in the last few decades, with a concomitant shift in attitudes towards greater acceptability; there is indeed no reason (apart from the prejudices which linger on to some extent in particular in the influential circles of the society) why its great potential as a means of communication with large segments of the population should not be exploited more for formal communicative purposes. I have also pointed out that though the majority of Nigerians continue to speak an indigenous language as their first language, there is a tendency in some multilingual urban communities for children to acquire a first language competence in NigP which may, but, as the example of Ajegunle in Lagos has shown, need not be matched by equal competence in an indigenous language (see 3.2.2, 3.3). However, these developments are not such that it would seem realistic to expect that NigP could displace English as Nigeria's official language, or that it could constitute a threat to the indigenous languages as a group (though perhaps to some minor individual ones), and it seems likely that in its basic form the situation will remain triglossic for the foreseeable future.

Mühlhäusler (1993) has argued that the ultimate line of development in established multilingual societies (e.g. in Melanesia, Africa) in which a P/C has developed is from multilingualism in a large number of indigenous languages to monolingualism in a world language: the P/C replaces the indigenous languages before it is, in the long run, itself replaced by the world language. Mühlhäusler focuses on the social process of language shift, but the outcome of a P/C being displaced in this way would be essentially the same as that envisaged by those who have proposed that under certain social conditions, a P/C will eventually merge with the superstrate through a linguistic process of depidginization/ decreolization. As Mühlhäusler (1993: 65) concludes: "Their [P/Cs'] ultimate role may be that of providing substratum features for shallow differences in the variants of large metropolitan languages such as World English or World French." In the Nigerian case, it has in fact been documented that there is, as elsewhere, a tendency for small languages to die out (according to Brenzinger, Heine & Sommer 1991: 27, a total of 27 Nigerian languages is either already extinct or in a process of extinction), and there is also the emphasis on the children's acquisition of English in some elite families which has been mentioned in 3.2.2. However, in view of the relatively small number of languages and speakers affected, these may, for now, still be considered developments at the margins of Nigeria's sociolinguistic configuration, and the scenario of large numbers of Nigerians being monolingual in English seems so removed from present-day realities that there is no need to speculate about it in the context of the present study.

Whether or not NigP will, from a sociolinguistic point of view, be able to withstand the pressure of English, as more and more Nigerians are provided with the opportunity to acquire a knowledge of the latter, is also an issue which I discussed with some of my informants in the interviews (Appendix C). In one case, a debate arose between a group of informants (Interview 1, ll 208-234, 281-305, 363-428), which clearly brought out the relevant factors. On the one hand, its prestigious status in Nigeria and its role as a world language will continue to provide a strong incentive for more and more Nigerians to learn English. On the other hand, it also seems very likely that NigP will continue to be widely spoken, not least because its use as an informal variety complementing English is already "engrained" in the country, "it's a culture", as two of my informants put it (Interview 1, ll 418-419).

8.4 Concluding remarks

> *[...] Pidgin is the most widely spoken and understood language in Nigeria. You don't need to be educated to be able to speak Pidgin. That's why the average Nigerian speaks Pidgin no matter the tribe, age, background and sex. With this view, I think Pidgin is already being taken as a national language, more or less.* (from the comments section of a language questionnaire filled in by an advertising practitioner in Lagos)

> *For people who are not educated, it's [Nigerian Pidgin is] the language they can use to speak to people who do not speak their language. And apart from that, even if everybody is educated, there will still be uses for it, people will still need to use Pidgin English, because it is used where formal English is not appropriate. And in Nigeria, there are many areas where formal English is not used.* (Interview 2, ll 581-585)

Whether NigP will rise beyond the status of an unofficial national language, as some like to see it, to become an officially recognized language in Nigeria is difficult to tell, intertwined as the issue is with socio-political developments. However, given its widespread nature, its vital function as a lingua franca – particularly in the growing urban communities ("Lagos will repeat itself", Interview 2, l 473) – and its increasing popularity among the educated as an informal language, it is hardly in doubt that for as long as one can foresee, NigP will continue to play an important role in Nigeria's sociolinguistic configuration. An additional reason to assert NigP's vitality has also become apparent in this study, namely that it has so far resisted a deep encroachment of English on its structure.

Appendix A: The questionnaires

<u>Language Questionnaire</u>

<u>place and date:</u> _____, _____ 1997
<u>personal data:</u>
age: _____
sex: male   female
occupation: _____
education: highest qualification held: _____
             if currently enrolled, at which level? _____

1. What is your <u>mother tongue</u>? _____
2. What <u>other languages</u> do you know? Please list all languages, and indicate in brackets whether you have a good knowledge (G) or only some knowledge (S):   _____
                                _____
                                _____
                                _____
                                _____

3. Some people say that <u>Pidgin</u> is the most widely spoken language in Nigeria. Do you agree with this view? _____

4. Do you speak <u>Pidgin</u> yourself?
    no   only a little   Yes, I speak Pidgin.
        I use it: often   sometimes   rarely

5. a. Can you give some typical <u>places</u> where Pidgin is spoken?
   _____
   _____

   b. Can you give some <u>situations</u> in which Pidgin is often used?
   _____
   _____

   c. Can you name some <u>professions</u> in which a knowledge of Pidgin is necessary or at least useful?
   _____
   _____

6. Some people say that Pidgin is only a corrupt form of English. What do you think about this notion?

   It is certainly correct.

   It is correct only to some extent. Pidgin is similar to English, but it does have its own grammatical rules.

   It is not correct. Pidgin is a language in its own right.

7. a. What do you think about the use of Pidgin in the media for comic purposes (e.g. in some of the popular television comedy series and newspaper columns or cartoons)?

   _____
   _____
   _____
   _____
   _____

   b. What do you think about the use of Pidgin in the media for serious purposes (e.g. newscasting)?

   _____
   _____
   _____
   _____
   _____

8. Some linguists say that Pidgin would be the most adequate candidate for a national language. Do you agree with this view? Please give your reasons!

   _____
   _____
   _____
   _____
   _____

Space for any comments you may wish to make:

_____
_____
_____

Thank you very much for your participation!

National Language Questionnaire

place and date: _____, _____ 1997

personal data:

age: _____

sex: male   female

occupation: _____

education: highest qualification held: _____

                  if currently enrolled, at which level? _____

1. What is your mother tongue? _____

2. What other languages do you know? Please list all languages, and indicate in brackets whether you have a good knowledge (G) or only some knowledge (S):
   _____
   _____
   _____
   _____
   _____

3. How important do you think it is for Nigeria to have a national language?
   very important
   rather important
   not very important, but may have certain advantages
   not important
   Please give the reasons for your answer:
   _____
   _____
   _____

4. If a national language was to be chosen, which of the following options would be most desirable from your personal point of view?
   a. English
   b. Pidgin
   c. Hausa
   d. Yoruba
   e. Igbo
   f. Hausa, Yoruba and Igbo as joint national languages
   g. any other language/ combination: _____

What are the reasons for your choice?
_____
_____

5. Which of the options in question 4 (above) do you consider the most <u>realistic</u>, although it may not be the most desirable from your personal point of view? Please give the appropriate letter from question 4: ____

   What are the reasons for your choice?
   _____
   _____

6. Some people say that <u>Pidgin</u> would be a good candidate for a national language because it is so widely spoken. If this language is not among your choices in questions 4/5, please give reasons:
   _____
   _____
   _____

Space for any <u>comments</u> you may wish to make:
_____
_____
_____
_____

Thank you very much for your participation!

Text Evaluation Sheet

| Name: _____ | Extract code: _____ |

1. LEXIS AND GRAMMAR:

1.1. Are <u>Standard English lexical words/expressions</u> used in this text instead of proper Pidgin ones?

☐ Yes, very frequently.   ☐ Yes, fairly frequently.   ☐ Only infrequently.   ☐ No, not at all.

Examples (if applicable):

Standard English	Pidgin equivalent (if any)

1.2. Are <u>Standard English grammatical words/constructions</u> used in this text instead of proper Pidgin ones?

☐ Yes, very frequently.   ☐ Yes, fairly frequently.   ☐ Only infrequently.   ☐ No, not at all.

Examples (if applicable):

Standard English	Pidgin equivalent (if any)

(please turn over)

1.3. Other peculiarities (if any):

_____

_____

_____

_____

_____

_____

_____

2. **OVERALL EVALUATION:**

2.1. How satisfactory do you find the language of this text as Pidgin?

☐ fully satisfactory
☐ fairly satisfactory
☐ largely unsatisfactory
☐ totally unsatisfactory

2.2. In your view, how intelligible would the language of this text be to a speaker of Pidgin who has little or no formal education?

☐ fully intelligible
☐ fairly intelligible
☐ largely unintelligible
☐ totally unintelligible

2.3. Any other comments:

_____

_____

_____

_____

_____

Background Information Sheet for Research Contributors

1. a. **Surname:** _____   b. **First name:** _____
   ☐ Tick the box if you do <u>not</u> want your name to appear in any **publication** of research results.

2. a. **Sex:** ☐ M   ☐ F   b. **Age group:** ☐ 16-19   ☐ 20-29   ☐ 30-39
   ☐ 40-49   ☐ 50 or over

3. a. **Occupation:** _____
   b. **Highest educational qualification:**
   ☐ secondary school certificate   ☐ O.N.D.
   ☐ first degree or H.N.D.   ☐ master's degree
   ☐ Ph.D.   ☐ other (specify: _____)

4. **Ethnic affiliation:** _____

5. a. **Place of birth:**
   ☐ Lagos   ☐ other (specify town or state: _____ ;
   country, *if outside Nigeria:* _____)
   At what age did you come to Lagos? _____
   b. Place where you grew up, *if different from place of birth:*
   _____

6. a. **First language(s)** you spoke as a child: _____
   b. *If Pidgin is not (among) your first language(s),* indicate approximate **age** at which you first came into contact with **Pidgin**:
   ☐ 0-5   ☐ 6-11   ☐ 12-17   ☐ 18 or over

7. a. **Knowledge of Pidgin:**
   ☐ very good   ☐ good   ☐ moderate   ☐ rudimentary
   b. Explain briefly how/where you came to know Pidgin:
   _____

8. Indicate whether you **use Pidgin**
   ☐ often   ☐ sometimes   ☐ occasionally   ☐ rarely.

(please turn over)

Any other relevant information:

_____

_____

I give **permission** for my contribution to be used for linguistic research and in publications of results thereof.

Signed: _____

Appendix B: Results of the questionnaire study of corpus extracts

Table B 1 Examples cited in Sections 1.1 and 1.2 of the questionnaire

Content of frequency columns:[1]
a: number of citations in questionnaire
b: number of occurrences in the corpus, of which number indicated in square brackets in parts of the corpus marked as non-NigP speech, and number indicated in round brackets in other items consisting of more than one (orthographic) word that were cited in the questionnaires
c: number of corpus texts in which item occurs

Example no.	Example English	Example NigP equivalent	Frequencies a	b	c
	1. Nouns				
1-1	government (V05/7, C01/5, N03/4)		5	220 [2] (52)	23
1-2	• local government (N02/2)		1	28	8
1-3	• federal government (V01/8)		1	24	9
1-4	guy (C04/5, C08/7, C09/7, C10/8)	bobo	4	73	9
1-5	problem (V01/1, V03/1, V05/8, D02/1, C09/4, R04/2)	wahala/palaver	7	69 (1)	23
1-6	union (R03/5)		2	53 (1)	6
1-7	• workers union (V01/8)		1	1	1
1-8	programme (D02/3, D02/5, C06/8, C08/4, A05/1) - [radio/television] (C06/8, A05/1)	talk-talk	8	45 (4)	19
1-9	• awareness programme (V01/2)		1	1	1
1-10	• professional programme (C07/6)		1	1	1
1-11	president (N03/7)	oga kpatakpata	2	38 [1]	11
1-12	• Senate president (C06/6)	oga kpatakpata for Senate	1	5	1
1-13	test (C03/4)		1	31	5
1-14	World Cup (A03/1)		1	23	1
1-15	union members (R04/7)	people	1	22	8
1-16	refuse (V02/3, V04/2, V04/3)	dirty	5	22 (4) [1]	2
1-17	• refuse bin (V02/4)	dustbin	1	2	1
1-18	• refuse disposal (V02/5)	(people wey dey) throway dirty	1	2 [1]	1
1-19	lecturer (C03/2, C03/4, C04/1, C04/2, C05/1, C07/3)	(teacher for university)	6	20 [1]	5
1-20	textbook (V04/5, C03/7, C06/1)		3	20	3
1-21	semester (C04/2, C04/3, C05/1, C06/1)		4	19	4
1-22	result (C03/8)		1	18 [1]	8
1-23	chairman (R03/5)		2	17[2]	7
1-24	period (C09/4)	time	1	17	7
1-25	education (N01/2)	school/book matter	2	16 (2)	6
1-26	• Universal Basic Education Programme (N02/7)		1	2	1
1-27	English (D02/5)	oyibo	1	15	6
1-28	democracy (V02/7, C03/1, N02/4, N04/6)	(government of talk make I talk)	5	14	8

---

[1] For a more detailed description of the content of the table and its arrangement see 5.3.3.
[2] Plus 174 occurrences as the name of a character in R01-05.

1-29	lecture (C04/1, N03/4)		2	14 [1]	5
1-30	parents (D04/2, C10/8)	papa and mama	2	14	5
1-31	professor (N03/4, N05/6)		2	14	5
1-32	brain (C07/8)	head	1	13 (1)	6
1-33	• brain drain (D05/5)		1	1	1
1-34	daughter (D04/2)	woman pikin	1	13	4
1-35	election (R02/3)		2	13	6
1-36	committee (N01/7, N04/7)		2	12	3
	- ten man committee (N01/7)	ten people			
1-37	cult (N05/6)		1	12	3
1-38	faculty (C04/1, C04/2, C05/1, C08/6)		4	12	6
1-39	issue (D01/1, D05/9, C09/4)	matter/thing	4	12 (1)	7
1-40	go make progress (C07/4)	go better	3	11 (5)	2
1-41	report (N01/3, N01/7, A03/5)	tory	3	11	5
1-42	research (D02/1, D02/4, D02/5, D03/5, C03/7)	(book work)	5	11	3
1-43	budget (D05/3, C01/4, C01/5)		3	10	2
1-44	sector (D05/1, D05/5, N02/3)	(place/matter)	4	10 (1)	5
1-45	job (V04/1)	work	1	9	7
1-46	maths (V04/4)		1	9	3
1-47	quiz (C05/2, C05/3)		2	9	1
1-48	security (V05/8)		2	9 (1)	4
1-49	• security system (V01/6)		1	1	1
1-50	situation (D01/4, R06/4, N01/4)		3	9	7
	- [adverse situation] (N01/4)	wahala			
1-51	amount (R09/2)		1	7	4
1-52	car (V02/6)	motor	1	7	5
1-53	contraband (R05/1)		1	7	1
1-54	degree (C08/5)		1	7	2
1-55	masses (V02/8, D05/3)	poor people	3	7 [1]	4
1-56	minimum wage (V01/7, N01/5)		2	7	3
1-57	my point (C06/3)	wetin I dey talk	1	7	2
1-58	treasurer (R03/6)		1	7	3
1-59	science (C05/1)		1	7	2
1-60	address (N05/6)	talk	3	6 (2)	4
1-61	• public address system (C06/5)	loudspeaker	1	2	1
1-62	• welcome address (N02/3)		1	1	1
1-63	authority/-ies (C06/5, N02/6)	oga dem	2	6	4
1-64	condition (V03/2, R03/8, N02/5)		4	6 (1)	4
1-65	operation (A02/8)		1	6	2
1-66	radio corporation (N04/8)		1	6[3]	1
1-67	solution (D01/8)		1	6 [1]	5
1-68	agency (N05/2)		1	5	3
1-69	commissioner (N02/6)	oga	1	5	5
1-70	criminal (C05/7)	thief	2	5	3
1-71	development (D05/4)		2	5 (1)	3
1-72	fader (R07/6)	papa	1	5	4
1-73	fashion (C02/8)	di thing wey dey reign	1	5	1
1-74	graduate (N05/7)	people wey don finish university	1	5	3
1-75	Lagosian (V01/1, V01/2)	Lagos people	2	5	1

---

[3] Of which 5 in *Federal Radio Corporation of Nigeria*.

1-76	*pregnancy* (D02/5)	belle (wey im/dem get)	4	5	2
1-77	*seminar* (C04/8, N05/6, N03/8)	talk-talk	3	5	4
1-78	di WAEC *staff* (V04/4)	people	2	5 (1)	4
1-79	• *staff quarters* (C08/6)	house wey workers dey stay	1	1	1
1-80	*assignment* (C03/7)	homework	2	4	1
1-81	*brewery* (N01/1)	place wey dem dey make beer	2	4 (2)	1
1-82	• *brewery industry* (N01/1)	people wey dey make beer	1	2	1
1-83	*commission* (R09/8)	(money)	1	4	4
1-84	im *constituency* (D05/7, D05/8)	people	2	4	1
1-85	*deliverance* (C02/2)		1	4	1
1-86	*economy* (D05/5)		1	4	2
1-87	*electricity* (V03/2)	light	2	4 (1)	3
1-88	your *expectation* (C06/1)	di thing wey you wan get	2	4	1
1-89	*financial secretary* (R03/6)		1	4	2
1-90	*House of Assembly* (N02/6)		1	4	2
1-91	*infection* (D02/1)	disease	3	4 (2)	1
1-92	• *sexually transmitted infection* (R08/6, R08/7)	sickness wey you get if you meet woman [for a man]/ waka-waka disease	2	2	1
1-93	*mercenary* (R07/2, R07/8)		2	4	1
1-94	*motion* (D05/7, N02/6)		2	4	3
1-95	*oracle* (R10/7)	juju	1	4	1
1-96	*organisation* (N01/7)	people	1	4	2
1-97	*permit* (D01/1)		1	4	1
1-98	*profession* (N02/5)	work	2	4 (1)	1
1-99	• *teaching profession* (N02/5)	teacher work	1	1	1
1-100	*pronunciation* (C03/8)		1	4	1
1-101	*provost* (N02/7)	oga	1	4	1
1-102	*railing* (A01/7, A01/8)		2	4	1
1-103	*recycling* (V02/1)		1	4	1
1-104	*stage* (V04/2)	time	1	4 (1)	3
1-105	*statement* (V04/5)		1	4	3
1-106	*United Nation(s)* (V04/8)		1	4	2
1-107	*activity* (N01/3, N05/6)	(thing)	2	3	3
1-108	*agriculture* (D05/4)	farm work	1	3	3
1-109	*approval* (R07/3)	agreement paper	1	3	1
1-110	*calculation* (C04/5)		1	3	1
1-111	*construction* work go start (N05/3)	dem go start dey build	1	3	3
1-112	*effect* (V04/7)		2	3 (1)	2
1-113	• *side effect* (D03/5)		1	1	1
1-114	*equation* (A01/2)		2	3 (1)	1
1-115	• *quadratic equation* (C04/2)		1	1	1
1-116	*healing* (C02/3)		1	3	1
1-117	*leniency* (V04/4)		1	3	2
1-118	*limit* (C07/6)	where e for stop	1	3	1
1-119	*maiden* (R07/5)	girl	1	3	1
1-120	*policy* (N01/7)		1	3	2
1-121	*protection* (R06/1)		1	3	1
1-122	*resources* (D05/4)		2	3	3
1-123	*set-up* (D05/7)		1	3	1
1-124	*stress* (C04/1)	wahala	1	3	1
1-125	*waste* (V02/6)	dirty	2	3 (1)	3
1-126	• *waste disposal* (V04/2)	(people wey dey) throway dirty	1	1	1
1-127	*workshop* (N01/7)	talk-talk	1	3	2
1-128	*allowance* (C07/3)		2	2 (1)	2
1-129	• *furniture allowance* (C06/8)	money for chair and table	1	1	1

1-130	*analysis* (C07/2)	*idea*	1	2	1
1-131	*behaviour* (A04/2)	*how dem dey do*	1	2	2
1-132	*board of trustees* (N02/7)		1	2	1
1-133	*bursary* (C05/6, N02/7)		2	2	2
1-134	*campaign* (N05/4)		1	2	2
1-135	*colleague* (D05/1)	*friend*	2	2	2
1-136	*community* (V02/7)	*people*	1	2	2
1-137	*competition* (V03/7, A03/7) - [among companies] (V03/7) - [sports] (A03/7)	*plenty sellers*	2	2	2
1-138	*conference* (N03/7)	*talk-talk*	2	2	2
1-139	*make <u>conspiracy</u>* (R03/8)	*make plan for person back*	1	2	2
1-140	*Constitution* (C04/6)		1	2	2
1-141	*convocation* (C04/5)		1	2	1
1-142	*corruption* (N05/5)	*wuruwuru*	1	2	2
1-143	*curfew* (C09/1)	*law wey dey say make people no waka for outside*	1	2	1
1-144	*<u>environment</u> go don change* (C06/3)	*things*	1	2	2
1-145	*excise duties* (N01/1)	*tax*	1	2	1
1-146	*excuse* (C05/6)	*tory*	1	2	2
1-147	*extent* (C10/2)		1	2	1
1-148	*fairness* (D03/4)	*yellow*	1	2	1
1-149	*future* (D03/1)		1	2	1
1-150	*gown* (C07/5)		1	2	1
1-151	*habit* (D02/6)		1	2	1
1-152	*hooligan* (R10/5)	*area boy*	1	2	1
1-153	*image* (C08/3)		1	2	1
1-154	*impeachment* (C06/6)	*dem don comot am*	1	2	2
1-155	*incinerator* (V02/3, V02/5)	*place wey dem dey burn dirty*	2	2	1
1-156	*di oder <u>lane</u>* (A01/8)	*side*	1	2	2
1-157	*union <u>levy</u>* (R04/4)	*money*	1	2	1
1-158	*Yoruba <u>lifestyle</u>* (C10/3)	*di way wey Yoruba people dey do*	1	2	1
1-159	*na di <u>logic</u> be dat* (C07/8)	*di thing wey dey inside*	1	2	1
1-160	*marginalization* (C09/7)		1	2	1
1-161	*measure* (N02/2, R05/7) - ['official action'] (N02/2) - ['measurements'] (R05/7)		2	2	2
1-162	*military* (C04/4)	*soldier*	1	2	1
1-163	*mirror* (R07/2, R08/4)	*glass*	2	2	2
1-164	*moderator* (V01/2)		1	2	1
1-165	*national rebirth* (N05/5)	*born again nation*	1	2	1
1-166	*offence* (V05/6)	*wuruwuru*	2	2 (1)	2
1-167	• *capital offence* (R05/9)		1	1	1
1-168	*parade* (R05/7)		1	2	1
1-169	*patience* (A04/2)		1	2	2
1-170	*peanut(s)* [fig.] (C05/7)	*nothing/small thing*	1	2	1
1-171	*football <u>pitch</u>* (C03/5)	*field*	1	2	1
1-172	*poverty eradication* (N03/2)	*comot sufferhead*	1	2	1
1-173	*start di <u>preparation</u>* [food] (A05/4)	*start to dey cook di food*	1	2	2
1-174	*rate* (V05/2)		1	2	2
1-175	*revenue* (D05/4)	*money*	1	2	2
1-176	*salvation* (C02/3)		1	2	1
1-177	*special adviser* (N04/1)		1	2	1
1-178	*standard* (C07/4)		2	2 (1)	2
1-179	*success* (N05/6)	*better*	1	2	2

1-180	*taste* (C02/8)		1	2	1
1-181	*urban drift* (V02/2)	*village people wey dey rush come town*	1	2	1
1-182	*accused* (R07/8)		1	1	1
1-183	*airspace* (N03/6)		1	1	1
1-184	*allegation* (R07/9)	*matter*	1	1	1
1-185	*anniversary* (N05/3)		1	1	1
1-186	*ambassador* (N05/6)		1	1	1
1-187	*arrangement* (A01/6)	*agreement*	1	1	1
1-188	*atrocity* (V04/5)	*bad bad thing*	1	1	1
1-189	*blood pressure* (V01/4)		1	1	1
1-190	*borehole* (V03/5)		1	1	1
1-191	*business administration* (C06/3)		1	1	1
1-192	*caliphate* (D05/7)		1	1	1
1-193	*canteen* (R10/7)	*buka*	1	1	1
1-194	*cerebral meningitis* (A03/2)		1	1	1
1-195	*commandment* (C02/2)		1	1	1
1-196	*communication gadget* (V01/5)		1	1	1
1-197	*your <u>concern</u>* (R03/7)	*your own*	1	1	1
1-198	*corporation director general* (N02/3)		1	1	1
1-199	*counselling clinic* (N05/6)		1	1	1
1-200	*counterpart* (N02/4)	*kind*	1	1	1
1-201	*course outline* (C04/1)		1	1	1
1-202	*cultism* (C04/8)		1	1	1
1-203	*dedication* (V01/6)		1	1	1
1-204	*destiny* (A04/8)		1	1	1
1-205	*diagram* (C05/1)		1	1	1
1-206	*disadvantage* (C10/8)		1	1	1
1-207	*discount* (R05/3)	*special price*	1	1	1
1-208	*distributor* (N01/1)	*dose wey dey help sell di drink*	1	1	1
1-209	*document* (R08/5)	*paper*	1	1	1
1-210	*drainage* (A01/1)	*gutter*	1	1	1
1-211	*drive* (N02/5)	*plan*	1	1	1
1-212	*na <u>drunk</u>* (C06/6)	*e dey drink well well*	1	1	1
1-213	*encouragement* (C10/1)		1	1	1
1-214	*essence* (C03/2)		1	1	1
1-215	*executive* (N03/7)		1	1	1
1-216	*go <u>exile</u>* (C10/3)	*anoder place*	1	1	1
1-217	*fellow* (C06/7)	*man*	1	1	1
1-218	*flaw* (C03/3)		1	1	1
1-219	*football politics* (A03/4)		1	1	1
1-220	*grain silo* (A02/3)		1	1	1
1-221	*gratuity* (N03/7)		1	1	1
1-222	*hygiene* (D01/6)		1	1	1
1-223	*ignorant* (R08/4)		1	1	1
1-224	*implication* (D02/6)		1	1	1
1-225	*inquiry* (R04/5)		1	1	1
1-226	*institution* (C07/4)	*school*	1	1	1
1-227	*instruction* (N04/6)	*command*	1	1	1
1-228	*interconnectivity* (V03/8)		1	1	1
1-229	*interview* (N05/2)	*talk*	1	1	1
1-230	*kombi bus* (A01/8)	*danfo*	1	1	1
1-231	*laboratory* (N03/1)		1	1	1
1-232	*enter <u>leadership position</u>* (C07/5)	*come be oga*	1	1	1
1-233	*legislative house* (N04/6)	*di people wey dey make law*	1	1	1

1-234	*Adolphus na letdown* (R01/3)	*yeye person*	1	1	1
1-235	*exam malpractice* (V04/4)	*wayo*	1	1	1
1-236	*method* (N01/1)	*kind way*	1	1	1
1-237	*model* (C10/6)		1	1	1
1-238	*moustache* (R02/1)	*bear-bear*	1	1	1
1-239	*mufti* (A04/6)		1	1	1
1-240	*get night blindness* (D01/3)	*no fit see for night*	1	1	1
1-241	*notice of increment* (R03/8)	*paper wey dey talk say dem don put money*	1	1	1
1-242	*shop occupant* (D01/1)	*people wey get shop*	1	1	1
1-243	*palace* (R02/4)	*king house*	1	1	1
1-244	*parastatal* (N04/7)		1	1	1
1-245	*partnership* (N03/7)	*dem join hand*	1	1	1
1-246	*pickpocket* (A04/5)	*thief*	1	1	1
1-247	*pledge* (N02/3)	*promise*	1	1	1
1-248	*poem* (C09/4)	*small tory*	1	1	1
1-249	*polythene* (V02/6)	*rubber*	1	1	1
1-250	*practical* (C03/7)		1	1	1
1-251	*prank* (C05/8)	*wayo*	1	1	1
1-252	*win Senate presidency* (C06/8)	*come be oga kpatakpata for Senate*	1	1	1
1-253	*privacy* (C10/8)		1	1	1
1-254	*professional* (N03/6)		1	1	1
1-255	*proposition* (R06/6)		1	1	1
1-256	*quadratic formula* (C04/2)		1	1	1
1-257	*rejection* (R07/1)		1	1	1
1-258	*relief* (V05/1)	*help*	1	1	1
1-259	*request* (N02/2)	*beg/beg-beg*	1	1	1
1-260	*restaurant* (A05/5)	*buka*	1	1	1
1-261	*retirement* (N04/1)		1	1	1
1-262	*make revenge* (R04/5)	*pay am back*	1	1	1
1-263	*stock* (D01/4)	*market*	1	1	1
1-264	*dem subjects* (N02/2)	*people*	1	1	1
1-265	*subsidy to take support fuel matter* (N04/5)	*money*	1	1	1
1-266	*government subvention for you* (C07/5)	*di money wey government dey give you*	1	1	1
1-267	*telephone* (V03/8)		1	1	1
1-268	*transformer* (V03/4)	*light engine*	1	1	1
1-269	*transporter* (V05/1)	*motor people*	1	1	1
1-270	*travelling mercies* (R06/1)		1	1	1
1-271	*treatment* (N03/4)		1	1	1
1-272	*troop* (V04/8)	*soldier*	1	1	1
1-273	*venereal disease* (D02/1)	*sickness wey you get if you meet man [for a woman]/ waka-waka disease*	1	1	1
1-274	*welfare* (N05/6)		1	1	1
1-275	*work ethics* (R06/6)		1	1	1

	2. Lexical verbs				
2-1	*know* (V01/4, V02/8, V03/7, V04/3, V04/6, C01/2, C02/4, C03/1, C03/3, C04/3, C04/6, C07/4, C07/6, C09/6, N02/4, A02/3, A04/7, A05/8)	*sabi*	20[4]	431 [5] (6)	40
2-2	*understand* (V01/6, V05/1, D02/3, D02/4, D03/5, C03/6, A05/4, R06/5, R07/7)	*know/sabi*	14	68 [24] (2)	16
2-3	*collect* (V05/4, C06/1, R07/3)	*take*	3	30	18
2-4	*live* (C01/4)	*stay*	1	26	17
2-5	*eat* (A05/2, R02/5)	*chop*	2	25	10
2-6	*spend* [money] (V02/6)	*use*	2	20 (1)	13
2-7	*cancel* (V04/5, V05/7, A03/2, A03/5)	*take comot/spoil/dabaru*	4	18	5
2-8	*look for* (C03/7)	*find*	1	17	14
2-9	*check* (N02/1)	*look*	1	14	9
2-10	*listen* (A04/1)	*hear*	1	14	11
2-11	*add* (A05/5)	*put*	1	13	6
2-12	*complain* (C06/2, C06/4)	*talk*	2	13	8
2-13	*feed* (C01/3, A04/1) - [itr.] (C01/3) - [tr.] (A04/1)	*chop* *give am food*	2	13	9
2-14	*organise* (A03/1, A03/5)		2	13	3
2-15	*remove* (V02/7)	*comot*	1	13	9
2-16	*solve* (N01/3)		1	13	7
2-17	*look at* (R01/8)	*see*	1	12	7
2-18	*advise* (A04/4)	*warn*	1	11	5
2-19	*encourage* (C09/4, C10/3, C10/5, R08/8) - *im just encourage me say look im like as I just dey enter school* (C09/4) - *dem go encourage am* (C10/3) - *na encourage you dey encourage me?* (R08/8)	 *tell* *tell am make e do am* *na power you dey give me?*	4	11	5
2-20	*increase* (V05/2, R08/6)	*carry go up*	3	11 (1)	3
2-21	*support* (C01/5)	*help*	1	11	9
2-22	*allow* (V04/5, V05/3, R07/9) - *you allow am finish dat paper* (V04/5)	*gree* *you gree make e finish dat paper*	3	10	8
2-23	*find out* (V03/4, C10/3, N03/4)	*see*	3	10	4
2-24	*recycle* (V02/5, V02/6)	*use am make anoder*	2	10	1
2-25	*continue* (V03/3, V05/3, V05/8) - *make NEPA continue like dis* (V03/3) - *if dis thing continue* (V05/3) - *make JAMB still continue* (V05/8)	 *dey be* *no stop* *dey*	3	9	7
2-26	*create* (D03/1, C09/1, N01/5) - *create plenty work tabi job* (N01/5)	*make* *bring*	3	9	5
2-27	*reduce* (V05/1, D03/7)		2	9	5
2-28	*resemble* (N02/3)	*be like*	1	9	6

---

[4] Of which 15 by one informant.

2-29	*watch* (C01/8)	see	1	9	7
2-30	*receive* (V03/8, N03/8)	get	2	8	3
2-31	*register* (N05/6)		1	8	3
2-32	*vote* (R07/4)		1	8	4
2-33	*tax* (D05/4)		1	7	2
2-34	*behave* (V05/1)	do	1	6	6
2-35	*discuss* (N02/3, N03/6, N03/8, R02/1, R09/8) - *discuss how* (N03/8)	talk find	5	6	5
2-36	*expect* (C06/1)	wan get	2	6 (1)	5
2-37	*explain* (N01/1, R07/2)	tell	3	6 (1)	5
2-38	*maintain* (D03/1, D03/5, N01/1) - [machines] (N01/1)	keep repair	3	6	3
2-39	*provide* (V04/2)	give	1	6	3
2-40	*suspend* (N03/2, A03/5)		2	6	2
2-41	*I trust you* (R08/1)	I know you well well	1	6	4
2-42	*develop* (D05/4, D05/9)	(make grow)	2	5	2
2-43	*excuse* (R08/3)		1	5	1
2-44	*impeach* (V02/8, C04/4, C06/6, D05/7)	comot	4	5	5
2-45	*relax* (C05/2)	rest	1	5	1
2-46	*represent* (D05/8, C04/1)		2	5	3
2-47	*resume* (C03/2)	begin	1	5	1
2-48	*separate* [a couple] (R07/1)	scatter	1	5	4
2-49	*shut up your mouth* (R04/2)	close your mouth/stop am	1	5	2
2-50	*survive* (C06/8, N01/7) - [itr., animate subject] (C06/8) - [itr., inanimate subject] (N01/7)	 live last	2	5	5
2-51	*award* (N03/8)	give	1	4	2
2-52	*charge* [somebody for something] (N01/1)	make dem pay	1	4	4
2-53	*ensure* (N03/3)	make sure	1	4	1
2-54	*di condition wey be say e no go favour dem* (V03/2)	good for	1	4	2
2-55	*interview* (C06/7)	talk to	1	4	3
2-56	*introduce* (C04/6, C09/2)	bring	2	4	4
2-57	*launch* (C01/5)	start	1	4	2
2-58	*mould* (D03/8)	make	1	4	2
2-59	*postpone* (A03/5, R04/6)	say I go do am anoder time	2	4	2
2-60	*report* (A02/6)		1	4	4
2-61	*retire* (N04/1, A02/6)		2	4	2
2-62	*round up* (C08/1)	catch	1	4	1
2-63	*balance* (A02/1, A03/5) - *if dem wan balance am, shebi dem for first ask us?* (A03/5)	 talk true	2	3	3
2-64	*close down* (C03/1)	close	1	3	2
2-65	*commit* [crime] (V04/5, V05/6)	do	3	3 (1)	3
2-66	*cooperate* (N04/3)	join hand	1	3	2
2-67	*donate* (C01/8)	give	1	3 [1]	2
2-68	*educate* (D03/5)	teach	1	3	3
2-69	*elect am Senate president* (C06/8)	make	1	3	3
2-70	*expose* (D01/6)	open	1	3	2
2-71	*flush out* (V01/6, D05/1)	comot/push comot	2	3	2

2-72	*graduate* (R06/5)	*finish school*	1	3	1
2-73	*investigate* (R07/9)	*look*	1	3	1
2-74	*lead* [somebody somewhere] (C01/8)	*carry*	1	3	3
2-75	*mix* (A05/5)	*join*	1	3	1
2-76	*notice* (C09/7)	*know/see*	1	3	2
2-77	*produce* (N01/1, R02/2)	*make*	2	3	2
2-78	*replace* (D05/1)	*change*	1	3	3
2-79	*respect* (C08/5)		1	3 [1]	3
2-80	*spread* (N04/3)	*scatter*	1	3	3
2-81	*stake* (R05/4)		1	3	1
2-82	*wonder* (C10/8)	*think*	1	3	3
2-83	*address* (N02/2)		1	2	2
2-84	*approve* (N05/8)	*gree*	2	2 (1)	2
2-85	*carry out* (A02/4)	*do*	1	2	2
2-86	*conduct* (V05/7, V05/8)	*do*	2	2	1
2-87	*connect* (V03/8)	*join*	1	2	1
2-88	*contribute* (N04/1)	*do deir own*	1	2	2
2-89	*e wan know wetin everyone decide* (R03/8)	*go do*	1	2	2
2-90	*establish* (C01/4)	*start*	1	2	2
2-91	*evacuate* (C03/1, C03/2) - *bring police make dem come evacuate student* (C03/1) - *e wan come evacuate us* (C03/2)	*drive/comot*	2	2	1
2-92	*hawk* (D02/6, D02/7)	*waka sell*	2	2	1
2-93	*imitate* (C02/7)	*follow*	1	2	1
2-94	*go improve* (V03/7)	*go better*	1	2	1
2-95	*let down* (R04/8)		1	2	1
2-96	*monitor* (N04/3)	*guard*	1	2	2
2-97	*own* (R08/5)	*get*	1	2	2
2-98	*pass out for di school* (N05/6)	*finish school*	1	2	1
2-99	*purge cultism* (C04/8)	*quench*	1	2	1
2-100	*scare* (C07/6)	*drive*	1	2	2
2-101	*set up* (N01/3)	*form*	1	2	2
2-102	*spark* (R07/4)		1	2	2
2-103	*tackle* [person] (R10/7)	*fight*	2	2 (1)	2
2-104	*na from Abuja de transfer am go Yola* (C09/4)	*send*	1	2	2
2-105	*view* (C06/1, C06/4)	*look/see*	2	2	1
2-106	*abstain* (R08/1)	*no do*	1	1	1
2-107	*fit afford* (V02/3)	*buy*	1	1	1
2-108	*allocate* (C06/8)	*give*	1	1	1
2-109	*analyse* (D02/4)	*talk am well*	1	1	1
2-110	*appreciate* (D05/9)	*like*	1	1	1
2-111	*avoid* (C02/3)	*no do*	1	1	1
2-112	*beat up* (R04/4)	*fight*	1	1	1
2-113	*breast-feed* (A04/1)	*give am breast*	1	1	1
2-114	*campaign* (C04/4)	*talk*	1	1	1

2-115	*checkmate* (C03/5)	stop	1	1	1
2-116	*chop your head comot* (R01/6)	cut	1	1[5]	1
2-117	*circulate* (D05/3)		1	1	1
2-118	*clamour* [for something] (C09/6)	ask	1	1	1
2-119	*commonize* (R01/1)		1	1	1
2-120	*compete* (A04/3)		1	1	1
2-121	*consider* (C08/5)	look	1	1	1
2-122	*decorate* (A01/7)	make fine	1	1	1
2-123	*destroy* (R06/6)	spoil	1	1	1
2-124	*differentiate* (C05/5)		1	1	1
2-125	*disagree* (C07/2)	no gree	1	1	1
2-126	*disappoint* (V03/2)	no do well for	1	1	1
2-127	*disburse* (C05/8)	give/pay	1	1	1
2-128	*discourage* (A05/7)		1	1	1
2-129	*disgrace* (R10/1)	shame	1	1	1
2-130	*dupe* (C04/4)	cheat	1	1	1
2-131	*embarrass* (C01/1)	give wahala/wahala [v.]	1	1	1
2-132	*embezzle* (R05/4)	steal/chop	1	1	1
2-133	*enact* (V01/2)	put for ground	1	1	1
2-134	*endanger* (D02/7)		1	1	1
2-135	*eradicate* (C04/8)	stop	1	1	1
2-136	*escape* (C08/8)	run go	1	1	1
2-137	*estimate* (C05/8)		1	1	1
2-138	*exchange* (N04/8)		1	1	1
2-139	*fluctuate* (C04/6)	change	1	1	1
2-140	*generate* (V04/3)	make	1	1	1
2-141	*dem hospitalize you* (R09/7)	you dey for hospital	1	1	1
2-142	*impress* (V01/5)		1	1	1
2-143	*insure* (A03/2)		1	1	1
2-144	*intimidate* (R07/3)	open eye	1	1	1
2-145	*invest money* (D05/5)	put	1	1	1
2-146	*lecture* (C04/1)	teach	1	1	1
2-147	*lodge* (R04/4)	put	1	1	1
2-148	*make up di soup* (A05/8)	cook	1	1	1
2-149	*mess* (R02/7)	dirty	1	1	1
2-150	*obey* (N02/6)	follow	1	1	1
2-151	*overlook* (A04/8)	(no mind)	1	1	1
2-152	*portray* (C08/3)	show	1	1	1
2-153	*preach* (C09/7)		1	1[5]	1
2-154	*promulgate* (V05/7)		1	1	1
2-155	*protest* (V01/8)	halla	1	1	1
2-156	*quadruple* (C07/2)	go up	1	1	1
2-157	*qualify* (N03/2)		1	1	1
2-158	*refurbish* (V02/8)	repair	1	1	1
2-159	*repent* (N05/6)		1	1	1
2-160	*require* (R08/5)		1	1	1
2-161	*resolve* (V05/2)	settle	1	1	1
2-162	*retrieve* (C06/6)	bring comot	1	1	1

[5] In the sense of 'cut'.

2-163	*scale through*[6] (C05/4)	*pass*	1	1	1
2-164	*sponsor* [a person] (C09/3)	*send*	1	1	1
2-165	*you wan make we starve* (R01/3)	*make we die/make hungry kill us*	1	1	1
2-166	*succeed* [plan] (N05/5)	*work*	1	1	1
2-167	*terrorise* (C09/3)	*wahala*	1	1	1
2-168	*transport* (N01/1)	*carry*	1	1	1
2-169	*wish* (C06/6)	*want*	1	1	1
2-170	*withdraw* (V03/2)	*comot*	1	1	1
	3. Adjectives				
3-1	*serious* (C04/3, C07/4) - *serious?* (C04/3) - *serious mistake* (C07/4)	*true?* *big*	2	21	12
3-2	*national* (N01/7, N03/8)		3	15[7] (2)	5
3-3	*important* (D04/3, R02/1)		4	14 (3)	8
3-4	*second-hand* [clothes] (R05/1, R05/3)	*okrika*	2	8	3
3-5	*normal* (C06/1, C10/3)		2	7	5
3-6	*so-called* (D03/6)		1	7	3
3-7	*useless* (V02/7, V04/8)	*yeye*	3	7 (1)	3
3-8	*compulsory* (C06/3)	*important well well*	1	6 [1]	1
3-9	*one particular road* (V02/3)	*one road like dat*	3	6 (2)	4
3-10	*e no quiet* (R10/5)	*close im mouth*	1	6	5
3-11	*terrible* (C03/4)	*bad (well well)*	1	6 [2]	3
3-12	*former* (R04/2)	*before before*	1	5	5
3-13	*jealous* (C03/2)		1	4	2
3-14	*objective* (C05/2)		1	4	1
3-15	*presidential* (D05/6)		1	4	1
3-16	*e dey urgent* (R03/7)	*we must do am quick quick*	2	4 (1)	2
3-17	*useful* (R06/4)	*kamkpe/better*	1	4	2
3-18	*criminal* (R06/6)		1	3	2
3-19	*difficult* (V04/2)	*hard*	2	3 (1)	3
3-20	*international* (N03/7)		1	3	3
3-21	*modern* (N05/3, R06/7)		2	3	2
3-22	*political* (R06/2)		1	3	3
3-23	*pregnant* (R09/3)	*wey get belle*	1	3	3
3-24	*unisex* (C02/6)	*man and woman own*	1	3	1
3-25	*corrupt* (C04/6)	*wowo/bad*	1	2	1
3-26	*expensive* (C06/2)	*dear*	1	2	1
3-27	*grated water yam* (A05/4)	*wey you don grind*	1	2	1
3-28	*impromptu* (C05/2)		1	2	1
3-29	*medium* (N05/2)		1	2	1
3-30	*we dey too money-conscious* (D05/8)	*we too like money*	1	2	1
3-31	*nice person* (C10/5)	*better*	1	2 [1]	2
3-32	*shameless* (R02/5)	*wey no get shame*	1	2	2
3-33	*stubborn* (C10/6)	*wey no dey hear word*	2	2	2
3-34	*advanced country* (D05/9)	*oyibo*	1	1	1
3-35	*arrogant* (C06/6)	*e dey make yanga*	1	1	1
3-36	*boring* (C06/4)	*dry*	1	1	1

---

[6] "A PNE [Popular Nigerian English] coinage which seems to be the result of confusing 'scale' (meaning 'climb') and 'sail through' (meaning 'move easily through')" (Jowitt 1991: 234).

[7] Of which 8 in names of official institutions and organisations.

3-37	how *capable* you be [as a student] (C08/5)	how you sabi/know book reach	1	1	1
3-38	*economic* (N04/1)		1	1	1
3-39	*elected* officer (R03/6)	wey una don elect	1	1	1
3-40	*essential* (C06/2)	important	1	1	1
3-41	*extra* money (N01/1)	anoder	1	1	1
3-42	*genuine* (V02/8)	true	1	1	1
3-43	*grown-up* pikin (A04/1)	big big	1	1	1
3-44	girl go dey *mature* (D02/4)	grow well	1	1	1
3-45	*possible* (C07/8)		1	1	1
3-46	*principal* (C07/3)	ogbonge/important	1	1	1
3-47	*qualified* nurse (D01/3)	ogbonge/better	1	1	1
3-48	*ready-made* [clothes] (C02/6)	oyibo make am	1	1	1
3-49	*separate* (A05/5)	different	1	1	1
3-50	*stable* (C04/6)		1	1	1
3-51	all di *total* money (N01/1)	all di money	1	1	1
4. Adverbs					
4-1	*why* (C03/5, R05/6, V02/7, C03/2)	wetin make	12	142 [1] (29)	31
4-2	*very* (D01/3, D02/5) - *very very* good (D01/3) - *very* well (D02/5)	better well well	16	57 [8] (13)	18
4-3	*maybe* (V01/2, V01/3, C07/3) - *maybe* government go make law (V01/3)	e fit be (say) government fit make law	3	43	16
4-4	*really* (C05/7, R10/3) - you *really* get belle problem (R10/3)	you get belle problem proper	2	35	17
4-5	*about* (D05/6, N05/1) - *about* fifteen thousand (D05/6) - *about* one million (N05/1)	like like fifteen thousand like one million	4	27 [1] (2)	17
4-6	*especially* (N03/8, A03/7)		2	17	8
4-7	*home*[8] (R03/4, R10/5) - come *home* (R03/4) - go *home* (R10/5)	house	2	10	7
4-8	*actually* [as sentence adverb] (C03/8, C04/8)	true true	3	9 [3] (2)	4
4-9	thirteen years *ago* (N01/4)	e don reach thirteen years	3	9 [2] (1)	8
4-10	*once* (V04/2)	one time	5	7 [1] (3)	5
4-11	*meanwhile* (V01/3, R07/9)	(for now)	2	5	4
4-12	*somehow* (C03/3, C06/8)		2	5	3
4-13	*exactly* [as reply] (D05/3, C06/7)	na im/yes	2	4	2
4-14	*somewhere* (A04/3)	for one kind place	1	4	4
4-15	*fully* (C05/1)		1	3	2
4-16	*twice* (C07/5)	two times	1	3	2
4-17	go *abroad* (C01/2)	obodo oyibo	1	2	1
4-18	listen *carefully* (R07/2)	well well	1	2	1
4-19	*henceforth* (D04/5)	from now	1	2	1
4-20	*completely* (C06/6)	kpatakpata	1	1	1

---

[8] As it was cited as an English element, I have included *home* in functions where it would be classified as an adverb in English in the list of adverbs, but since in NigP, verbs of motion can be complemented by NPs (cf 5.5.2), *home* can in fact be regarded as a noun in all functions.

4-21	*immediately* (V03/8)	*fiam*	1	1	1
4-22	*initially* I dey think say di man go do small (C07/2)	*when e come*	1	1	1
4-23	*mistakenly* (C04/3)	*by mistake*	1	1	1
4-24	*mostly* (V03/3)		1	1	1
4-25	*occasionally* (V03/7)	*sometimes*	1	1	1
4-26	*properly* (V04/3)	*well well*	1	1	1
4-27	*psychologically* (V01/6)	*for (dem) head*	1	1	1
4-28	*recently* (C07/5)	*e never tay*	1	1	1
4-29	*regularly* (V03/1)	*all di time*	1	1	1
4-30	*right from* (C07/8)	*from*	1	1	1
4-31	*secondly* (C06/6)	*di second one be*	1	1	1
4-32	*smoothly* (D05/2)	*well well*	1	1	1
4-33	*tonight* (R01/8)	*for dis night*	1	1	1
4-34	*totally* (C04/8)	*kpatakpata*	1	1	1
4-35	*whereby* (V02/2)	*wey*	1	1	1
	5. Interjections				
5-1	*Congratulations!* (R06/7, R07/7)	*I salute you*	2	3	2
5-2	*hello* (C06/1)	*I greet o*	1	1	1
5-3	*Oh dear!* (R05/8)	*Chei!*	1	1	1
	6. Prepositions				
6-1	*of* (V02/3, D05/1, N01/1, N01/4, D05/2, C03/5, R04/4) - talk *of* (V02/3) - one year *of* (D05/1) - di mouth *of* di Nigerian Breweries Association (N01/1) - di wife *of* di man (N01/4) - dat kind *of* thing (D05/2, C03/5) - out *of* union levy (R04/4)	 *about* *one year don reach wey* *for* *di man im wife* *dat kind thing* *from union money*	58	568 [11] (82)	40
6-2	*to* (N03/1, A05/3, R02/4) - come *to* camp (N03/1) - give *to* your husband (A05/3) - di sister *to* Sergeant Innocent (R02/4)	 *come camp* *give your husband* *Sergeant Innocent sister*	17	243 [6] (20)	38
6-3	*from* (A03/1, C09/4)	*for*	2	181 [1]	38
6-4	*about* (D03/1, C07/5, C09/7, A03/2) - I wan talk *about* (D03/1) - dat thing *about* gown (C07/5) - im talk *about* marginalization (C09/7) - talk *about* am (A03/2)	 *my tory concern* *wey concern* *im say na* *talk am*	9	104 [5] (4)	29
6-5	*in* (D05/9, C08/4, C08/5, N02/7)	*for*	23	86 [6] (43)	28
6-6	• *wey dey in charge of* (A03/2)	*wey be oga for*	2	8 (1)	3
6-7	• *in line with* God (C02/4)	*as God want am*	1	1	1
6-8	*at* (V03/7, V04/3, C09/8, A04/1)	*for*	12	77^9 [3] (53)	24

---

[9] Plus 82 occurrences in *at all*, which is a well-established item in NigP (often spelled as one word, cf e.g. Agheyisi 1971: 148 and Faraclas 1996: 23). (Occurrences in *at all* are also not included in the count for the preposition *at* in the ICE-GB subcorpus provided for comparison in Figure 5.2, because in ICE *at all* is treated as a multi-word adverb.)

6-9	by (R08/8) - go by night bus (R08/8)	take night bus	6	65 (8)	25
6-10	• according by (N01/3, N01/6)	as ... talk am/... talk say	2	5[10]	3
6-11	into (V01/3, D05/4, N02/9, A04/2) - enter into (V01/3, N02/9) - look into (D05/4, A04/2)	inside/Ø enter (inside) look (inside)	6	24 [4] (1)	12
6-12	during Alao time (C07/3)	for	2	17[11] (1)	7
6-13	over four weeks (C08/1)	four week don pass	3	11 (2)	10
6-14	as per (V01/3, C08/3)	as e concern/for	3	9 [1]	7
6-15	dem dey around am (D05/2)	with	1	8	7
6-16	among (R08/6)	inside	1	4	4
6-17	through (C06/1, V04/4) - na through di textbook sha we just try do di exam (C06/1) - e go leak out through di WAEC staff (V04/4)	na di textbook we dey use try do di exam sha from	2	4	4
7. Conjunctions					
7-1	because (A03/2)	sake of say	1	279 [5] (1)	37
7-2	when (V01/1, V02/3)	di time wey	2	254 [1]	38
7-3	or (V04/3, C01/3, C05/2, C08/6, A04/7) - make dem repair am or make dem buy anoder one (V04/3) - buy tomatoes or pepper (C01/3) - shey na fill in di answer or options dey? (C05/2) - Wednesday or Thursday (C08/6) - when you dey leave dem [children], say your sister or you get housegirl (A04/7)	abi	6[12]	142 [1] (1)	35
7-4	so dat/that (V01/3)	make	3	50 [1] (2)	20
7-5	until [negated verb in main clause] (V01/2)	na when [without negation]	2	17 (2)	12
7-6	once I sow my yam (R08/5)	when I sow my yam finish	2	15 (1)	7
7-7	dat/that (R03/5, R04/4)	say	2	12 [2]	8
7-8	as long as (C05/4)	so far	1	7	3
7-9	aldough (D05/1, C02/8)	even dough	2	4	4
7-10	dough/though (D05/4)		1	4 [1]	3
7-11	since [causative] (N03/1)	as	1	4	3
8. Determiners					
8-1	some (D05/4, C03/5, C08/8 (2 citations), R04/8) - e get some towns (D05/4) - some oder place (C08/8)	e get town dem anoder	5	157 [2]	33
8-2	a(n) (R09/2, R02/6) - thirty times a day (R09/2) - a good papa (R02/6)	for one day good papa	30	89 [27] (19)	25
8-3	every (V02/3)	all di	1	55 (1)	28
8-4	many (D04/2)	plenty	1	49	22

---

[10] Plus 9 instances of according to.
[11] Of which 8 in during by.
[12] Of which 5 (all the direct citations) by the same informant.

8-5	*each* (N02/2)	*every*	1	9	6
8-6	*enough ...* (C04/1, C04/4)	*plenty .../... reach*	2	6	5
8-7	*most* (D02/5)	*plenty*	1	5	4
8-8	<u>*few*</u> *people* (C01/8)	*people wey no plenty*	1	4	2
	9. Noun inflections				
9-1	*-s* [plural] (V01/6, V01/8, V02/2, V02/3, V02/5, V02/6, V02/7, V04/1, V04/5, V04/8, D01/1, D04/2, D05/1, D05/2, D05/4, D05/6, C03/5, C04/6, C05/1, C07/3, C08/1, C08/5, C08/7, C09/1, N02/1, N02/2, N03/1, N03/4, N04/7, N05/5, A02/8, A04/1, A04/5, R05/8, R07/6, R08/1, R08/8)	*dem*/Ø	50[13]	741 [29] (24)	40
9-2	*children* (V01/2, V04/5, V04/8, V05/7, D04/2, A04/3, A04/5, R01/8)	*pikin dem*	8	58	17
9-3	*-'s* [genitive] (R01/5) - *God's* (R01/5)	*God im*	3	16[14] (2)	8
	10. Pronouns				
10-1	*our* (N02/4, A03/8, A04/7)	*we*	3	230	35
10-2	*deir/their* (V04/5)	*dem*	1	174 [5] (2)	31
10-3	*de/they* (N01/1, N02/7, N05/8)	*dem*	5	114 [13] (2)	22
10-4	*everybody* (R02/5)	*person*	1	74	30
10-5	*she* (R01/8)	*e*	2	73 [3]	16
10-6	*you* [pl.] (C05/1, A04/2)	*una*	2	56 [2]	14
10-7	*nobody* (R05/6)	*person no*	2	46 [1]	20
10-8	*what* (R02/5, R03/8) - *I go leave house go look for what everybody go eat* (R02/5) - *How I go pay? Pay for <u>what</u>?*(R03/8)	*wetin*	13	46[15] [4] (14)	17
10-9	*anybody* (A04/3, R05/6)	*person*	2	38 [1]	21
10-10	*somebody* (R10/6)	*person*	2	21 (2)	12
10-11	*your* [pl.] (N02/1, A04/2)	*una*	2	14	5
10-12	*everywhere* (A02/8)	*every place*	1	13[16]	8
10-13	*her* (N01/4, R10/5)	*im*	2	7	4
10-14	*everyone* (R03/8)	*everybody*	1	1	1
	11. Verb inflections and auxiliaries				
11-1	*is/'s* [copula] (N05/1, N05/4) - *my name <u>is</u>* (N05/1, N05/4)	*na/be*	36	121 [38] (40)	32
11-2	*suppose (to)* (C07/8, A03/2) - *you <u>suppose</u> dey* (C07/8) - *di thing wey we don <u>suppose to</u> do* (A03/2)	*for*	2	84	24
11-3	*you <u>must</u> pay* (A05/5)	*go*	1	33	18

---

[13] Of which 22 (19 of the direct citations) by one informant who had himself done research on NigP.
[14] Of which 4 each in *Children's Day* and *master's (degree)* and 1 each in *Lord's Prayer* and *Lady's Queen of Nigeria* (name of a cathedral).
[15] Of which 10 in *what of* (cf Faraclas 1996: 27).
[16] Plus 13 occurrences as adverb.

11-4	V*ing* in nonfinite VPs (R10/1) - *stop to dey disgracing me* (R10/1)	*shame*	14	22 [4] (12)	12
11-5	*are/'re* [copula] (D05/6) - *all our senators [...] are fuck up* (D05/6)	*dey*	12	20 [7] (8)	9
11-6	*can* (V04/1, V05/8, C07/5, R09/7)	*fit*	8	14 [8] (1)	9
11-7	*will/'ll* (V04/5, D04/5)	*go*	8	12 [4] (4)	8
11-8	inflected *be* + V*ing* [progressive] (D03/8, C08/5) - *are dying* (D03/8) - *were talking* (C08/5)	*dey die* *dey talk*	7	12 [8] (1)	7
11-9	*-ed* [past tense] (C09/4) - *Yoruba man used O.P.C.* (C09/4)	*use*	3	9 [5]	5
11-10	*was* [copula] (C04/4, R06/5) - *and dat was how di whole thing take be like dat* (C04/4) - *my own boot was green* (R06/5)	*na* *be*	4	8 [3]	6
11-11	*be able to* (V05/3)	*fit*	2	3 [1]	2
	12. *to* [particle]				
12-1	*to* [particle][17] (V01/2, V01/6, D05/1, C01/4 (2 citations), C04/1, C10/4, N01/1, A02/6, A03/1 (4 citations), A03/2, A03/7, A04/1, A05/3)		40	538 [12] (18)	40
	- in nominal *to*-infinitive clause as object (C10/4, (A02/6, A03/1 (2 citations)) - *want to marry* (C10/4) - *try to save* (A02/6) - *reach to organise* (A03/1) - *prepare to organise* (A03/1)	 *want marry* *try save* *reach organise* *prepare organise*	10	114 [5] (6)	36
	- in adverbial clause of purpose (A03/1 (2 citations)) - *di money wey dese people go borrow from bank to take prepare dem hotel* (A03/1) - *pump heavy money to take prepare for di thing* (A03/1)	 *make dem take* *make dem take*	3	104 [1] (1)	26
	- in postmodification of noun (D05/1, N01/1, A03/2) - *next thing to do* (D05/1) - *money to put inside di business* (N01/1) - *FIFA give Chile di power to organise World Cup* (A03/2)	 *wey e go do* *wey dem fit put* *make e organise*	12	87 (8)	33
	- in nominal *to*-infinitive clause as subject (V01/2, C01/4 (2 citations), C04/1) - *to clear am [...] na wahala* (V01/2)	 *make we clear*	4	32 [1]	17

---

[17] I have analysed as *to* [particle] all non-prepositional uses of *to*, including 15 occurrences in *if to say* 'if', where it links the subordinators *if* and *say*. (*If to say* may in fact be regarded as a complex subordinator in NigP; cf also Agheyisi (1971: 138) who uses the spelling *iftose*.)

	- *to* borrow-- *for you to see person wey go borrow you money self e dey hard* (C01/4) - *to lecture you/* zero (C04/1) - in *wh-*infinitive clause (V01/6, A04/1, A05/3) - *understand how to fight* (V01/6) - *di thing wey we go talk put today, na how to train una pikin dem* (A04/1) - *I wan teach una how to cook ekpang kukwo* (A05/3)	*make you borrow-- make you see person* *make dem lecture you* *how dem go take fight* *how una fit* *how una go take cook*	4	28 [1]	14
	- in other contexts[18]		7	172 [4] (3)	40
	13. Comparative/superlative forms of adjectives/adverbs				
13-1	*-er* [comparative] (D02/2) - *easier* (D02/2)	*pass* *easy pass*	5	9[19] [1] (3)	7
13-2	*best* (V05/8, R01/3)	*better*	2	8	5
13-3	*-est* [superlative] (D03/6) - *cheapest* (D03/6)	*pass* *cheap pass*	2	2[20] (1)	2
13-4	• *di most dirtiest hostel* (V02/4)	*di hostel wey dirty pass*	1	1	1
	14. Negation				
14-1	*noto* (R01/4, R03/2, R05/6, R05/9)	*(e) no be*	4	33	6
14-2	*no* [negative determiner] (N01/3) - *no good road* (N01/3)	*good road no dey*	6	32 [1] (3)	19
14-3	*don't* (C03/3, R04/4)	*no*	4	10 [2] (1)	9
	15. Discourse chunks/ idiomatic expressions				
	15.1 Clauses/larger segments				
15-1-1	*you understand (me) (now)?* (C05/7, C05/8, C10/4, C10/5)	*you hear?*	4	25 [24]	4
15-1-2	*can you imagine?* (D05/4, D05/6, C03/3)	*you fit believe am?*	3	4 [4]	2
15-1-3	*God forbid!* (R07/9)	*God no go gree.*	1	3 [3]	4
15-1-4	*I see no reason* (V05/5)	*I no see why*	1	2	1
15-1-5	*let's be very frank* (D04/3)	*make we talk true*	2	2 [2]	1
15-1-6	• *they are trying let's be very frank* (D04/7)	*dem dey try, make we talk true*	1	1 [1]	1
15-1-7	*they should try* (V05/3)	*make dem try*	1	2 [2]	1
15-1-8	*all power belongs to God* (C01/6)	*na God get all di power*	1	1 [1]	1
15-1-9	*America is a very great country* (D05/9)	*America na big country*	1	1 [1]	1
15-1-10	*and they will now make it compulsory* (C06/2)	*dem go say you must*	1	1 [1]	1
15-1-11	*Are you seeing what I'm seeing?* (R07/5)	*You dey see di thing wey my eye dey see?*	1	1 [1]	1

---

[18] Contexts other than those mentioned in which *to* as particle occurs include nominal *to-*infinitive clauses as subject complement and as adjectival complementation and modal expressions like *suppose to* (cf 5.5.5) or *be able to*.

[19] Excluding *later* and *earlier* not functioning as comparatives of *late* and *early*.

[20] Excluding *newest* in *Newest Hall* (proper name) and *latest* 'most recent'.

15-1-12	as if I no get any right over what I want to do with my life (R02/4)	like say I no suppose talk wetin I go do for my life	1	1	1
15-1-13	as we were saying (C09/8)	as we been dey talk	1	1 [1]	1
15-1-14	because he is a useless man (V02/7)	because na yeye person	1	1	1
15-1-15	before you know it (D03/5)	before you open eye	1	1	1
15-1-16	Come in, the door is open. (R10/6)	Make you come inside o, we no lock door.	1	1 [1]	1
15-1-17	di guy is just trying to advertise himself (C09/7)	di guy just wan make people know am	1	1	1
15-1-18	di higher you go di cooler di thing go become (C07/8)	if you go up e go better	1	1	1
15-1-19	even though it's bad people need to talk about it (C08/3)	even dough e bad people go talk about am	1	1 [1]	1
15-1-20	everywhere was just terrible (C08/7)	everywhere dey bad well well	1	1 [1]	1
15-1-21	he is a man of God (C02/1)	im be man of God	1	1 [1]	1
15-1-22	how much is that? (C06/3)	how much e be?	1	1 [1]	1
15-1-23	I can't imagine (D05/5)	I no fit see	1	1	1
15-1-24	if you are an English person you come out able to present yourself (C08/4)		1	1	1
15-1-25	if you have the stuff man that means you are a student (C08/5)		1	1 [1]	1
15-1-26	Is this time for donation? (R06/7)	Time don reach to give money?	1	1 [1]	1
15-1-27	it's a blessing (D04/6)		1	1 [1]	1
15-1-28	it's a different ball game altogether when you just get in (C07/5)	if you enter na anoder thing e go be	1	1 [1]	1
15-1-29	it's a good thing (C10/3)	na good thing	1	1 [1]	1
15-1-30	it's a temporary place (D04/8)	e no go tay before you go die	1	1 [1]	1
15-1-31	it's a very serious thing (C06/8)	na serious thing be dat	1	1 [1]	1
15-1-32	it's a very shameful thing (C10/1)	na shameful thing	1	1 [1]	1
15-1-33	it's not good for the masses (V05/1)	e no good for poor people	1	1 [1]	1
15-1-34	JAMB has to be blamed (V05/6)	na JAMB we go blame	1	1 [1]	1
15-1-35	na jiving around (C04/2)	waka waka about	1	1	1
15-1-36	let's just face the fact (V05/6)	make we look am well well self	1	1 [1]	1
15-1-37	life begins at fifty (R07/4)	na when you be fifty life dey begin	1	1 [1]	1
15-1-38	Look, you are a common dispenser. (R08/4)	You no be proper doctor.	1	1 [1]	1
15-1-39	making progress [elliptical, no subject] (C07/1)	life don dey better well well	1	1	1
15-1-40	me I don't know how to describe the man (V05/4)	I no know how I go talk am	1	1 [1]	1
15-1-41	Nigerians we believe in spending money for irrelevant things (V02/6)	we Nigeria people like to use money for yeye things	1	1 [1]	1
15-1-42	Nzeribe got his money (V02/7)	Nzeribe get im money	1	1 [1]	1
15-1-43	once you are dere (C08/4)	when you don dey dere	1	1	1
15-1-44	one good turn deserve anoder (R10/8)		1	1	1
15-1-45	opportunity comes but once (R07/1)		1	1 [1]	1
15-1-46	she rightly said (D02/4)	e talk am correct correct	1	1 [1]	1
15-1-47	so dat de will monitor di activities of di exam (V05/8)	make dem dey look wetin dem dey do for di exam	1	1	1
15-1-48	so dat di thing will not leak again (V05/7)	make di thing no comot again	1	1	1
15-1-49	that is the meaning of Nzeribe (V02/8)	na im be wetin e mean	1	1 [1]	1
15-1-50	that is the way me I see it (V05/3)	na so I see am	1	1 [1]	1

15-1-51	that man is he a credible man? (V02/7)	dat man na better person?	1	1 [1]	1
15-1-52	The more we are together, the merrier we shall be. (R06/2)	If we plenty we go happy well well.	1	1 [1]	1
15-1-53	there was no light (C08/7)	light no dey	1	1 [1]	1
15-1-54	They did now, papa. (R02/2)	Dem teach me now, papa.	1	1 [1]	1
15-1-55	they will be able to sell at a reasonable price (V05/3)	dem go fit sell for money wey no too much	1	1 [1]	1
15-1-56	this is life (D04/8)	na so life be	1	1 [1]	1
15-1-57	time waits for nobody (C01/2)	time no dey wait for person	1	1 [1]	1
15-1-58	to be very frank (D04/3)	if we go talk true	1	1 [1]	1
15-1-59	give dem law _to do dat_ (N01/2)	make dem do am	1	1	1
15-1-60	time _to get married_ (C10/8)	time wey dem fit marry	1	1	1
15-1-61	we ourselves Nigerians we are very dirty (V02/4)	we Nigeria people dirty well well	1	1 [1]	1
15-1-62	what actually happened (C08/6)	wetin happen self	1	1 [1]	1
15-1-63	what do you call it (V05/7)	wetin dem dey call am	1	1	1
15-1-64	what you make out of it (A04/3)	wetin you make am	1	1	1
15-1-65	when you are in di university (C08/4)	when you dey for university	1	1	1
15-1-66	which is better? (C07/5)	which one dey better?	1	1 [1]	1
15-1-67	which is even more than what the federal government wanted to pay (V05/4)	wey even pass wetin federal government talk say dem go pay	1	1 [1]	1
15-1-68	why should I be grateful? to who? (C07/8)	wetin go make me thank somebody? who I go thank?	1	1 [1]	1
15-1-69	you are on your own (C10/7)	you dey answer for yourself	1	1	1
15-1-70	You met me some months ago. (R08/1)	E never tay wey you know/ meet me.	1	1 [1]	1
15-1-71	you're well educated (C08/4)	you sabi book well well	1	1	1
	15.2 Noun phrases/ noun phrase fragments				
15-2-1	wetin you want? _intellectual progress?_ (C07/1)	make book matter dey better	1	4	1
15-2-2	a lot of (V05/7, C08/7)	plenty/plenty plenty	2	3 [1]	3
15-2-3	unwanted pregnancy (D02/6, C10/1, C10/5)	belle wey im/dem no want	3	3	2
15-2-4	a particular school (V05/8)	one kind school	1	2	1
15-2-5	democratic process (D05/5)		1	2	1
15-2-6	male hostel (C03/4)		1	2	1
15-2-7	next patient (R08/6)	anoder person	1	2	1
15-2-8	somebody to talk to (R01/1)	person wey go follow me talk	1	2	1
15-2-9	traditional ruler (N02/2)		1	2	1
15-2-10	dem give you _a peaceful atmosphere_ (C07/8)	dem put you for better place	1	1	1
15-2-11	a very bigger success (D05/1)		1	1	1
15-2-12	about three assignments (C03/4)		1	1	1
15-2-13	all of us (A03/2)	we all	1	1	1
15-2-14	all sorts of (D05/4)	different different	1	1	1
15-2-15	we no get _any money to waste on any stubborn child_ (R02/3)	we no fit throway our money for pikin wey no dey hear word	1	1	1
15-2-16	arms and ammunition (V02/7)		1	1	1
15-2-17	condition of service (N02/5)		1	1	1
15-2-18	cultural troupe (N03/3)		1	1	1
15-2-19	e be like _di case of di person_ wey (A03/1)	person	1	1	1

15-2-20	*different version of* story (C08/7)	anoder	1	1	1
15-2-21	*dis Enwenrem of a guy* (D05/7)	dis Enwenrem wey dem dey talk	1	1	1
15-2-22	*dis oil price of a thing* (V05/1)	di money for petrol	1	1	1
15-2-23	*di stuff you're made of* (C08/4)	as you be	1	1	1
15-2-24	*di wrong thing and di right thing to do* (A04/1)	di thing wey e no suppose do and di one wey e suppose do	1	1	1
15-2-25	*enemy of democracy* (N05/5)		1	1	1
15-2-26	*every one of dem* (D05/9)	dem all	1	1	1
15-2-27	*female hostel* (C03/4)		1	1	1
15-2-28	*first year of nation's return to* (N02/8)	one year wey our country don dey (for)	1	1	1
15-2-29	*general performance* (C04/2)		1	1	1
15-2-30	*harassment of* motor people (N02/6)	wahala wey dem dey give motor people	1	1	1
15-2-31	*harden criminal* (R07/3)		1	1	1
15-2-32	*honourable caretaker* (D01/1)		1	1	1
15-2-33	*joint session* (N03/3)	big meeting	1	1	1
15-2-34	*just a minute now e don take cross two o'clock* (N02/1)	na small time	1	1	1
15-2-35	*metric tons of* (N03/4)		1	1	1
15-2-36	your *moder's relation* (R02/4)	your mama broder/sister	1	1	1
15-2-37	dat one go cost di state government *more money dan de expect* (C05/6)	pass wetin dem think say e go cost	1	1	1
15-2-38	*most of deir passenger* (D03/6)	plenty people	1	1	1
15-2-39	*most of your colleagues* (C06/3)	di people wey you and dem dey read	1	1	1
15-2-40	*my beloved ladies and gentlemen* (R06/7)		1	1	1
15-2-41	*no alignment for deir shoe* (R09/8)	e bend bend	1	1	1
15-2-42	*no way to communicate with police* (V01/5)	nothing dey wey dem fit take call police	1	1	1
15-2-43	*nothing to write home about* (D04/4)		1	1	1
15-2-44	*official procedure* (R07/9)		1	1	1
15-2-45	*per cent of* (N01/1)		1	1	1
15-2-46	e read sotay e come reach *Ph.D. level* (C07/8)	where book for stop	1	1	1
15-2-47	*physical structure* (C07/1)	thing	1	1	1
15-2-48	*political rally* (N03/3)		1	1	1
15-2-49	*poor electricity supply* (N01/3)	light wey no dey steady	1	1	1
15-2-50	*private sector people* (N04/3)	people wey no dey government work	1	1	1
15-2-51	*psychological orientation* (V01/3)		1	1	1
15-2-52	*real digit* (C04/2)		1	1	1
15-2-53	get *regular supply* for dat kind good cloth (R05/7)	get dat kind good cloth every time	1	1	1
15-2-54	you no get *right to force me to do what I don't want to do* (R02/4)	you no fit make me do wetin I no wan do	1	1	1
15-2-55	*round-table conference* (N01/6)	face-me-I-face-you talk-talk	1	1	1
15-2-56	*sale of clothes* (R05/8)	wey I sell cloth	1	1	1
15-2-57	*theoretical part* (C08/4)		1	1	1
15-2-58	*tribunal for di anti-corruption* (N03/8)	court for wuruwuru people	1	1	1
15-2-59	*West African subregion* (V04/8)		1	1	1
15-2-60	*word of advice* (A04/1)	better word	1	1	1
15-2-61	*word of elders* (A04/1)	wetin our papa dem talk	1	1	1

	15.3 Verb phrases/verb phrase fragments				
15-3-1	sit down (V05/3, C01/6, A04/3)	siddon	3	20	12
15-3-2	come out (C04/8)	comot	3	19 (1)	12
15-3-3	take care of (D04/3)		1	16	6
15-3-4	give birth to (D04/1, D04/2)	born	2	5	1
15-3-5	let Nigeria know (N05/5)	tell	1	5	4
15-3-6	get married (D02/4, C10/7)	marry	3	3 (1)	2
15-3-7	do something about it (D02/5)		1	2 [1]	1
15-3-8	go out (C06/4)	comot	1	2	1
15-3-9	pick my pocket (R06/2)	thief my thing	1	2	1
15-3-10	remind of (R06/5)	make remember	1	2	2
15-3-11	approve di construction of (R07/3)	gree make dem build	1	1	1
15-3-12	commit my life into God hand (C05/3)	put for	1	1	1
15-3-13	explain yourself to me (R07/2)		1	1	1
15-3-14	give peace a chance (N02/2)	live well with your neighbour	1	1	1
15-3-15	gloat over his election (C06/7)	make yanga sake of say dem choose am	1	1	1
15-3-16	go fight against any attempt (N03/8)	no go gree	1	1	1
15-3-17	hold ... responsible (N02/6)		1	1	1
15-3-18	impose am on you (C06/3)	force am for your head	1	1	1
15-3-19	if person don get sexually transmitted disease like gonorrhea before, e dey increase dat person risk of contracting H.I.V. (R08/6)	e fit make dat person catch H.I.V. quick quick	1	1	1
15-3-20	Unilag ... is always di school (C08/4)	na im better pass	1	1	1
15-3-21	is worth billions of naira (D05/5)	cost plenty plenty money	1	1	1
15-3-22	government go let us understand (C05/8)	tell	1	1	1
15-3-23	like to spend money (A01/2)	wan use	1	1	1
15-3-24	lose control of (A01/8)	no fit manage	1	1	1
15-3-25	make a living (D05/9)	work	1	1	1
15-3-26	I don make up my mind (R08/8)	I don know wetin I go do	1	1	1
15-3-27	needs urgent attention (D05/5)	we must look am quick quick	1	1	1
15-3-28	anything like dat pertaining to exam (V05/7)	wey concern	1	1	1
15-3-29	plot against (C06/7)	make plan for person back	1	1	1
15-3-30	put finishing touches (C09/5)	complete am	1	1	1
15-3-31	satisfy my expectation (C06/1)	give me di thing wey I wan get	1	1	1
15-3-32	sign into law (N05/4)		1	1	1
15-3-33	stand up (A03/2)	tanda	1	1	1
15-3-34	take advantage of (D04/3)		1	1	1
15-3-35	una take di decision to marry (R07/7)	una come gree say una go marry	1	1	1
15-3-36	talking about (C07/1)	when we dey talk about	1	1	1
15-3-37	walk out of my house (D04/5)	carry yourself comot for	1	1	1
15-3-38	will be very happy to do anything (A05/3)	go happy and e go do anything	1	1	1
15-3-39	will stop di problem of cheating (V05/8)	go stop di wayo wey dem dey do	1	1	1
15-3-40	wipe away (N05/5)	comot	1	1	1

	15.4 Adjective phrases/adjective phrase fragments				
15-4-1	dey <u>grateful to</u> (C07/6)	thank	2	3 (1)	1
15-4-2	• dey <u>grateful to God for giving you di resources</u> (C07/8)	thank God wey give you di thing wey you dey use	1	1	1
15-4-3	very very important (D02/4, D02/5)		2	3	1
15-4-4	armed and dangerous (R07/8)		1	1	1
15-4-5	di <u>most difficult</u> thing (C06/1)	di thing wey hard pass	1	1	1
	15.5 Adverb phrases/adverb phrase fragments				
15-5-1	first of all (A01/5, A03/2)	di first thing/number one (be say)	2	5	5
15-5-2	thank you <u>very much</u> (D02/5, R10/1)	plenty plenty	2	4	3
15-5-3	here and dere (V05/1, C04/6)	(for) everywhere	2	3	3
15-5-4	a year later (C10/6)	one year after	1	2	1
15-5-5	once and for all (V05/5)	kpatakpata	1	2	1
15-5-6	about two weeks ago (C04/8)	e don reach like two weeks now	1	1	1
15-5-7	once a week (V04/2)	one time for every week	1	1	1
15-5-8	once in a while (C09/1)		1	1	1
	15.6 Prepositional phrases/ prepositional phrase fragments				
15-6-1	at least (D03/5)		1	27	11
15-6-2	in fact (D04/5, C05/2, C07/6, R10/6)	true true	4	18	11
15-6-3	at times (A01/5, A05/6)	sometime	2	12	4
15-6-4	of course [as reply] (C04/6, C07/1, C08/7, R06/4)	na im now	4	7	5
15-6-5	for instance (D05/3, D05/9)	make we take ... do example	1	3	2
15-6-6	in di morning (A04/6)	for morning	1	3	3
15-6-7	Nigeria <u>as a whole</u> (V02/6)	for all di place	1	2	1
15-6-8	in di night (C01/1)	for night	1	2	1
15-6-9	in disguise (C04/4)	wey we no know	1	2	1
15-6-10	in dose days (C10/5)	before before	1	2	2
15-6-11	of nowadays (C02/7)	wey dey today	1	2	2
15-6-12	on di long run (V05/6)	after now	1	2	1
15-6-13	as a sign of (N02/9)	to show say	1	1	1
15-6-14	as per to run di country in a very smooth way (D05/2)	how e go rule well well	1	1	1
15-6-15	as usual (R05/5)		1	1	1
15-6-16	at di earlier stage (D03/5)	before before	1	1	1
15-6-17	at dis particular time (D05/5)	now now	1	1	1
15-6-18	between di two of you (R04/4)	for you and im	1	1	1
15-6-19	by all means (D04/2)	anyhow	1	1	1
15-6-20	by burning (V02/5)	burn am	1	1	1
15-6-21	by so doing (D05/1)	if e dey do dat one	1	1	1
15-6-22	during his time [as vice chancellor] (C07/1)	for di time wey im be oga	1	1	1
15-6-23	for sure [as reply] (C10/3)	true	1	1	1
15-6-24	in charge of social development (N02/9)		1	1	1
15-6-25	e no dey <u>in circulation</u> (C01/8)	e no dey town	1	1	1
15-6-26	in di first instance (V02/7)	number one be say	1	1	1
15-6-27	in his time [as vice chancellor] (C07/1)	for di time wey im be oga	1	1	1
15-6-28	rough <u>in riding</u> okada (D03/7)	when dem dey ride	1	1	1
15-6-29	way <u>of driving</u> (D03/7)	wey dem dey drive	1	1	1
15-6-30	of recent (V03/4)	e never tay	1	1	1

15-6-31	on dis issue (V05/6)	for dis matter	1	1	1
15-6-32	full to di brim (C06/5)	kpatakpata	1	1	1
15-6-33	up to standard of oders (C06/3)	like	1	1	1
	15.7 Other discourse chunks/idiomatic expressions				
15-7-1	dat's why/dat is why (V05/1, D03/1, D03/6, A04/7, R01/3, R04/4, R07/3) - dat's why e good (A04/7)	na im make na im e take good	7	28	14
15-7-2	it's (V04/7, C10/3)	na	9	17 [11]	11
15-7-3	which means (V05/6, V05/8)	na im be say	2	7	3
15-7-4	what if (R07/7, R08/8)	wetin go happen if/wetin you go do if	2	6	2
15-7-5	not to (C07/6, C07/8) - not to dose barawos (C07/6) - not to government (C07/8)	no be for	2	5	1
15-7-6	and so on (A01/7)		1	3	3
15-7-7	as neighbour is concerned (R05/3)	sake of say we be neighbours	1	2	2
15-7-8	not until (V03/8)	na after	1	2	2
15-7-9	What about ...? (R01/8)	... nko?	1	2	2
15-7-10	dere is no way (V05/6)	dem no go fit	1	1	1
15-7-11	di more di merry (R03/4)	as people plenty, na im e dey better	1	1	1
15-7-12	... or what? (R09/2)	... abi na wetin?	1	1	1
15-7-13	e fit do something to actually tackle (D05/2)	make e solve	1	1	1
15-7-14	what's (C07/4)	wetin be	1	1	1
15-7-15	you are actually ... (C08/4)	you dey ... be dat	1	1	1

Table B 2 Responses in Sections 1.3 and 2.3 of the questionnaire

Extract	Responses
1. Interviews	
V01/7	Being a burning issue, the extract's technical terms (*minimum wage*, especially) appear through popular usage, to have passed into the Pidgin vocabulary. [2.3]
V02/1	The extract has several rhetorical questions, which represent an important aspect of Nigerian Pidgin speech [1.3]
V03/1	The respondent here is a proficient speaker of Pidgin. [2.3]
V03/3	This extract is in what could be regarded as "normal" Pidgin. It is devoid of the embellishment that newscasters sometimes bring into the language. Fully comprehensible, though it has the features of uncoordinated speech. [2.3]
V03/4	Use of typical Pidgin expressions such as *oga, kamkpe* [1.3]
V03/6	The text seems to meet the proper Pidgin standard, though it is still somewhere between fully satisfactory and fairly satisfactory. [2.3]
V03/7	(a) The use of typical Pidgin expressions such as *oga* and *chop* [1.3] (b) Although the text employs technical terms, they do not impair intelligibility. [2.3]
V04/6	Simple and straightforward expressions understandable to the least educated speaker of the language [1.3]
V04/8	Use of repetition to indicate the degree of greatness (in this particular example): *baba baba baba power* [1.3]
V05/1	(a) The speaker here displays strong ability at code switching and code mixing. [1.3] (b) While the extract is comprehensible to a large extent, the user of Pidgin unfamiliar with standard English is likely to have problems with some lexical items. [2.3]
V05/7	This speaker demonstrates many features of creative use of language common among students e.g. borrowing, slang (e.g. *expo* meaning 'cheating/exam malpractice') and repetitions. The speaker also exhibits characteristics of educated speech which informs his lexical choice, as observed overleaf. [1.3]
2. Discussions	
D01/5	This extract satisfies to a large extent the pattern of Pidgin usage that is likely in use in Nigeria. It fits into the pattern of everyday Pidgin usage. [2.3]
D02/3	This text strikes me as a good example of how someone with a fair background in standard English and excellent foundation in Pidgin, speaks. [2.3]
D04/3	Emphasis is achieved by repetition – *so so woman woman woman woman woman* etc. [1.3]
D05/1	Constant interference of standard English [1.3]
D05/6	An observation on question 2.2: A speaker of Pidgin may have little or no formal education, but could have been so exposed to those with formal education that he/she might find the passage largely intelligible. Yet the passage appears quite distant from countryside Pidgin. Here again we get back to the issue of varieties of Pidgin. [2.3]
D05/9	This text suggests that not all subjects can be handled or domesticated to meet the simple requirements of Pidgin. Notice how the speaker makes an effort to communicate, to translate standard English words into Pidgin. How, for instance, do you translate *brain drain* into Pidgin? [2.3]
3. Conversations	
C01/1	The features highlighted above, in my opinion, represent characteristics of educated speech and indicate the social status or educational attainment of the speakers, hence the occasional intrusion of standard English forms of usage. [1.3]
C01/3	The orthography of the text has a high correlation with some of the supposedly accepted spellings (Pidgin). [2.3]
C02/4	(a) It captures the spoken features of the language. For instance, the repetition of some adjectives for emphasis, e.g. *bad bad things*. [1.3] (b) The lowest speaker of Pidgin may not have any difficulty comprehending this discourse because of its subject matter: religion. [2.3]

C03/1	The context of this conversation influenced the choice of standard English lexical expressions. [2.3]
C03/4	(a) The topic is special (lecture), therefore the register is also special, and can be called borrowing or loans, e.g. *assignments, lecturer, test, Newest Hall* (proper name), *female hostel, male hostel.* [1.3] (b) The two speakers in the text are competent speakers of Pidgin. See the underlined expressions for example [*dis uh Newest Hall/ wey be say na female hostel before/ you come see as dem dey change am to male hostel?; dat place na one kind terrible place now; boys wey just dey for dat place eh/ na so so noise dem just dey make*]. They are beautiful Pidgin phrases in spite of the code-switching in the arrowed segment [*about three assignments*]. The most beautiful expressions in this text come from speaker A. Note that any non-comprehension on the part of someone with little formal education will stem from "specialist register" and "specialist topic". [2.3]
C04/2	The speakers' speech clearly depicts their environment and they use lexical items to indicate this. [2.3]
C04/3	Audience not exposed to the language register of campus setting may have a little difficulty grasping some of the words [2.3]
C04/4	The present political dispensation in the country makes the text to be a fairly familiar one to the majority of speakers of Pidgin. [2.3]
C04/5	This text illustrates the infiltration of standard English into Pidgin because the speakers are students. [2.3]
C04/8	(a) The speech style seems to have been influenced heavily by setting and topic (e.g. lexical items and code alternation). [1.3] (b) This is an interesting text. It is natural. A dominates the conversation. They are at home with the language (Pidgin), but because they have got formal education up to post-secondary level, the influence of English is perceptible in their code-mixing. [2.3]
C05/2	There is no clearer way this discourse could have been presented because its context is academics. [2.3]
C05/6	(a) This text employs some of the typical vocabulary of Pidgin, for example *yarn patashi, nyafunyafu.* [1.3] (b) The word *broder* is better written as *broda*; *because*, as *becos*. [2.3]
C05/7	Although a dialogue, B virtually said everything, leaving A to say only about 15 words. B is efficient but her/his interjection is always in standard English, just like a speaker of Igbo will always say *you know* or *you understand* or *I mean*. Her/his interjection is *you understand me (now)?* [1.3]
C05/8	Repetition of the tag *you understand me now?* [1.3]
C06/2	The context of the discourse permitted the use of some lexical items that may pose a little difficulty to the audience who are not familiar with it. [2.3]
C07/4	The use of the English idiomatic expression *cut your coat according to your size* [1.3]
C07/5	We also find traces of standard English constructions in this text. It is also the type of Pidgin popular amongst the enlightened circle. [2.3]
C07/6	Speakers with little or no formal education would have difficulty comprehending this discourse because of its academic setting. [2.3]
C08/3	Possibly because the participants are university students, their Pidgin is significantly influenced by their knowledge of, and regular use of standard English. [2.3]
C08/4	Intra-sentential switching e.g. *once you are dere man dat means* (English) *say* (Pidgin) *you are actually* ... (English) [1.3]
C08/6	The use of language register comprehensible to speakers who are used to campus setting e.g. *faculty, H.O.D.* etc. [1.3]
C08/7	Inter-sentential switching e.g. *light no dey/* (Pidgin) *there was no light there* (English) [1.3]
C10/1	The use of *pikin* and *cooleh*, which are typical Pidgin expressions [1.3]
C10/5	Tag-switching e.g. ... *go marry am/* (Pidgin) *you understand?* (English) [1.3]
C10/7	This seems to be good Pidgin. Occasional standard English interference results from the speakers' background. [2.3]

C10/8	The Pidgin used in this text is not like the original Pidgin. It is adulterated. However its adulteration can be attributed to the social circle. This type of Pidgin is common among young educated men. [2.3]

4. News

N01/1	(a) Use of repetitions for different purposes e.g. *e don dey cry <u>well well</u>, make e dey grow <u>well well</u>, <u>many many</u> things, <u>different different</u> place* [1.3] (b) Local expressions (*ogbonge, oga*), which add colour to the piece [1.3] (c) The occurrence of *o* at some points does not seem to sound intelligible enough. Some examples are its occurrence in l. 4, 5, 7, 10 etc. I think the text will read better if the *o*'s are removed. [2.3]
N01/3	(a) This extract is verbose. The bracketed words [*(especially) especially*; *don dey beg (plenty beg)*; *dey suffer (serious suffer suffer no be small)*; *cry (better cry)*] could have been omitted with no serious effect on meaning. [1.3] (b) The degree of verbosity and repetition seems to suggest that serious issues such as news cannot be treated in Pidgin, though that is not the case. Generally, the extract is artificial in tone, for no normal discourse in Pidgin takes this form. [2.3]
N01/4	(a) *Gberere* is an intrusion from a local language. Its use here is unnecessary. [1.3] (b) The news item here could have been expressed in very few words. Extract characterized by unnecessary circumlocution, e.g. *wey don marry <u>come do "I do I do"</u>*; *no pikin wan land deir doormouth* (for *dem no born pikin*) [2.3]
N01/6	*According by* is pretentious, for no genuine speaker of Pidgin uses such. It was popularized by Zebrudaya in the TV soap *Masquerade*, who hardly spoke Pidgin. [1.3]
N02/2	Words or phrases like *subjects, give peace a chance, measure, traditional ruler* are undiscriminating carry-overs from standard English. [1.3]
N02/4	The text exhibits the features of repetition for emphasis (especially with adjectives) and choice of words peculiar to the language such as *tranga* and *ogbonge*. [1.3]
N02/5	Somewhat pretentious and vague use of Pidgin, e.g. *dem throway dis kind abeg o for Abuja*; *teach dose wey go be greater tomorrow* [2.3]
N02/6	Repetition, as a process of laying emphasis in Pidgin, is apparent in this piece – *at all at all* .... [1.3]
N02/8	(a) The expression *di ones dem wey I go call "<u>khaki no be leader</u> [[FROM "LEATHER"]]" inside di news* [for 'headlines'] is an attempt to impress the listener that fell flat. For, in the context, it is absolutely meaningless. [1.3] (b) The Pidgin here is unnatural, that is, not free flowing, an attempt by a speaker of standard English to impress the listener with his condescension. [2.3]
N04/1	This news item is well received in Pidgin. It's a model for Pidgin news broadcast unblemished by the unnecessary digression and verbosity which characterized some news texts. The standard English words used here, such as *retire, economic*, are lexical items that are fully known in Pidgin, even to those who are not speakers of standard English. [2.3]
N04/2	The use of adages in Pidgin: *I no bellefull o, na im make Oliver Twist ask for more o* and *na for dry season, ant dey gader dem food dey put for inside hole o*. [1.3]
N04/3	Words like *ogbonge, oturugbeke, okamuka* are dialectal intrusions. But while the first, *ogbonge*, has been fully integrated into Pidgin, the others task comprehension, though in the context, they serve only as intensifiers. [1.3]
N04/6	This news extract hardly reads like a news item. The attempt at making a meaning resulted in oversimplification. In the end, it reads more like an unstructured conversation. [2.3]
N05/3	The text is highly pretentious, tedious and does not reflect the real form of Pidgin as it is used by ordinary people in Nigeria, e.g. the expression *during by di time*. [2.3]
N05/4	The attempt to pidginize made this newscaster resort to much creativity. The end result is Pidgin that can hardly find any basis in reality. (See for example expressions like *launch-launch* and *all dis katakata oturugbeke wahala and okpotu*.) [2.3]
N05/6	There are instances of the use of terms from local Nigerian languages – *kpatakpata, ogbonge, fiam*. [1.3]

N05/8	There is excess repetition and a strong desire to impress the listener with Pidgin skills and to suggest that the listener is not intelligent enough. That is why almost every major statement tends to get repeated. [2.3]	
	5. Advice	
A01/2	This is a standard Pidgin text except for the problem of knowing how words which were spelt in standard English orthography were rendered in the Pidgin when read aloud. [2.3]	
A01/3	Some words are written in standard English although there are accepted Pidgin spellings instead. For instance *because* is usually written as *becos* in Pidgin and *thing* may be written as *ting*. [2.3]	
A01/5	Masterful piece [2.3]	
A01/7	Appropriate and normal Pidgin use [2.3]	
A01/8	Nature of topic makes it easily understandable to all listeners [2.3]	
A02/3	(a) The use of adages (*ground no level for everybody; too much gain e dey wound throat; na small small water dey take full bucket*) makes the text more familiar to the audience. [1.3] (b) The goal of the discourse is to enable the audience to reflect on issues and thereafter effect a change. The language allows for such a development. [2.3]	
A02/4	Clear presentation of ideas [2.3]	
A02/6	Idiomatic expression: *Money for hand, back for ground.* [1.3]	
A03/5	This text is written in good Pidgin. Except for few, the standard English words which occurred here do not, as yet, have Pidgin equivalents. [2.3]	
A03/6	Absolutely superb [2.3]	
A03/7	Idiomatic expression: *Person wey dem cut im head still fit no die o!* [1.3]	
A03/8	An example of a good text in Pidgin. [2.3]	
A04/3	*Anybody wey no quick quick lick hot soup, e go cool down lick cold one* (proverb) [1.3]	
A04/5	(a) Retention of the plural marker *–s* in the nouns (*pickpockets dem, girls dem*) is a common feature of contemporary Nigerian Pidgin. [1.3] (b) This speaker, in my opinion, consciously adheres to the local Pidgin forms though there is an indication that she is an educated speaker. I believe this is informed by the need to communicate effectively to her Pidgin audience. [2.3]	
A04/7	(a) The use of adages: *Na make dis person bring am, make dis person bring am, na im go make am better for all of us.* [1.3] (b) Popular expressions employed in the text drive home the point being made by the producer of the programme. [2.3]	
A05/1	Language use here is natural, free flowing. The speaker seems adept and seems to refrain from the pretensions that often characterize Pidgin on the radio. [2.3]	
A05/2	Like in most Pidgin usage, repetition also abounds here: e.g. *well well, pieces pieces.* [1.3]	
A05/4	Good Pidgin text, but like most programmes of the sort, it is laced with repetitions, though this is only tangential to the issue. [2.3]	
A05/7	The speaker has a very good knowledge of Pidgin. [2.3]	
A05/8	Simple and straightforward expressions [1.3]	
	6. Drama	
R01/5	This extract seems to me to capture the speech nuances of Pidgin speakers appropriately. A near perfect example of Pidgin unhindered by the sophistication that comes with familiarity with standard English. [2.3]	
R01/7	The use of Pidgin is quite okay and natural. [2.3]	
R02/1	The only peculiarity here is the accurate representation of the quoted speech [in English], which is quite unusual for a speaker of Pidgin, considering that most speakers who use Pidgin as represented are assumed to be not-so-literate. [1.3]	
R02/2	The Pidgin used in the extracts from the drama presentations seems to reflect standard usage more than that in the news broadcasts. The latter sound somewhat artificial, especially with the unnecessary addition of *o* at the end of many statements. [2.3]	
R02/5	There is an instance of the idiomatic *till thy kingdom come.* [1.3]	

R03/4	Highly commendable and natural [2.3]
R04/3	Extract shows evidence of Yoruba-based Pidgin, with the insertion of Yoruba words and phrases [1.3]
R05/3	This seems a good text in Pidgin. [2.3]
R05/5	The use of Pidgin in the text indicates the exposure of the speakers to urban life and some degree of formal education or experience with people who have had some formal education in English. The text is good Pidgin, but indicates a measure of refinement which would probably make it different from the Pidgin spoken in places such as Benin, Warri, Calabar etc. [2.3]
R05/7	This is a good example of Nigerian Pidgin. It has both the rhythm and the local idiom. [2.3]
R06/1	Expressions from Yoruba [1.3]
R06/3	This is one of the best of the texts. The Pidgin used is nearly excellent. [2.3]
R06/5	Instances of code-mixing such as *onile olola di di, mo mo bo se wa* (Yoruba expressions) [1.3]
R07/3	The characters here are very "sophisticated". It is difficult to ascertain what the playwright wants to point out in this exchange, but the speech pattern here shows a lot of inconsistency. The expressions underlined [*collect approval*; *dat is why I rush back*; *approve di construction of dis our road*; *intimidate*] are hardly available to an ordinary speaker of Pidgin. If the aim is to show the characters as uneducated, this is a serious artistic flaw in terms of the realism of the language. [2.3]
R07/6	There are instances of code-mixing and switching as in lines 5, 7-8, 13-14 [Yoruba expressions] [1.3]
R07/9	(a) The use of *reprimand* (instead of *remand*) is particularly effective in the context as it delineates character, showing the Chief's struggle to show sophistication; malapropism. [1.3] (b) *Iro ni, laye, wo* are influences from Yoruba. [1.3] (c) The speakers are handicapped by officialese and an attempt to be sophisticated. That explains the heavy presence of standard English in the extract. [2.3]
R08/8	On the whole, the conversation here smacks of one conducted in a language that is useful for its nostalgic effect The two characters imply, by their speech pattern, that they are returning to a language they have outgrown. See expressions like *I don make up my mind, what if, I want two days off, encourage*. These expressions sound artificial and could cast doubt on the creative ability of the artist. [2.3]
R09/3	It contains many instances of code-mixing (Yoruba). [1.3]
R10/3	Good Pidgin [2.3]
R10/6	There are instances of code-mixing: *Why? Ki lo de?* (English/Yoruba); *Ah na fever be dat. Ako iba nu.* (Pidgin/Yoruba) [1.3]

Appendix C: Interviews (summary only)

Below is a list of the interviews with a brief description of their content. The complete version of Appendix C, with transcriptions of all interviews, is available only on the CD.

Interview 1

Place and date: University of Lagos, 17 July 1997
Speakers: Mostapha Agbolade, Ofure Aito, Francis Mogu, Patrick Oloko, Harry Olufunwa (Department of English, University of Lagos); Dagmar Deuber
Language: English
Topics: Status and functions of NigP, attitudes towards the language, prospects for its future development

Interview 2

Place and date: University of Lagos, 21 July 1997
Speakers: Anthony Okeregbe (Department of Philosophy, University of Lagos); Patrick Oloko, Harry Olufunwa (see interview 1); Dagmar Deuber
Language: English
Topics: Use of NigP in Ajegunle (Lagos); language use in education; personal use of NigP by the interviewees; use of NigP on the University of Lagos campus; status and functions of NigP, attitudes towards the language, prospects for its future development; varieties of NigP and standardization

Interview 3

Place and date: Lagos (Ajegunle), 23 July 1997
Speakers: A, a young man from Ajegunle enrolled in a vocational school at the time of the interview; B, friend of A; Dagmar Deuber
Language: English
Context: The speakers are walking to the secondary school which A attended, where he wants to arrange an interview with a teacher for D. Deuber (see Interview 4).
Topics: Use of NigP in the school environment in Ajegunle; attitudes towards NigP and English in Ajegunle; personal language use of speaker A

Interview 4

Place and date: Lagos (Ajegunle), 23 July 1997
Speakers: T, teacher; Dagmar Deuber
Language: English
Setting: Secondary school in Ajegunle, staff room
Topics: Personal language use of T and his family; use of NigP in Ajegunle; language use in education; prospects for NigP in education and for its general future development

Interview 5

Place and date: Lagos (Ajegunle), 23 July 1997
Speakers: A, B (see Interview 3); F, friend of A and B; M, F's mother; Dagmar Deuber
Language: NigP
Setting: In the home of F and M
Topics: Personal language use of F and M; historical development and present-day status and functions of NigP

Interview 6

Place and date: Lagos, 29 July 1997

Speakers: E, official at the Ministry of Information; Patrick Oloko (see interview 1); Dagmar Deuber

Language: English

Context: D. Deuber and P. Oloko have come to the ministry to inquire about publications in NigP.

Topics: Use of NigP by the Ministry of Information in publications and information campaigns; translating information into NigP; prospects for government support of NigP

Interview 7

Place and date: Lagos, 30 July 1997

Speakers: J, journalist with a major newspaper; Dagmar Deuber

Language: English

Topics: Uses and prospects of NigP in newspapers; attitudes towards the language; prospects for a language policy encouraging NigP

Interview 8

Place and date: Lagos, 25 July 1997

Speakers: G, official at the National Television Authority, Lagos; C, colleague of G; Dagmar Deuber

Language: English

Topics: Language use on television; status and functions of NigP, attitudes towards the language; personal use of NigP by speaker G

Interview 9

Place and date: Lagos, 29 July 1997

Speakers: Ndidi Osaka, broadcaster at Radio Nigeria 2; Dagmar Deuber

Language: English

Topics: Language use on Radio Nigeria 2; NigP programmes on Radio Nigeria 2; selection of NigP presenters; varieties of NigP and standardization

Interview 10

Place and date: Lagos, 11 August 2000

Speakers: Smart Esi, Head of the Pidgin Section at Radio Nigeria 3; Dagmar Deuber

Language: NigP

Topics: Use of NigP on Radio Nigeria 3; selection of NigP presenters; standards of correctness in NigP; varieties of NigP and standardization; NigP orthography

Interview 11

Place and date: University of Lagos, 17 October 2000

Speakers: Emmanuel Mbah, Austin Nwagbara, Patrick Oloko, Harry Olufunwa, Babatunde Opeibi (Department of English, University of Lagos); David Aworawo (Department of History, University of Lagos); Nkechi Okoroanyanwu (Department of African and Asian Studies, University of Lagos); Raphael Uzoezie (Department of English, University of Lagos and Nnamdi Azikiwe University, Awka); Uduopegeme Yakubu (Department of English, Olabisi Onabanjo University, Ago-Iwoye); Dagmar Deuber

Language: English

Topics: Results of the questionnaire study of corpus extracts, in which most of the speakers participated; varieties of NigP and standardization

Appendix D: Samples of written Nigerian Pidgin

Text D 1 News script

The following is the first page of the script for the NigP news on Radio Nigeria 3, Lagos, on 17 May 2000, copied from the newscaster's handwritten version. The full text, as transcribed from the broadcast, is part of the corpus (Text N04-1). It also appears on the CD as a sound sample.

BROKIN NEWS
RN-3 IKOYI
LAGOS
17-05-Y2K
(1)

1. Dẹn dọn retire some pipo for petroleum ministry.
2. One ogbongẹ oga wọn look for money to repair F.R.C.N. & N.T.A.
3. De dọn set task force wey go follo put eye for dorty mata for Lagos Mainland Local Govt.
4. Igbo pipo wọn celebrate Igbo day for on 29th of May Y2K.

Na feda wey nọ good, E go dey pluck trowey-o.
Naim make di department of petroleum resources wey bi pipo wey tanda ontop petroleum mata, dọn retire some pipo wey dey work with dẹm. Dẹn retire dẹm to make di department dey kampe pass as b/4. Na di mouth of di special adviser ontop petroleum and energy mata dis order fall comọt. E say, dis retirement go continue until dẹm see say, petroleum dọn dey contribute dẹm own part well well for our economic mata.

I nọ bẹllẹfull, naim make Oliver Twist ask for more.
Di oga ontop ofofo and tọk-tọk mata Prof Jerry Gana say, E go soon write anoda give me money paper go give National Assembly so dat dẹm fit bring money wey Ein go take buy things and repair Federal Radio Corporation of Nigeria and N.T.A. property dẹm. Di oga tọk dis word by di time wey Ein carry waka come look di working property wey dey for F.R.C.N. compound for Lagos here. By di time wey our newtorey man Chika Emerenwah dey take question dey jam di oga bodi, E say, Ein go change all di F.R.C.N. equipment dẹm to chabẹ wey dẹm dey use nowadays.

Na for dry season, ant dey gada dẹm food for inside hole-o.
Naim make di Govt of Benue State dọn bring out fifty-nine million naira to buy fertilizer to divide for di farmers wey dey dẹm state for dis farming season. Na di oga madam ontop agriculture mata for B/State Mrs Elizabeth Shuluwa tell our new-torey pipo for Makurdi say, dẹn go use new style to dey divide fertilizer give farmers for di state as from now, so dat dẹn go make sure say fertilizer reach many farmers hand.

Text D 2 Public enlightenment: Facts for Life

Facts for Life: A Communication Challenge by UNICEF, WHO, UNESCO and UNFPA (1993; first published in 1990) is a handbook on child health intended for organizations, institutions and individuals in the developing world who can communicate the messages to families. Translations or adaptations are available in over 170 languages. In Nigeria, Hausa, Yoruba, Igbo and NigP adaptations have been produced. The NigP edition (UNICEF, WHO and UNESCO 1991) is entitled *True Word dem for Beta Life: How to Make People Sabi dem*. Below I have juxtaposed the NigP version of an excerpt from the handbook with the English version. The excerpt (pp xvi f in both editions) is an introductory overview of the main information in the book.

True Word Dem for Beta Life - **DI BIG TEN THING DEM**	Facts for Life - **THE TOP TEN**
Dis be di big ten thing dem wey we gader from TRUE WORD DEM FOR BETA LIFE.	*The following are the top ten messages distilled from Facts for Life.*
1 Our mama and pikin dem go get strong body if mama dem dey born pikin every 2-2 year. Our mama dem body go dey kampe if dem no get belle bifor dem reach 18 year and dem life go beta if dem no get belle pass 4 time.	**1** The health of both women and children can be significantly improved by spacing births at least two years apart, by avoiding pregnancies before the age of 18, and by limiting the total number of pregnancies to four.
2 Make our mama dem wey get belle dey go hospital so dat nurse go put eye for dem body and make dem go hospital if dem wan born pikin. Dis tory dey important well well bicos if our mama dem dey go hospital bifor dem born pikin and after dem born finish sef, dem wahala no go plenty at all.	**2** To reduce the dangers of childbearing, all pregnant women should go to a health worker for prenatal care and all births should be assisted by a trained person.
3 Anoda important message be say make our mama dem give pikin dem breast for 6 month after dem don born.	**3** For the first few months of a baby's life, breastmilk *alone* is the best possible food and drink. Infants need other foods, in addition to breastmilk, when they are about six months old.
4 Make our mama dem dey give pikin dem wey never reach 3 year plenty food to dey chop, make di food good well well o and make e get oil.	**4** Children under the age of three have special feeding needs. They need to eat five or six times a day and their food should be specially enriched by adding mashed vegetables and small amounts of fats or oils.
5 Belle wey dey run wey dey make pikin dem go toilet everytime fit kill. Make our mama dem dey give their pikin	**5** Diarrhoea can kill by draining too much liquid from a child's body. So the liquid lost each time the child

wey belle dey run, plenty breast, soup, food and wetin our dokinta dey call ORS. Some kind drink wey dem make with water, sugar and salt.

6 Injection dem wey no dey make pikin dem get bad disease good well well. Injection dem no dey make pikin die. E dey make pikin grow well well. E dey important make pikin dem get dis injection bifor dem reach 1 year. Every woman wey dey get belle must to get injection wey no go make poison enter im body should in case e get wound.

7 Cough and cold dem fit go even if dem no use melecine for am but if pikin get bad cough and cold e ku ku good make we carry am go hospital quick quick. If our pikin dem get cough togeder with cold, make we dey give dem plenty food chop with water wey clean.

8 Na mouth disease dey follow enter body wey dey cause sickness, we fit to stop dis bad thing if we dey wash our hand dem after we don use latrine - make we dey wash our hand dem bifor we touch food wey we wan chop. Make our food and water dem dey clean, make we dey cook water wey we dey drink for fire if we no get pump water.

9 Sickness no dey make pikin dem grow well. If pikin sick and after e don well, make we give am plenty food every day for one week, make e for grow well well.

10 Pikin dem wey dem just born and wey never reach three year, we must to put dem for scale every month to see how dem heavy reach. If dem body no heavy put for 2 month, den small wahala dey be that o.

passes a watery stool must be replaced by giving the child plenty of the right liquids to drink - breastmilk, diluted gruel, soup, or a special drink called ORS. If the illness is more serious than usual, the child needs help from a health worker - and the special ORS drink. A child with diarrhoea also needs food to make a good recovery.

6 Immunization protects against several diseases which can cause poor growth, disability, and death. All immunizations should be completed in the first year of a child's life. Every woman of child-bearing age should be immunized against tetanus.

7 Most coughs and colds will get better on their own. But if a child with a cough is breathing much more rapidly than normal, then the child is seriously ill, and it is essential to go to a health centre quickly. A child with a cough or cold should be helped to eat and drink plenty of liquids.

8 Many illnesses are caused because germs enter the mouth. This can be prevented by using latrines; by washing hands with soap and water after using the latrine and before handling food; by keeping food and water clean, and by boiling drinking water if it is not from a safe piped supply.

9 Illnesses hold back a child's growth. After an illness, a child needs an extra meal every day for a week to make up the growth lost.

10 Children from birth to the age of three years should be weighed every month. If there is no gain in weight for two months, something is wrong.[1]

---

[1] In the revised edition from which the English text is taken, this information is subsumed under point 9, and a new item about AIDS has been added as point 10. I have adjusted the text to the NigP version.

Text D 3 Newspaper Column: Popular Side

Popular Side by Henry Chandy is a column in the weekly sports newspaper *Sporting Champion*. The text presented here appeared in the edition of 8 August 1997 (p 16).

[original version]

DIS KATAKATA FIT SPOIL SOMETHING

For last week, we carry something like dis kwa for *Popular Side* but dat one na football e concern. For dis week own na sports ministry and Nigeria Olympic Committee (NOC) matter na im I bring come for una.

Dis matter don cos plenty thing but people no know. Even sef press people just comot dem eye for dis matter as dem no wan enter court case becos of dis tory wey manpikin no know how to put mouth inside am.

But as *Popular Side* wey im motto na "Hand no de cover pregnancy" we must open fowl nyash when breeze blow for una wey de read us to know wetin de shele around us. Una know say no be one one type of soup person de eat everyday as manpikin go de like to change im soup at least for every 3 - 3 days.

True-true dis matter na big case wey if we no settle am. Naija go lose plenty thing. Shebi we don de enjoy our gold medal from Ajunwa and our U-23 dream team own. For say we carry katakata go Atlanta Olympics, you think say we go get anything for there? Lai-lai.

Dis matter start when sports ministry talk say dem wan hold election for chairman of association wey be people wey de head other sports association minus soccer for dis obodo Naija. Hockey, boxing, karate, judo, tennis, wrestling, weightlifting, handball, and plenty other association wey sports ministry wan help conduct election for dem to get chairman dem wey go head dem for two years.

[translation]

THIS PROBLEM COULD HAVE SERIOUS CONSEQUENCES

Last week we had a similar story to this one in *Popular Side* but that one was about football. What I bring you this week is the problem between the sports ministry and the Nigeria Olympic Committee (NOC).

This problem has had numerous consequences but people are not aware. Even journalists no longer concern themselves with the problem, as they are afraid of litigation over this controversial matter.

But since the motto of *Popular Side* is "you can't hide a pregnancy by covering your belly with your hands", we must expose the rump of the fowl when the breeze is blowing for you as our readers to understand what is happening around us. You know that one doesn't eat the same meal every day, as people want to change their meal at least every three days.

The truth is that this problem will result in a big scandal if it is not resolved. Nigeria will lose a lot of things. Haven't we been rejoicing over the gold medals won by Ajunwa and our U-23 dream team? If we had gone to the Atlanta Olympics in disagreement, do you think we would have won anything there? No way!

The conflict started when the sports ministry announced its intention to hold elections for the chairmen of sports associations, that is, those who are in charge of sports associations except soccer in our country Nigeria. Hockey, boxing, karate, judo, tennis, wrestling, weight lifting, handball and many other associations [are the ones] that the sports ministry wants to help conduct elections for chairmen who will head them for two years.

But my broda and sister, our Nigeria Olympic Committee (NOC) wey be like say dem dey dem own separate, no come gree with wetin sports ministry talk as dem say dem hand suppose dey for de election more than de ministry own. Dis disagreement cos katakata wey make sports ministry to begin show NOC say na dem be oga for anything wey concern sports while NOC de show sports ministry say shebi na dem go carry all de association go register for Olympic and Commonwealth Games, since na only dem NOC na im the International Olympic Committee, IOC, na im sabi no other body or person.

Dis katakata continue sotey sports ministry come hold de election and come get new chairman of de associations. The ministry come from dat time begin call NOC to carry dem office from Lagos come Abuja but NOC no gree with dat order wey come make sports ministry to begin declare NOC illegal if dem continue to de stay for Lagos. [...]

Now, IOC don hear wetin de go on for Naija and just de wait make complaint come to dem table.

Abeg o, our people, make una leave all dis katakata as e no go fit help us. At least we don see how our people take flop for Athens. Dat one na small. Manpikin dey with wetin Reverend Moses Iloh talk say make our people comot monkey hand for soup make e no be like person own. E say if dis wahala continue IOC fit no allow us to come Sydney for year 2000 Olympics. Person wey get ear make e hear.

But my brothers and sisters, our Nigeria Olympic Committee (NOC), which wants to see itself as independent, opposed the sports ministry's plan, insisting that it has more important part to play in the elections than the ministry. This disagreement has caused a controversy in which the sports ministry is trying to show the NOC that it is the highest authority in sports matters, while the NOC is trying to make it clear to the sports ministry that it is responsible for registering all the associations for the Olympic and Commonwealth Games, since it is the only body recognized by the International Olympic Committee, IOC.

This controversy continued until the sports ministry held the elections and got new chairmen of the associations. The ministry then ordered the NOC to move its office from Lagos to Abuja, and when the NOC did not comply with that order, the sports ministry threatened to declare the NOC illegal should it remain in Lagos.

The IOC has now got word of what is going on in Nigeria and is only waiting for a complaint to be lodged.

I appeal to you, our people, to stop this useless wrangle. At least we have seen how our athletes flopped in Athens. And that is a relatively minor problem. I agree with Rev. Moses Iloh who said that we should remove the hand of the monkey from the soup bowl so that it is not mistaken for a human being's. That is, if this problem continues, the IOC might not allow us to participate in the 2000 Olympics in Sydney. Whoever has ears should listen.

Text D 4 Poem by Ezenwa-Ohaeto

Ezenwa-Ohaeto has published poems in NigP in two of his poetry collections, *I Wan Bi President: Poems in Formal and Pidgin English* (1988) and *If to Say I Bi Soja: Poems in Pidgin English* (1998). The following poem is taken from *If to Say I Bi Soja* (pp 33ff).

[original version]

POLITICIAN NA WIND

Dem say trap no fit catch
Wind wey dey blow,

E get wind wey go blow
You no go see as e take pass,

5 Politician na like wind
Dem just dey blow dey pass,

Politician go promise everything
E fit promise say e go bring God,

Politician go promise everything
10 E fit promise say e go fight war
When him no get even knife,

Politician go promise food
When him no get yam
When him no get cassava,

15 Politician get uniform
E go wear one big dress
E go buy one big car
E go get body wey fat,

Politician go do like money na water
20 If people dey look e go comot money

When people look for anoder place
E go take back him money quick,

Politician go promise
Say e go give you development
25 Den him go build private house
Wey big pass King him palace
E go take your very plenty money
Make chieftaincy title for every corner,

Den dem go begin praise am
30 Dem go call am *Baba ke*
Dem go call am *Igwekala*,

Politician na wind
Wey dey blow wey no get direction.

[translation]

POLITICIANS ARE WIND

They say a trap cannot catch
The wind that is blowing,

There is a wind that will blow
You won't notice it when it blows by,

Politicians are like the wind
They just blow by,

A politician will promise everything
He may promise that he will bring God,

A politician will promise everything
He may promise that he will fight a war
When he doesn't even have a knife,

A politician will promise food
When he doesn't have yam
When he doesn't have cassava,

A politician has a uniform
He will be dressed in sumptuous attire
He will buy a big car
He will have a fat body,

A politician will act as if money was water
If people are looking his way he will bring
    out money

When people are looking another way
He will quickly take his money back,

A politician will promise
That he will give you development
Then he will build a private house
That is bigger than the King's palace
He will take a lot of money from you
And acquire chieftaincy titles everywhere,

Then they will start to praise him
They will call him *Baba ke*
They will call him *Igwekala*,

Politicians are wind
Blowing without direction.

References

Abdulaziz Mkilifi, M H 1972 Triglossia and Swahili-English bilingualism in Tanzania. *Language in Society* 1: 197-213.

Abiodun, Josephine Olu 1997 The challenges of growth and development in metropolitan Lagos. Rakodi, Carol (ed.) *The Urban Challenge in Africa: Growth and Management of Its Large Cities.* Tokyo: United Nations University Press, 192-222.

Adegbija, Efurosibina 1994 The candidature of Nigerian Pidgin as a national language: Some initial hurdles. *International Review of Applied Linguistics* 105-106: 1-23.

Adekunle, Mobolaji 1972 Multilingualism and language function in Nigeria. *African Studies Review* 15: 185-207.

Agheyisi, Rebecca N 1971 *West African Pidgin English: Simplification and Simplicity.* PhD thesis, Stanford University. Ann Arbor: UMI.

—— 1977 Language interlarding in the speech of Nigerians. Kotey & Der-Houssikian (eds) 97-110.

—— 1984a Linguistic implications of the changing role of Nigerian Pidgin English. *English World-Wide* 5: 211-33.

—— 1984b Minor languages in the Nigerian context: Prospects and problems. *Word* 35: 235-53.

—— 1988 The standardization of Nigerian Pidgin English. *English World-Wide* 9: 227-41.

Akere, Funso 1981 Sociolinguistic consequences of language contact: English versus Nigerian languages. *Language Sciences* 3: 283-304.

—— 1995 Languages in the curriculum: An assessment of the role of English and other languages in the education delivery process in Nigeria. Bamgbose, Banjo, & Thomas (eds), 178-99.

Akinnaso, F Niyi 1990 The politics of language planning in education in Nigeria. *Word* 41: 337-67.

—— 1991 Toward the development of a multilingual language policy in Nigeria. *Applied Linguistics* 12: 29-61.

Alleyne, Mervyn C 1971 Acculturation and the cultural matrix of creolization. Hymes (ed,) 169-86.

—— 1980 *Comparative Afro-American. An Historical-Comparative Study of English-Based Afro-American Dialects in the New World.* Ann Arbor: Karoma.

Amuda, Ayoade A 1986 Yoruba/English code-switching in Nigeria: Aspects of its function and form. PhD thesis, University of Reading.

—— 1994 Yoruba/English conversational code-switching as a conversational strategy. *African Languages and Cultures* 7: 121-31.

Awonusi, Victor O 1985 Issues in language planning: An examination of the continued role of English as Nigeria's lingua franca. *Sociolinguistics* 15: 25-30.

—— 1987 The identification of standards within institutionalised non-native Englishes: The Nigerian English experience. *Lagos Review of English Studies* 9: 47-63.

—— 1990 Planning for a National (Nigerian) Language. Eruvbetine (ed.), 113-19.

Bailey, Beryl L 1971 Jamaican Creole: Can dialect boundaries be defined? Hymes (ed.) 341-48.

Baker, Philip 1997 Developing ways of writing vernaculars: Problems and solutions in a historical perspective. Tabouret-Keller, Le Page, Gardner-Chloros, & Varro (eds), 93-141.

—— & Corne, Chris 1982 *Isle de France Creole. Affinities and Origins.* Ann Arbor: Karoma.

Bamgbose, Ayo 1967 *A Short Yoruba Grammar.* Ibadan: Heinemann.

—— 1982 Standard Nigerian English: Issues of identification. Kachru, Braj B (ed.) *The Other Tongue: English across Cultures.* Urbana: University of Illinois Press. 99-111.

—— 1991 *Language and the Nation: The Language Question in Sub-Saharan Africa.* Edinburgh: Edinburgh University Press.

—— 1992 Corpus planning in Yoruba: The radio as a case study. *Research in Yoruba Language and Literature* 2: 1-13.

—— 1996 Post-imperial English in Nigeria 1940-1990. Fishman, J A, Conrad, A W & Rubal-Lopez, A (eds) *Post-Imperial English: Status Change in Former British and American Colonies, 1940-1990.* Berlin: Mouton de Gruyter. 357-72.

——, Banjo, A, & Thomas, A (eds) 1995 *New Englishes: A West African Perspective.* Ibadan: Mosuro.

Banjo, Ayo 1971 Towards a definition of standard Nigerian spoken English. *Actes du Huitième Congrès International de Linguistique Africaine.* Abidjan: Université d'Abidjan, 165-75.

—— 1986 The influence of English on the Yoruba language. Viereck & Bald (eds), 533-45.

—— 1987 Varieties of English in a multilingual setting in Nigeria. Battestini, Simon P X (ed.) *Developments in Linguistics and Semiotics, Language Teaching and Language Learning, Communication across Cultures.* Washington, DC: Georgetown University Press, 37-50.

—— 1993 An endonormative model for the teaching of the English language in Nigeria. *International Journal of Applied Linguistics* 3: 261-75.

Barbag-Stoll, Anna 1983 *Social and Linguistic History of Nigerian Pidgin English: As Spoken by the Yoruba with Special Reference to the English Derived Lexicon.* Tübingen: Stauffenberg.

Barbour, K M, Oguntoyinbo, J S, Onyemelukwe, J O C, & Nwafor, J C 1982 *Nigeria in Maps.* New York: Africana Publishing Company.

Biber, Douglas 1995 *Dimensions of Register Variation: A Cross-Linguistic Comparison.* Cambridge: Cambridge University Press.

Bickerton, Derek 1973a The nature of a creole continuum. *Language* 49: 640-69.

—— 1973b The structure of polylectal grammars. Shuy (ed.) 17-42.

—— 1975 Can English and Pidgin be kept apart? McElhanon, K A (ed.) *Tok Pisin I Go We?* Port Moresby: Linguistic Society of Papua New Guinea. 21-27.

—— 1975b *Dynamics of a Creole System.* Cambridge: Cambridge University Press.

—— 1980 Decreolisation and the creole continuum. Valdman & Highfield (eds) 109-27.

—— 1983 Review of Baker & Corne, Isle de France Creole. *The Carrier Pidgin* 13.4: 8-9.

—— 1984 The language bioprogram hypothesis. *The Behavioral and Brain Sciences* 7: 173-221.

—— 1988 Creole languages and the bioprogramme. Newmeyer, Frederick J (ed.) *Linguistics: The Cambridge Survey.* Vol. 2: *Linguistic Theory: Extensions and Implications.* Cambridge: Cambridge University Press. 268-84.

Blom, Jan-Petter & Gumperz, John J 1972 Social meaning in linguistic structure: code-switching in Norway. Gumperz, J J & Hymes, Dell (eds.) *Directions in Sociolinguistics: The Ethnography of Communication.* New York: Holt, Rinehart & Winston, 407-34.

Bokamba, Eyamba G 1988 Code-mixing, language variation, and linguistic theory: Evidence from Bantu languages. *Lingua* 76: 21-62.

Bourgault, Louise M 1995 *Mass Media in Sub-Saharan Africa.* Bloomington: Indiana University Press.

Brann, Conrad M B 1975 Standardisation des langues et éducation au Nigeria. *African Languages/Langues Africaines* 1: 204-23.

—— 1989 Lingua minor, franca and nationalis. Ammon, Ulrich (ed.) *Status and Function of Languages and Language Varieties.* Berlin: de Gruyter, 372-85.

—— 1990 The role and functions of languages in government: language policy issues in Nigeria. *Sociolinguistics* 19: 1-19.

Brenzinger, M, Heine, B & Sommer, G 1991 Language death in Africa. *Diogenes* 153: 19-44.

Brosnahan, L F 1958 English in Southern Nigeria. *English Studies* 39: 97-110.

Carayol, Michel & Chaudenson, Robert 1977 A study in the implicational analysis of a linguistic continuum: French - Creole. *Journal of Creole Studies* 1: 179-218.

—— 1978 Diglossie et continuum linguistique à la Réunion. Gueunier, N, Genouvrier, E, & Khomsi, A (eds) *Les Français devant la norme.* Paris: Champion, 175-89.

Central Intelligence Agency 2003 Nigeria. *The World Factbook*. Washington DC: Central Intelligence Agency. <http://www.cia.gov/cia/publications/factbook/geos/ni.html>

Chafe, Wallace L 1993 Prosodic and functional units of language. Edwards & Lampert (eds), 33-43.

Chaudenson, Robert 1974 *Le lexique du parler créole de la Réunion.* Paris: Champion, 2 vols.

—— 1979 *Les créoles français.* Paris: Nathan.

—— 1992 *Des îles, des hommes, des langues: Essai sur la créolisation linguistique et culturelle.* Paris: L'Harmattan.

Cheshire, Jenny (ed.) 1991 *English around the World. Sociolinguistic Perspectives.* Cambridge: Cambridge University Press.

Couper-Kuhlen, Elizabeth 1986 *An Introduction to English Prosody.* Tübingen: Niemeyer.

Craig, Dennis R 1977 Creole languages and primary education. Valdman, Albert (ed.) *Pidgin and Creole Linguistics.* Bloomington: Indiana University Press. 313-32.

—— 1980 Models for educational policy in creole-speaking communities. Valdman & Highfield (eds) 245-65.

Crozier, D H & Blench, R (eds) 1992 *An Index of Nigerian Languages.* Dallas: Summer Institute of Linguistics, 2nd edn.

Cruttenden, Alan 1997 *Intonation.* Cambridge: Cambridge University Press, 2nd edn.

Crystal, David & Davy, Derek 1969 *Investigating English Style*. London: Longman.

Cyffer, Norbert 1982 Sprachpolitik in Nigeria - Realität oder Utopie? Bruchhaus, Eva-Maria (ed.) *Afrikanische Eliten zwanzig Jahre nach Erlangung der Unabhängigkeit*. Hamburg: Buske. 187-200.

Dada, Ayorinde 1985 The new language policy in Nigeria: Its problems and its chances of success. Wolfson, Nessa & Manes, Joan (eds) *Language of Inequality*. Amsterdam: Mouton, 285-93.

Dadzie, A B K 1985 Pidgin in Ghana: A theoretical consideration of its origin and development. Ugboajah (ed.), 113-21.

—— 1990 Meaning in Pidgin English in Nigeria: Its processes and function. Eruvbetine (ed.), 23-29.

DeCamp, David 1971 Toward a generative analysis of a post-creole speech continuum. Hymes (ed.) 349-70.

Dejean, Yves 1983 Diglossia revisited: French and Creole in Haiti. *Word* 34: 189-213.

—— 1993 An overview of the language situation in Haiti. *International Journal of the Sociology of Language* 102: 73-83.

Deuber, Dagmar 1998 Nigerian Pidgin: Current sociolinguistic status and prospects for development. MA thesis, University of Freiburg.

—— 2002 'First year of nation's return to government of make you talk your own make I talk my own': Anglicisms versus pidginization in news translations into Nigerian Pidgin. *English World-Wide* 23: 195-222.

Deuber, Dagmar & Oloko, Patrick 2003 Linguistic and literary development of Nigerian Pidgin: The contribution of radio drama. Mair, Christian (ed.) *The Politics of English as a World Language: New Horizons in Postcolonial Cultural Studies*. Amsterdam: Rodopi, 289-303.

Devonish, Hubert 1991 Standardisation in a creole continuum situation: The Guyana case. Cheshire, J (ed.) 585-94.

Donwa-Ifode, Shirley 1984 Is Nigerian Pidgin English creolizing? *Journal of the Linguistic Association of Nigeria* 2: 199-203.

Du Bois, J W, Schuetze-Coburn, S, Cumming, S, & Paolino, D 1993 Outline of discourse transcription. Edwards & Lampert (eds), 45-89.

Ebam, Oru O 1990 On the search for a lingua franca in Nigeria: a case for the minority language option. Eruvbetine (ed.), 105-12.

Edwards, Jane A & Lampert, Martin D (eds) 1993 *Talking Data: Transcription and Coding in Discourse Research*. Hillsdale: Lawrence Erlbaum.

Egbe, D 1980 Some Linguistic Characteristics of Nigerian Pidgin English. *Lagos Review of English Studies* 2: 53-76.

Elugbe, Ben 1995 Nigerian Pidgin: Problems and prospects. Bamgbose, Banjo, & Thomas (eds) 284-306.

—— & Omamor, Augusta P 1991 *Nigerian Pidgin: Background and Prospects*. Ibadan: Heinemann.

Emenanjo, E Nolue 1975 Central Igbo - An objective appraisal. Ogbalu, F C & Emenanjo, E N (eds) *Igbo Language and Culture*. Ibadan: Oxford University Press. 114-37.

―― 1991 Language modernization from the grass-roots: the Nigerian experience. Cyffer, N, Schubert, K, Weier, H-I, & Wolff, E (eds) *Language Standardization in Africa*. Hamburg: Buske. 157-64.

―― (ed.) 1990 *Multilingualism, Minority Languages, and Language Policy in Nigeria*. Agbor: Central Books.

Eruvbetine, Agwonorobo E (ed.) 1990 *Aesthetics and Utilitarianism in Languages and Literatures*. Ojo: Lagos State University, Dept. of Languages and Literatures.

Essien, Okon 1995 The English language and code-mixing: a case study of the phenomenon in Ibibio. Bamgbose, Banjo, & Thomas (eds) 269-83.

Eze, Smart N 1980 *Nigerian Pidgin Sentence Complexity*. Vienna: Afro-Pub.

Ezenwa-Ohaeto 1988 *I Wan Bi President: Poems in Formal and Pidgin English*. Enugu: Delta Publications.

―― 1998 *If to say I Be Soja: Poems in Pidgin English*. Enugu: Delta Publications.

Falola, Toyin 1999 *The History of Nigeria*. Westport: Greenwood.

Faraclas, Nicholas 1984 Rivers Pidgin English: Tone, stress, or pitch-accent language? *Studies in the Linguistic Sciences* 14: 67-76.

―― 1986 Pronouns, creolization and decreolization in Nigerian Pidgin: A pilot study. *Journal of West African Languages* 16.2: 3-8.

―― 1987 Creolization and the tense-aspect-modality system of Nigerian Pidgin. *Journal of African Languages and Linguistics* 9: 45-59.

―― 1988 Nigerian Pidgin and the languages of southern Nigeria. *Journal of Pidgin and Creole Languages* 3: 177-97.

―― 1991 The pronoun system in Nigerian Pidgin: A preliminary study. Cheshire (ed.), 509-18.

―― 1996 *Nigerian Pidgin*. London: Routledge.

――, Ibim, O, Worukwo, G, Minah, A, & Tariah, A 1984 Rivers State Pidgin English. *Journal of the Linguistic Association of Nigeria* 2: 187-98.

Fasold, Ralph 1984 *The Sociolinguistics of Society*. Oxford: Blackwell.

―― 1990 *The Sociolinguistics of Language*. Oxford: Blackwell.

―― 1997 Motivations and attitudes influencing vernacular literacy: Four African assessments. Tabouret-Keller, Le Page, Gardner-Chloros, & Varro (eds), 264-70.

Fayer, Joan M 1990 Nigerian Pidgin English in old Calabar in the 18th and 19th centuries. Singler, John V (ed.) *Pidgin and Creole tense-mood-aspect systems*. Amsterdam: Benjamins, 185-202.

Federal Republic of Nigeria 1998 *National Policy on Education*. Lagos: NERDC Press, 3rd edn.

―― 1999 *Constitution of the Federal Republic of Nigeria 1999*. Lagos.

Ferguson, Charles A 1959 Diglossia. *Word* 15: 325-40.

―― 1968 Language development. Fishman, Ferguson, & Das Gupta (eds), 27-35.

Fishman, Joshua A 1967 Bilingualism with and without diglossia; diglossia with and without bilingualism. *Journal of Social Issues* 23.2: 29-38.

―― 1971 National languages and languages of wider communication in the developing nations. Whiteley, W H (ed.) *Language Use and Social Change: Problems of Multilingualism with Special Reference to Eastern Africa*. London: Oxford University Press, 27-56.

——, Ferguson, C A, & Das Gupta, J (eds) 1968 *Language Problems of Developing Nations.* New York: Wiley.

—— & Lovas, John 1970 Bilingual education in sociolinguistic perspective. *TESOL Quarterly* 4: 215-22.

——, Tabouret-Keller, A, Clyne, M, Krishnamurti, B, & Abdulaziz, M (eds) 1986 *The Fergusonian Impact: In Honor of Charles A. Ferguson on the Occasion of His 65th Birthday.* Vol. 2: *Sociolinguistics and the Sociology of Language.* Berlin: Mouton de Gruyter.

Forde, Daryll (ed.) 1956 *Efik Traders of Old Calabar.* London: Oxford University Press.

Gani-Ikilama, T O 1990 Use of Nigerian Pidgin in education? Why not? Emenanjo (ed.) 219-27.

Gilman, Charles 1979 Cameroonian Pidgin English, a neo-African language. Hancock, I F (ed.) *Readings in Creole Studies.* Ghent: Story-Scientia. 269-80.

Goke-Pariola, Abiodun 1983 Code-mixing among Yoruba-English bilinguals. *Anthropological Linguistics* 25: 39-46.

Görlach, Manfred 1991 Scotland and Jamaica: Bidialectal or bilingual? Görlach, *Englishes: Studies in Varieties of English 1984-1988.* Amsterdam: Benjamins. 69-89.

—— 1994 Texts: Broken English from Old Calabar. *English World-Wide* 15: 249-52.

—— 1998 Nigerian English: Broken, pidgin, creole and regional standard? Görlach, *Even More Englishes: Studies 1996-1997.* Amsterdam: Benjamins. 119-51.

Greenbaum, Sidney (ed.) 1996 *Comparing English Worldwide: The International Corpus of English.* Oxford: Clarendon.

Grimes, Barbara (ed.) 2000 *Ethnologue: Languages of the World.* Dallas: Summer Institute of Linguistics. 14th edn (web ed. <http://www.ethnologue.com>).

Gumperz, John J 1982 *Discourse Strategies.* Cambridge: Cambridge University Press.

—— & Berenz, Norine 1993 Transcribing conversational exchanges. Edwards & Lampert (eds) 91-121.

Hall, Robert A 1962 The life cycle of pidgin languages. *Lingua* 11: 151-56.

—— 1966 *Pidgin and Creole Languages.* Ithaca: Cornell University Press.

Hancock, Ian F 1986 The domestic hypothesis, diffusion and componentiality: An account of Atlantic anglophone creole origins. Muysken, Pieter & Smith, Norval (eds) *Substrata versus Universals in Creole Genesis: Papers from the Amsterdam Creole Workshop, April 1985.* Amsterdam: Benjamins. 71-102.

Haugen, Einar 1950 The analysis of linguistic borrowing. *Language* 26: 210-31.

—— 1953 *The Norwegian Language in America: A Study in Bilingual Behavior.* Vol. 2: *The American Dialects of Norwegian.* Philadelphia: University of Pennsylvania Press.

Haust, Delia & Dittmar, Norbert 1998 Taxonomic or functional models in the description of codeswitching? Evidence from Mandinka and Wolof in African contact situations. Jacobson, Rodolfo (ed.) *Codeswitching Worldwide.* Berlin: Mouton de Gruyter. 79-90.

Hellinger, Marlis 1986 On writing English-related Creoles in the Caribbean. Görlach, M & Holm, J (eds) *Focus on the Caribbean.* Amsterdam: Benjamins. 53-70.

Holm, John A 1988 *Pidgins and Creoles.* Vol. 1: *Theory and Structure.* Cambridge: Cambridge University Press.

—— 1989 *Pidgins and Creoles* Vol. 2: *Reference Survey.* Cambridge: Cambridge: Cambridge University Press.

Huber, Magnus 1999 *Ghanaian Pidgin English in Its West African Context: A Sociohistorical and Structural Analysis.* Amsterdam: Benjamins.

—— & Görlach, Manfred 1996 Texts: West African Pidgin English. *English World-Wide* 17: 239-58.

Hudson, Richard A 1996 *Sociolinguistics.* Cambridge: Cambridge University Press, 2nd edn.

Hymes, Dell (ed.) 1971 *Pidginization and Creolization of Languages.* Cambridge: Cambridge University Press.

Jibril, Munzali 1990 Minority languages and lingua francas in Nigerian education. Emenanjo (ed.), 109-17.

—— 1995 The elaboration of the functions of Nigerian Pidgin. Bamgbose, Banjo, & Thomas (eds) 232-47.

Johnson, Alex C 1992 Varieties of Krio and standard Krio. Jones, E D, Sandred, K I & Shrimpton, N (eds) *Reading and Writing Krio.* Stockholm: Almqvist & Wiksell. 21-30.

Johnson, Bruce C 1978 Stable triglossia at Larteh, Ghana. *West African Journal of Modern Languages* 3: 128-36.

Jones, Frederick C 1990 The development of the *#s* plural in Sierra Leone Krio. Edmondson, J A, Feagin, C, & Mühlhäusler, P (eds) *Development and Diversity: Language Variation across Time and Space.* Dallas: Summer Institute of Linguistics. 309-22.

Jowitt, David 1991 *Nigerian English Usage: An Introduction.* Lagos: Longman Nigeria.

—— 1995 Nigeria's national language question: Choices and constraints. Bamgbose, Banjo, & Thomas (eds), 34-56.

Klein, Wolfgang 1986 *Second Language Acquisition.* Cambridge: Cambridge University Press.

Kloss, Heinz 1969 *Research Possibilities on Group Bilingualism: A Report.* Quebec: International Center for Research on Bilingualism.

Kotey, Paul F & Der-Houssikian, Haig (eds) 1977 *Language and Linguistic Problems in Africa.* Columbia: Hornbeam.

Labov, William 1966 *The Social Stratification of English in New York City.* Washington, DC: Center for Applied Linguistics.

—— 1982 Building on empirical foundations. Lehmann, W P & Malkiel, Y (eds) *Perspectives on Historical Linguistics.* Amsterdam: Benjamins. 17-92.

—— 1994 *Principles of Linguistic Change.* Vol. 1: *Internal Factors.* Oxford: Blackwell.

—— 2001 *Principles of Linguistic Change.* Vol. 2: *Social Factors.* Oxford: Blackwell.

Lafont, Robert 1971 Un problème de culpabilité sociologique: la diglossie franco-occitane. *Langue française* 9: 93-99.

Lavandera, Beatriz R 1978 Where does the sociolinguistic variable stop? *Language in Society* 7: 171-82.

Lawton, David 1980 Language attitude, discreteness, and code-shifting in Jamaican Creole. *English World-Wide* 1: 211-26.

Lefebvre, Claire 1974 Discreteness and the linguistic continuum in Martinique. *Anthropological Linguistics* 16: 47-78.

Le Page, Robert B & Tabouret-Keller, Andrée 1985 *Acts of Identity. Creole-Based Approaches to Language and Ethnicity.* Cambridge: Cambridge University Press.

Mackey, William F 1986 The polyglossic spectrum. Fishman, Joshua A et al. (eds), 237-43.

Madaki, Rufa'i Omar 1983 *A Linguistic and Pragmatic Analysis of Hausa-English Code-Switching*. PhD thesis, University of Michigan. Ann Arbor: UMI.

Mafeni, Bernard 1971 Nigerian Pidgin. Spencer, John (ed.) *The English Language in West Africa*. London: Longman, 95-112.

Mair, Christian 1992 The new Englishes and stylistic innovation: Ken Saro-Wiwa's *Sozaboy: A Novel in Rotten English*. Collier, Gordon (ed.) *Us/Them: Translation, Transcription and Identity in Post-Colonial Literary Cultures*. Amsterdam: Rodopi. 277-87.

—— 1993 Can Caliban be made to speak German? On some problems arising in the translation of African writing in English, with special reference to Wole Soyinka's *The Road*. Fill, A, Bahn-Coblans, S, Ganner-Rauth, H, & Ramsey-Kurz, H (eds) *New-Found-Lands: Festschrift für Harro Heinz Kühnelt zum 70. Geburtstag*. Tübingen: Narr. 219-29.

Mann, Charles C 1993a Polysemic functionality of prepositions in pidgins and creoles: The case of 'fọ̀' in Anglo-Nigerian Pidgin. Byrne, F, & Holm, J (eds) *Atlantic Meets Pacific: A Global View of Pidginization and Creolization*. Amsterdam: Benjamins. 57-67.

—— 1993b The sociolinguistic status of Anglo-Nigerian Pidgin: An overview. *International Journal of the Sociology of Language* 100-101: 167-78.

—— 1996 Anglo-Nigerian Pidgin in Nigerian education: A survey of policy, practice and attitudes. In Hickey, T & Williams, J (eds) *Language, Education and Society in a Changing World*. Dublin: IRAAL/Multilingual Matters. 93-106.

—— 1998 Language, mass communication and national development: the role, perceptions and potential of Anglo-Nigerian Pidgin in the Nigerian mass media. International Conference on Language in Development (3rd (1997: Langkawi, Malaysia)). *Language in Development: Access, Empowerment, Opportunity*. Kuala Lumpur: National Institute of Public Administration, 136-44.

—— 2000 Reviewing ethnolinguistic vitality: The case of Anglo-Nigerian Pidgin. *Journal of Sociolinguistics* 4: 458-74.

—— 2001 Anglo-Nigerian Pidgin in competition: a survey of female attitudes in urban, southern Nigeria. Paper presented at the Nigerian Millennium Sociolinguistics Conference, Lagos, 16-18 August.

McWhorter, John 1995 Sisters under the skin: a case for genetic relationship between the Atlantic English-based creoles". *Journal of Pidgin and Creole Languages* 10: 289-333.

—— 1998 Identifying the creole prototype: Vindicating a typological class. *Language* 74: 788-818.

—— 2000 Defining 'creole' as a synchronic term. Neumann-Holzschuh & Schneider (eds) 85-123.

Milroy, Lesley 1987 *Observing and Analysing Natural Language: A Critical Acount of Sociolinguistic Method*. Oxford: Blackwell.

Modigie, Clara Bolanle 1997 A descriptive linguistic analysis of Pidgin in Nigerian public health enlightenment literature. MA thesis, University of Benin.

Moravcsik, Edith A 1978 Language contact. Greenberg, J H (ed.) *Universals of Human Language.* Vol. 1: *Method and Theory.* Stanford: Stanford University Press. 95-122.

Moser, Claus A & Kalton, Graham 1971 *Survey Methods in Social Investigation.* London: Heinemann, 2nd edn.

Mufwene, Salikoko S 1986a Les langues créoles peuvent-elles être définies sans allusion à leur histoire? *Études créoles* 9: 135-50.

—— 1986b Number delimitation in Gullah. *American Speech* 61: 33-60.

—— 1994 On decreolization. The case of Gullah. Morgan, Marcyliena (ed.) *Language and the Social Construction of Identity in Creole Situations.* Los Angeles: Center for Afro-American Studies, 63-99.

—— 1996 The founder principle in creole genesis. *Diachronica* 13: 83-134.

—— 1997 Jargons, pidgins, creoles and koines: What are they? Spears, Arthur K & Winford, Donald (eds) *The Structure and Status of Pidgins and Creoles: Including Selected Papers from the Meetings of the Society for Pidgin and Creole Linguistics.* Amsterdam: Benjamins. 35-69.

—— 2000 Creolization is a social, not a structural, process. Neumann-Holzschuh & Schneider (eds) 65-84.

—— 2001 *The Ecology of Language Evolution.* Cambridge: Cambridge University Press.

Mühlhäusler, Peter 1981 The development of the category of number in Tok Pisin. Muysken, Pieter (ed.) *Generative Studies on Creole Languages.* Dordrecht: Foris, 35-84.

—— 1982 Tok Pisin in Papua New Guinea. Bailey, Richard W & Görlach, Manfred (eds) *English as a World Language.* Ann Arbor: University of Michigan Press, 439-66.

—— 1986 English in contact with Tok Pisin (Papua New Guinea). Viereck & Bald (eds) 550-70.

—— 1993 The role of pidgin and creole languages in language progression and regression. Hyltenstam, K & Viberg, Å (eds) *Progression and Regression in Language.* Cambridge: Cambridge University Press. 39-67.

—— 1997 *Pidgin and Creole Linguistics.* Expanded and revised edition. London: University of Westminster Press.

Muysken, Pieter 1984 Linguistic dimensions of language contact. The state of the art in interlinguistics. *Revue québécoise de linguistique* 14.1: 49-76.

Myers-Scotton, Carol 1992 Comparing codeswitching and borrowing. *Journal of Multilingual and Multicultural Development* 13: 19-39.

—— 1993a Common and uncommon ground: social and structural factors in codeswitching. *Language in Society* 22: 475-503.

—— 1993b *Duelling Languages: Grammatical Structure in Codeswitching.* Oxford: Clarendon.

—— 1993c *Social Motivations for Codeswitching: Evidence from Africa.* Oxford: Clarendon.

National Population Commission [Nigeria]. 2000. *Nigeria Demographic and Health Survey 1999.* Calverton, Maryland: National Population Commission and ORC/Macro.

Ndolo, Ike S 1989 The case for promoting the Nigerian Pidgin language. *Journal of Modern African Studies* 27: 679-84.

Ndukwe, Pat 1982 Standardizing Nigerian languages. *Journal of the Linguistic Association of Nigeria* 1: 141-46.

Nelson, Gerald 1996 The design of the corpus. Greenbaum (ed.) 27-53.

Neumann-Holzschuh, Ingrid & Schneider, Edgar W (eds) 2000 *Degrees of Restructuring in Creole Languages.* Amsterdam: Benjamins.

"Nigeria" 2003 *Africa South of the Sahara 2004.* London: Europa, 817-57, 33rd edn.

Nitzl, Irene 1999 *Formen und Funktionen des Pidgin im zeitgenössischen nigerianischen Drama.* Aachen: Shaker.

Nwachukwu-Agbada, J O J 1990 Nigerian Pidgin proverbs. *Lore and Language* 9.1: 37-43.

Nwoga, Donatus I 1994 From dialectal dichotomy to Igbo standard development. Ogbaa, Kalu (ed.) *The Gong and the Flute: African Literary Development and Celebration.* Westport: Greenwood. 103-17.

Nwoye, Onuigbo Gregory 1993 Code-switching as a conscious discourse strategy: Evidence from Igbo. *Multilingua* 12: 365-85.

Obilade, Anthony 1978 The stylistic function of Pidgin English in African literature: Achebe and Soyinka. *Research in African Literatures* 9: 433-44.

—— 1980 Pidgin English as a medium of instruction: the Nigerian experience. *Africana Marburgensia* 13.1: 59-69.

O'Connor, Anthony 1983 *The African City.* London: Hutchinson.

Odlin, Terence 1989 *Language Transfer: Cross-Linguistic Influence in Language Learning.* Cambridge: Cambridge University Press.

O'Donnell, William Robert & Todd, Loreto 1991 *Variety in Contemporary English.* London: HarperCollins, 2nd edn.

Ofuani, Ogo A 1981a Future time expression in Nigerian Pidgin. *Papers in Linguistics: International Journal of Human Communication* 14: 309-26.

—— 1981b Pidgin in Nigerian journalism. *Papers in Linguistics: International Journal of Human Communication* 14: 327-46.

Ofuokwu, Dili 1990 Ethnolinguistic vitality and language planning: The Nigerian situation". Emenanjo (ed.), 73-80.

Oladejo, James 1991 The national language question in Nigeria: Is there an answer? *Language Problems and Language Planning* 15: 256-67.

Oloruntoba, Christiana Iyetunde 1992 *Sociocultural Dimensions of Nigerian Pidgin Usage (Western Niger Delta of Nigeria).* PhD thesis, Indiana University. Ann Arbor: UMI.

Omamor, Augusta P 1997 New wine in old bottles? A case study of Ẹnpi in relation to the use currently made of it in literature. *Arbeiten aus Anglistik und Amerikanistik* 22: 219-33.

Oreh, O O 1985 *Masquerade* and other plays on Nigerian television. Ugboajah (ed.), 108-12.

Osaji, Debe 1991 The place of broadcasting translation in multilingual Nigeria. *Babel* 37: 54-62.

Parkvall, Mikael 2000 Reassessing the role of demographics in language restructuring. Neumann-Holzschuh & Schneider (eds) 185-213.

Pasch, Helma 1997 The choice of lingua francae in triglossic environments in Africa. Pütz, Martin (ed.) *Language Choices: Conditions, Constraints, and Consequences.* Amsterdam: Benjamins. 45-54.

Patrick, Peter L 1997 Style and register in Jamaican Patwa. Schneider, Edgar W (ed.) *Englishes around the World: Studies in Honour of Manfred Görlach.* Vol. 2: *Caribbean, Africa, Asia, Australasia.* Amsterdam: Benjamins, 41-55.

—— 1999 *Urban Jamaican Creole: Variation in the Mesolect.* Amsterdam: Benjamins.

Peil, Margaret 1991 *Lagos: The City is the People.* London: Belhaven.

Poplack, Shana 1980 Sometimes I'll start a sentence in Spanish Y TERMINO EN ESPAÑOL: Toward a typology of code-switching". *Linguistics* 18: 581-618.

—— 1985 Contrasting patterns of code-switching in two communities. Warkentyne, H J (ed.) *Papers from the Fifth International Conference on Methods in Dialectology,* 363-85.

—— & Sankoff, David 1984 Borrowing: the synchrony of integration". *Linguistics* 22: 99-135.

——, Sankoff, David, & Miller, Christopher 1988 The social correlates and linguistic processes of lexical borrowing and assimilation. *Linguistics* 26: 47-104.

—— & Tagliamonte, Sali 1996 Nothing in context: Variation, grammaticization and past time marking in Nigerian Pidgin English. Baker, Philip & Syea, Anand (eds) *Changing Meanings, Changing Functions.* London: University of Westminster Press, 71-94.

——, Wheeler, S & Westwood, A 1987 Distinguishing language contact phenomena: Evidence from Finnish-English bilingualism. Lilius, Pirkko & Saari, Mirja (eds) *The Nordic Languages and Modern Linguistics 6: Proceedings of the Sixth International Conference of Nordic and General Linguistics in Helsinki, August 18-22, 1986* Helsinki: Helsinki University Press, 33-56.

Quirk, R, Greenbaum, S, Leech, G, & Svartvik, J 1985 *A Comprehensive Grammar of the English Language.* London: Longman.

Rickford, John R 1979. *Variation in a Creole Continuum: Quantitative and Implicational Approaches.* PhD thesis, University of Pennsylvania. Ann Arbor: UMI.

—— 1980 Analyzing variation in creole languages. Valdman & Highfield (eds) 165-84.

—— 1983 What happens in decreolization. Anderson, Roger W (ed.) *Pidginization and Creolization as Language Acquisition.* Rowley: Newbury House, 298-319.

—— 1986 Some principles for the study of black and white speech in the South. Montgomery, Michael B & Bailey, Guy (eds) *Language Variety in the South: Perspectives in Black and White.* Alabama: University of Alabama Press, 38-62.

—— 1987 *Dimensions of a Creole Continuum: History, Texts and Linguistic Analysis of Guyanese Creole.* Stanford: Stanford University Press.

—— 1988 Connections between sociolinguistics and pidgin-creole studies. *International Journal of the Sociology of Language* 71: 51-57.

Romaine, Suzanne 1981 *On the Problem of Syntactic Variation: A Reply to Beatriz Lavandera and William Labov.* Austin: Southwest Educational Development Laboratory.

—— 1984 On the problem of syntactic variation and pragmatic meaning in sociolinguistic theory. *Folia Linguistica* 14: 409-37.

—— 1992 *Language, Education and Development: Urban and Rural Tok Pisin in Papua New Guinea.* Oxford: Clarendon.

—— 1995 *Bilingualism.* Oxford: Blackwell, 2nd edn.

Rufai, Abba 1977 The Question of a national language in Nigeria: Problems and prospects". Kotey & Der-Houssikian (eds), 68-83.

Samarin, William J 1971 Salient and substantive pidginization. Hymes (ed.) 117-40.

Sankoff, Gillian 1973 Above and beyond phonology in variable rules. Bailey C-J N & Shuy, R W (eds) *New Ways of Analyzing Variation in English.* Washington, DC: Georgetown University Press, 44-61.

—— 1977 Review of Bickerton, *Dynamics of a Creole System. Journal of Linguistics* 13: 292-306.

Saro-Wiwa, Ken 1985 *Sozaboy.* Port Harcourt: Saros.

Schmied, Josef 1991 *English in Africa: An Introduction.* London: Longman.

Schwegler, Armin 2000 The myth of decreolization: The anomalous case of Palenquero. Neumann-Holzschuh & Schneider (eds) 409-36.

Scotton, Carol Myers 1975 Multilingualism in Lagos - What it means to the social scientist. Herbert, Robert K (ed.) *Patterns in Language, Culture, and Society: Sub-Saharan Africa.* Columbus: Ohio University Press. 78-90.

—— 1983 The negotiation of identities in conversation: A theory of markedness and code choice. *International Journal of the Sociology of Language* 44: 115-36.

—— 1986 Diglossia and code switching. Fishman et al. (eds), 403-15.

—— 1988a Code switching and types of multilingual communities. Lowenberg, Peter H (ed.) *Language Spread and Language Policy.* Washington, DC: Georgetown University Press 61-82.

—— 1988b Code switching as indexical of social negotiations. Heller, Monica (ed.) *Code-switching: Anthropological and Sociolinguistic Perspectives.* Berlin: Mouton de Gruyter. 151-86.

Sebba, Mark 1997 *Contact Languages: Pidgins and Creoles.* Basingstoke: Macmillan.

Shnukal, Anna & Marchese, Lynell 1983 Creolization of Nigerian Pidgin English: A progress report. *English World-Wide* 4: 17-26.

Shuy, Roger W (ed.) 1973 *Sociolinguistics: Current Trends and Prospects.* Washington, DC: Georgetown University Press.

Siegel, Jeff 1997 Pidgin and English in Melanesia: is there a continuum? *World Englishes* 16: 185-204.

Simpson, Ekundayo 1985 Translating in the Nigerian mass media: A sociolinguistic study. Ugboajah (ed.) 133-52.

Singler, John Victor 1997 The configuration of Liberia's Englishes. *World Englishes* 16: 205-31.

Smith, Geoff P 2000 Tok Pisin and English: The current relationship. Siegel, Jeff (ed.) *Processes of Language Contact: Studies from Australia and the South Pacific.* Quebec: Fides. 271-91.

—— 2002 *Growing up with Tok Pisin: Contact, Creolization and Change in Papua New Guinea's National Language.* London: Battlebridge.

Statistisches Bundesamt [Federal Statistical Office, Germany] 1983 *Länderkurzbericht Nigeria 1983.* Stuttgart: Kohlhammer.

―― 1993 *Länderbericht Nigeria 1992.* Stuttgart: Metzler-Poeschel.

Stewart, William A 1964 Urban Negro speech: Sociolinguistic factors affecting English teaching. Shuy, Roger W (ed.) *Social Dialects and Language Learning: Proceedings of the Bloomington, Indiana, Conference 1964.* Champaign: National Council of Teachers of English, 10-18.

Swigart, Leigh 1994 Cultural creolisation and language use in post-colonial Africa: The case of Senegal. *Africa* 64: 175-89.

Tabouret-Keller, A, Le Page, R B, Gardner-Chloros, P & Varro, G (eds) 1997 *Vernacular Literacy: A Re-Evaluation.* Oxford: Clarendon.

Tagliamonte, Sali A 2000 The story of *kom* in Nigerian Pidgin English. McWhorter, John (ed.) *Language Change and Language Contact in Pidgins and Creoles.* Amsterdam: Benjamins. 353-82.

――, Poplack, Shana & Eze, Ejike 1997 Plural marking patterns in Nigerian Pidgin English. *Journal of Pidgin and Creole Languages* 12: 103-29.

Thomason, Sarah G & Kaufman, Terrence 1988 *Language Contact, Creolization and Genetic Linguistics.* Berkeley: University of California Press.

Todd, Loreto 1974 *Pidgins and Creoles.* London: Routledge.

―― 1994 Pidgins and creoles. Asher, R E (ed.) 1994 *The Encyclopedia of Language and Linguistics.* Oxford: Pergamon, 10 vols, 3177-81.

―― & Jumbam, Martin 1992 Kamtok: Anatomy of a pidgin. *English Today* 29: 3-10.

Trudgill. Peter 1972 Sex, covert prestige and linguistic change in the urban British English of Norwich. *Language in Society* 1: 179-95.

―― 1995 *Sociolinguistics: An Introduction to Language and Society.* Harmondsworth: Penguin, revissed edition.

Ugboajah, Frank Okwu (ed.) 1985 *Mass Communication, Culture and Society in West Africa.* Oxford: Zell.

UNICEF, WHO, & UNESCO 1991 *True Word Dem for Beta Life: How to Make People Sabi Dem.* Lagos: UNICEF Nigeria Country Office. (Translated by Olatilo, B, Shaba, S, Okoru, O, & Okpala, C.)

UNICEF, WHO, UNESCO & UNFPA 1993 *Facts for Life: A Communication Challenge.* Oxford: P&LA, revised edition.

United Nations 2004 *Urban Agglomerations 2003.* New York: United Nations, Department of Social and Economic Affairs.
<http://www.un.org/esa/population/publications/wup2003/2003urban_agglo.htm>

Uwabor, Iwebunor 1995 *Radio Drama: Growth and Contributions to National Development.* Lagos: Vitanor Communications.

Uzoezie, Raphael Udeoye 1986 Code-mixing and code-switching in the speech of educated Igbo-English bilinguals: A socio-linguistic perspective. MA thesis, University of Lagos.

Valdman, Albert 1968 Language standardization in a diglossia situation: Haiti. Fishman, Ferguson & Das Gupta (eds) 313-26.

―― 1973 Some aspects of decreolization in Creole French. Sebeok, Thomas A (ed.) *Current Trends in Linguistics.* Vol. 11: *Diachronic, areal, and typological linguistics.* The Hague: Mouton. 507-35.

―― 1989 Aspects sociolinguistiques de l'élaboration d'une norme écrite pour le créole haitien". Ludwig, Ralph (ed.) *Les créoles français entre l'oral et l'écrit.* Tübingen: Narr. 43-63.

―― 1991 Decreolization or dialect contact in Haiti? Byrne, Francis & Huebner, Thom (eds) *Development and Structures of Creole Languages: Essays in Honor of Derek Bickerton.* 75-88.

―― & Highfield, Arnold (eds) 1980 *Theoretical Orientations in Creole Studies.* New York: Academic Press.

Verhaar, John W M 1995 *Toward a Reference Grammar of Tok Pisin: An Experiment in Corpus Linguistics.* Honolulu: University of Hawai'i Press.

Viereck, Wolfgang & Bald, Wolf-Dietrich (eds) 1986 *English in Contact with Other Languages: Studies in Honour of Broder Carstensen on the Occasion of His 60th Birthday.* Budapest: Akadémiai Kiadó.

Weiner, E Judith & Labov, William 1983 Constraints on the agentless passive. *Journal of Linguistics* 19: 29-58.

Weinreich, Uriel. 1953. *Languages in Contact: Findings and Problems.* The Hague: Mouton.

――, Labov, W & Herzog, M I 1968 Empirical foundations for a theory of language change. Lehmann, W P & Malkiel, Y (eds) *Directions for Historical Linguistics.* Austin: University of Texas Press, 95-188.

Whinnom, Keith 1971 Linguistic hybridization and the 'special case' of pidgins and creoles. Hymes (ed.) 91-115.

Whiteley, W H 1973 Sociolinguistic surveys at the national level. Shuy (ed.) 167-80.

Whitney, W D 1881 On mixture in language. *Transactions of the American Philological Association* 12: 5-26.

Williams, Wayne R 1975 Variation in the Krio speech community. Herbert, R K (ed.) *Proceedings of the Sixth Conference on African Linguistics.* Columbus: Ohio State University. 279-93.

Williamson, Kay 1990 Development of minority languages: Publishing problems and prospects. Emenanjo (ed.) 118-44.

Winford, Donald 1984 The linguistic variable and syntactic variation in creole continua. *Lingua* 62: 267-88.

―― 1991 The Caribbean. Cheshire (ed.) 565-84.

―― 1993 *Predication in Caribbean English Creoles.* Amsterdam: Benjamins.

―― 1997 Re-examining Caribbean English creole continua. *World Englishes* 16: 233-79.

Wolfram, Walt 1993 Identifying and interpreting variables. Preston, Dennis R (ed.) *American Dialect Research.* Amsterdam: Benjamins, 193-221.

Wurm, Stephen A 1980 Standardization and instrumentalization in Tok Pisin. Valdman & Highfield (eds) 237-44.

Youssi, Abderrahim 1995 The Moroccan triglossia: Facts and implications. *International Journal of the Sociology of Language* 112: 29-43.

Zabus, Chantal 1992 Mending the schizo-text: Pidgin in the Nigerian novel. *Kunapipi* 14: 119-27.

Index

A

Abdulaziz Mkilifi, M 30-31, 35, 53, 255
Abiodun, J 6-7, 255
Abuja 7
Achebe, C 22, 49, 196
accountability 41
Adedebu, R 71
Adedun, E 71
Adegbesan, R 71
Adegbija, E 4, 185, 187-88, 255
Adheke Joseph, G v, 93-94
Adekunle, M v, 46, 255
Adetugbo, A v
adjectives, adjective phrases 229-30, 239
adverbs, adverb phrases 230-31, 238
Africa(n) vi, 1-3, 8, 18, 25-26, 30-32, 49, 56, 185, 204, 208
African American 25
African languages 3; *see also* Nigerian (indigenous) languages, *and* Swahili.
Agbolade, M 247
Agege 7
Agheyisi, R 1, 3-5, 7, 10, 23, 43, 46, 49, 51, 53, 62-65, 70, 84, 86-88, 90, 95, 100-01, 103, 105, 107, 115-16, 121-23, 128, 130, 132, 134-35, 144, 190, 193, 198-99, 203, 207, 231, 234, 255
Aito, O 247
Aiyegbusi, T 53, 77
Ajayi, K 187
Ajegunle xi, 7, 55, 207, 247
Akere, F 48, 59, 61, 63, 255
Akinnaso, F 46-51, 255
Akwa Ibom State ix, 76
Alaba, O 11
Alleyne, M 18, 25, 107, 255
American 27
Amerindian 14
Amuda, A 59-63, 255
anglophone Caribbean 14, 16-18, 20, 22-23, 28-29, 155-56, 180, 202, 204
Anyokwu, C 71
Apapa 7, 55
Arabic 29-30, 192

Atlantic Creoles 106-07, 113, 128; *see also* Caribbean Creoles, and under individual or place names: Barbados, Dominica, Gullah, Guadeloupe, Guyanese, Haitian, Jamaican, Krio, Martinique, Saint Lucia, Surinam, Trinidad
Awonusi, V 64-65, 184, 185-89, 255
Aworawo, D 71, 248

B

Bailey, B 16, 256
Baker, P vi, 19, 21-22, 191, 256
Bamgbose, A 46-50, 63-64, 77, 92, 192, 196, 256
Banjo, A 59, 61-65, 179, 205-07, 256
Barbados 14, 19
Barbag-Stoll, A 49, 256
Barbour, K xi, 256
Bariga market ii, xiii
Belize 14, 16
Bendel State viii, 3, 51, 108, 196, 198
Benin (City) viii, 5, 189, 246
Berenz, N 79
Biber, D 43, 256
Bickerton, D 15-16, 18-22, 25-26, 28, 40-41, 108, 119, 124, 130, 135, 169, 202-03, 205, 256-57
Blench, R 46
Blom, J-P 32, 34, 257
Bokamba, E 32, 257
Borno State viii, 48
borrowing 16, 35-39, 80, 82, 84, 87-89, 95, 103, 105, 120, 142, 155, 158, 179-81, 202-03
Bourgault, L 49, 257
Brann, C 46, 52, 257
Brenzinger, M 208, 257
British 2-3, 21, 26-27, 100, 197
Broken (English) 1, 49, 67, 69, 124, 163, 203
Brosnahan, L 65, 257

C

Calabar viii, 3, 5, 7, 45, 124, 183, 246
Cameroon(ian) (Pidgin) 2-3, 23-25, 27
Canada 5
Canadian French 38, 40, 85
Carayol, M 21, 257
Caribbean (Creoles) 6, 14, 19, 21-25, 27, 125, 130, 134, 155, 197, 201; *see also* Atlantic Creoles, and under individual or place names: Barbados, Dominica, Guadeloupe, Guyanese, Haitian, Jamaican, Martinique, Saint Lucia, Trinidad
CD details iv, 247-48 (The CD is located inside the back cover.)
Central Intelligence Agency 46, 257
Chafe, W 79, 257
Chandy, H 252
Chaudenson, R 19, 21, 257
Christian 49, 86, 170-71, 178
code choice 59-63
code-mixing 32, 242
code-shifting 16-17, 32
code-switching 32-36, 59-63, 79-80, 136-44, 155, 181, 204, 242-43
comparatives 131-33, 235
conjunctions 61, 103-05, 232
constitution 46-47, 50
contact studies 14, 59
continuum 13-25, 27-29, 36, 40, 42, 119, 130, 134, 155-56, 169, 179-81, 198, 201-05
copula 63-64, 127-30
Corne, C 19, 21
corpus 71-78, 80-82, 140, 147-48
corpus planning 191-200
Couper-Kuhlen, E 79, 257
Craig, D 190-91, 257
Creole/creolization 1, 13-16, 18, 20, 22-23, 25, 36, 39-40, 55-56 114, 155, 199, 202-03
Cross River (State) viii, 1, 3, 51, 76

Crozier, D 46, 257
Cruttenden, A 79, 257
Crystal, D 43, 258
Cyffer, N 185, 258

D

Dada, A 50, 185-87, 189, 258
Dadzie, A 56, 193, 258
Davy, D 43, 258
DeCamp, D 15-18, 20, 22, 25, 203, 205, 258
decreolization 13-14, 18-20, 22-23, 25, 36, 42, 108, 202-05, 208
Dejean, Y 20
Delta, *see* Delta State or Niger Delta
Delta State 76, 156, 161, 195
demography 19, 20
depidginization 202-05, 208
determiners 105-06, 232-33
Deuber, D 45, 74, 94, 140, 145-47, 157-58, 162-63, 183, 200, 247-48, 258
Deutscher Akademischer Austauschdienst v
Devonish, H 198, 258
Dibie, M 71
Diejomaoh, E 71
diglossia 20, 29, 52, 59, 207
discourse features 136-146, 235-37, 241
Dittmar, N 30
Dominica 14
Donwa-Ifode, S 4, 47, 56, 258
Du Bois, J 79, 258

E

Ebam, O 185, 258
Ebhomien, E 71
Ebute Metta xi, 162
Edime, Mr v
Edo x, 46, 52, 76, 195
education 8, 22, 48, 65, 71-159, 161-77, 181, 184, 189-90, 242, 247
Edwards, J 9, 258
Efik x, 46, 52, 76
Egbe, D 4, 193, 258
Egwu, A 71
Ejeh, S v
Elugbe, B 2-5, 7, 9-10, 46-47, 51, 53, 103, 105, 107-08, 115-16, 122, 128, 180, 184, 187, 193-94, 258
Emananjo, E 52, 258
English [Comparison is made between NigP and English throughout the entire book so no individual page references are given.]
English-based P/Cs 14, 21-22, 24, 29, 107, 109, 130, 205; *see also* Barbados, Cameroonian PE, Dominica, Ghanaian PE, Gullah, Guyanese, Jamaican, Krio, Kru PE, Liberian, Melanesian PE, Saint Lucia, Surinam, Tok Pisin, Trinidad, West African PE
English World-Wide xii
Esan x, 76, 195
Esi, S v, 193, 198, 248
Essien, O 59, 61-62, 259
European 1-3, 18-19, 25-27, 204
expanded pidgin(s) 1, 13
Eze, S 4-5, 103-05, 108-10, 179, 193, 259
Ezenwa-Ohaeto 254, 259

F

Falola, T ix, 259
Family Planning posters 58
Faraclas, N 2-5, 9-10, 23-24, 46, 87-91, 100-01, 103-06, 108-09, 115-16, 120-123, 126-29, 132, 134-35, 144, 170, 179-80, 193-94, 198, 204, 231, 233, 259
Fasold, R 30, 56, 192, 259
Fayer, J 124, 259
Federal Republic of Nigeria 259
Ferguson, C 20, 29-31, 52, 191, 199, 259
FESTAC Town 176-77
Fishman, J 30, 185, 190, 259-60
Forde, D 2, 124, 260
France 21
Freetown 2, 26
French 20-22, 24, 29, 38, 48, 208
French-based Creole(s) 14, 20-22; *see also* Dominica, Guadeloupe, Haitian, Indian Ocean Creoles, Martinique, Mauritius, Reunion, Rodrigues, Saint Lucia, Seychelles.
Fulfulde x, 46

G

Gambia 26
Gandu Street 53
Gani-Ikilama, T 4, 184, 190, 260
gender 56-57, 72, 76
German 2
Ghana(ian) (Pidgin) 3, 14, 24-27, 56-57, 105, 129
Gilman, C 52, 260
Goke-Pariola, A 59, 61, 260
Gold Coast, *see* Ghana
Görlach, M 5, 32, 87, 157, 197, 201, 260-61
grammar 78, 80, 99-135, 147
graphization, *see* orthography
Greek 29
Greenbaum, S 100, 260
Grimes, B 46, 260
Guadeloupe 21
Gullah 27, 107-08
Gumperz, J 32, 34, 79, 137-38, 140, 257, 260
Guosa 185
Guyana, Guyanese 14-18, 21-22, 40-42, 119, 124, 130, 134-35, 169, 205

H

Haitian Creole 20-21, 29, 197
Hall, R 18, 191, 260
Hancock, I 26-27, 260
Haugen, E 35-36, 260
Hausa x, 45-46, 48-50, 52-53, 55, 61, 77, 84, 136, 163, 184-86, 188
Haust, D 30, 260
Heine, B 208, 257
Hellinger, M 197, 260
Herzog, M 41, 268
Hinrichs, L vi
Holm, J 1-3, 15, 21, 25, 27, 106-07, 128, 130, 260
Huber, M 2-3, 5, 7, 24, 26-27, 56-57, 87, 105, 129, 261
Hudson, R 23, 261

I

Ibadan viii, 186
Ibibio x, 61, 76
idiomatic expressions 235-37, 241
Ifukor, P 71
Igbo x, 45-46, 48-50, 52-53, 55, 60-61, 68, 76-77, 109, 136, 145, 161, 184-85, 188, 195-96, 198, 243

Ijo 2, 46, 52
Ikeja viii, xi, 7, 75
Ikoyi xi, 7
Ilorin viii, 187
Ilupeju xi, 75
implicational scaling 16-18, 21
Indian Ocean (Creoles) 21-22, 25-26
interference 16, 23, 39
interjections 231
interviews 247-48
IPA = International Phonetic Alphabet 9
I Salute Una 54
Islamic 77
Iyana-Ipaja expressway xiii
Izon x, 46

J

Jamaica(n) (Creole) 14-21, 24, 26-27, 42, 107, 124, 134, 158, 205
jargon 1-3
Jibril, M 5-6, 49, 108, 184, 261
John Benjamins Publishing Co. xii
Johnson, A 24, 261
Johnson, B 30, 261
Jones, F 107-08, 261
Jowitt, D 49-50, 52, 64-65, 137-38, 185, 189, 229, 261
Jumbam, M 24, 267

K

Kalton, G 45, 263
Kamerun, *see* Cameroon
Kamtok = Cameroonian (Pidgin English)
Kano viii, 52
Kanuri x, 46, 48
Kaufman, T 35-36, 155, 267
Ketu xi, 75
Kim, J ii
Klein, W 39, 261
Kloss, H 183, 261
Krio 1-4, 24-27, 107-08, 199, 204
Kru PE 25
Kwara State 161-62

L

Labov, W 39-41, 261, 268
Lafont, R 30, 261

Lagos viii, xi, 2-9, 11, 27, 45, 54-56, 72-73, 75-77, 92-93, 121, 138, 148, 161-62, 164-66, 173, 177, 183, 195, 198, 247-48
Lagos Weekend 53
Lampert, M 9, 258
language planning 4, 183-200, 247-48
Lavandera, B 40, 261
Lawton, D 16, 261
Lefebvre, C 20-21, 261
Le Page, R 16, 261
lexicon 78, 80, 82, 84-99, 147, 219-46
Liberia(n) 25
life cycle (of P/Cs) 18, 20, 22-23, 28
Lovas, J 190, 260

M

Mackey, W 30, 262
Madaki, R 59, 61, 63, 262
Mafeni, B 4, 7, 47, 107, 193, 262
Mair, C vi, 49, 196, 262
Make We Think Small 77, 96
Makwemoisa, A 71
Mann, C vi, 1, 3-5, 7, 43, 47, 49-50, 53, 56, 95, 100-01, 184, 187-89, 262
Marchese, L 4, 47-48, 56, 184, 189-90, 266
Martinique 21
Masquerade 53, 102, 157, 244
Mauritius 21-22
Mbah, E 71, 248
McWhorter, J 13, 26-27, 262
Melanesia(n) (Pidgin English) 29, 204, 208
methodology 99-100
Miller, C 36-37, 84-85, 265
Milroy, L 72, 262
Ministry of Information 248
Modigie, C 49, 71, 262
Mogu, F 247
Moravcsik, E 35, 263
Morocco 30
Moser, C 45, 263
Mufwene, S 13-14, 19-20, 25-26, 107-8, 203, 263
Mühlhäusler, P 1, 22, 28, 107-08, 208, 263
Mushin xi, xiii, 7
Muslim 170-71
Muysken, P 35, 263
Myers-Scotton, C 32-34, 36, 38-39, 50, 55, 263

N

Nash, G vi
national language 185-89, 209
National Policy on Education 47-50, 189
National Population Commission 8, 263
Ndolo, I 4, 184-86, 263
Ndukwe, P 52, 264
negation 62, 133-35, 235
Nelson, G 75, 264
newspapers 5, 9, 53, 248
New World 25-27
Niger-Congo 61
Niger Delta 1, 3-5, 7, 55, 189, 198-99
Nigeria(n) 1-9, 13, 22-25, 42-43, 45-47, 50-54, 56, 59-70, 77, 145, 183, 189, 192
Nigerian (indigenous) languages 3-4, 9, 14, 45-47, 49-50, 52, 59, 62-63, 76, 140, 153, 155-56, 184, 186, 202, 204-05, 207-08, 244. *See also individual entries for* Edo, Efik, Esan, Fulfulde, Hausa, Ibibio, Igbo, Ijo, Izon, Kanuri, Tiv, Urhobo, Yoruba.
NigP = Nigerian Pidgin
Nitzl, I 49, 264
Noserime, E 71
nouns 83-86, 219-24, 233
noun phrase 105-122, 237-38
Nova Scotia(n) 27
Nwachukwu-Agabada, J 145-46, 264
Nwafor, J 256
Nwagbara, A 71, 248
Nwankpa, A 71
Nwoga, D 52, 264
Nwoye, O 50, 59-60, 63, 264

O

o 144-45
Obakoya, A 11, 71
Obilade, A 48-49, 264
O'Connor, A xi, 264
Odlin, T 39, 264
O'Donnell, W 24, 264
official language 185-89
Ofuani, O 4-5, 49, 53, 122, 193, 196, 264
Ofuokwu, D 186-87, 264
Ogbulogo, C 71
Ogunjobi, K v, 77, 141
Ogunsanya, K 71
Oguntoyinbo, J 256

Ogun State viii, 56
Ohali, E 71
Ojuelegba Motor Park xiii
Okeregbe, A 247
Okoroanyanwu, N v, 71, 248
Oladeji, K 11
Oladejo, J 184-85, 187, 264
Oloko, P v, 71, 140, 147, 158, 247-48, 258
Oloruntoba, C 4, 49, 63, 189, 264
Olufunwa, H v, 71, 247-48
Omamor, A 1-5, 7, 9-10, 47, 49, 53, 103, 105, 107-08, 115-16, 122, 128, 156-57, 180, 184, 187, 193-94, 196, 199, 206, 258, 264
Ondo State ix, 46
One Thing at a Time v, 56, 74, 77, 97, 118, 136, 140-41, 146, 153-54, 164
Onyemelukwe, J 256
Opeibi, B 248
Oreh, O 53, 264
orthography 9-11, 52, 191-97, 248-254
Osaji, D 49, 264
Osaka, N 199, 248
Osoba, J 71
Owerri viii, 45
Oyo viii, 52

P

Pacific 1, 22
Palenquero 204-05
Papua New Guinea 22, 28, 192, 197, 201. 204
Parkvall, M 20, 264
Pasch, H 30, 265
pass (serial verb) 131-33
Patrick, P 17-18, 42, 124, 135, 158, 265
P/C = Pidgin(s) and/or Creole(s)
PE = Pidgin English
Peil, M xi, 7-8, 27, 55, 265
pidgin(s) 1-2, 13-14, 158, 202-03
pidginization 22-23, 89-94, 111, 152-53, 157, 206
Pidgin Portuguese 1
plantation Creoles 25
plurality 62, 106-14
Poplack, S 4-5, 32-34, 36-37, 84-85, 108-10, 122, 124, 137, 139, 179, 265
Popular Side 49, 252-53
Port Harcourt viii, 2, 4-5, 87
Portuguese 10, 87

possessives 114-22
(post-)P/C continuum, *see* continuum
prepositions, prepositional phrases 100-102, 231-32, 240
pronouns 115-22, 233
proverbs 145-46, 158
pseudopidgin 5-6, 156-57, 199, 206

Q

quantitative studies 18, 39-41, 55, 80
questionnaire 8-9, 45, 55, 57, 74, 77-82, 84-89, 103, 130, 139, 142-43, 146-54, 183, 211-46, 248

R

radio 5-6, 8-9, 22, 49, 53, 55, 71-72, 74-75, 77, 96-98, 100, 102, 120, 137, 140, 146, 149-54, 156-59, 183, 190, 195-96, 198-99, 205-06, 244-45, 248-49
Rainbow City v, 56, 74, 77, 84, 97, 118, 140, 146, 153-54, 158, 167, 197
reduplication 90-91, 242, 244
register 158-59, 205-07, 243
Réunion (Creole) 21-22
Rickford, J 13, 16, 18, 107-08, 135, 265
Rivers State viii, 3-4, 23, 46, 51, 198
Rodrigues 21
Romaine, S 28, 35, 40, 108, 197, 265-66
Rufai, A 185, 266

S

Safe Journey 5, 22, 53, 157
Saint Lucia 14, 16
Samarin, W 158, 266
Sand, A vi
Sankoff, D 36-37, 84-85, 265
Sankoff, G 40, 266
Sapele 3, 47, 189, 198
Saro-Wiwa, K 49, 266
Schmied, J 56, 266
Schneider, E vi
Schwegler, A 204-05, 266
Scotton, C, *see* Myers-Scotton
Sebba, M 14-15, 23, 107, 191, 266
Sedlatschek, A vi

semi-Creole 21
Settler English 25
Seychelles 21
Shnukal, A 4, 47-48, 56, 184, 189-90, 266
Shodipe, M 71
Shomolu xi, 7, 161, 173
Siegel, J 28-29, 204, 266
Sierra Leone(an) 1-3, 24-27, 199, 204
Simpson, E 77, 196, 200, 266
Singler, J 25, 266
Smith, G 28, 108, 266
Society for Family Health v
sociolinguistics 13, 16, 29-32, 35, 39-40, 45-57, 71-72, 76, 183, 191-92, 194, 207-09, 247
Sommer, G 208, 257
Soyinka, W 22, 49, 185, 196
Spanish 14, 37, 204-05
Sporting Champion 49, 252
standardization 197-200, 247-48
Statistisches Bundesamt viii, 6, 266-67
status planning 184-90
Stewart, W 16, 267
Studienstiftung des deutschen Volkes v
substrate 2, 4, 24, 204, 208
superlative 235
superstrate 24
Surinam 192
Surulere 7, 75
Swahili 31-32, 185
Swigart, L 56, 267
Swiss German 29

T

Tabouret-Keller, A 16, 261
Tagliamonte, S 4-5, 108-10, 122, 124, 179, 265, 267
Tanzania 30-31, 35, 53
target language 39
television 49, 53
tense/aspect/modality 80, 122-27, 144, 155
tertiary hybridization 2-3
Thomason, S 35-36, 155, 267
Tiv x, 46, 52
to 130-31, 234-35
Todd, L 22-24, 105, 122, 179, 192, 194, 267
Togo 2
Tok Pisin 1, 22, 26, 28-29, 107-08, 197, 201, 204
triglossia 30, 59, 207-08

Trinidad 14
Trudgill, P 43, 56, 267
Tuggar, K v

U

Uduma, L 71
UNFPA 250, 267
UNESCO 250, 267
UNICEF 250, 267
United Nations 7, 267
University of Lagos v, 11, 55, 75, 78, 247-48
Upper Guinea 26
Urhobo x, 76, 195
Uwabor, I 53, 267
Uzoezie, R v, 59-61, 71, 248, 267

V

Valdman, A 20-21, 197, 267-68
VARBRUL 111-13
variables, variants, variation 39-42, 56, 72, 158-59, 205-07
verbs, verb phrase 83, 86-88, 225-29, 233-34, 238-39
Verhaar, J 197, 268
Victoria Island xi, 7
Virginian Black English 27

W

Wakabout 5, 53, 87
Warri 2-3, 5, 47, 161, 166, 189, 198, 246
Washbourne, J vi
Weiner, E 40, 268
Weinreich, U 39, 41, 268
West Africa(n) 1, 22, 24-26, 109
West African PE 2-3, 25, 27, 204
West Indies, *see* Caribbean
Westwood, A 36-37, 265
Wheeler, S 36-37, 265
Whinnom, K 2, 268
Whiteley, W 30, 268
Whitney, W 35, 268
WHO (= World Health Organization) 250, 267
Williams, W 24, 268
Williamson, K 52, 268
Winford, D 14, 16-18, 40, 268
Wolfram, W 41, 268
Woman Corner 77
written NigP, *see* orthography
Wurm, S, 197, 268

Y

Yaba xi, 7, 45
Yakubu, U 71, 248
Yoruba x, 3, 7, 11, 45-46, 48-50, 52-55, 60-63, 67, 72, 76-77, 85, 92-93, 103, 136, 141-42, 145, 155, 163-64, 173, 184-86, 188, 195-96, 198, 200, 205-06, 246
Youssi, A 30, 268

Z

Zabus, C 49, 268
Zaria 186